MODERN MANAGEMENT

Theory and Practice
for Irish Students

Dr Siobhán Tiernan
Michael Morley
Edel Foley

D1464495

GILL & MACMILLAN

Gill & Macmillan Ltd
Goldenbridge
Dublin 8
with associated companies throughout the world
© Dr Siobhán Tiernan, Michael Morley, Edel Foley 1996
0 7171 2366 9

Index compiled by
Helen Litton

Design and print origination by
O'K Graphic Design, Dublin

Printed by
ColourBooks Ltd, Dublin

A catalogue record is available for this book from the
British Library.

To Kevin and Baby Luke (ST)

To Noreen (MM)

To James, Deirdre and Conor (EF)

CONTENTS

Preface

Managers in Ireland today face a rapidly changing world. Changes over the last decades in Irish business mirror international developments. New organisational forms, new approaches to management and rapid technological developments reflect the strategic imperative of the 1990s and challenge our traditional assumptions in relation to organisation and management. There is a sense in which managers cannot look to past practices in order to chart a course for the future.

Any summative account of management in Ireland cannot claim to be all inclusive. Managerial backgrounds and styles, organisational practices and business environments vary widely. This book is intended as an introductory text for Irish students. A mixture of theory and practice has been employed in the completion of this work. Theoretical principles are supported by Irish case examples and data where available. The fourteen chapters trace the history of management thought, examine the business environment, discuss key managerial roles (planning, decision making, organising, motivating, leading and controlling), review core managerial functions (financial, production, personnel and marketing), and discuss contemporaneous issues relating to entrepreneurship and the management of change. Readability of the text is enhanced by the inclusion of a summary of key propositions at the end of each chapter and student revision is facilitated by the provision of end of chapter discussion questions and a glossary of key managerial terms. Terms that occur in the glossary appear in italics in the text. Where appropriate, appendices are used to expand on the sources cited in the text.

There are a number of people who have provided valuable assistance in the preparation of this book and we take this opportunity to place on record our thanks to them.

Prof. Noel Whelan, Dean of the College of Business, Prof. Donal Dineen, Associate Dean, David McKevitt, Head of the Department of Management & Marketing and Paddy Gunnigle, Head of the Department of Personnel & Employment Relations, all of the University of Limerick.

John Geraghty, Lecturer in Personnel Management, Eddie Laverty, Director of the Bolton Trust and Margaret Field, Chief Librarian, all of the Dublin Institute of Technology, Aungier St, Kate Gallagher, Lecturer in Marketing, Laura Cuddihy, Lecturer in Marketing and Tom Cooney, Lecturer in Enterprise Development, all of the Dublin Institute of Technology, Mountjoy Square.

Helena Lenihan, Una Brady, Camilla Noonan, Terence Sheridan, Eugene Power, Noreen Heraty, Tom Garavan, Patrick Flood, Brega Hynes, Jim Donoghue, Roy Hayhurst, Sarah Moore, Tom Turner and Joe Wallace, all of the College of Business at the University of Limerick, Yvonne McMahon, Dublin Institute of Technology and Frank DeRisi of Dun & Bradstreet are also thanked for their help and encouragement.

The staff at the following institutions were always courteous and helpful when dealing with our enquiries: The Government Publications Office; Forfas; The Central Statistics Office; The Department of Enterprise & Employment; The Labour Relations Commission; An Board Trachtala; Department of Tourism & Trade; The Companies Office; Office of the Revenue Commissioners; Shannon Development Company.

Siobhán Tiernan
Michael Morley
Edel Foley

Limerick and Dublin
September 1995

1

An Introduction to Management

1.1 INTRODUCTION

This chapter provides an introduction to the topic of *management*. Firstly, a definition of management is provided and its nature and importance in modern society is explained. The main functions and skills of all *managers* are outlined. The different roles played by managers at all levels are explained and the characteristics of effective managers are considered. Finally, the chapter looks at management in Ireland and explains the structure of this book.

1.2 THE NATURE AND IMPORTANCE OF MANAGEMENT

Drucker (1988), one of the most influential management theorists, has stated that over the last 150 years management has revolutionised the social and economic fabric of the developed regions of the world. Management has also made the structure of modern industry possible. Prior to the advent of management, society could only support small groups of workers. It has enabled large numbers of knowledgable and skilled employees to achieve organisational goals. As a result, effective management has become one of the most important resources of the developed world and one which most developing regions seek eagerly.

Defining management adequately is not always easy as the term has often been used in a variety of ways. Management can refer to the process that managers go through to achieve organisational goals. It can refer to a body of knowledge which provides information about how to manage. Management can also be used to denote individuals who guide and control organisational activities. Finally, management can refer to a career which involves guiding and controlling organisations. For the purposes of this book, management is viewed as the process in which managers engage to achieve organisational goals. In this respect, numerous definitions of management exist, though most have three common characteristics:

1. Management is viewed as a process or series of continuing and related activities.
2. Management is viewed as involving the achievement of organisational goals.
3. Management reaches such organisational goals by working with and through people.

One of the best definitions available at present defines management as 'the process of achieving desired results through an efficient utilisation of human and material resources'. (Bedeian 1993) Managers can thus be viewed as individuals within organisations whose principal aims are to achieve organisational goals by holding positions of authority and making decisions about the allocation of resources.

The organisation can be viewed as a system which is designed and operated to achieve specific organisational objectives. Organisations are consciously and formally established to achieve goals that their members would be unable to achieve by working on their own. Management is universal in that it occurs in all types of organisation whether public or private, large or small, profit or non profit. While the techniques and emphasis may vary, the general principles of management can be used in all organisations. The top thirty Irish organisations as classified by turnover in 1994 are shown in Figure 1.1.

Figure 1.1 The Top Thirty Irish Organisations by Turnover in 1994

	Name	Turnover IR Millions	Activity
1.	CRH	1427.16	Building materials
2.	Jefferson Smurfit	1317.34	Print and packaging
3.	ABF Retail *	1280.00	Supermarkets
4.	The Irish Dairy Board	1214.00	Export of dairy produce
5.	Avonmore Foods	1129.40	Dairy and pig meat processing
6.	Dell	950.00	PC manufacture and sales
7.	ESB	942.68	Electricity supply
8.	Dunnes Stores	925.00	Retailing
9.	Kerry Group	879.88	Food processing
10.	Telecom Eireann	871.30	Telecommunications
11.	Apple Computers	850.00	Computer manufacture
12.	Aer Lingus	817.10	Air transportation
13.	Goodman	800.00	Meat process/export
14.	Microsoft	800.00	Software mfr/distribution
15.	Waterford Foods	689.66	Food products
16.	Guinness Ireland	636.00	Brewing
17.	Fyffes	611.40	Fruit and vegetables
18.	Dairygold	516.50	Dairy products
19.	Intel	500.00	Computer manufacture
20.	Musgrave	498.00	Wholesale grocery
21.	IAWS	479.00	Food/agribusiness
22.	Coca Cola Atlantic	425.00	Soft drink concentrate
23.	Golden Vale	423.20	Dairy products
24.	Greencore	404.50	Food processing distribution
25.	Irish Distillers	340.00	Distillers
26.	The Gilbey Group	340.00	Alcoholic beverages
27.	DCC	335.57	Industrial and financial holding co.
28.	Waterford Wedgewood	319.20	Crystal and ceramics
29.	Fitzwilton	305.74	Industrial holding co.
30.	Glen Dimplex	300.00	Electrical appliances

* Includes Quinnsworth, Crazy Prices and Primark

Source: Business and Finance, 26 Jan 1995.

As all organisations exist for a purpose, managers have the responsibility of combining and using organisational resources to ensure that the organisation achieves its purpose. If these activities are designed effectively, the output of individual workers represents a contribution towards the achievement of organisational goals. Management tries to encourage individual activity that will lead to reaching organisational objectives and tries to discourage individual activity that hinders organisational goal attainment.

1.3 THE FUNCTIONS OF MANAGEMENT

In order to achieve organisational goals all managers perform several major functions or activities: planning, organising, staffing and personnel, leading, and controlling.

1.3.1 Planning
Planning is the process of establishing goals and objectives and selecting a future course of action in order to achieve them. Plans are developed throughout the organisation including business units, work groups and individuals. Such plans can have a long-term orientation of between five and fifteen years, a medium-term orientation of one to five years, or a short-term orientation of less than one year. Managers have responsibility for gathering and evaluating the information on which the plans are based, setting the goals that need to be achieved and deciding how such goals should be achieved through the implementation of plans.

1.3.2 Organising
Once the plans have been established, it is necessary to allocate adequate resources to ensure that they can be achieved. Organising, therefore, constitutes the next logical step in the management process. It involves dividing tasks into sub tasks and allocating resources to achieve such tasks and, finally, co-ordinating employees. Organising also involves establishing managerial authority.

1.3.3 Staffing
The staffing and personnel function ensures that effective employees are selected, trained and developed and then rewarded for accomplishing organisational goals.

1.3.4 Leading
The fourth main function of management is leading. This involves inducing individuals or groups to assist willingly and harmoniously in the attainment of organisational goals. Leading usually means that the manager has to direct, motivate and communicate with employees. The leading function is almost entirely concerned with managing the people within the organisation.

1.3.5 Controlling
The final function of management is control, which is the process of monitoring progress made by the organisation, business unit or individual and, where necessary, taking action to ensure goals match targets. The previous four management functions concentrated on developing plans, organising the resources needed to put the plans into practice and directing and motivating employees towards their realisation. However, good plans, solid organisation and effective leaders are no guarantee of success unless the various activities are measured, evaluated and corrected. Successful organisations pay close attention to the control function to make sure that they are on target for achieving goals.

These five management functions are carried out by all managers and are interrelated. They make up a set of interdependent activities that shape the *management process* as shown in Figure 1.2.

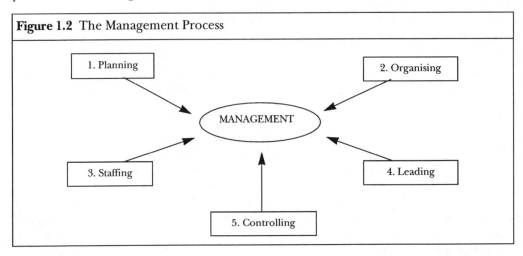

Figure 1.2 The Management Process

While the various functions take place concurrently throughout most organisations they follow a logical sequence. Planning establishes the direction of the organisation. Organising divides organisational activities among work groups and co-ordinates results. Staffing allocates the right people to achieve specific tasks. Leading motivates employees to achieve organisational goals. Finally, control measures and evaluates organisational performance.

1.4 MANAGEMENT LEVELS

Managers are located at different levels in the organisation. Typically, managers at different levels perform a range of different activities. Three distinct but sometimes overlapping levels of management can be identified in most organisations, as shown in Figure 1.3.

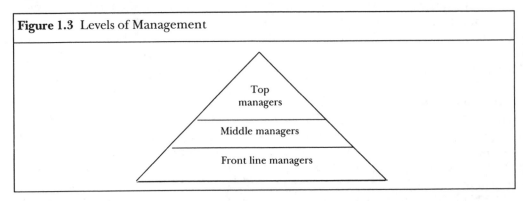

Figure 1.3 Levels of Management

1.4.1 Top managers

Top managers (sometimes referred to as strategic managers) are the top executives in the organisation. They include the Chief Executive Officer, President, Chairman, Chief

Operating Officer, Directors and members of the Board. These managers are responsible for the overall mission and direction of the organisation. Top managers shape organisational goals, provide resources, monitor progress and make strategic decisions. In this sense they act as the interface between the organisation and its external environment. They represent the organisation at outside meetings and develop customer and supplier relationships.

Mintzberg (1973) identifies ten different but interrelated roles undertaken by top managers in the course of their activities, as shown in Figure 1.4.

Figure 1.4 Roles Performed by Top Managers	
Interpersonal	Figurehead Leader Liaison
Informational	Monitor Disseminator Spokesperson
Decisional	Entrepreneur Disturbance handler Resource allocator Negotiator

Top managers have an interpersonal role which usually comes from their formal authority. They are figure-heads serving as organisational representatives in social, economic and legal areas. Top managers are leaders in that they have to influence the activities of employees. These managers also have a liaison function and are required to interact with peers and colleagues in other organisations.

The second major role undertaken by top managers is communicating information. Top managers are monitors; they collect information that enables them to deal with both internal and external developments. As disseminators, top managers transmit information to those inside the organisation. Finally, top managers act as spokespeople for their organisations when dealing with external bodies.

The final top managerial role is decision making. In their roles as entrepreneurs, top managers initiate changes to improve organisational performance. As disturbance handlers, they deal with unforeseen events. As resource allocators, they decide where the organisation should allocate its resources. As negotiators, top managers bargain with influential groups such as trade unions.

1.4.2 Middle managers
Middle managers are also called tactical managers and are responsible for translating the general plans and objectives developed by top managers into specific objectives and ways of achieving them. In this way middle managers occupy positions above front line managers and below top managers. Middle managers include Plant Managers, Business Unit Managers, Operations Managers, Superintendents and Senior Supervisors. Middle managers integrate the activities of different work groups to ensure co-ordination. They provide the link between top managers and front line mangers and, in this manner, they transfer information and communications between the levels. In recent years they have become more involved in strategy formulation. However, top managers still have primary responsibility for strategic planning and decision making.

During the 1980s, many middle managers lost their jobs as organisations down sized and delayered. The main casualties in these delayering programmes were Superintendents and Senior Supervisors. Such moves were brought about by the need to reduce costs and to become more competitive. Developments in information technology have meant that middle managers are no longer required to serve as information and communications channels between top managers and front line managers. Many organisations have not replaced the middle managers and are unlikely to do so in the future.

1.4.3 Front line managers

Front line managers form the largest group of managers in most organisations. They are responsible for directly supervising and managing operating employees and resources. They ensure that the plans developed by top managers are fulfilled by those employees who produce the organisation's goods and services. Front line managers are a critically important group as they are the link between management and non-management personnel. How they interpret information and pass it on to employees has an important impact on employees' reactions.

While the number of middle managers has been reduced, the role of front line managers has changed, too. Many of the responsibilities of the traditional middle manager have been passed to the front line manager who has become increasingly responsible for shop floor operations and has been given more authority and responsibility. Some observers have predicted that no job is going to change more over the next decade than that of the front line manager.

1.5 MANAGEMENT SKILLS

While management functions are the cornerstone of the manager's job, certain skills are needed to ensure that managers carry out their functions effectively. Skills are the abilities developed by managers through knowledge, information, practice and aptitude. Management skills can be divided into three categories — technical, interpersonal and conceptual.

1.5.1 Technical

A technical skill is the ability to perform a specialised task involving a particular method or process. Most employees develop a set of technical skills as they start their careers. For example, business graduates have technical skills in accounting, finance, marketing and Human Resource Management (HRM). The daily activities of most managers involve the use of some technical skills. However, as managers rise within the organisation they spend less time using these skills. For example, when recruited, an engineer relies heavily on technical skills, however, as he/she is promoted and manages other employees, other skills become more important.

1.5.2 Interpersonal

In order to work well with other people a manager needs good interpersonal skills, sometimes called human skills. Most top managers spend about half of their time dealing with other people (Mintzberg, 1975). If managers are to deal with employees effectively, they must develop their abilities to motivate and communicate with those around them. Interpersonal skills are required by all managers as they all have to deal with other people.

1.5.3 Conceptual

Conceptual skills involve the ability to see the organisation as a whole, to recognise complex and dynamic issues, and to examine factors that influence these problems and resolve such situations. As managers are promoted up the organisation they depend more and more on conceptual skills. In fact, most managers are promoted because of their ability to make sound decisions and their vision and ability to chart the organisation's future. While conceptual skills are used by most managers, top managers require them most, particularly when making strategic decisions.

Figure 1.5 shows the variations in skills necessary at different management levels. As the diagram shows, the most important skills for front line managers are technical and interpersonal. For middle managers, interpersonal skills are the most important with medium amounts of technical and conceptual input. For top managers, the most important skills are conceptual and interpersonal, with little need for technical input.

Figure 1.5 Management Skills at Different Levels

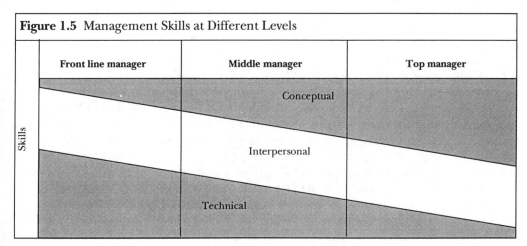

1.6 EFFECTIVE MANAGERS

Figure 1.6 The Effective Manager

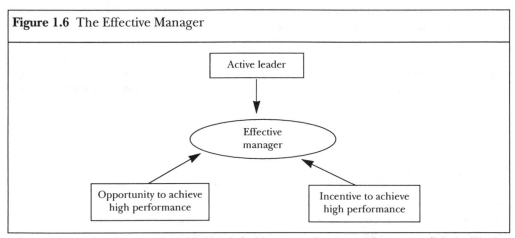

Source: Adapted from Bateman, T. and Zeithaml, C., *Management: Function and Strategy*, page 7, Irwin, Illinois 1993.

In addition to the execution of the four management functions with the use of three types of skills, effective managers have a number of important characteristics. Bateman and Zeithhaml (1993) argue that effective managers are active leaders who create both the opportunity and incentive to achieve high performance, as shown in Figure 1.6.

1.6.1 An active leader

To be effective a manager should be an active leader. As we have seen, leading is one of the key functions of management. The main difference between managers and leaders is that managers do things right whereas leaders do the right things. (Bennis and Nanus 1985) In this way, leaders have a vision which they communicate successfully to employees. Active leaders concentrate on achieving the task at hand in an active rather than passive manner. They participate in the activities of the organisation at business unit and work group levels. In this way, they are highly visible to employees and demonstrate their thorough knowledge of the business. Michael Smurfit of the Smurfit Group and Fergal Quinn of Superquinn are good examples of managers who are active leaders.

1.6.2 Opportunity to achieve high performance

In order to provide the opportunity for high performance, both managers and employees must understand their jobs and what they do as opposed to what they should do. They should also have a sense of the future for their particular task. Involving employees in the design and execution stages is one method of providing the opportunity to achieve high performance. The Japanese have used this philosophy very effectively especially in relation to quality circles. Japanese managers work closely with employees to plan and implement changes for the benefit of everyone. Management can also ensure the opportunity to achieve high performance by making sure that all employees have the necessary resources. Effective managers are constantly searching for ways to help employees do their jobs well and focus their activities and efforts on production matters.

1.6.3 Incentive to achieve high performance

In order to provide incentives for employees to achieve high performances, the manager needs to identify the factors that motivate employees and build those factors into the work environment. Incentives can include rewards such as money and promotions, a challenging job or relationships with co-workers. Having identified the factors that motivate employees, the manager needs to link these factors to clear objectives. In other words, effective managers identify the important objectives they need to achieve and focus everyone's efforts towards achieving those objectives.

1.7 THE IRISH CONTEXT

Ireland is a late developing economy, with most industrial development occurring since the 1960s. As a small open economy, Ireland is highly dependent on foreign trade and sensitive to developments in the world economy. Since the mid-1960s, Government policy has focused on attracting foreign direct investment (FDI) to Ireland by using tax and financial incentives, and on building the physical and human-capital support infrastructures (Gunnigle 1992).

Possibly the most remarkable feature of Ireland's social and economic history is the decline in the country's population since the mid-1800s, with a decrease from over 6 million in 1841 to some 3.5 million in 1991. Emigration is also a characteristic of Irish life, particularly to the UK and the USA.

In terms of employment distribution, there has been a progressive decline in the numbers employed in agriculture and industry and a growth in the services sector. The other characteristic feature of Irish employment patterns is the high levels of unemployment and the growth of unemployment since the 1970s, in particular. Standing at almost 13 per cent of the labour force as of April 1995 (Central Bank of Ireland: Irish Economic Statistics, Autumn 1995), Irish unemployment is very high by EU standards.

Since the mid-1960s, Irish Government policy has been to actively encourage foreign investment. There are now over 1000 overseas companies operating in Ireland with particular focus on the engineering (including electronics) and chemicals sectors. These companies employ some 90,000 people.

Ireland has a unique set of cultural characteristics that are important in the context of understanding Irish management. Dineen and Garavan (1994) draw upon the work of a number of international researchers to summarise these characteristics.

Figure 1.7 Prominent Cultural Characteristics Found in Ireland

Cultural characteristic	How it manifests itself in Ireland
Individualism versus collectivism	Relatively moderate degree of individualism
Pride in the country	Moderate to high
Attitude to time	Plenty of time, not viewed as tangible commodity
Attitude to work and achievement	Reasonable work ethic, but ambivalent towards achievement
Uncertainty avoidance	High degree of uncertainty avoidance
Relationships to nature	High attachment to nature
Youth orientation of society	Considerable extolling of youth values
Attachment to hierarchy	Very high attachment
Attitude to competition	Competition not overemphasised
Talent for motivating a workforce	Moderate ability
Formality/informality	Relatively informal in one-to-one relationships
Reputation for marketing push	Very poor
Masculine/feminine values	Predominantly masculine values
Creativity and willingness to exploit innovation	Moderate willingness
Acceptance of business by the public	High level of acceptance
Co-operation/conflict	High degree of co-operation encouraged
Attitude towards foreign influences	Healthy attitude
Willingness to delegate authority	Poor

Source: Dineen, D. and Garavan, T., 'Ireland: The Emerald Isle: Management Research in a Changing European Context', *International Studies of Management and Organisation*, Vol.24, Nos.1–2.

There is a push for economic growth and prosperity and a respectability attached to business and management among the Irish public. However, given the culture, key questions concern the extent to which the attachment to hierarchy impacts upon the introduction of innovations in work design and organisation structures, the applicability of American and Japanese approaches to management in the Irish context and the extent to which prevailing attitudes influence employment equality and affirmative action programmes.

Management training is provided in the main by the Irish Management Institute (IMI), third level institutions and private organisations. The cost of management training is subsidised by the national training agency (FAS) under the Training Support Scheme and state support for the IMI and third level institutions. In the public sector the Institute of Public Administration (IPA) provides most management training.

The first significant Government attempt to analyse the Irish system of management training and development was undertaken as recently as 1988 under the auspices of the Advisory Committee on Management Training. This Committee's report noted that economic performance is significantly influenced by the quality of management. With the onset of the single European market and greater international trade, the report highlighted the need to improve the quality of Irish management. A number of key strengths and weaknesses of the Irish system of management training were outlined. The main strengths identified were the quality of the key providers, the standard of general education, and the wide choice of provision and experimentation with different delivery systems. A number of significant weaknesses were also highlighted. In particular, the report identified a low level of commitment to management development in many Irish organisations. Few organisations recognised the investment value of management development and expenditure in the area was very low: over one-fifth of the country's top 1000 companies spent nothing on management development and over half spent less than IR£5000; foreign-owned organisations spent on average 50 per cent more than indigenous firms; new organisations spent considerably less than established firms. The report also identified a lack of customer focus by providers, an inadequate supply of trainers and an inability to link management development with other strategic considerations in the organisation.

In relation to career progression, the report identified three routes to management in Irish organisations: (i) *the specialist route* whereby professionals such as engineers or computer specialists acquire management positions by virtue of their particular expertise; (ii) *the business qualification route* whereby people with qualifications in business disciplines, most commonly finance and accounting, gain management positions (a particularly common route to management positions); (iii) *the generalist route* whereby management positions are gained on the basis of general work and organisational experience only (five–ten years).

Recent trends indicate higher levels of participation by managers in post-experience tertiary education. In particular, there has been a marked increase in managerial participation in post-experience part-time vocational diplomas/certificates, business studies degrees and MBA level programmes. There is also evidence of a greater participation by new managers in management development programmes.

A traditional criticism of the culture for business in Ireland is that it has not always encouraged enterprise and innovation. This trait was felt to be attributed to Ireland's relatively late independence which created, what some have termed, a 'dependence mentality'. However, there is growing evidence that an 'enterprise culture' is taking root in Ireland. Levels of productivity and export performance have increased dramatically and compare very favourably with international standards. Recent studies have noted the flexibility of the Irish workforce and the relevance of coherent and strong corporate culture formation among Irish organisations. Characteristics of Irish organisations with strong corporate cultures include the pivotal influence of the company founders, the presence of a coherent and explicit company philosophy, the existence of a well-developed personnel function and sophisticated personnel practices and a degree of community involvement. (Gunnigle and Morley 1996) Kakabadse (1991) identified four predominant styles: (i) valuing performance and professionalism; (ii) sensitivity to people; (iii) rules and regulations oriented; (iv) power oriented. The predominant style identified was one of valuing performance and professionalism, which was characterised by a focus on mission statement, an attention to relationships within the top team, attempts to ensure an absence of sensitivities concerning the way the business is run, and an emphasis on improving employee morale and practices to ensure staff retention.

Figure 1.8 Management Styles in Irish Organisations (% of Respondents)

MANAGERIAL STYLE	% of Respondents
Valuing performance and professionalism	53 %
Sensitivity to people	23 %
Rules and regulations oriented	22 %
Power oriented	19 %

Source: Kakabadse, A., 'The Cream of Irish Management.' Paper presented to the 23rd Irish Institute of Training and Development National Conference, Limerick, April 1991.

A number of points can be made about current management issues in Ireland. The Irish economy is now in a much healthier position than at any stage since the early 1970s. Particular strengths are low labour costs, low inflation and a young and highly skilled labour force. At the macro level, the single greatest challenge facing the Irish economy is the need to tackle effectively the persistently high level of unemployment. Despite a pervasive feeling that the fundamentals of the Irish economy are sound (low inflation, stable currency, balance of payment surpluses, good industrial relations, solid GNP growth), the country has struggled to provide jobs for its young, well educated workforce. The openness of the Irish economy also means that any downturn in the world economy impacts significantly upon the domestic economic performance, particularly in relation to export growth and emigration opportunities. Other important policy concerns at the macro level are the need for tax reform (particularly in reducing personal income tax), continued infrastructural development and increased concern with environmental issues (Gunnigle 1992).

At the micro level, important management concerns include the need to increase quality levels, the introduction of new information technology, the growth of atypical employment forms and the development of more innovative personnel policies tailored to achieve competitive advantage. Other important factors include organisational restructuring to devolve more responsibility to strategic business units, the increasing importance of culture and mission in focusing management effort and guiding decisions on resource allocation, a possible tightening in some segments of the Irish labour market, and increased education levels among Irish managers.

1.8 THE STRUCTURE OF THE BOOK

CHAPTER 2 provides a synopsis of the history of management thought. The earliest approaches, classical thinking and modern approaches are all examined.

CHAPTER 3 examines the business environment. The external environment is divided into the macro environment and the task environment. The concept of competitive analysis is introduced as a means of determining the level of competition in the environment and a possible tool for managing this environment.

CHAPTER 4 focuses on the key managerial activities of planning and decision making. It considers the importance of planning, different types of planning and various approaches that can be utilised to facilitate good planning. Decision making is considered an integral part of the planning process and the various stages of decision making are considered. Both individual and group modes of decision making are presented.

CHAPTER 5 is dedicated to the process of organising. Organisational structure as the framework for organising is examined in detail. Both classical and more recent approaches to structuring, including network, cluster and high performance design are all considered.

CHAPTER 6 discusses two concepts that are central to the management process, namely motivation and leadership. The link between motivation and leadership theory and management practice is central to management's success. Furthermore, these are two interdependent concepts when it comes to the study of management in the sense that a good leader may well be a good leader because he/she understands the principles of motivation, while conversely high levels of motivation may exist as a result of effective leadership.

CHAPTER 7 focuses on the process of control. Control ensures the achievement of organisational objectives and goals by measuring actual performance and taking corrective action where necessary. Various types of control are considered and the characteristics of effective controls are highlighted.

CHAPTER 8 deals with financial management. The chapter centres around two key issues, namely the sources of finance (short-, medium- or long-term) and how the organisation should invest spare funds with particular reference to working capital, inventory, cash and debts.

CHAPTER 9 examines issues in production and operations management with specific reference to Total Quality Management (TQM) and quality systems, Just-In-Time (JIT) manufacturing and, finally, technology and innovation in organisations.

CHAPTER 10 deals with the fourth management function — personnel management and staffing. An overview of the historical development of the personnel function is provided. Human resource planning, recruitment, selection, pay and benefits, performance appraisal and training and development are all discussed. Where available, research data is incorporated into the chapter.

CHAPTER 11 focuses on employee relations in Ireland. The nature and context of employee relations are sketched briefly with particular reference to organisational level developments in recent years. The structure of employee relations is discussed. Trade unions, employer organisations and state institutions as parties to the labour process are all examined.

CHAPTER 12 deals with marketing management. Because of Ireland's export dependency and its entry into the European Union (EU) in 1973, marketing awareness was heightened. Here, we discuss the marketing concept, how to conduct a market analysis, marketing planning and the marketing mix. Pricing, promotion and distribution are also examined.

CHAPTER 13 deals with entrepreneurship and small business management. It explores the origins of enterprise, the structure of small businesses in Ireland and Government policy on entrepreneurship. The characteristics of entrepreneurs are presented and the process of small business formation is examined.

CHAPTER 14 deals with the issue of managing change. Due to the dynamic nature of the business environment, the management of change has become a priority for all managers and organisations. The broad forces driving change are identified in this chapter and the key potential sources of resistance to change are presented. A model of strategic change is then presented. Finally, factors which seem to contribute to the successful management of change are considered.

1.9 SUMMARY OF KEY PROPOSITIONS

- Management has been largely responsible for the development of the pattern of industry as we know it today. Management has facilitated the co-ordination of people with different skills and knowledge to achieve organisational goals.
- Management is the process of achieving desired results through an efficient utilisation of human and material resources. Managers are individuals within organisations who are responsible for the process of management.
- Management typically has five main functions which logically follow on from one another; firstly, planning, which involves establishing what needs to be done; secondly, organising, which establishes how tasks should be completed; thirdly, staffing and personnel, which ensure the availability of human resources to achieve such tasks; fourthly, leading, which involves directing and motivating employees towards the attainment of organisational goals; finally, control, which involves measuring actual performance against desired performance and taking corrective action.
- There are three management levels — top managers, middle managers and front line

managers, all of whom have slightly different roles and responsibilities. Top managers are responsible for the overall direction and mission of the organisation. Middle managers translate such objectives into achievable targets. Front line managers develop operational plans to achieve such targets.

- Effective managers are active leaders who try to create the opportunity and the incentive to achieve high performance.
- While traditionally management practice in Ireland has been based more on pragmatism than professionalism, with common sense and experience being considered more important than education, there is evidence that this is changing, mainly as a result of the influence of foreign, multi-national corporations.
- A traditional criticism of the culture for business in Ireland is that it has not always encouraged enterprise and innovation. This trait was attributable to Ireland's relatively late independence which created, what some have termed, a 'dependence mentality'.

DISCUSSION QUESTIONS

1. Define the terms management and manager.
2. How important is the management function to society?
3. List and define the five management functions.
4. What are the three main levels of management? What are the responsibilities associated with each level?
5. Explain the three management skills. With which levels of management are the skills normally associated?
6. What are the characteristics of an effective manager? Can you identify an Irish manager with these qualities?
7. Write an essay on 'Current Management Issues in Ireland'.

REFERENCES

Bateman, T. and Zeithaml, C., *Management: Function and Strategy*, page 7, Irwin, Illinois 1993.

Bedeian, A., *Management*, Dryden, New York 1991.

Bennis, W. and Nanus, B., *Leaders*, Harper Row, New York 1985.

Business and Finance, January 1995, 'Top 1000 Irish Companies'.

Dineen, D. and Garavan, T., 'Ireland The Emerald Isle: Management Research in a Changing European Context', *International Studies of Management and Organisation*, Vol.24, No.1–2, 1994.

Drucker, Peter, 'Management and the Worlds Work', *Harvard Business Review*, Vol.66, No.6, 1988.

Gunnigle, P., 'Ireland' in Brewster, C., Hegewisch, A., Holden, L. and Lockhart, T. (eds), *The European Human Resource Management Guide*, Academic Press, London 1992.

Gunnigle, P. and Morley, M., 'Republic of Ireland' in *International Encyclopedia of Business and Management*, Routledge, London 1996.

Kakabadse, A., 'The Cream of Irish Management'. Paper presented to the 23rd Irish Institute of Training and Development National Conference, Limerick, April 1991.

Mintzberg, H., *The Nature of Managerial Work*, Harper Row, New York 1973.

Mintzberg, H., 'The Managers Job: Folklore and Fact' *Harvard Business Review*, Vol.53, No.5, 49–61, 1975.

2

History of Management Thought

2.1 INTRODUCTION

Attempts to understand and develop a *theory* of management can be traced back to man's earliest efforts to achieve goals by working in groups. However, the advent of the Industrial Revolution heightened awareness and interest in management theory and practice as managers sought to achieve internal *efficiency*. The opportunities created by the Industrial Revolution at the turn of the twentieth century led to a period of considerable debate on the most effective management theory and practice, which resulted in what we now term classical approaches to management.

A thorough knowledge and understanding of the classical approaches to management are necessary as they laid the foundations for many of the modern theories. In fact, the most modern approaches to management have integrated and expanded the key concepts developed within the classical approach. This chapter will examine the earliest contributions to management thought, the classical approaches and the modern approaches that are available to managers today.

2.2 EARLY MANAGEMENT THOUGHT

For thousands of years man has faced the same issues and problems that confront managers today. The earliest thoughts and ideas in relation to management can be traced back to the written records of the Sumerians (5000 BC), who documented the formation of their government, tax gathering systems and the conduct of commerce. The clearest example of such management thought lies with the Ancient Egyptians (4000 BC–2000 BC), who used managerial skills to build vast pyramids, giving rise to the first real nation state. The construction of the Great Pyramid involved over 100,000 workers of various trades using levers and rollers and took nearly thirty years to complete. To co-ordinate and manage such a vast exercise, the Egyptians developed managerial skills to organise human labour and found that hierarchy was the best way of delegating the multitude of tasks required to complete the undertaking.

Greek civilisation (circa 500 BC–300 BC) also contributed to early management thought with the development of separate courts, an administration system and an army, highlighting the need for different management functions. Early Greek philosophers, such as Socrates, differentiated between management and other technical functions, providing the first written example of the concept of management as a separate and specialist skill.

The Roman Empire (circa 300 BC–AD 300) provides further evidence of the development of management thought. Because the Roman Empire extended over such a vast area, the Romans faced the problems of management and control of their conquests. In order to manage the empire effectively, delegation of power and the *scalar principle of authority* were used, coupled with a system of communication between the outposts and the central command. The Roman Empire could then maintain control over its regions due to this tight organisation.

One of the most enduring examples of early management thought and certainly the most prevalent in Ireland can be found in the Catholic Church, which combined managerial skills with a spiritual message to successfully convey its objectives. The techniques included a strict hierarchy of authority and the specialisation of members along a functional basis. The Catholic Church became a model for the management of other religious organisations and the army, who developed further the concepts of leadership, *unity of command* and line and *staff authority*.

In the 1300s, flourishing Venetian merchants made their contribution to management thought by establishing the legal foundations of the enterprise. Financial records were formalised into double entry book keeping, first described by Pacioli in 1494. Machiavelli, who published *The Prince* in 1532, further developed management thought in relation to political organisation. He suggested that the prince or leader should build a cohesive organisation, binding his allies with rewards and making sure they knew what was expected of them. Machiavelli's ideas on leadership and consent of the masses for effective rule still have relevance in today's environment.

Collectively, the contributors to the development of early management thought have produced many ideas and concepts which are relevant to modern theory and practice. However, early managers tended to operate on a trial and error basis. Communication and transport problems prevented the widespread growth of business ventures which meant that advances in management techniques and skills could not significantly improve performance. The advent of the Industrial Revolution changed the situation and led to the development of management as a formal discipline.

2.3 THE INDUSTRIAL REVOLUTION

The Industrial Revolution marked a major watershed in the development of management thought. Up until the 1700s, large organisations were mainly military, political or religious rather than industrial. Most skilled work was performed by craft workers, working alone using fairly simple tools to produce clearly identifiable goods such as watches or clothing. These goods were then sold directly to individual customers within the locality of the craft worker.

The Industrial Revolution significantly changed this pattern of industrial activity. The invention of machines such as Watt's Steam Engine (1765), Arkwright's Water Frame (1769) and Cartwright's Power Loom (1785) effectively transferred skills from the craft worker to the machine. These new machines required only an unskilled worker to insert raw materials and extract the finished goods. Eventually, fully automated machines were developed which no longer required any worker input. Such developments also made possible the establishment of large-scale factories, which stood in marked contrast to the local nature of craft work.

As a result of these advances the *productivity* of both humans and animals was increased greatly. Industry began to feel the benefits of *economies of scale*, whereby the average unit cost of producing an item decreases as the volume of production increases. Consequently, prices fell and consumption rose. Developments in transportation and communications opened up new markets and promoted economic growth. Industry and commerce boomed and entrepreneurs formed the new social class — the bourgeoisie. The growth of industry gave people the opportunity to leave the country and move to cities to work in the new factories. The social implications of the Industrial Revolution were enormous as people left their homes to work long hours for poor pay and conditions.

Prior to the Industrial Revolution in Ireland, agriculture was the main form of occupation though some of the larger towns had small, water-powered factories which produced beer, whiskey and flour. Only about one in ten people lived in towns, most of whom were craft workers. The impact of the Industrial Revolution in Ireland was less evident than in the UK or the USA in terms of industrialisation. In fact, Irish industry suffered from competition in the UK, particularly in the woollen and cotton industries which virtually collapsed in the mid 1800s. The impact of the industrial revolution was most marked in the linen industry, where production moved from the home to large-scale factories. Ireland, however, remained an agricultural economy and only experienced the shift to industrial employment in the 1950s.

As industry and commerce expanded to capitalise on new markets and production processes, organisations became increasingly large and complex. New management techniques had to be developed to cope with the problems and opportunities presented by industrialisation. As early as 1776, Adam Smith produced the *Wealth of Nations* advocating that the key to profitability lay in the specialisation of labour, whereby workers should be assigned a specific task to complete, ensuring a sharp division of labour.

The Industrial Revolution created huge opportunities for mass production and, coupled with the increasing size and complexity of organisations, resulted in an upsurge of systematic thought on the key managerial problems presented by industrialisation, namely production, efficiency and cost savings. An era of renewed interest and debate ensued which led to the emergence of management as a formal discipline distinct from other technical areas.

Figure 2.1 The Evolution of Management Thought	
1700s	Industrial Revolution
Classical Approaches	
1898	Scientific management
1916	Administrative management
1920s	Bureaucracy
1927	Human relations
Modern Approaches	
1950s	Systems theory
1960s	Contingency theory
1970s	Total Quality Management
1980s	Organisational culture

The year associated with each school of thought is the year that the approach began. The beginning of the next school of thought does not, however, denote the end of the previous one.

The evolution of management thought since the Industrial Revolution can be divided into classical approaches and modern approaches. Figure 2.1 provides a historical picture of the evolution of management thought. Many of the approaches were developed simultaneously and, therefore, have affected one another. On the other hand, some of the approaches were developed as a direct response to weaknesses in earlier approaches. The remainder of this chapter will concentrate on the contribution of both the classical and modern approaches to the study of management.

2.4 THE CLASSICAL APPROACHES

The classical approach to the study of management was devised at the end of the nineteenth century, as a response to the managerial challenges posed by over a century of intense industrialisation. The major approaches associated with this era are scientific management, bureaucracy, administrative management and human relations — many of which were based on the personal experiences of key contributors. In order to avoid confusion about dates throughout the various approaches, it is important to distinguish between the date the work was written, the date it was translated into English and the date the work became popular in management thought. For many of the approaches each of these categories will have a different date.

2.4.1 Scientific management

Scientific management is concerned with the development of the single best way to perform a task through the application of *scientific methods*. The concept of scientific management is attributed to Frederick Taylor (1856–1917), whose ideas were developed in two books *Shop Management* (1903) and *Principles of Scientific Management* (1911). (Both of these books were combined and published in 1947 under the title *Scientific Management*.) Taylor trained in the USA as an engineer and, after finishing his apprenticeship, he joined the Midvale Steel Company where he rose to the rank of Chief Engineer. His first-hand experience at Midvale led him to conclude that both productivity and pay were poor, operations were inefficient and wasteful, and that relations between workers and management were antagonistic, a picture which he believed reflected the wider state of industry at the time.

According to Taylor, the principle objective of management should be to secure the maximum prosperity for the employer coupled with the maximum prosperity for each employee. This prosperity did not just mean profit, but the development of the employee to perform the highest grade of work for which he/she was able. In order to achieve this end, he advocated that scientific methods should be used to analyse the single best way to perform tasks scientifically.

In 1898, Taylor was employed as a consultant by the Bethlehem Steel Works Company, where he applied his principles of scientific management most visibly. Production within the company focused on two processes, the handling of pig iron blocks on to railroad cars and shovelling fuel (sand, limestone, coal and iron ore) into blast furnaces. Pig iron handling was a very physical job and the management at Bethlehem found that they could do nothing to persuade employees to work faster. By studying pig iron handlers over a period of time, Taylor concluded that with better, less tiring work methods and frequent breaks daily output per worker could be quadrupled. In order to do this, a piece rate pay system was developed whereby workers were paid extra when their output exceeded a standard level. The results were staggering; not only did output per worker increase from twelve and a half tons to forty-seven and a half, but wages per day increased from $1.15 to $1.85.

Taylor then proceeded to tackle the problem of shovelling which was completed by work groups of fifty to sixty men under a single foreman. *Time and motion studies* were used by Taylor to establish the best way of shovelling. The studies also examined the most suitable type of shovel, which Taylor believed depended on the raw material used. As a result of his findings, a tool room was established and each morning workers were given written instructions stating what tools were needed for the day. A piece rate system was also introduced. Once again the results were outstanding. Output increased from 16 tons to 59 tons per day and wages increased from $1.15 to $1.88.

Taylor's experience at Bethlehem led him to develop four main principles of management which became the cornerstones of scientific management.

1. **The development of a true science of work**: Taylor believed that both workers and management were essentially unaware of what a fair day's work was and, consequently, this gave employers room for complaint about employee inadequacies. Taylor, therefore, argued that rules of thumb should be replaced by a scientific approach to work, whereby each task could be broken down into basic movements. These could then be timed to determine the best way of doing the task. In this way, a worker would know what constituted a fair day's work, for which he/she would receive a fair day's pay. The level of pay would be higher than in unscientific factories, but if workers failed to perform they would lose income.

2. **The scientific selection and development of workers**: Taylor was aware of the importance of hiring and training the appropriate worker for the job with regard to physical and mental aptitudes. Having matched the worker to the job he/she could then be developed to the highest capacity by a piece rate system of pay. Taylor believed that as workers were motivated by money, both workers and managers would benefit by increased productivity.

3. **The co-operation of workers and management in studying the science of work**: Taylor believed that management and workers should co-operate to ensure that the job matched plans and principles. To achieve this, he advocated standardised tools, instruction cards to assist workers and breaks to reduce tiredness.

4. **The division of work between management and the workforce**: Taylor believed that both workers and management should do the tasks for which they were best equipped. In this regard, managers would direct and allocate work and workers would complete the tasks.

The *principles* of scientific management were widely accepted and one of the most famous applications of the approach was in Henry Ford's Model T factory. Other proponents of scientific management included Henry Gantt and Frank and Lillian Gilbreth. Gantt (1861–1919), a contemporary and acquaintance of Taylor, modified some of the latter's ideas. He proposed that every worker should be entitled to a set wage rate, with a bonus if output was exceeded. This would allow supervisors to spend more time coaching the less able worker or, in other words, apply the principle of *management by exception*. Such an approach left room for more initiative and discretion.

Frank Gilbreth (1868–1924) and his wife, Lillian (1878–1972) were also contemporaries of Taylor. They were primarily concerned with the elimination of waste and, like Taylor, discovering the single best way to do a job. They believed that in finding this one way, an individual's personal potential could best be achieved. Frank Gilbreth, who owned a construction company in Boston, began to analyse each task he performed, trying constantly to eliminate unnecessary work movements. He identified seventeen hand motions which he called therbligs (a slightly altered backward spelling of the family name). Frank believed that by isolating the therbligs in a task one could eliminate or shorten them. In applying this system to brick laying, he reduced the motions or therbligs from eighteen to four and a half.

After her husband's death, Lillian continued his pioneering work. As an industrial psychologist, she emphasised the need for understanding workers' personalities and needs, and pioneered the development of human resource management. Her interests lay in the human factor and the scientific selection, training and development of workers. The Gilbreths proved to be a formidable team in terms of their contribution to management thought and the handling of materials, monotony and modern human resource management.

Scientific management and its advocates had a phenomenal effect on managerial practices at the turn of the century. Taylor's *Principles of Scientific Management* was first published in 1911 and within a few years had been translated into eight different languages. Scientific management spread as far as the Soviet Union, where the principles were incorporated into the various five-year development plans. It dramatically improved productivity and efficiency in manufacturing organisations and introduced scientific analysis into the world of work. The piece rate pay system gained wide acceptance due to the link between effort and reward. Scientific management instilled a sense of co-operation between workers and management and the concept of a management specialist gained widespread acceptance.

However, scientific management was not without its critics. In emphasising the link between worker effort and monetary reward, Taylor assumed that people were motivated solely by money. Worker motivation is, however, far more complex and involves job-related social and psychological factors which Taylor ignored. The application of a single best way of completing a task meant that jobs frequently became routine and machine-like, leading to boredom and apathy among the workforce.

Trade unions strongly opposed scientific management techniques. They viewed the piece rate system as a return to the 'sweat shop' exploitation of labour by management. Scientific management techniques frequently resulted in lay offs and, as a result, unions feared that their application would lead to widespread job losses. While dealing with the issues of internal efficiency, scientific management failed to deal with the relationship between the organisation and the environment, such as competitors and regulators, especially at the senior level of the organisation.

Despite these criticisms the legacy of scientific management is pervasive. It formally established management as a specialist area, introduced scientific analysis to the work-place and provided a framework for solving the managerial problems of efficiency and productivity. While Taylor was accused of causing unemployment, his own aim was to cause a mental revolution so that both sides could take their eyes off the division of the surplus as the all important matter and, together, turn their attention towards increasing the size of the surplus (Taylor 1947).

2.4.2 Administrative management

Administrative management was based on the personal experiences of its key advocates. It focused on senior managers and the policy issues they faced. In doing so, administrative management offered *universal principles of management.* The most important contributor was Henri Fayol (1841–1925), commonly known as the father of modern management. Unlike previous management theorists who were American, Fayol was French and worked independently during the same period that scientific management was gaining momentum. Fayol, a mining engineer, came to realise that managing an enterprise required a host of other, non technical, skills. In 1916 he produced *Administration Industrielle et Generale,* later published in English during the 1930s as *General and Industrial Management,* which established him as the pioneer of European management in the early 1900s.

Unlike Taylor, who concentrated on work group management, the focus of Fayol's work was the senior executive of the organisation, which reflected his own managerial experiences. Concentrating on the problems faced by the senior executive in managing the organisation, Fayol concluded that all business activities could be divided into six essential areas: **technical** (production and manufacturing); **commercial** (buying, selling and exchange); **financial** (funding and using capital); **security** (guarding property); **accounting** (costing and stock-taking); **managerial** (planning, organising, controlling, commanding and co-ordinating).

The inclusion of management as a separate business activity with five main functions gained Fayol widespread recognition. He believed that each of the six groups of activities were interdependent and all needed to run effectively for the organisation to prosper. Figure 2.2 outlines a manager's main activities according to Fayol. It is interesting to note the similarity between Fayol's five main managerial activities and the modern five functions of management (planning, organising, staffing, leading and controlling) discussed in the first chapter.

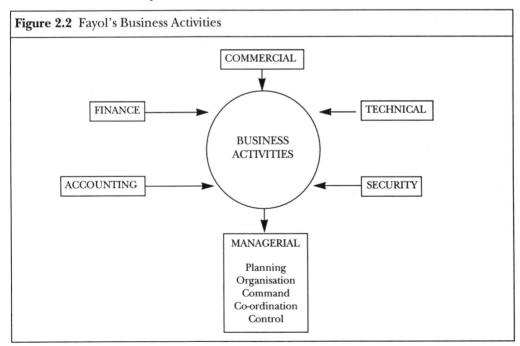

Figure 2.2 Fayol's Business Activities

In addition to the five management functions, Fayol identified fourteen basic principles of management which he had found to be most useful during his career. Figure 2.3 presents Fayol's management principles.

Figure 2.3 Fayol's Fourteen Management Principles

1. **Division of labour**: Divide work into specialised tasks and assign responsibility to individuals.
2. **Authority**: Equal delegation of responsibility and authority.
3. **Discipline**: Establish clear expectations and penalties.
4. **Unity of command**: Each employee should report to one supervisor.
5. **Unity of direction**: Employee efforts should be guided to achieve organisational goals.
6. **Subordination of individual interest to general**: Group interests should not precede the general interests of the organisation.
7. **Remuneration**: Equitable rewards for work.
8. **Centralisation**: Decide the importance of superior and subordinate roles.
9. **Scalar chain**: Lines of authority and communications from the highest to the lowest level.
10. **Order**: Order tasks and materials to support organisational direction.
11. **Equity**: Treat employees fairly.
12. **Stability of tenure**: Minimise turnover to ensure loyalty of personnel.
13. **Initiative**: Employees should have freedom and discretion.
14. **Esprit de corps**: Unity of interest between management and workers

---

Fayol emphasised that such principles of management should be applied in a flexible manner. His principles remain important not only because of the influence of Fayol on succeeding generations of managers, but also because of the continuing validity of his work. While many of the principles are out of date, several, such as unity of command and scalar principle, will be referred to in later chapters.

Other executives used their personal experiences to contribute to administrative management. Chester Barnard (1886–1961) produced *The Functions of the Executive* in 1938 which highlighted the importance of the mission and purpose of the organisation, hiring specialists and an effective communications system. During the 1920s, Mary Parker Follet (1868–1935) produced *The Dynamic Administration* (published in 1941 after her death) which emphasised the changing situations faced by managers. She pointed out that all managers want flexibility and also distinguished between the motivation of individuals and groups.

In 1947, Lyndall Urwick published *Elements of Administration* which emphasised the social responsibility of managers towards their employees. Urwick produced ten principles for good organisation which focused on responsibility, job definition and spans of control. As an employee of Rowntree in the UK, Urwick was influenced by the company's humane management policy, which became a trail blazer for many of today's human resource policies. Cadbury and Guinness were among the first companies in Ireland to adopt these policies.

The key contribution of administrative management was the recognition of management as a profession, much like law or medicine, in which people could be trained and developed. Advocates of administrative management offered recommendations based on their personal experience of managing large organisations and focused on senior level managers and the policy issues faced by them. Administrative management also offered universal principles of management, in other words, principles that were believed to work in all situations.

The main criticism levelled at the approach is that universal principles do not take account of variations in the environment, technology or personnel which may require alternative management action. Administrative management is remembered for its enormous influence on successive generations of managers due to the continued relevance and validity of its principles, particularly Fayol's.

2.4.3 Bureaucracy

Max Weber (1864–1920) was a German sociologist who wrote most of his work at the turn of the century, later translated into English during the 1920s. While Taylor's and Fayol's attention focused on the problems of effectively managing the organisation, Weber concentrated on how to structure organisations for success. He outlined the key elements of an ideal structure which he believed would promote efficiency, and called it *bureaucracy*. It is important to note that while the term bureaucracy may have negative connotations in today's society, at the turn of the century it was viewed as the ultimate structure which would provide efficiency and stability.

Weber's ideal bureaucracy had six main elements:

1. **Division of Labour**: Tasks were divided and delegated to specialists so that responsibility and authority were clearly defined.
2. **Hierarchy**: Positions were organised in a hierarchy of authority from the top of the organisation to the bottom, with authority centralised at the top.
3. **Selection**: Employees were recruited on the basis of technical qualifications rather than favouritism.
4. **Career orientation**: Managers were viewed as professionals pursuing careers rather than having ownership in the organisation.
5. **Formalisation**: The organisation was subject to formal rules and procedures in relation to performance.
6. **Impersonality**: Rules and procedures were applied uniformly to all employees.

Weber's ideal bureaucracy gained widespread acceptance as soon as his work was translated in the 1920s and 1930s. The structure was used extensively in large-scale organisations around the world due to the fact that it allowed them to perform the many routine activities necessary for survival. Bureaucracy was particularly popular for public organisations and civil service-type organisations. Many of the early Irish semi-state bodies and the Civil Service were structured along bureaucratic lines, including Aer Lingus and Iarnrod Eireann (formerly part of CIE).

The bureaucratic structure had a number of important advantages for large organisations. The division of labour increased efficiency and expertise due to repetition of each task. Hierarchy allowed a *chain of command* to develop in line with Fayol's scalar chain idea. Formal selection meant that employees were hired on merit and expertise only.

Career orientation ensured that professionals would give the organisation a degree of continuity in operations. Rules and procedures controlled employee performance and increased efficiency. The impersonality of the organisation ensured that rules were applied across the board without personalities or influence getting in the way.

While bureaucracy might be an extremely rational and efficient form of organisation, it has a number of disadvantages. The extensive rules and procedures can sometimes become ends in themselves. In other words, obeying rules at all costs becomes important irrespective of whether such action helps to achieve organisational goals. Bureaucracy promotes stability, but over time things can become very rigid. Rules and procedures are applied blindly to all situations even though they may not be the most appropriate. Consequently, the organisation comes to believe that what has worked well in the past will continue to do so in the future, despite changed conditions.

Delegation of authority in the bureaucratic organisation can lead to a situation where the goals of the work groups become more important than organisational goals, adversely affecting the organisation in the long run. The strict division of labour can lead to routine and boring jobs where workers feel apathetic and demotivated. The extensive rules can cause workers to establish a minimum acceptable standard as laid down by the rules, above which they will not go. So, instead of acting as a controlling device, the rules can actually reduce performance.

The fact that elements of Weber's bureaucratic structure can be found in so many organisations today is testimony to the importance of his work. Bureaucracy is both rational and efficient. However, organisations need to understand bureaucracy in order to avoid being controlled by it. Like Taylor and Fayol, Weber's work had an enormous influence on management thought and is still relevant in today's business environment, particularly for organisations operating in a stable environment such as McDonalds.

2.4.4 Human relations

The human relations (or behavioural) approach to management emerged in the 1920s and 1930s. In contrast to previous approaches, the human relations movement concentrated on the human side of management and sought to understand how psychological and social factors interacted with the work environment to influence performance. The approach built on the ideas and concepts developed by the foregoing approaches, most notably Gantt and the Gilbreths' scientific management.

The human relations approach emerged from a research study that began as a scientific management application to determine the impact of working conditions on performance and ended up discovering the effect of the human factor on productivity. Elton Mayo (1880–1949) and Fritz Roethlisberger, both Harvard researchers, were employed in 1927 by the Western Electric Company to study the effect of physical working conditions on worker productivity and efficiency. Commonly known as the Hawthorne Studies, and chronicled by Roethlisberger and Dickson in *Management and the Worker* (1949), they marked one of the most important watersheds in the evolution of management thought.

Western Electric (now AT&T Technologies) manufactured equipment for the telephone industry. Between 1924 and 1932, a series of studies were carried out within the company. The Hawthorne Studies can be divided into three main phases, with each phase adding to the knowledge gained previously: The Illumination Experiments 1924–1927; The Relay Assembly Room Experiments 1927–1932; and The Bank Wiring Observation Room Experiments 1931–1932.

• THE ILLUMINATION EXPERIMENTS 1924–1927
Prior to the arrival of Mayo and his research team, an investigation by the US National

Research Council had marked the first stage of the Hawthorne Studies. Between 1924 and 1927, the Illumination Experiments were conducted in several departments employing female coil winders, relay assemblers and small parts inspectors. The investigation was designed to determine how the level of lighting affected worker output, with the researchers expecting that better lighting would increase output. Two groups were isolated: the conditions in one were held constant, while the level of light was systematically changed in the other. The results, however, showed that output increased in both groups. When Mayo and his research team were employed in 1927, they concluded that there was no simple cause and effect relationship between illumination and productivity, and that the increase in output was caused by the fact that the workers were aware of being observed. This phenomena was called the Hawthorne Effect, whereby workers were influenced more by psychological and social factors (observation) than by physical and logical factors (illumination).

• THE RELAY ASSEMBLY ROOM EXPERIMENTS 1927–1932

The Relay Assembly Room Experiments were designed to study the effect of rest breaks, length of working day, refreshments and incentive payments on productivity. Six skilled women involved in the assembly of phone relays were selected and placed in a test room without their usual supervisor. An observer was placed in the test room to record observations and to create a friendly and relaxed atmosphere. The various changes were introduced with the women's knowledge and consent. The result was that output increased. The next stage was to return the women to their original conditions — a forty-eight hour, six-day week, without refreshments, incentives or breaks — and, once again, output increased.

In trying to explain these results, Mayo concluded that, unintentionally, the research team had changed the human relations of the work group under observation. The test room was significantly different to regular departments in four main ways. Firstly, the supervisory style in the test room, with the absence of a formal supervisor, was more open and friendly and workers enjoyed being the centre of attention. Secondly, the test room was less controlled than regular work groups and the women actually participated in decisions affecting their jobs and set their own work pace. Thirdly, group formation resulted in a cohesive, loyal and co-operative group. Finally, the attitudes of the women were different as they felt involved, and not simply part of a large department subject to managerial control. Consequently, this affected their job satisfaction.

Mayo was rather puzzled and surprised by the results of his observations and decided to interview the factory workers about their conditions. From this he found that many of the management's problems were related to human factors. In other words, people were under-productive because of things they felt were wrong, rather than because of ignorance about the company's objectives. This went against the grain of Taylorism, which claimed that once a worker was convinced of the one best way, he/she would adopt it.

• THE BANK WIRING OBSERVATION ROOM EXPERIMENTS 1931–1932

The final experiment was the Bank Wiring Observation Room Experiments, involving fourteen men. The men remained in their natural work setting (i.e. non experimental) with an observer but with no changes in their working conditions. The aim of the study was to analyse the behaviour of the work group and how it functioned. Observation and interviewing showed that the group had well-established norms or rules of behaviour. The results showed that the men restricted their output: not one worker exceeded the group standards for output. They had their own idea of what constituted a fair day's work and employees who exceeded the agreed daily output were called 'rate busters' and those producing below it were called 'rate chisellers'. These norms were enforced by the group through sarcasm and 'binging', whereby a group member hit another on the arm to show displeasure. Group members were united in their opposition to management and were indifferent to the financial incentive scheme offered for higher output. All of these observations led Mayo to conclude that informal work group relations had enormous influence on motivation and performance.

When Mayo reviewed the overall findings, he concluded that an 'informal organisation' existed among the workers, in addition to the 'formal organisation' recognised by management. From his research, Mayo produced four important findings which challenged prevailing assumptions of the time.

1. Personal and social factors have an important role to play in motivation and performance.
2. Individual attitudes are important in determining employee behaviour and performance. (Relay Room Experiments)
3. Supervision has an important role to play in employee job satisfaction and productivity. (Illumination Experiments)
4. Informal work groups have an important influence on employee performance. (Bank Wiring Room Experiment)

The important contribution made by the Hawthorne Studies was to recognise that social needs took precedence over economic needs and that the informal work group could exert control over employee behaviour and performance. Consequently, Mayo argued that managers should focus on motivation, communication and employee welfare to gain the co-operation of the group and promote job satisfaction and norms consistent with the goals of the organisation.

Another key contributor to the human relations approach to management was Abraham Maslow. Maslow was concerned with the issue of worker motivation and sought

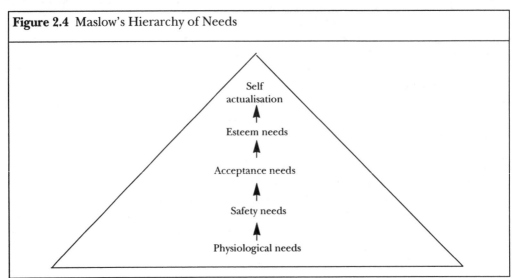

Figure 2.4 Maslow's Hierarchy of Needs

Self actualisation

Esteem needs

Acceptance needs

Safety needs

Physiological needs

to explain how workers could be motivated to achieve higher performance. In 1943, Maslow's studies led him to propose a theory of human motivation which is still referred to in current discussions of management. He believed that people try to satisfy a hierarchy of needs as shown in Figure 2.4.

The various needs which he identified started with physiological needs, such as food and shelter. Safety needs refer to feelings of security and physical protection. Acceptance needs concern the need to relate to and be accepted by other people. Esteem needs include the need for self respect and for the esteem of others. Finally, self actualisation refers to the needs for self-achievement and fulfilment. The first three have been termed deficiency needs as they need to be satisfied for basic comfort, while the last two are growth needs as they focus on growth and development.

Maslow argued that people try to satisfy their needs systematically, starting from the bottom and working up, so that once a given level of needs has been satisfied it no longer acts as a motivator and people move on to higher order needs. For example, people try to satisfy food and shelter needs before considering love and esteem. These basic needs can be applied to the organisational setting to discover more about what motivates people. Figure 2.5 provides an example of *Maslow's hierarchy of needs* as applied to the organisation and shows what basic needs the worker has and what has to be satisfied before moving on to the next level.

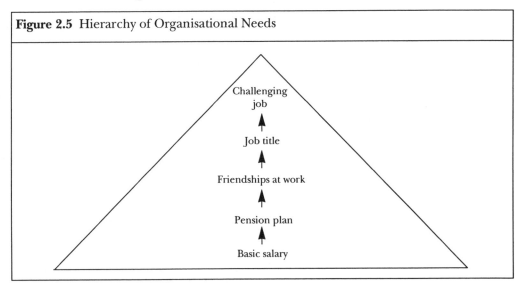

Figure 2.5 Hierarchy of Organisational Needs

Challenging
job

Job title

Friendships at work

Pension plan

Basic salary

It has been concluded that in many instances managers help workers to satisfy the first three needs but neglect the last two. Consequently, many employees remain under-motivated. Maslow's research gave important managerial insights into how people seek self actualisation in their work: many regard it as a way of satisfying physiological and safety needs, and seek self fulfilment in their hobbies or interests.

Other researchers belonging to the human relations school of thought include Hertzberg and McGregor, both of whom are discussed in detail in Chapter 6. The primary contribution of the human relations movement was its emphasis on the importance of the human factor in the work environment. The movement highlighted the role played by social and psychological processes and the satisfaction of needs in determining performance. As with the previous approaches, it also drew criticism. The

Hawthorne Studies, it was claimed, were unscientific in that many of the conclusions reached did not necessarily follow the evidence. The human relations approach in general has been criticised for its apparent neglect of the more rational side of workers and the important characteristics of the formal organisation. Despite criticisms, the human relations movement had a phenomenal impact on management thought and encouraged managers and researchers to consider psychological and social factors that might influence performance.

2.4.5 The classical approaches: a summary

The various classical approaches to the study of management laid the foundations for the management of organisations which still exist today. Figure 2.6 provides a summary of the main contributions and limitations of the various approaches.

Figure 2.6 The Classical Approaches: A Summary

School of Thought:	Scientific Management: 1898–Present
Proponents:	Taylor, Gantt and the Gilbreths
Contribution:	Application of scientific principles to the study of work through work studies and incentives
Limitations:	Simplistic view of motivation and ignored the role of the external environment
School of Thought:	Administrative Management: 1916–Present
Proponents:	Fayol, Follet, Barnard and Urwick
Contribution:	Universal principles of management for senior executives
Limitations:	Ignored environmental differences
School of Thought:	Bureaucracy: 1920s–Present
Proponent:	Weber
Contributions:	Bureaucratic structure emphasising efficiency and stability
Limitations:	Ignored the human element and the role of the external environment
School of Thought:	Human Relations: 1927–Present
Proponents:	Mayo, Roethlisberger and Maslow
Contributions:	Importance of social and psychological factors in influencing work performance
Limitations:	Ignored the role of the formal work group and worker rationality

---

The approaches were designed to provide managers with the necessary skills and techniques to confront the important issues of the time, namely productivity and efficiency. Primarily based on the personal experience of key contributors, they focused on the basic managerial functions, co-ordination of work and supervision. Apart from the human relations school and elements of administrative management, they concentrated on formal aspects of the organisation. With the benefit of hindsight some of the approaches take a simplistic view of the needs and interests of workers and fail to address the important issue of the role of the external environment in determining success. The more modern approaches to the study of management attempt to further these basic concepts and overcome key criticisms.

2.5 THE MODERN APPROACHES

Since the 1950s, modern approaches to the study of management have sought to build on and integrate many of the elements of the classical approaches and, in so doing, provide a framework for managing a modern organisation. As industries have matured and evolved and competition has steadily increased, researchers and practitioners have become more concerned about how to manage for competitive success. As a result, there has been an increasing amount of literature on management. The next section concentrates on four critically important approaches, namely systems theory, contingency theory, Total Quality Management and organisational culture, which mark the most dominant and influential theories on management, rather than an exhaustive list of all of the contributions.

2.5.1 Systems theory
The systems approach originated in the work of Barnard (1938) and came to the fore of management literature in the 1950s. Many of the classical approaches had ignored the role of the *external environment* and tended to concentrate on particular aspects of the organisation rather then viewing it as a whole. In the 1950s, management theorists began to consider the organisation as a whole system and developed systems theory as a means of interpreting organisations.

A system is a set of interdependent parts or elements which function as a whole in achieving certain goals or objectives. Systems theory argues that organisations should be seen as systems that transform inputs from the external environment into outputs back to the external environment. Figure 2.7 outlines the basic model of systems theory.

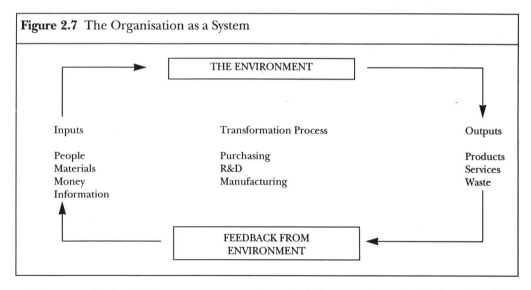

Figure 2.7 The Organisation as a System

THE ENVIRONMENT

Inputs

People
Materials
Money
Information

Transformation Process

Purchasing
R&D
Manufacturing

Outputs

Products
Services
Waste

FEEDBACK FROM
ENVIRONMENT

The organisation's inputs are commonly termed 'factors of production' and include materials, money, information and people. The organisation transforms such inputs into outputs in the form of goods or services to be exchanged in the external environment. Such outputs provide feedback for the organisation, enabling it to begin the whole process again. Figure 2.8 provides an example of the application of systems theory to an Irish university or third level institution.

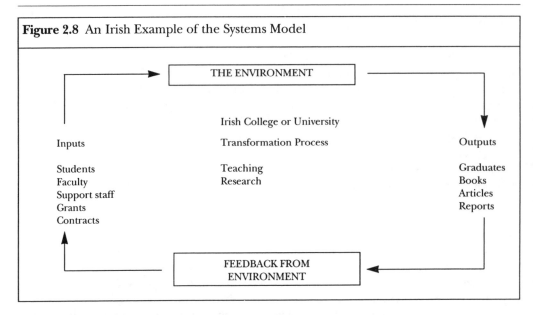

Figure 2.8 An Irish Example of the Systems Model

The above example shows how the organisation can be viewed as a system using various inputs and producing outputs for the external environment through its transformation process. The cycle of inputs, transformation and outputs must be maintained if the organisation is to stay in existence. The organisation will be profitable when the value created, or what customers are willing to pay, is greater than the cost of inputs and transformation.

One of the key elements of systems theory is that organisations should be viewed as *open systems* rather than *closed systems*. Many of the classical approaches treated organisations as closed systems which meant that the organisation did not depend on interactions with the external environment for survival and, in this sense, acted as a closed entity. The classical approaches, in concentrating on closed systems and internal efficiency, ignored the fact that the organisation depends on the environment for inputs and a market for outputs.

Systems theory advances the idea of the organisation as an open system which depends on other systems. For example, universities or third level institutions all depend on inputs in the form of students and faculty. In addition, they are dependent on the environment to sell or market their outputs in the form of graduates and research. So, if the organisation is to survive it must not only be aware of, but also respond to systems that it supplies and which supply it.

In viewing organisations as closed systems, many of the classical approaches were concerned solely with internal efficiency. By taking an open systems view another important dimension for managers becomes apparent — effectiveness. This is the extent to which the organisation's outputs match the needs and wants of the external environment. The effectiveness of a university or third level institution examined earlier, can be determined by the extent to which the external environment needs and wants students and research. If the environment neither needs nor wants the outputs, then the organisation cannot be effective no matter how efficient it is.

As all systems tend to have sub systems, the organisation can be viewed as a series of sub systems. Each sub system itself can be viewed as a system with its own sub systems.

The organisation can also be viewed as a sub system of a wider system. For example, the world economy can be viewed as a system with each of the national economies as sub systems. In turn, the Irish national economy is made up of various sub systems including industries. Avonmore as the organisation is a sub system of the wider food industry. The realisation that the organisation is both a system and a sub system encourages it to think in whole terms. As a result, it should be easier for the organisation to see the effect of any single action on its ability to achieve wider organisational goals.

Systems theory also highlights the point that if the performance of the organisation is the product of interactions of its various parts, it is possible for the action of two or more parts to achieve more than either is capable of individually. This concept is referred to as synergy and means that the creation of a whole is often greater than the sum of its parts. Therefore, the performance of the organisation as a whole depends more on how well its parts relate than on how well each operates. The implication for management is that organisations need to be managed in terms of their interactions, not independent actions.

The most important contribution made by systems theory is its recognition of the relationship between the organisation and its environment, especially in terms of achieving organisational *effectiveness*. Viewing the organisation as an open system emphasises the importance of the external environment both for inputs and markets for outputs. As a system the organisation also has various sub systems which must interact well with each other, sometimes achieving a synergy where the whole is greater than the sum of the parts.

One limitation of the approach is that it does not provide details on the functions and duties of managers working in open systems. Nonetheless, systems theory marked a step away from a sole focus on internal operations, to one which incorporated the external environment.

2.5.2 Contingency theory

The second modern approach to the study of management has attempted to integrate the concepts of earlier approaches, especially systems theory. Contingency theory advocates that managerial practice depends on the situation facing the organisation. Advocates of contingency theory argue that it is impossible to specify a single way of managing that works best in all situations, because the circumstances facing organisations are significantly different. In this sense, contingency theory rejects the idea of universal principles of management which can be applied in every case.

Contingency theory accepts that every organisation is distinct, operating in a unique environment with different employees and objectives. Such differences mean that managers have to consider the circumstances of each situation before taking action. The different circumstances are called *contingencies*. Managerial response depends on identifying key contingencies in the organisational setting. The main contingencies are:

1. The rate of change and complexity of the external environment.
2. The types of technology, tasks and resources used by the organisation.
3. The internal strengths and weaknesses of the organisation.
4. The values, skills and attitudes of the workforce.

These various contingencies affect the type of managerial action required by the organisation and its degree of success. For example, a universal strategy of low cost products will only be effective if the market is cost conscious. If the market emphasises quality then such a strategy will not be effective for the organisation. In this example, the success of the strategy is contingent upon the demands of the external environment. It should be noted, however, that low costs do not necessarily lead to poor quality but high quality is usually associated with higher costs.

Only when a manager understands the contingencies facing the organisation is it possible to identify which situations demand particular managerial action. Depending on the contingency, the organisation can categorise the situation and use an appropriate form of structure, managerial process or competitive strategy. Much of the research conducted within the contingency framework concentrated on how different environments and technologies affect the structure and processes of the organisation.

In 1969, Lawrence and Lorsch, both from the Harvard Business School, argued that the structure of the organisation is contingent upon the environment within which it operates. Their approach to structure was based on research undertaken in ten organisations in three different industrial sectors — plastics (six organisations), food (two) and containers (two).

In order to deal effectively with the external environment, organisations develop segmented units to deal with specific aspects. For example, organisational functions are typically divided into production, sales, research and development (R&D), and finance, each of which has to cope with different sub sections of the environment. Lawrence and Lorsch used the term differentiation to describe this segmentation or breaking down of functions. They defined differentiation as 'the differences in cognitive and emotional orientation of managers in various functional areas' (Lawrence and Lorsch 1969).

However, organisations also need to be co-ordinated to achieve effective transaction with the environment. Such co-ordination and collaboration is achieved through integration, which Lawrence and Lorsch define as 'the quality of the state of collaboration existing among departments that are needed to achieve unity of effort demanded by the environment' (1969:11). Integration can be achieved through mechanisms such as direct managerial contact, hierarchy, formal and informal communication, and through more sophisticated devices such as permanent integrating teams and an integrative department.

During the course of their research, Lawrence and Lorsch found that the greater the level of uncertainty in the environment, the greater the diversity or differentiation among organisational sub units. For example, organisations in the plastics industry facing a high degree of uncertainty, significantly differentiated between sales, R&D, finance and production. In contrast, organisations in the container industry facing a more certain environment, required less differentiation.

Greater differentiation, however, creates the potential for conflict between sub units as the specialist groups develop their own ways of dealing with uncertainty in the environment. Consequently, highly differentiated organisations require appropriate methods of integration and conflict resolution. Lawrence and Lorsch found that the greater the degree of differentiation, the greater was the need for integration. For example, high performing organisations within the plastics sector, which had the highest level of differentiation, used a variety of integrative mechanisms including direct managerial contact, hierarchy, communications, permanent cross functional teams and an integrative department. In contrast, the container industry, with lower levels of differentiation, required less integration in the form of direct managerial contact, hierarchy and communications.

Lawrence and Lorsch concluded that effective organisational functioning depended on an appropriate three-way relationship between uncertainty and diversity within the environment, the degree of differentiation and the state of integration achieved. In this way, the structure of a successful organisation was contingent upon its environment as shown in Figure 2.9.

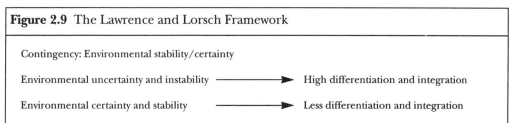

Figure 2.9 The Lawrence and Lorsch Framework

Contingency: Environmental stability/certainty

Environmental uncertainty and instability ⟶ High differentiation and integration

Environmental certainty and stability ⟶ Less differentiation and integration

In relation to technology, Burns and Stalker (1961) argued that the structure of the organisation was contingent upon the rate of technological change, as shown in Figure 2.10. Based on research in the UK, they found that if the rate of technological change is slow the most effective structure is mechanistic, but if the rate of change is rapid then a more flexible type of structure is required, called organic, which allows flexibility demanded by the pace of change.

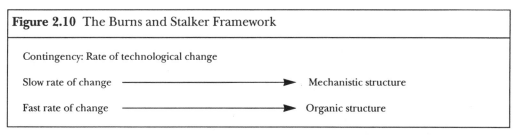

Figure 2.10 The Burns and Stalker Framework

Contingency: Rate of technological change

Slow rate of change ⟶ Mechanistic structure

Fast rate of change ⟶ Organic structure

A mechanistic form of structure is mainly hierarchical in nature with communications and interaction occurring vertically. In this form of structure, knowledge is concentrated at the top and continued membership of the organisation is based on obedience and loyalty. Therefore, the mechanistic form of structure is similar to a bureaucracy. In contrast, the organic structure is like a network with interactions and communications occurring both horizontally and vertically. Knowledge is based wherever it is most suitable for the organisation, and membership requires commitment to the organisation.

Lawrence and Lorsch, Burns and Stalker and another influential theorist on the relationship between structure and technology, Woodward, are discussed in more detail in Chapter 5.

An example of an Irish company which took a contingency approach to its structure is Team Aer Lingus. Up until 1990, Team was the Maintenance and Engineering (M&E) department of the national airline involved in aircraft maintenance of the Aer Lingus fleet and outside contracts. The external environment facing M&E remained relatively stable during the 1960s and 1970s, which suited the department's bureaucratic structure. However, once the environment became more dynamic and competitive in the mid-1980s, it was forced to change its structure in order to take advantage of market opportunities. As a result, Team was formed as a separate company with its own internal business unit structure. Layers of hierarchy were eliminated and job design was widened to give more flexibility in meeting the demands of the competitive environment.

The main contributions of contingency theory are that it recognised the limitations of universal principles of management and identified contingencies under which different actions are required. These ideas gained widespread acceptance especially in relation to the roles of technology and the external environment. The main problems associated with the approach is that it may not be applicable to all managerial issues and it is almost impossible to identify all contingencies facing organisations. Despite these problems, contingency theory is still popular today, emphasising the need for managers to be flexible and adaptable to changing conditions. In recognising that the world is too complex for there to be one best way of managing, contingency theory has provided much food for thought in contemporary management.

2.5.3 Total Quality Management

Improving the quality of products and services is not a new idea, but since the 1950s there has been an upsurge of interest in the role quality improvement can play in organisational success. Traditionally, quality was seen as the responsibility of the Quality Control Department, whose role was to identify and weed out mistakes after they had occurred. However, controlling mistakes after they had been made meant that many of the quality defects were already embedded in the product and were essentially hidden and difficult to locate. Organisations, therefore, did the best they could to uncover mistakes, but were resigned to the fact that certain problems would remain undetected. Total Quality Management, however, emphasised preventing mistakes rather than finding or correcting them. In order to achieve this, responsibility for quality shifted from Quality Control to all members of the organisation. This led many organisations to alter their operations fundamentally.

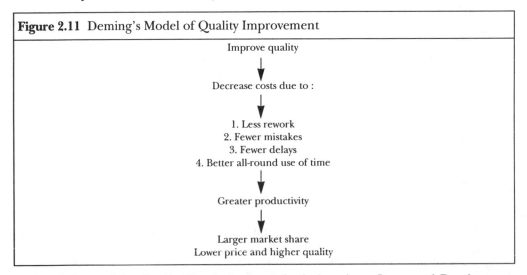

Figure 2.11 Deming's Model of Quality Improvement

Improve quality

Decrease costs due to :

1. Less rework
2. Fewer mistakes
3. Fewer delays
4. Better all-round use of time

Greater productivity

Larger market share
Lower price and higher quality

The fathers of the Quality Revolution were both American, Juran and Deming, yet, ironically, it was the Japanese who embraced their ideals in the 1950s. Much of Japan's post war manufacturing success has been attributed to both Deming and Juran. Deming believed that by improving quality, costs would decrease due to less rework, fewer mistakes, fewer delays and better all-round use of time. This would, he believed, result in greater productivity and enable the organisation to capture a larger share of the market with lower prices and higher quality as illustrated in Figure 2.11. Therefore, the more the idea of quality became embedded in the organisation, the less it would cost over time.

Deming produced a list of fourteen points which he believed were the essential ingredients for achieving quality within the organisation. He emphasised that organisations should cease to rely on inspection to ensure quality, but that quality should be built into every stage of the production process with statistical controls to prevent defects rather than detect them. Deming also believed that the cause of inefficiency and poor quality lay with the systems used and not the people using them. Therefore, it was management's responsibility to correct the systems to achieve high quality. He further stressed the importance of reducing deviations from standards and distinguished between special causes of variation (correctable) and common causes of variation (random).

Juran also taught quality to the Japanese and argued that 80 per cent of quality defects were correctable and, therefore, controllable by management. Consequently, he believed it was management's responsibility to correct this problem. Quality, he believed, revolved around three areas:

1. Quality planning to identify the processes which would be capable of achieving standards.

2. Quality control to highlight when corrective action was required.

3. Quality improvement to identify ways of doing things better.

The successful application of these concepts in Japan by the 1970s resulted in increasing their power in the US steel, auto and electronics markets. As a result, organisations world-wide attempted to copy the Japanese success and adopted total quality initiatives aimed at helping organisations cope with increased competition.

The term Total Quality Management has come to mean the organisation's philosophy and efforts to achieve a total quality product/service by the involvement of the entire organisation with customer satisfaction as the driving force. The TQM approach involves a number of steps as shown in Figure 2.12.

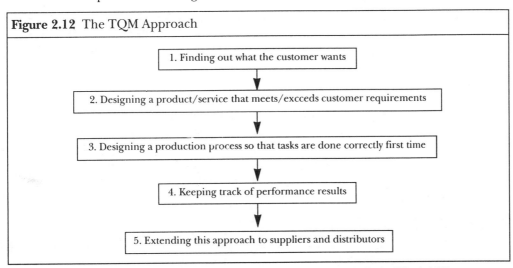

Figure 2.12 The TQM Approach

1. Finding out what the customer wants

2. Designing a product/service that meets/excceds customer requirements

3. Designing a production process so that tasks are done correctly first time

4. Keeping track of performance results

5. Extending this approach to suppliers and distributors

Source: Stevenson, W., *Production/Operations Management*, page 104, Irwin, Illinois 1989.

The first step involves finding out about customer requirements. This can be achieved by the use of surveys and focus group interviews. Following on from this, a product/service is designed to meet customer requirements focusing on easy use and easy production. The production process must then be designed to determine where mistakes are likely to occur and how to prevent them. Performance results are gathered and monitored to make sure that continuous improvement takes place. Finally, organisations that have developed TQM attempt to extend the principles to those who supply them with raw materials and those who distribute the final goods/services.

An important feature of the TQM approach is that the entire organisation is involved in the search for quality improvement and nothing is regarded as untouchable. Members of a TQM organisation view themselves as internal customers. In this sense, different areas within the organisation can be viewed as customers. For example, the Materials Department supplies the Production Department with raw materials. So, in this regard, Production is a customer of the Materials Department. By focusing on what is needed to satisfy these internal customers, it is quite frequently possible to improve the system, and thereby increase external customer satisfaction.

Within a TQM system each employee is responsible for the quality of his/her work and is expected to produce goods/services that meet specifications and to find mistakes. The emphasis is on producing goods and services correctly the first time rather than identifying faults that have already been made. In this way, each employee becomes a quality inspector for his/her own work. When the work is then passed on to the next internal customer in the process, the employee is certifying that the goods/services meet quality standards.

According to Stevenson (1993) there are five important elements to any Total Quality Management approach.

1. **Continual improvement**: The quest to improve quality must be never ending.
2. **Competitive benchmarking**: This involves finding another organisation which is the best at doing something and then using it as a model.
3. **Employee empowerment**: Workers must be given responsibility and autonomy to make changes where necessary.
4. **Team approach**: Teams promote participation and co-operation which is essential for quality improvement.
5. **Knowledge of tools**: Everyone in the organisation should be trained in the use of quality control and improvement tools, such as statistical quality control. This involves determining how many products from a larger number should be inspected to calculate the probability that the total number of products meets organisational quality standards.

Total quality, as advocated by Deming and Juran, has become a vital ingredient for corporate success. It has become one of the most important tools in achieving competitive advantage and is seen as an important way for the organisation to differentiate itself from competitors. On the whole it has created a revolution in the way quality can be managed and improved and has become a cornerstone in modern management thought.

2.5.4 Organisational culture
The final approach examined in this chapter is *organisational culture* and its affect on

management. The organisation's culture is concerned with the shared values, beliefs and assumptions of its members commonly communicated through symbolic means. Schein (1985) provides a useful definition of organisational culture: 'Organisational culture is the pattern of basic assumptions that a given group has invented, discovered or developed in learning to cope with its problems of external adaptation and internal integration.'

The culture of the organisation develops over time from a unique blend of three interdependent elements as shown in Figure 2.13.

Figure 2.13 The Formation of an Organisation's Culture

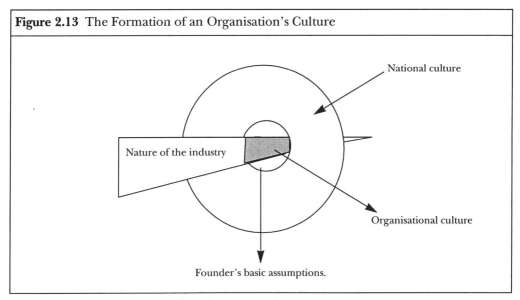

Source: Adapted from Ott, *The Organisational Culture Perspective*, page 83, Irwin, Illinois 1989.

Firstly, the organisation's culture is developed by the prevailing national culture within which it operates. Secondly, the nature of the industry acts as a determinant of the organisation's culture. Specific industries have certain cultural characteristics which become manifest in the organisation's culture. Gordon (1991) argues that organisational culture is shaped by the competitive environment and the degree to which the organisation is in a monopoly situation or faced by many competitors. Similarly, customer requirements in the form of reliability versus novelty shape the organisation's culture. Finally, society holds certain expectations about particular industries which influence the values adopted. Both the role of national culture and industry characteristics reflect the view that the organisation is shaped by its environment in line with Katz and Kahn's (1966) open systems theory. The final element shaping the organisation's culture is the role of its founders. Founder members shape organisational culture by their own cultural values which they use to develop assumptions and theories when establishing the organisation. Therefore, organisational culture is developed from three interdependent sources all of which influence the beliefs, values and assumptions of the organisation.

Organisational culture was catapulted to the forefront of management literature with the publication of four books in the early 1980s —*The Art of Japanese Management*

(Pascale and Athos 1981), *In Search of Excellence* (Peters and Waterman 1982), *Theory Z* (Ouchi 1981) and *Corporate Cultures* (Deal and Kennedy 1982). These and subsequent publications have tried to explain why some organisations are more successful than others and have pin-pointed aspects of culture which, they argue, contribute to organisational performance. The organisational culture perspective, therefore, maintains that many of the behaviours within the organisation are predetermined by the patterns of basic assumptions in the organisation, i.e. its culture. Effective management, therefore, should focus on the culture of the organisation rather than on its structures and systems.

Ouchi (1981) analysed the organisational cultures of three groups of organisations which he characterised as typical American organisations, typical Japanese organisations and Type Z American organisations. Through his analysis Ouchi developed seven cultural factors with which these three types of organisation could be compared. He believed that the cultures of both the typical Japanese organisation and the Type Z American organisation were very different to the typical American organisation. Ouchi argued that the differences in culture explained the success of Japanese and Type Z organisations at the expense of typical American organisations. The seven points of cultural comparison developed by Ouchi are shown in Figure 2.14.

Figure 2.14 The Ouchi Framework			
Cultural value	**Japanese Co.**	**Type Z**	**Typical US Co.**
Commitment to employees	Lifetime employment	Long-term employment	Short-term employment
Evaluation	Slow and qualitative	Slow and qualitative	Fast and quantitative
Careers	Very broad	Moderately broad	Narrow
Control	Implicit and informal	Implicit and informal	Explicit and formal
Decision making	Group consensus	Group consensus	Individual
Responsibility	Group	Group	Individual
Concern for people	Holistic	Holistic	Narrow

Source: Ouchi, W., *Theory Z: How American Business can meet the Japanese Challenge*, Addison-Wesely, Massachussetts 1981.

Peters and Waterman (1982) focused more specifically on the relationship between organisational culture and performance. They chose a sample of highly successful organisations and tried to describe the management practices that made them so successful. They identified eight cultural values that led to successful management practices which they called excellent values. These are listed in Figure 2.15.

According to the organisational culture perspective, successful management resulted from the development of key cultural values rather than any innovations in structure and systems. The key contribution made by the approach was the recognition of the importance of the role of organisational culture within the organisation. Limitations of the approach are that it is unscientific, organisational cultures are not easily identifiable and that many of the excellent organisations identified in the research (especially by Peters and Waterman) have subsequently performed badly. The approach also largely ignores the role of structures and systems within the organisation and their part in achieving organisational success.

Figure 2.15 The Peters and Waterman Framework

Characteristics of the Excellent Organisation

1. **Bias for action**: Managers are expected to make decisions even if all of the facts are not available.
2. **Stay close to the customer**: Customers should be valued over everything else.
3. **Encourage autonomy and entrepreneurship**: The organisation is broken into small, more manageable parts and these are encouraged to be independent, creative and risk taking.
4. **Encourage productivity through people**: People are the organisation's most important asset and the organisation must let them flourish.
5. **Hands-on management**: Managers stay in touch with business activities by wandering around the organisation and not managing from behind closed doors.
6. **Stick to the knitting**: Reluctance to engage in business activities outside of the organisation's core expertise.
7. **Simple form, lean staff**: Few administrative and hierarchical layers and small corporate staff.
8. **Simultaneously loosely and tightly organised**: Tightly organised in that all organisational members understand and believe in the organisation's values. At the same time, loosely organised in that the organisation has fewer administrative overheads, fewer staff members and fewer rules and procedures.

2.5.5 The modern approaches: a summary

Systems theory, contingency theory, Total Quality Management and organisational culture have dominated the field of management thought since the 1950s and are still influential both in theory and practice. The key contributions and limitations of the various approaches are outlined in Figure 2.16.

Figure 2.16 Modern Approaches: A Summary

School of Thought:	Systems Theory: 1950s–Present
Proponents:	Barnard and Katz and Kahn
Contribution:	Organisation seen as an open system interacting with the environment; organisation is both a system and a sub system; synergies exist and multiple ways to achieve the same outcome
Limitation:	No specific guidelines on the functions and duties of managers
School of Thought:	Contingency Theory: 1960s–Present
Proponents:	Burns and Stalker and Lawrence and Lorsch
Contribution:	Appropriate managerial action depends on situational contingencies; no one best way of managing
Limitation:	Not possible to identify all contingencies; may not apply to all managerial issues
School of Thought:	Total Quality Management: 1970s–Present
Proponents:	Deming and Juran
Contribution:	Quality is an important means of achieving competitive advantage; emphasises Total Quality Management throughout the organisation and on doing things right first time
Limitation:	Ignores other issues such as structure and strategy
School of Thought:	Organisational Culture: 1980s–Present
Proponents :	Peters and Waterman, Ouchi, Deal and Kennedy and Pascale and Athos
Contribution :	Highlighted the importance of organisational culture in an organisation's success
Limitation :	Largely unscientific approach, culture difficult to identify and some research within the school has been discredited

Systems theory recognised the organisation as an open system depending on the external environment for survival and emphasised that efficiency alone was not sufficient for survival. In order to be successful, organisations have to be effective in ensuring a match between what they produce and what the external environment wants and needs.

Contingency theory argues that best management practice depends on or is contingent upon the situation at hand. The technology employed by the organisation and the environment within which it operates often influence the managerial action required for success.

Total Quality Management emphasises the importance of improving quality to achieve competitive advantage. It was argued that Total Quality Management could significantly reduce costs, focus on customer satisfaction and lead to huge quality gains, all of which benefit the organisation. In terms of management, the focus is on building total quality into every aspect of the organisation and at every level so that it becomes everyone's responsibility not just that of the Quality Control Department.

Organisational culture emphasises the role that the organisation's culture can play in shaping its success. It is argued that managers should shift their focus from structures and systems and concentrate their efforts on developing and sustaining cultural values which contribute to organisational success.

These approaches are still popular today in the field of management thought and represent four of the most critical issues facing managers as they try to achieve an advantage in the increasingly competitive external environment. Systems theory highlights the importance of the environment for organisational survival. Contingency theory emphasises that best management practice depends on the situation which must be evaluated by the manager. Total Quality Management focuses on the role quality can play in reducing costs and improving the goods/service. Finally, organisational culture emphasises the importance of the organisation's basic values and assumptions and the important role they play in its success. All of these factors need to be adequately addressed by managers in today's environment if the organisation is to be successful. These points will be developed further throughout the book.

2.6 SUMMARY OF KEY PROPOSITIONS

• The earliest contributions to management thought can be traced back to the Sumerians, Ancient Egyptians and Romans. One of the most enduring examples of early management practice is the Catholic Church.

• The Industrial Revolution marked a watershed in the development of management thought. As industries expanded to take advantage of new markets and technological innovations, organisations became larger and more complex. This led to the development of new management techniques to cope with the issues presented by industrialisation — production, efficiency and cost savings.

• In response to the managerial challenges posed by industrialisation, the classical approach to management emerged at the turn of the century. The major schools of thought associated with this approach are: scientific management, administrative management, bureaucracy and human relations.

• Scientific management emphasised the development of the single best way of performing a task through the application of scientific methods. The origin of scientific management is attributed to Taylor and his pioneering work in the Bethlehem Steel Works.

•Administrative management was based on the personal experiences of its key proponents and focused on senior managers and the policy issues they faced. The father of administrative management was Fayol who identified management as a separate business activity with five functions. Fayol also developed fourteen principles of management.

• Max Weber concentrated on how organisations should be structured to ensure efficiency. He developed what he perceived to be the ideal form of structure and called it bureaucracy. The bureaucratic structure emphasised detailed rules and procedures, hierarchy and impersonal relationships between organisational members.

• The human relations movement concentrated on the human side of management and tried to understand how social and psychological factors influence performance. Mayo and his associates conducted the Hawthorne Studies which proved that social needs took precedence over economic needs and that the informal work group exerts control over employee performance.

• The modern approaches to management have developed from the 1950s and include, systems theory, contingency theory, Total Quality Management and organisational culture. Systems theory argues that organisations should be viewed as systems that transform inputs into outputs to the environment. Consequently, the organisation constantly interacts with its environment. Key advocates of this approach include Barnard and Katz and Kahn.

• Contingency theory argues that there is no single best way of managing due to the different situations or contingencies facing organisations. The most common contingencies are the external environment, technology, internal strengths and weaknesses of the organisation and the values and skills of the workforce. Burns and Stalker and Lawrence and Lorsch examined the contingencies affecting structure.

• Total Quality Management (TQM) was pioneered in Japan by Americans Juran and Deming. They argued that quality was the key to organisational success. The TQM approach they developed emphasised the prevention rather than correction of mistakes. In order to achieve this, responsibility for quality shifted from the Quality Control Department to all members of the organisation.

• The organisational culture approach emphasises the importance of culture in influencing behaviour within the organisation. Advocates of this approach such as Peters and Waterman and Ouchi argue that effective management should focus on culture rather than structures and systems.

• All of the issues raised by the various approaches need to be considered by managers when striving to compete in the present business environment.

DISCUSSION QUESTIONS

1. What was scientific management? Why was it so popular.?
2. What effect did the Industrial Revolution have on management?
3. Compare and contrast scientific and administrative management.
4. What were the Hawthorne Studies? Why were they so important to the development of management thought?
5. What are the main elements of bureaucracy? What are its advantages and disadvantages?
6. How did systems theory try to overcome the limitations of earlier approaches?
7. Explain why contingency theory has become so popular.
8. What is Total Quality Management? What does it try to achieve?
9. How do the modern approaches to management differ from the classical approaches?
10. Taylor and Fayol have been accused of seeking a single best way of managing the organisation. To what extent is this statement true?
11. Why is the organisational culture of the organisation important for managers to consider?

REFERENCES

Barnard, Chester, *The Functions of the Executive*, Harvard University Press, Cambridge, Massachussetts 1938.

Baughman, J. (ed), *The History of American Management Thought*, Prentice-Hall, New Jersey 1969.

Burns, T. and Stalker, G., *The Management of Innovation*, Tavistock, London 1961.

Deal, T. and Kennedy, A., *Corporate Culture: The Rites and Rituals of Corporate Life*, Wesely, Massachussetts 1982.

Deming, W., *Quality Productivity and Competitive Position*, MIT, Cambridge, Massachussetts 1982.

Drucker, Peter, *Managing in Turbulent Times*, Heinemann, London 1980.

Drucker, Peter, *The Frontiers of Management*, Heinemann, London 1949.

Fayol, Henri, *General and Industrial Management*, Pitman, London 1949. Translation of *Administration Industrielle et Generale* (1916).

Gordon, G., 'Industry Determinants of Organisational Culture' *Academy of Management Review*, Vol.16, No.2, 339–358, 1991.

Handy, Charles, *Understanding Organisations*, Penguin, London 1993.

Juran, J., 'The Quality Trilogy' *Quality Progress*, Vol.19, No.8, 19–24, 1986.

Katz, D. and Kahn, R., *The Social Psychology of Organisations*, John Wiley, New York 1978.

Koontz, Harold, 'The Management Theory Jungle Revisited' *Academy of Management Review*, April, 175–187, 1980.

Lawrence, P. and Lorsch, J., *Organisations and Environment: Managing Differentiation and Integration*, Irwin, Illinois 1969.

Machiavelli, Niccolo, *The Prince*, Penguin, London 1985. Originally published in 1532.

Maslow, Abraham, *Motivation and Personality*, Harper Row, New York 1954.

Maslow, Abraham, 'A Theory of Human Motivation' *Psychological Review*, Vol.50, No.2, 370–396, 1943.

Mayo, Elton, *The Human Problems of an Industrial Civilisation*, Macmillan, New York 1949.

Metcalf, Henry and Urwick, Lyndall (eds), *Dynamic Administration: The Collected Papers of*

Mary Parker Follet, Harper Row, New York 1941.

Ott, M., *The Organisational Culture Perspective*, Irwin, Illinois 1989.

Ouchi, W., *Theory Z: How American Business can Meet the Japanese Challenge*, Addisan-Wesely, Massachussetts 1981.

Pascale, R. and Athos, A., *The Art of Japanese Management: Applications for American Executives*, Harper Row, New York 1981.

Peters, Tom and Waterman, Robert, *In Search of Excellence*, Harper Row, New York 1982.

Pugh, D. and Hickson, D., *Writers on Organisations*, Penguin, London 1989.

Roethlisberger, E. and Dickson, W., *Management and the Worker*, Harvard University Press, Cambridge, Massachussetts 1939.

Schein, E., *Organisational Culture and Leadership*, Jossey Bass, California 1985.

Smith, A., *An Inquiry into the Nature and Causes of the Wealth of Nations*, Modern Library, New York 1937. Originally published in 1776.

Stevenson, W., *Production/Operations Management*, Irwin, Illinois 1993.

The Sunday Business Post, selected articles, April to July 1993.

Taylor, F., *Scientific Management*, Harper Row, New York 1947.

Urwick, L., *The Elements of Administration*, Pitman, London 1973.

Weber, Max, *The Theory of Social and Economic Organisation*, Henderson and Talcott translation, Free Press, New York 1947.

Weinhrich, H. and Koontz, H., *Management. A Global Perspective*, McGraw-Hill, New York 1993.

3

The Business Environment

3.1 INTRODUCTION

This chapter analyses the business *environment* within which all organisations operate. It is possible to consider the external environment in two main sections: a macro environment and a task environment. In the current business environment the most important area to consider is that of competitors or rivals. Competitive analysis can be undertaken to determine the degree of competition in the market-place and to assess whether the environment is favourable or unfavourable. Based on this analysis, the organisation can then make attempts to manage its external environment.

3.2 THE BUSINESS ENVIRONMENT

Organisations, regardless of their size or whether they are public or private enterprises, domestic or international, all operate within the context of an external environment. The external business environment includes all factors which affect the organisation yet which lie outside its boundary, i.e. all factors that are external to the organisation. In order to fully understand the challenge faced by managers, it is important to come to terms with the relationship between the organisation and its external environment.

Systems theory, which was introduced and discussed in Chapter 2, highlighted the importance of the external environment in viewing the organisation as an open system. All organisations must have inputs (people, money, information and materials) from their external environment and, in turn, exchange the finished goods and services for continued existence. Managerial performance often depends on knowing how the organisation influences and is influenced by its external environment. No organisation can be viewed as having enough power and influence to be able to ignore environmental pressures.

Factors contained in the external environment are essentially uncontrollable from the organisation's point of view. For example, there is very little the organisation can do to prevent the onset of a recession. However, this does not mean that the organisation can ignore such factors. For example, many Irish organisations were severely affected by the recent interest rate and currency crises. To survive in the current business environment the organisation needs to be able to manage its environment by being aware of current developments and, where possible, anticipating future developments to ensure a speedy and accurate response to the situation at hand.

The external business environment consists of two main elements: the macro environment is the most general part of the environment, containing, for example, the political and economic environments and other fundamental factors which generally affect all organisations; the task environment is more specific and includes competitors, suppliers, customers, trade unions and regulators, all of whom interact with the organisation. Figure 3.1 illustrates the external environment facing organisations.

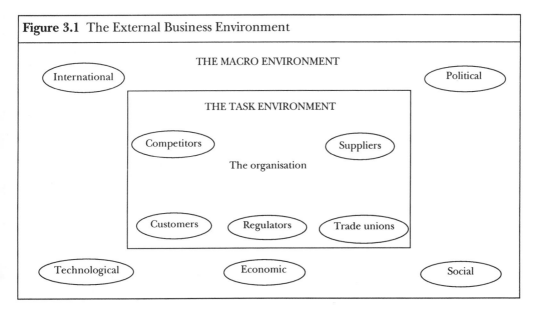

Figure 3.1 The External Business Environment

THE MACRO ENVIRONMENT

International

Political

THE TASK ENVIRONMENT

Competitors

Suppliers

The organisation

Customers

Regulators

Trade unions

Technological

Economic

Social

3.3 THE MACRO ENVIRONMENT

The macro environment contains general factors which affect all organisations and includes the international environment, political and economic factors, technology and social factors. The macro environment facing most organisations is quite similar, given the general nature of the various factors. For example, developments in the international environment affect most organisations. How organisations perceive and react to these factors, however, accounts for the variations in organisational performance in relation to the external environment. Each of the elements of the macro environment are discussed below.

3.3.1 The international environment
The international environment concerns events which transcend national boundaries. Developments in this environment have important ramifications for organisations operating in international markets. However, domestic organisations should also be aware of developments on the international front, in order to facilitate future decisions on international expansion and to keep abreast of developments which may lead to new entrants on to the domestic market.

The current international environment is characterised by three important emerging trends: the formation of the *Single European Market,* the opening up of the former

Eastern European markets and the increasing importance of the Asia/Pacific region.

In 1992, the member states of the European Community (now known as the European Union) integrated economically. Trade barriers between the member states have been eliminated and capital and labour can now flow freely between the states with no restrictions. The issue of a common European currency has not been agreed upon to date. However, it is likely that in the future member states will operate a common currency.

As a result, the European Union (EU) has emerged as one of the largest markets in the world with a population of 346 million (Eurostat 1994). It is also becoming far more competitive on a global basis, pursuing an active policy to enhance its competitiveness in a number of key industries, including information technology, defence and aerospace. An example is the success of Airbus Industries, involved in the manufacture of civil aircraft, which has captured a 30 per cent share of the world-wide market since its formation in the early 1970s. The emergence of the EU has been a cause for concern in the USA as its exports and employment could suffer severely (Yochelson and Lesser 1990).

While the EU is becoming a more potent force in the global market in terms of its competitiveness, its development also presents threats and opportunities for individual member states like Ireland. In terms of opportunities, the establishment of the Single European Market has opened up vast European markets for Irish organisations. Non EU countries have come to view Ireland as an important base from which to aggressively pursue the EU market. For example, many US organisations, especially in the aerospace and electronics industries, have set up operations in Ireland to form a strategic base to capture EU market share. Acromil, located in Shannon, produces structural components for the aircraft industry. It established operations in Ireland hoping to win important subcontract work from Airbus, which would have been impossible to achieve from a US base. Therefore, the emergence of the Single European Market has afforded Ireland numerous opportunities. However, at the same time the opening up of Irish markets to EU competitors marks an important threat to established Irish markets.

The second major development has seen the break-up of the former Communist-controlled Eastern Europe. The Soviet Union has been disbanded and been replaced by a Commonwealth of Independent States (CIS). Germany was reunified and many former communist nations, such as Romania and Poland, denounced communism and moved towards capitalism with the *privatisation* of many state industries.

These developments are providing huge, previously untapped markets for goods and services. Organisations world-wide are investigating new business and investment opportunities. Many Irish organisations have also sought to expand in order to capture a share of these markets. An example of an Irish company expanding into Eastern European markets is Beeline Healthcare, established in 1989 to produce vitamins and supplements. The company has recently developed markets in both the Czech and Slovak Republics, Hungary and Poland (Finn 1994). Sales of Guinness have also grown significantly in Eastern Europe, and the region has become an important target export market (*Irish Times* 1994). So, the emergence of Eastern Europe has opened up many opportunities for Irish organisations. Along with such opportunities there are threats, however. The former communist countries are potential competitors for Irish companies in many markets, with their huge sources of cheap labour and raw materials. According to Schares (1991), many Polish organisations have already started to enter international markets.

The final trend has seen the development of a strong industrial and technological base in the Asia/Pacific region. Just as the Japanese threatened US dominance in the 1970s and 1980s, the 'four dragons' — South Korea, Taiwan, Singapore and Hong Kong — are emerging as strong challengers on the international front. Other Asian countries whose economies are growing include Thailand, Malaysia and the Philippines; their collective trade with the USA in 1990 was greater than that of Japan (Peters 1990). These countries are, therefore, increasing the competitiveness of many international markets. Africa and Latin America are two enormous markets whose economic potential has not yet been realised. When these markets start to develop and become more open they too will provide opportunities and threats.

3.3.2 The political environment

The political environment is shaped by the activities of governments at both national and international levels. The environment consists of the governments of different countries who have an enormous impact on the business environment in terms of economic policies, international trade policies and tax laws. The economic environment is also shaped by the activities of various governments and is discussed in the next section. On a national level, a government can affect business through its policies in relation to industrial/services development and, in particular, by various tax incentives, capital grants and expansion schemes. On an international level, the political environment influences business through policies in relation to international trade and deregulation/liberalisation.

One of the main ways that governments seek to influence international trade is their input into the General Agreement on Trade and Tariffs (GATT). GATT comprises ninety-seven member countries, including Ireland, and is the main multilateral body concerned with international trade. It recognises the right of governments to levy duties to offset export subsidies or dumping (selling goods and services at less than a fair value). In 1994, a new round of GATT was agreed with the aim of allowing more trade between member states. Individual governments and international agencies, such as the United Nations (UN), can also impose trade embargoes or sanctions on trade with particular countries. Iraq, South Africa and Libya have all had trade sanctions imposed on them in the past.

The political environment has also affected the business environment with moves towards deregulation in certain markets. Deregulation attempts to remove restrictions on trade within particular industries. Recent developments in the EU have seen moves towards the deregulation of financial markets and the airline industry, aimed at removing protective restrictions on operations to allow greater competition. The monopoly position currently enjoyed by Telecom Eireann, for instance, will cease by the year 2003, when the Irish industry will be deregulated and opened up to international competition (Magee 1994).

Due to the fact that Ireland is an export dominated economy, the Irish Government, both at national and international levels, tries to promote trade to ensure that Ireland can increase its exports to other markets. Ireland currently has a Balance of Trade surplus, which means that more goods are exported than imported. The Government tries to promote exports by ensuring a stable exchange rate which affects the cost of exports, and by trying to keep inflation down to stimulate demand and to keep exports competitive.

The developments in the political environment, including the new GATT agreement and moves towards deregulation and liberalisation, all result in the opening up of new markets and increased competition in existing markets.

3.3.3 The economic environment

The economic environment is shaped by the general state of individual economies, by the economic policies pursued by their respective governments and by the position of the various economies in relation to others, particularly trading partners. In effect, the economic environment consists of complex interconnections between the economies of different countries.

Governments pursue different economic policies which affect key areas like inflation (changes in prices levels from one year to the next), interest rates (the cost of borrowing money) and wage rates (levels of pay). Variations in these key areas have important effects on the business environment. Interest rates determine the extent of the organisation's loans and investments. In general, high interest rates deter organisations from heavy investment. Inflation and wage rates can be considered together. Increased inflation is usually followed by demands from workers for increased wages, because as inflation increases the purchasing power of the consumer declines. In other words, their wages buy fewer products and services.

Wage levels also affect the organisation's cost structure in that high wages mean high costs. Wage levels also determine the amount of disposable income, i.e. the amount customers can spend on goods and services which affects demand for the organisation's product. Finally, exchange rates have a huge impact on organisations which export large amounts of their produce and/or import large quantities of raw materials. When the value of the home country's currency rises in relation to the country to which they export, the organisation's goods and services become more expensive, thereby reducing their competitiveness. Therefore, variations in these areas affect the business environment within which organisations operate.

The current Irish economic environment has improved since the early 1980s and economic growth is stronger than in other EU member states. Inflation is low and stable, Government borrowing has been brought under control and the balance of payments is in surplus. The major problem is the high level of unemployment (17.9 per cent in 1994 makes it the second highest in Europe after Spain) and the ratio of debt to *Gross National Product.* Irish economic policy has centred around keeping finances under control, a firm exchange rate and low inflation to ensure growth. Wage increases under the Programme for National Recovery (1987) and the subsequent Programme for Economic and Social Progress (1990) were modest and designed to ensure that Irish products were competitive. This means that Irish organisations should be operating in an environment which allows them to compete favourably on the international market with competitive wage rates and a stable exchange rate.

One of the most important developments in relation to the economic environment has been the emergence of global interdependencies between different economies. This development is particularly important given that Ireland is a *small open economy.* National economies no longer operate in isolation; today they are interdependent. In other words, events in one economy impact on other economies.

For example, a recession in the UK affects the economies of other countries, particularly Ireland which has close trading links with the UK. Within the EU the currency crisis of 1993 highlighted how interdependent the various national economies have become. In the case of Ireland, a devaluation of the Punt was necessary to restore competitiveness in the Irish export market. Similarly, German interest rates have a huge impact on Irish interest rates through the exchange rate mechanism of the EU. Therefore, developments in one economy have enormous implications for others, which means that organisations have to keep up to date on growth and recession both domestically and internationally. Organisations which operate on an international basis must be aware of the economic conditions in both their parent and host nations. The main result of growing interdependencies between economies is that the complexity of conducting business increases.

3.3.4 The technological environment

The technological environment is concerned with technological developments and the pace of such developments. It is a critically important part of the macro environment as no organisation is immune to the effects of technological developments. Technological innovation, such as the development of the Walkman by Sony, leads to the creation of new industries, markets and competitive niches. Currently, technological innovation is occurring at a far greater pace than in previous decades, which is having an enormous impact on markets and whole industries. The lead times associated with such innovation are also decreasing. Lead time refers to the amount of time between the inception of the idea and its final production. One of the key results of the increase in the pace of technological change is that organisations can no longer rely on technological innovation to provide them with long-term success. Competitors can quickly imitate the innovation and eliminate any advantage the innovating organisation had. Organisations have to stay at the leading edge of technological change in order to enjoy any form of long-term success.

Technology affects the production techniques used by organisations. Technological innovations in the use of computers have resulted in computers being used increasingly for product design and manufacturing. A technique called *Computer Aided Design* (CAD) uses computer graphics for product design. *Computer Aided Manufacturing* (CAM) uses computers to assist in the manufacture of goods and services. Both CAD and CAM techniques are used in the automotive and electronics industries. Guinness has recently replaced its older brewing equipment with state of the art technology. Such new technology, particularly information technology and computers, has resulted in the complete automation of the brewing production process (*Irish Times* 1994). Robots have also been used increasingly in the manufacture of products. Figure 3.2 outlines the number of robots per 100,000 people in 1991 in a number of countries.

Figure 3.2 Industrial Robots per 100,000 People	
UK	125
Norway	130
France	173
USA	174
Finland	191
Italy	254
Germany	429
Sweden	479
Singapore	692
Japan	2,620

Source: Fortune 1994.

Technology affects the management and communications within the organisation. The more sophisticated the technology the easier it is to communicate and thereby manage large organisations. Systems such as Financial Information Systems (FIS) and Management Information Systems (MIS) mean that data can be acquired at the push of a button rather than having to sift through mounds of paper. Such systems also permit calculations to be computed on the data, which previously took a considerable time to achieve.

As a result of these changes, the technological environment is becoming increasingly complex and organisations need to keep up to date with developments. In the current business environment organisations need to incorporate technology into strategies to ensure survival. This is especially important for organisations involved in technological industries, but also has implications for all organisations in terms of production techniques and communications. Examples of Irish-based subsidiaries of US firms that are technological leaders in their industries include Intel, which is involved in the manufacture of micro chips, and Motorola, which is involved in the manufacture of mobile phones.

3.3.5 The social environment

The social environment is concerned with the attitudes and behaviour of members of society. An important influence on people's attitudes and behaviours is the demographic profile of the society in question. Demographics identify the characteristics of the people making up society's social units. Demographic groups include work groups, organisations, countries, markets and societies and can be measured in terms of age, gender, family size, education and occupation. These are the measures which are normally used in a population census.

Demographics affect the business environment in two important ways: the workforce employed by organisations and the consumers who purchase final goods and services. Organisations need to be aware of the workforce demographics when formulating plans for recruitment, selection, training and motivating staff. Consumer demands are largely a function of the demographics of a society. Large numbers of lone parent and dual income families with children have led to the development of crèche facilities and numerous disposable items such as nappies and ready-made baby foods. In Ireland the large number of highly skilled people available for work has meant that the labour market is very much a buyer's market. As a result, organisations do not need to focus on planning their manpower requirements to the same extent that they would have to if labour was scarce. Demographics also affect consumer demand. For example, radio stations such as 98 FM and FM 104 cater specifically for the musical tastes of the large proportion of the population who grew up in the 1960s and 1970s. Therefore, demographics affect human resource policies and the nature of products and services produced.

Developments in the wider social environment which affect people's attitudes and behaviour are also critically important for organisations to understand. As with demographics, developments in the social environment have implications for organisations in the attitudes and behaviour of the workforce and consumers. In relation to the workforce, the major social change over the past decade has been the emergence of large numbers of mothers working outside of the home. Organisations have had to introduce supportive policies regarding maternal and paternal leave, flexible working hours and child care. In 1994, for example, paternal leave became compulsory in Sweden for working fathers.

Social changes in relation to consumer demand have been equally important. One of the main developments has been the emergence of a more environmentally aware consumer. This has led to the development of new industries such as vegetarian and organic food markets. An Irish example can be seen in the expansion of the Dublin Trading Co-operative which has a sizeable market in organic food produce (O'Raghallaigh 1994). Other organisations have also been forced to become more environmentally aware by using recyclable materials, particularly for packaging.

Increasing crime and violence in society is also driving change with the emergence of whole new industries and the development of existing industries. For example, the increase of crime in the USA has led to the emergence of a whole new industry producing non lethal crime-fighting devices. Honeywell, ADT Security and AT&T all concentrate on the burglar alarm market where sales have increased from US $4 billion in 1986 to US $6 billion in 1993. (Serwer 1994)

Taken collectively, the five components of the macro environment are giving rise to an increasingly competitive, complex and changing business environment. Organisations operating in both domestic and international markets need to be aware of such developments and adopt pertinent strategies which reflect these developments.

3.4 THE TASK ENVIRONMENT

The task environment consists of factors which are directly relevant to the organisation. In contrast to the macro environment, which is a broad environment, the task environment is the more immediate environment in which the organisation operates. All organisations operating in a similar industry face the same task environment. It is important to remember that while it is possible to distinguish clearly between macro and task environments, the boundaries between them should not be viewed as static. Changes in the macro environment inevitably force change in the task environment. For example, the Gulf War in 1992, a feature of the macro environment, had a huge effect on the task environment of many organisations, particularly the tourist business which suffered greatly as demand plummeted. Each element of the task environment will now be discussed.

3.4.1 Competitors

The first component of the task environment, and probably the most important one given the increased competitiveness of the macro environment, is competitors. Unless operating in a monopoly situation, organisations face competition. When organisations compete for the same customers and the same market they must react to and anticipate their competitors' actions in order to remain competitive.

In attempting to compete with other organisations, a company tries to develop a competitive advantage. In other words, it must develop some form of advantage over its rivals. Porter explains the concept of competitive advantage as follows: 'Competitive advantage grows fundamentally out of the value a firm is able to create for its buyers that exceeds the firm's cost of creating it. Value is what buyers are willing to pay, and superior value stems from offering lower prices than competitors for equivalent benefits or providing unique benefits that more than offset a higher price.'

Therefore, to achieve a competitive advantage, the organisation must either provide equal product value while operating more efficiently than rivals, thus enabling it to charge a lower cost, called *cost leadership*, or operate in a unique manner and create greater product value that commands a premium price, called *differentiation*. Organisations that are unable to develop a competitive advantage through either cost leadership or differentiation will find that the law of the market-place dictates that they must change their product line or risk going out of business.

In order to compete effectively in a product market and develop a sustainable competitive advantage, the organisation clearly has to analyse its competitive environment. The final section of the chapter will examine how the organisation can analyse its competitive environment which forms such an important part of its task environment.

3.4.2 Suppliers

In line with systems theory, organisations must have inputs from the external environment and convert these into products and services. Suppliers provide these sources of raw materials including people (schools and universities), capital (banks and other lending agencies) and inputs required for the manufacturing process (producers, wholesalers and distributors). Therefore, organisations are extremely dependent on suppliers, who form an integral part of the task environment.

The choice of supplier is critically important for any organisation. Favourable supplier relations can lead to improved quality, better shipping arrangements, improved manufacturing time, early warning of price changes and information about developments in the market-place. There has been a recent trend towards establishing more long-term partnerships with suppliers. Many organisations have selected just a few suppliers and developed closer links with them. For example, Boeing have thousands of suppliers who produce small component parts. Recently, the organisation has reduced this number significantly and has developed closer links with certain suppliers, especially in the area of quality. Motorola, which has a subsidiary in Ireland, has also forged closer contacts with suppliers. The company now sends its design and manufacturing engineers to assist suppliers with any problems.

3.4.3 Customers

Customers are the people who end up buying the product or service produced by the organisation and, consequently, are a critically important element of the task environment. Final customers purchase a final product such as a car or a meal. Intermediate customers buy wholesale products and then sell to final customers. An example is a clothes wholesaler who buys from the manufacturer and then sells to specific clothes outlets.

In competitive markets, organisations realise that giving customers a top quality service is critical if the organisations are to get repeat trade. Providing a quality customer service includes the speed of filling and delivering the order, willingness to meet emergency requests, products delivered in good condition, willingness to rectify faults quickly and the availability of repair service and spare parts. In order to develop customer loyalty, the organisation needs to be fully aware of who its customers are and what products and services they need.

Many organisations are turning to customer groups to find answers. A key example of an Irish organisation with a strong customer focus is Superquinn. In striving to improve the quality of the product and service, customer groups are frequently interviewed and asked for their suggestions. One suggestion which came out of group discussion was the need to provide scissors for cutting or breaking certain fruits, such as grapes. Superquinn realises that something so simple can make a difference (Quinn 1990).

3.4.4 Regulators

Regulators are generally government organisations whose function is to regulate and control aspects of certain industries. Due to the fact that regulatory bodies deal specifically with certain issues, they form part of the immediate task environment rather than the political environment.

Regulatory bodies exist at both national and international level. An example of an international regulatory body is the International Civil Aviation Organisation (ICAO), which is the intergovernmental body concerned with technical and safety issues for the airline industry. On a national level some examples of Irish regulatory bodies include the Employment Equality Agency, whose function is to ensure equal employment opportunities, and the Environmental Protection Agency, whose function is to ensure environmental awareness.

3.4.5 Trade unions

As a vast number of employees world-wide are trade union members, unions form an important part of the organisation's task environment. The role of trade unions is to recruit members, collect dues and represent and protect employees. Unions aim to ensure that employees are treated fairly in their jobs.

Traditionally, manufacturing has been the most unionised industrial sector. However, clerical workers, teachers, nurses and professionals are also catered for by trade unions. Many organisations find that their employees are represented by a number of trade unions, according to the different classifications of workers.

Historically, relations between organisations and trade unions have been adversarial. In other words, the two groups have often been in conflict with each other. Poor industrial relations create costs for the organisation, especially during strikes and go slows. More recently, trade unions and organisations have tried to work together to ensure that organisations survive. This trend is particularly noticeable in the USA where companies such as General Motors and Ford have allowed more union involvement in decision making.

In Ireland, 44 per cent of the workforce is unionised and, consequently, unions represent a key element in the task environment of many organisations, particularly semi-state bodies. These organisations, including Aer Lingus, Iarnrod Eireann, Bus Eireann and Dublin Bus, have to deal with numerous trade unions and tend to have a poor industrial relations record. Other, newer organisations like Shannon Aerospace have just one union representing their workforce — SIPTU — in an attempt to have better and more manageable industrial relations. Trade union issues will be discussed further in Chapter 11.

3.5 COMPETITIVE ANALYSIS

The most widely used technique for analysing the competitive environment was developed by Michael Porter in his famous books *Competitive Strategy: Techniques for Analysing Industries and Competitors* (1980) and *Competitive Advantage: Creating and Sustaining Superior Performance* (1985). Porter is a professor at the Harvard Business School and has had a phenomenal impact on management thinking and practice in the past decade. He believes that the most important thing for the organisation to consider when formulating strategy is how to deal with the competition. Porter argues that five forces shape the degree of market competition operating within the organisation's task environment:

1. The degree of rivalry among existing competitors
2. The threat of substitute products and services
3. The threat of new entrants into the market
4. The bargaining power of suppliers
5. The bargaining power of buyers/customers.

The combined power of these five forces determines the profit potential of an industry by shaping the price the organisation can charge and the costs and investment required to compete. Figure 3.3 illustrates Porter's five forces model for competitive analysis

Figure 3.3 The Five Competitive Forces that Determine Industry Profitability

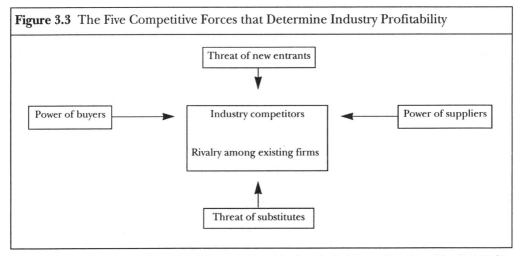

Source: Porter, M., *Competitive Advantage: Creating and Sustaining Superior Performance*, Free Press, New York 1985.

3.5.1 Rivalry among existing firms

Organisations in direct competition with each other use tactics such as price competition, advertising campaigns, new product launches and increased customer service or warranties to gain an advantage over rivals. Rivalry occurs because at least one competitor comes under pressure or feels that there is an opportunity to gain market share. Competition and rivalry are most intense when there are many direct competitors (domestic or international) and when the industry displays slow growth. New, high growth industries offer organisations the opportunity to make good profits. However, as an industry matures the excess profits attract new entrants, thereby making the industry more competitive. As the industry then reaches maturity the intense competition causes an industry shakeout, whereby weaker companies are eliminated.

In industries characterised by a high degree of rivalry, market actions by one competitor provoke countermoves by other competitors. Washing detergent is an example of a highly competitive international market. The main rivals are Proctor and Gamble and Unilever. Figure 3.4 lists the products manufactured by each rival.

Figure 3.4 Washing Detergent Products and their Manufacturers	
Proctor and Gamble	**Unilever**
Bold	Radion
Ariel	Persil
Fairy	Lux
Daz	Surf

The world-wide market for washing detergent is worth US $25 billion. Proctor and Gamble have captured 24 per cent of this market and Unilever have 20 per cent (*The Economist* 1994). Moves by either of these companies leads to a response from the competitor; for example, the introduction of liquid detergents and special detergents for coloured clothes by both Proctor and Gamble and Unilever. Traditionally, Europe has been the stronghold for Unilever and Proctor and Gamble have held the largest market share in the USA. However, recently, Proctor and Gamble's European market share has increased to 32 per cent while Unilever's has plummeted to 23 per cent. Unilever's response to the slip in market share was to introduce Persil Power.

In Ireland an example of a highly competitive industry is the supermarket sector with Dunnes Stores, Crazy Prices, and Quinnsworth engaged in intense rivalry. Price wars have been a constant feature of this industry sector with each competitor attempting to match price reductions by their rivals. Figure 3.5 shows the market share of the grocery sector held by the main competitors. Crazy Price's increased market share is due primarily to the fact that it has been competing on price with Dunnes.

Figure 3.5 Percentage Market Share of the Main Competitors in the Irish Grocery Industry			
Year	**Dunnes Stores**	**Quinnsworth**	**Crazy Prices**
1989	25.3	18.9	3.7
1991	21	14.9	5.6
1992	22.2	11.9	8.9
1993	23.2	11.2	11.2
1994	22	13.5	11.8

Source: Business and Finance, 1994.

However, rivalry and its associated intense competition, should not necessarily be viewed as a bad thing. Good competition can stimulate and motivate the organisation and thereby improve its performance. For example, if faced with a healthy competitor, the organisation has a strong impetus to reduce costs, improve the quality of goods and services and keep pace with technological developments.

3.5.2 The threat of substitutes
Organisations compete not only with other organisations providing similar products and services but also with those which produce substitute products and services. For example,

shipping companies like Irish Ferries and Stena Sealink compete directly with each other and also with organisations involved in substitute forms of transport such as airlines.

The availability of substitutes can severely limit an industry's potential unless organisations become involved in aggressive marketing campaigns and continue to improve product quality. For example, butter manufacturers Avonmore, Kerrygold and Mitchelstown have to compete directly with substitute products like Flora and new dairy spreads. The market share for dairy spreads has increased significantly since their introduction at the expense of butter. In order to compete more effectively, manufacturers have run successful advertising campaigns to promote sales of butter.

3.5.3 The threat of new entrants

New entrants come into an industry segment and compete directly with existing organisations. If there are few barriers to entry the threat of new entrants can become serious.

A government can limit or prevent new entrants to a particular industry. This is most notable in the airline industry, though deregulation is making this less of a problem. Capital requirements for certain industries can be so high that organisations are unable to raise sufficient capital to finance set-up costs. For example, the costs of establishing a national network for supplying electricity such as the ESB's would certainly put off other organisations from entering the market. Another barrier to entry is brand identification; new organisations would have to spend considerable amounts of money on advertising to develop customer loyalty. For example, the brand name Tayto is synonymous with potato crisps, so much so that customers frequently ask for Tayto's when referring to crisps. New entrants like Sam Spudz have had to spend a lot of money on advertising to develop market share. Another example of a new entrant pursuing an aggressive advertising campaign is Lipton which is trying to take market share from both Barrys and Lyons Tea.

Cost advantages also act as a barrier to entry in that existing organisations may have favourable locations or existing assets which give them a cost advantage over newer rivals. Finally, distribution channels can act as a barrier to entry to new companies trying to get their products and services to customers. For example, existing supermarket products are allocated a certain shelf space and position and if a new entrant is to make headway it will have to undertake promotions, price cuts and intensive selling campaigns to displace existing products.

If the organisation can overcome the barriers to entry and break into a market the result is normally an increase in the supply of the product, with the new entrant using considerable resources to gain market share. As a result, market prices usually fall which has a negative impact on the profitability of all organisations.

3.5.4 The bargaining power of suppliers

Suppliers are critically important to the organisation because of the resources that they supply. Suppliers can exert their power on the organisation by threatening to raise prices or to reduce product quality. If the organisation is unable to recover these increased costs through its own price increases, then its long-term profitability will suffer, making it all the more difficult to compete.

The organisation is at an extreme disadvantage if it is overly dependent on one supplier. In contrast, the supplier is in a powerful situation if the organisation has few sources of supply or if the supplier has many other customers. It is also very powerful if it has built up switching costs, i.e. fixed costs that organisations face if they change supplier. For example, if a company is used to purchasing and operating a particular brand of computer, changing to another type may involve switching costs if the existing software packages also have to be changed.

However, organisations can be in a strong situation if they are the dominant customer for a supplier. In that situation, the organisation is in a strong position to demand not only credit arrangements, but that the supplier goes through inspection and education processes to ensure acceptable quality of supplies. An example of a supplier in a poor position is Golden Vale, which provides cheese for McDonalds. Although Golden Vale is the sole supplier of McDonalds in Ireland, it has come under increasing pressure from the US giant, Schreiber, which has established a joint venture in Europe. Schreiber, therefore, is in a strong position to aggressively pursue the market for supplying McDonalds Ireland. In order to retain the McDonalds business, Golden Vale has been forced to reduce its prices resulting in a £500,000 to £1 million reduction in profits (*Sunday Tribune* 1994). All in all, the stronger the power of the buying organisation, the weaker the position of the supplier.

3.5.5 The power of buyers

Without buyers or customers the organisation will go out of business. Customers can put pressure on organisations by demanding lower prices, higher quality or additional services. Customers can also play competitors off against one another. For example, when purchasing durable goods of a high cost or even finding a mortgage, the buyer can collect different offers and negotiate the best possible deal.

Organisations have problems if they depend on a few strong customers. Customers are powerful if they make large purchases of the product either in monetary or volume terms, or if they can easily find alternatives. When the customer is powerful he/she can exert pressure on the organisation and is in a better position to negotiate a good deal than a minor customer.

Analysing these five environmental factors enables the organisation to identify its competitive strengths and weaknesses in relation to the external environment and to understand the nature of the competitive environment in which it is located. Competitive analysis helps to guide strategic decisions, such as whether to acquire a company in another industry or whether to divest a particular business interest. It also facilitates an evaluation of the potential for different business ventures by assessing their competitive environment.

Based on this analysis it is possible to identify favourable and unfavourable competitive business environments which may confront organisations. Figure 3.6 outlines the characteristic features of both types of environment. It should be noted that often the organisation's competitive environment contains favourable and unfavourable elements and, consequently, the organisation has to make sound decisions on future directions. However, the classification serves as a useful guideline.

Porter concludes that when formulating strategies based on competitive analysis, organisations should consider moving into industries with limited competition and many customers and suppliers. Similarly, organisations should avoid industries in more difficult or unfavourable competitive environments.

Figure 3.6 Favourable and Unfavourable Competitive Environments

Factor	Favourable	Unfavourable
1. Competitors	Few; high growth industry	Many; low growth industry
2. Threat of new entrants	Low threat, many barriers	High threat, few barriers
3. Substitutes	Few	Many
4. Power of suppliers	Many, low bargaining power	Few, high bargaining power
5. Power of customers	Many, low bargaining power	Few, high bargaining power

Source: Porter, M., *Competitive Advantage: Creating and Sustaining Superior Performance*, Free Press, New York 1985.

3.6 COMPETITIVE ANALYSIS: AN IRISH EXAMPLE

It is possible to apply Porter's five forces model to analyse the nature of the competitive environment in any industry. Here, it is used to analyse and illustrate the nature of the competitive environment faced by Ryanair. Ryanair is an appropriate choice due to the fact that it competes directly with another Irish organisation, Aer Lingus, along with international operators such as British Airways and British Midland, in a highly competitive and high growth industry. In fact, the world's air transport market is set to grow by 5.5 per cent per annum up to the year 2000 (Doganis 1993).

Ryanair commenced operations in 1985 operating a fifteen-seat aircraft between Waterford Regional Airport and Gatwick Airport. Currently, it operates six Boeing 737 aircraft along with older BAC 1–11s and provides services between Ireland and the UK. In 1993, Ryanair carried 1,125,000 passengers, capturing roughly 30 per cent of the Dublin–London route, one of the busiest in Europe.

3.6.1 Rivalry among existing firms

The Ireland–UK route provides one of the most competitive and keenly contested markets in Europe. The intense competition and rivalry is caused mainly by the fact that airlines have high fixed costs in terms of wages, fuel and insurance and this puts pressure on airlines to fill all the seats on their flights.

There are five main competitors all pursuing the same market: Aer Lingus, British Midland, Ryanair, British Airways (BA) Express and Cityjet. Figure 3.7 illustrates the airports served by each of the main competitors.

Figure 3.7 Airports Served by Competitors on the Dublin–London Route

Airline	Airport
Aer Lingus	LHR
Ryanair	Stansted/Luton/Gatwick
British Midland	LHR
BA Express	Gatwick
Cityjet *	London City

Source: Sunday Tribune, 16 Jan 1994.

Figure 3.8 shows the market share captured by Ryanair on the Dublin–London route since 1987.

Figure 3.8 Ryanair Market Share of the Dublin–London Route 1987–1995

Year	Percentage market share of Dublin–London route
1987	14
1988	14
1989	11
1990	11
1991	15
1992	24
1993	29
1994	32
1995	38 (e)

(e) denotes estimate

Source: Business and Finance, May 1995.

The main competitive strategies used by the airlines are *price competition* and product differentiation. All of the five airlines engage in price competition offering over fifty-three different types of fare on the Dublin–London route. Figure 3.9 outlines the range of fares for each airline including the business fare.

Figure 3.9 Fares on the Dublin–London Route

Airline	Range £	Business Fare
Aer Lingus	84–312	237
British Midland	69–237	237
Ryanair	59–312	199
BA Express	89–326	236
Cityjet	99–312	237

Source: Sunday Tribune, 16 Jan 1994.

The above figures illustrate clearly that Ryanair is pursuing a policy of cost leadership by offering the lowest fares for both business and non business passengers. Price competition is intense among the other rivals and if one competitor reduces fares it is likely that the rest will follow. Airlines also reduce fares when new entrants emerge. For example, when Cityjet joined in 1994, British Midland introduced a £69 fare with an overnight Saturday restriction and also reduced its advance purchase requirement on APEX fares. Ryanair extended its £59 fare to all routes and reduced its advance purchase on this fare from seven to five days.

The airlines also compete in terms of product/service differentiation. Competition based on product differentiation is undertaken mainly by Aer Lingus, British Midland, BA Express and Cityjet. Ryanair operates a cost leadership strategy and does not engage in product differentiation to any great extent. The remaining four airlines compete in terms of the frequency of flights, airports served and in flight entertainment. For example, Aer Lingus has tried to differentiate its product by having regular hourly flights from Dublin to Heathrow and by providing good inflight meals. Aer Lingus also has a frequent flyer programme, Travel Award Bonus (TAB), designed to build up customer loyalty.

3.6.2 The threat of substitutes

Substitutes for the products provided by Ryanair are other forms of transport which include the services offered by Stena Sealink and Irish Ferries. The substitutability of the airline product depends very much on price. When Ryanair and Aer Lingus were engaged in strong price competition in 1986, the demand for sea travel declined significantly. The product offered by the substitute companies has one significant drawback — the length of time taken up by the trip. Air travel is much quicker than sea travel, as it takes three hours just to cross the Irish Sea by ferry, and one and a half hours with the new Sea Cat. Travelling by air takes the customer to his/her final destination rather than to either Fishguard or Holyhead. This is inappropriate for business travellers and is the least preferred option for leisure travellers. As long as the additional cost of flying can be offset against the time savings, then the power of alternative forms of travel is limited. The only advantage that sea travel has is the ability to bring a car. However, car rental companies offer good deals which diminishes the advantage.

3.6.3 The threat of new entrants

Increased liberalisation of the Ireland–UK market means that Ryanair is open to the threat of new entrants. However, the barriers to entry into the airline industry are still very high by industry standards.

The capital requirements of entry are extremely high and include the costs of acquiring aircraft, maintenance provisions, training of crew and landing slots at airports. Ryanair have estimated that their start-up costs were in the region of £20 million. Economies of scale represent another barrier to entry. Economies of scale refer to the advantages attached to large-scale organisation. Examples in the aviation industry include bulk discounts in purchasing fuel, maintenance and catering supplies. If organisations already within the industry exhibit economies of scale it will act as a deterrent to potential new entrants, because it will force them to come in at a larger scale or to accept cost disadvantages.

State aid to airlines can be viewed as another barrier to entry. National airlines like Aer Lingus and Air France have received considerable amounts of money from their respective governments, although this can no longer continue under new EU rules. Such state aid discourages new entrants who perceive that they would be at an immediate disadvantage, especially if these subsidies were used to offset losses made by offering lower fares. The final barrier to entry is brand identity. Organisations with established brand names or high levels of customer loyalty present a huge barrier to a new entrant. In effect, it means that the new entrant will have to invest heavily in advertising and promotion to develop the market. So, while deregulation is encouraging new entrants, the barriers to entry are still extremely high. An important point to note is that Cityjet has recently moved into the market under a franchise from Virgin which means that it did not face the same barriers to entry.

3.6.4 The bargaining power of suppliers

Airlines like Ryanair tend to have five main sources of supply: aircraft leasing companies, fuel suppliers, catering companies, airport management companies and travel agents. Ryanair has arrangements with British Airways and Atlantic Aviation, a US company, to ensure the supply of aircraft. Apart from individual airlines who lease aircraft there are also specialist companies like GPA. With so many aircraft available to lease, the power of the aircraft leasing companies is limited.

The power of suppliers of aviation fuel can be strong in times of oil shortages. However, under normal conditions there is an abundant supply of distributors who do not wield significant power. Catering companies are plentiful, offering a wide choice for airlines and do not have significant power. This is especially true for Ryanair which operates a 'no frills' service with minimum catering facilities.

Airport management companies can possess significant power in determining what airline flies into what airport. For example, slots at Heathrow are in great demand, thereby increasing the power of airport management companies. However, Ryanair operates mainly from Stansted where slots are plentiful, giving a cost saving of £9 per passenger over Heathrow. Therefore, airport management companies do not exert significant power over Ryanair. Travel agents supply the critical component — passengers. All travel agents handle Ryanair flights as it would not be in their interests to lose out on low cost customers. Therefore, because of the vast number of travel agents all equally dependent on Ryanair for business, they do not exert significant power.

3.6.5 The power of buyers

Because Ryanair does not depend on a few large customers, the bargaining power of its customers is not that strong. Individual customers do not deal directly with the company but go through travel agents and rarely engage in any form of bargaining on price or quality. As Ryanair does not cater for the charter market, generally it does not deal with group travel and, therefore, would not offer discounts.

The nature of the market catered for by Ryanair does not lend itself to strong buyer power. Most of its customers are leisure travellers who want a 'no frills' service at the lowest possible cost. Executive travellers have a higher degree of buyer power if they have corporate accounts with airlines. Corporate accounts can negotiate for a lower price or a better deal. However, as it does not specifically cater for the business traveller, this issue is not that important for Ryanair. Buyers in this market have very low switching costs which means that there is little cost in changing airlines. All in all, the bargaining power of buyers in the airline market is very weak.

In summarising the nature of the competitive environment facing Ryanair, it is useful to consider whether it is a favourable or unfavourable one. Figure 3.10 outlines its competitive environment.

Figure 3.10 Competitive Environment for Ryanair

1. Threat of substitutes	Little threat
2. Threat of new entrants	Low threat; many barriers
3. Power of suppliers	Low power
4. Power of customers	Low power
5. Competitive rivalry	Intense; high growth

As we can see, the competitive environment facing Ryanair satisfies four out of the five conditions for favourable environments. The bargaining power of both suppliers and buyers is low, many barriers exist for potential new entrants and there is little threat from substitute products. In its favour, Ryanair operates a distinct strategy catering for a distinct market which seems to be quite effective. However, it is always open to the threat of other airlines reducing their fares and competing directly with Ryanair which Aer Lingus does frequently. All in all, Ryanair is well placed in the market but is involved in a highly competitive industry which is open to constant change.

3.7 Managing the External Environment

Having analysed the macro and task environments within which it operates, the organisation can then move on to consider ways of managing the external environment. *Environmental management* refers to strategies aimed at changing the environmental context within which the organisation operates. Zeithhaml and Zeithhaml (1984) suggest that there are three methods that organisations can employ when managing their external environments.

3.7.1 Strategic manoeuvring
This involves the organisation attempting to alter the boundaries of its task environment. Typical ways of doing this involve diversification into different types of business, i.e. different geographic regions, different products or using different technologies, mergers or acquisitions, selling one or more businesses or entering markets with limited competition and high growth. Aggressive competitors constantly seek to change the boundaries of the task environment, thereby placing other competitors under pressure.

3.7.2 Independent strategies
In contrast to strategic manoeuvring which involves changing the boundary of the external environment, organisations can also seek to change the existing environment within which they operate. An independent strategy means that the organisation acts on its own to alter the environment. Examples include public relations exercises to reinforce a favourable image of the company in the public mind, political action to create a more favourable business climate or to reduce competition, or taking legal action against a competitor.

3.7.3 Co-operative strategies
While the previous two approaches involve organisations working alone, co-operative strategies involve two or more organisations working together to change their environment. The rationale is that joint action will reduce the costs and risks and co-operation should increase power. Examples of this type of approach include the emergence of *joint venture* arrangements and the formation of industry associations.

In choosing which alternative to pursue, organisations should attempt to change appropriate elements of the environment, choose appropriate strategies that focus on the important elements and implement strategies which are most beneficial at the lowest cost. The bottom line for all organisations, however, as they attempt to manage their environment, is the need to achieve competitive advantage. As the nature of the external business environment is changing all the time, this task becomes all the more daunting for organisations which have to constantly update strategic decisions. The importance of the changing nature of the business environment and the need to achieve competitive advantage is a recurring theme throughout the book.

3.8 SUMMARY OF KEY PROPOSITIONS

• All organisations operate within an external business environment which is a critically important area. The external environment has two main parts — a macro and a task environment.

• The macro environment is made up of factors that effect all organisations and in this sense is very broad. These factors include the international, political, economic, technological and social environments. All of these factors are forcing change for organisations by increasing competitiveness and complexity.

• The task environment is the immediate environment facing the organisation. Organisations operating within the same industry have a similar task environment. Factors included are competitors, suppliers, customers, regulators and trade unions.

• As the current business environment has become increasingly competitive, organisations need to undertake a competitive analysis of their industry to work out how they can achieve a competitive advantage.

• When analysing the competitive environment, the following factors have to be considered: the degree of rivalry among existing competitors; the threat of new entrants and substitute products and services; and the bargaining power of suppliers and customers.

• Favourable competitive environments are high growth markets with few competitors, high barriers to entry, few substitute products and services, and suppliers and customers with little power over the organisation.

• Unfavourable competitive environments are low growth industries which have many competitors, few barriers to entry, many substitute products and services, and customers and suppliers with strong power over the organisation.

• Having analysed the external environments, both macro and task, and considered the nature of the competitive environment, organisations can examine ways of managing the external environment.

• Strategic manoeuvring means that the organisation tries to alter the boundaries of its task environment by either diversifying or merging.

• Independent strategies mean that the organisation tries to change the existing environment within which it operates. This can be done by public relations exercises or political action.

• Co-operative strategies mean that one organisation works with another to change its environment. This can be done by entering into a joint venture to reduce costs and spread risks.

DISCUSSION QUESTIONS

1. What do you understand by the term business environment and why is it important for organisations to consider?
2. Explain the difference between the macro and the task environment.
3. Of the three main changes in the international environment, which do you consider to be the most important for Irish organisations?
4. Select a company that you are familiar with and describe the macro environment within which it operates.
5. Select a company that you are familiar with and describe the task environment within which it operates.
6. Why are competitors so important for organisations to consider?
7. Apply Porter's five box model of competitive analysis to any Irish organisation/ industry.
8. Consider the soft drinks market in Ireland. Evaluate whether the current competitive environment is favourable or unfavourable.
9. How would you characterise the rivalry between your nearest competing supermarkets? What action has been taken recently by one competitor that has provoked counter moves by other competitors?
10. You are considering setting up your own pizza restaurant in your home town. Undertake a competitive analysis of the industry in the locality and examine whether you would establish or not, based on your analysis.
11. Overall, how would you describe the external business environment affecting Irish organisations operating domestically or internationally?
12. How can organisations try to manage their external environments?

REFERENCES

Barrett, S., 'International Competitiveness and the Semi State Sector'. Paper presented to the Economics Workshop, Kenmare 1993.

'Cityjet Joins the Fray' *Business and Finance*, 6–7, 6 January 1994.

'Dunnes Profits Top £70 million' *Business and Finance*, 30–31, 17 November 1994.

'Central Bank of Ireland Annual Report', Dublin, 1994.

Doganis, F., *Flying Off Course: The Economics of International Airlines*, Routledge, London 1993.

Facts Through Figures: A Statistical Portrait of the European Union, Eurostat, Luxembourg 1994.

Finn, G., 'Beeline: The New Buzz Word' *Checkout*, Vol.20, 8–9, 2 March 1994.

'Dog Fight for Survival in the Skies' *Irish Independent*, 5 October 1993.

'Great Air Race of 1994: Dublin to London — Airlines Compete' *Irish Independent*, 4–5, 11 January 1994.

'Special Supplement on Guinness' *Irish Times*, 29 June 1994.

McGee, J., 'Telecom's £1.2 Billion Challenge' *Business and Finance*, 6, 24 November 1994.

O'Raghaillaigh, L., 'Food for Thought' *Checkout*, Vol.20, 20–21, 2 March 1993.

Peters, T., 'Prometheus Barely Unbound' *Academy of Management Executive*, Vol.4, No.4, 70–84, 1993.

Porter, M., *Competitive Strategy: Techniques for Analysing Industries and Competitors*, Free Press, New York 1980.

Porter, M., *Competitive Advantage: Creating and Sustaining Superior Performance*, Free Press, New York 1985.

Quinn, F., *Crowning the Customer: How to Become Customer Driven*, Dublin 1990.

Schares, G., 'Reawakening: A Market Economy takes Root in Europe' *Business Week*, 46–50, 15 April 1991.

Serwer, A., 'Crime Stoppers Make a Killing' *Fortune*, 67–70, 4 April 1994.

Stewart, T., 'The Information Age in Charts' *Fortune*, 55–59, 4 April 1994.

'Speculation Continues as Ryanair Rejects Aer Lingus Wooing' *Sunday Business Post*, 10 October 1993.

'Hightime to Get to London: Aer Lingus Faster in the Dash' *Sunday Times*, 16 January 1994.

'Golden Vale Cheese in McDonalds Sandwich' *Sunday Tribune Business Section 1*, 1994.

'Tales from the Washroom' *The Economist*, 65, 11 June 1994.

Yochelson, J. and Lesser, E., 'Overview of EC 1992' in Perez-Lopez, P. and Yochelson, J. (eds), *EC 1992: Implications for Workers* , IS Department of Labour, Washington DC 1992.

Zeithaml, C. and Zeithaml, V., 'Environmental Management: Revising the Marketing Perspective' *Journal of Marketing*, Vol.48, No.2, 46–53, spring 1984.

4

Planning and Decision Making

4.1 INTRODUCTION

This chapter focuses on the first managerial function — planning. It considers the importance of planning for the organisation, the types of planning that can be undertaken and the various approaches that can be used to facilitate planning. Drawing all of these factors together, a corporate planning process is presented which outlines the numerous stages that the organisation goes through for successful planning. Decision making is strongly related to the area of planning and is the focus of the second section of the chapter.The chapter concludes with a discussion of group versus individual modes of decision making.

4.2 THE NATURE AND IMPORTANCE OF PLANNING

Planning is perhaps the most basic of all management functions. It can be defined as 'the systematic development of action programmes aimed at reaching agreed business objectives by the process of analysing, evaluating and selecting among the opportunities which are foreseen' (Jones 1974). Planning is, therefore, the process of establishing aims and objectives and choosing a course of action to ensure that they are achieved. This process serves to bridge the gap between where the organisation is and where it would like to be.

Planning is undertaken by all managers irrespective of their position in the hierarchy and is one of the most important managerial functions. Planning generally precedes all other management functions. In other words, before the organisation can organise, staff, lead and control it has to identify objectives and how to achieve them. Only by planning can the organisation decide what form of organisational structure, what people, what form of leadership and what means of control will be most effective.

Planning seeks to reduce the amount of uncertainty faced by the organisation. While no organisation can predict future events with certainty, without planning things are left to chance. As Michiels (1986) states: 'an enterprise without a plan is like a ship sailing in dense fog without any navigational means — the only thing it can possibly be sure about is whether it is afloat or not.' Organisations need plans to guide future action. Typically, organisations have a number of different contingency plans which are put into operation depending on the situation, thus ensuring that the organisation is prepared for all eventualities. Plans, therefore, should have an inbuilt flexibility, so that they can take account of unforeseen events such as changes in the price of raw materials.

An example of an Irish organisation which foresaw changes in its product market and made appropriate contingency plans is Dawn Farm Foods situated in Naas, Co. Kildare. The company manufactures ingredient meats and toppings for branded ready meals, most notably Green Isle and Heinz. Recently, the company began to realise that the principal manufacturers that they supplied were increasingly outsourcing ingredients and reducing their involvement in final assembly and product marketing. In response to these trends, Dawn began to develop contingency plans, developing its research and development, introducing ISO (an international quality standard), World Class Manufacturing and long-term relationships with clients. These plans paid off when Dawn Farm Foods beat six major European competitors to win a contract with Pizza Hut to supply meat topping to its 800 outlets in Europe, the Middle East and Africa. Planning for such market changes was critical to Dawn's success.

Planning sets up the skeleton around which the organisation's activities can be built. It sets the scene for the type of business which will be conducted and the *strategy* which will be pursued. If, for example, it is foreseen that demand for an organisation's present product range will remain buoyant, then this will have a positive effect on the forecast of net income, profit and cash flow. It might also enable the organisation to pursue a strategy of *diversification* into product lines complementary to its existing *portfolio*.

There are three main types of planning undertaken by the organisation.

1. **Strategic planning** involves issues of strategic direction and normally takes place at top level. Strategic planning has a long-term orientation (greater than five years) and focuses on the organisation's basic mission, establishing organisational objectives, conducting internal analysis, assessing the external environment and developing strategic business plans. It serves to guide issues such as mergers, acquisitions, investment and divestment and areas for future expansion.

2. **Tactical planning** is concerned with the current operations of the various component parts of an organisation and has a medium-term orientation (one to five years). This type of planning normally takes place at middle management level. It involves interpreting strategic plans by formulating tactical plans to achieve strategic objectives, outlining functional roles and responsibilities and developing tactical responses to medium-term business problems facing the organisation, such as a decline in market share for a particular product.

3. **Operational planning** is concerned with short-term planning of day to day functions and serves to guide immediate action undertaken by the organisation. Consequently, it is undertaken by front line supervisors who are in a position to make plans about short-term operations. Operational planning involves establishing short-term business unit or departmental targets, budgets and specific programmes of action geared towards the achievement of tactical plans.

Most organisations use all three types of planning to guide their future actions. However, for these programmes to be successful, each level of planning must be strongly related. In other words, operational plans must be related to and reflect tactical plans. Similarly, tactical plans must reflect overall strategic plans. All managers are involved in planning. However, as we have seen, the type of planning undertaken depends on the manager's position in the hierarchy.

The amount of time spent on planning also varies depending on the manager's position. Top management has the overall responsibility for seeing that the planning function is carried out. Generally these managers have more time to spend on planning and usually have the best understanding of the organisational situation as a whole and, therefore, are better equipped to make long-term strategic plans. Middle managers spend less of their time planning and focus more on operational issues. Middle managers have the best knowledge of the operations of the various areas and are therefore in a better position to make medium-term plans. Finally, lower level front line supervisors spend even less time planning due to their focus on day to day operations. Such a focus means that they are best able to determine what can be done in the short term to achieve organisational objectives. Figure 4.1 shows the increased time spent by managers on planning.

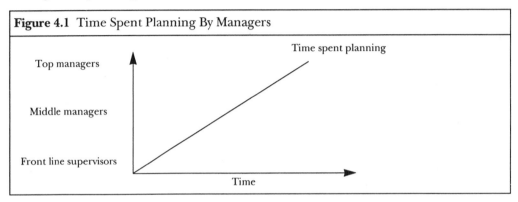

Figure 4.1 Time Spent Planning By Managers

4.3 Types of Plan

A plan is a statement of action to be undertaken by the organisation aimed at helping it achieve its objectives. Planning results in the formation of statements of recommended courses of action — namely plans. According to Kast and Rosenweig (1985) plans have a number of important dimensions — repetitiveness, time, scope and level.

The repetitiveness dimension concerns the extent to which a plan is used over and over again. Some plans apply to certain situations only and tend to have a short time frame and are essentially non repetitive. However, some plans apply to many situations and have a longer time frame. Such plans are repetitive by their very nature. The time dimension refers to the length of time associated with the plan. Some plans are short term and associated with operational planning, while others have a longer time frame and are associated with strategic planning.

Scope refers to the elements of the organisation that are affected by the plan. Some plans have a broad nature and serve to guide the organisation as a whole. Others focus on particular functions or departments and, therefore, have a narrower scope. The final dimension is the level of the organisation towards which the plan is directed. Plans differ in the extent to which they focus on top, middle or lower levels of the organisation. However, most plans, irrespective of the level they are aimed at, will have an effect on all levels due to their interdependence.

Organisations typically use a wide variety of plans to assist their planning processes. Weihrich and Koontz (1993) argue that planning can be a difficult process when managers fail to recognise that there are a number of different plans all of which have a future orientation. They state that there are eight different types of plan which form a hierarchy as shown in Figure 4.2. Each of the different types is discussed below.

Figure 4.2 The Hierarchy of Plans

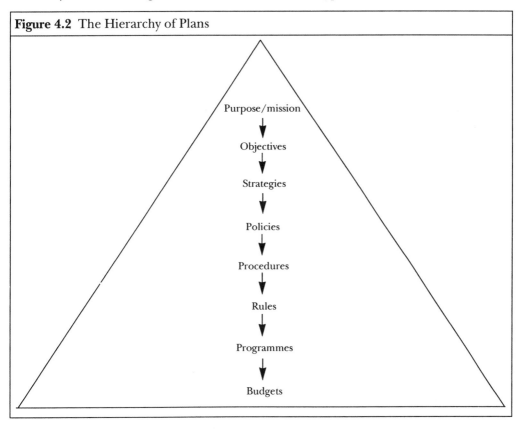

Purpose/mission

Objectives

Strategies

Policies

Procedures

Rules

Programmes

Budgets

4.3.1 Purpose or mission

David (1989) defines a mission as an enduring statement of purpose that distinguishes one organisation from other similar enterprises. The mission or purpose is, therefore, the organisation's reason for being. Drucker (1973) has argued that only a clear definition of the mission and purpose of the organisation makes possible clear and realistic business objectives. The mission is the most fundamental organisational plan of all, laying the foundation for all subsequent plans.

Figure 4.3 Examples of Irish Organisations' Mission Statements

Aer Rianta:	Aer Rianta wants to establish itself as the best organisation in the world in the field of managing airports and related commercial activities.
Ballygowan:	To substantially grow the Irish bottled water market and to grow Ballygowan's share of that market.
Irish Permanent:	To provide better retail financial services and to become and remain more profitable than the associated banks.
ESB:	We in the ESB will provide our customers with quality energy services at a competitive price with due care for the natural environment. We will also promote national economic progress by engaging in profitable ancillary activities.
Golden Vale:	Golden Vale will be a major force in the European dairy food market and acknowledged by all customers as innovative and responsive, a socially and environmentally responsible leader, trustworthy and fun to do business with.

The mission or purpose involves looking at the scope of the business the organisation is involved in and the organisation's future direction. Consequently, the organisation must decide on desirable directions for growth, market niches, worthwhile pioneering aims and which synergisms with other missions to develop. Figure 4.3 provides examples of the mission statements of a number of Irish organisations, which outline their basic mission as an organisational entity.

4.3.2 Objectives

Objectives and goals are terms used interchangeably to describe what must be undertaken by the organisation to achieve its basic mission or purpose. Objectives provide specific aims within the broader framework of goals and usually involve a specific time frame. Objectives, therefore, outline more precisely how the organisation seeks to achieve its mission and, according to Thompson and Strickland (1990), breathe life into the mission by training the energies of each part of the organisation in what needs to be achieved.

Objectives can be general, applied to the whole organisation (corporate objectives) or specific, focusing on one functional area. An example of a corporate objective would be 'to achieve a return on investment of 15 per cent at the end of the financial year'. An example of an objective specific to a production area would be 'to increase production by 50 per cent by 1 June 1996 without additional costs at the current level of quality'. According to Drucker (1954) there are a number of areas in which objectives and performance need to be set including market standing, physical and financial resources, innovation, productivity, profitability, manager performance and development, worker performance and attitude and public responsibility.

4.3.3 Strategies

A strategy is the programme of activities formulated in response to objectives. In other words, it answers the question 'How are we going to get where we want to go?' Many dictionaries define strategy in military terms and this is accurate for business. Strategy preparation means that the organisation must examine its own strengths and weaknesses and analyse the external environment to find out how both can be harnessed to achieve objectives.

The main purpose of strategy is to build on the objectives and to communicate through a system of major objectives and policies the direction the organisation wants to go. Strategies, by their very nature, do not attempt to outline exactly how the organisation is to accomplish its objectives. This role is achieved by numerous other major and minor supporting plans. Strategies, therefore, serve as important guides for planning.

4.3.4 Policies

Policies are general guidelines for decision making throughout the organisation. They provide a direction for managers when using their judgement to achieve objectives. Policies help to establish a consistency in decision making. However, they are only broad guidelines and managers can exercise discretion in their interpretation. For example, a policy might state that preference should be given to Irish raw materials suppliers when ordering stock. A policy written in such terms allows a degree of managerial discretion to determine the extent and degree of preference.

Policies can be couched in two forms — express and implied. An express policy is a written or verbal statement which guides managers in their decision making. For example, a personnel manual may state that the organisation is an equal opportunities employer, regardless of gender, race or creed. Implied policy is inferred from looking at the organisation's behaviour and actions. Referring to the previous example, an analysis of the workforce may reveal that all employees are white, middle class males and that there are no female managers, which means that the expressed policy is not being adhered to but has been replaced by an implied policy of hiring and promoting white, middle class males. Sometimes expressed and implied policies may conflict or contradict each other, with the organisation pursuing an expressed policy openly yet secretly applying an implied policy, as in the above example.

4.3.5 Procedures

Procedures are plans that outline methods for handling certain situations. In this sense they serve to guide thinking rather than action and detail the precise manner in which activities are to be carried out. Policies and procedures are quite similar in that they both seek to influence certain decisions. However, procedures frequently involve a series of related steps which have to be undertaken unlike policies which address single issues. For example, the organisation may have a stated policy in relation to grievances and discipline. To back up this policy, the organisation will have set procedures for dealing with these issues which normally follow a step by step approach. Other examples of procedures include purchasing equipment, hiring of staff and authorisations for travel expenses. Procedures, therefore, leave little room for discretion and ensure that all similar situations are handled consistently.

Procedures exist at all levels of the organisation but are more prevalent at the lower levels due mainly to the need for tighter control. Weihrich and Koontz (1993) argue that procedures become more numerous at lower levels due to the economic advantages of spelling out actions in detail for employees, because managers at lower levels need less leeway and, finally, because routine jobs can be completed most effectively when management details the best way to carry them out.

Well-established procedures are commonly termed Standard Operating Procedures. Organisations use these procedures in a routine manner. However, it should be remembered that procedures should be updated and reviewed to ensure that they remain appropriate. Mistakes frequently occur when procedures become obsolete and no longer contribute to the achievement of organisational objectives.

4.3.6 Rules

Rules are statements that either prohibit or prescribe certain actions by specifying what employees can and cannot do. Rules apply to situations regardless of the particular individuals involved, such as a 'No Smoking' rule. Rules differ from both policies and procedures in a number of important areas. Unlike procedures, rules do not contain a specific time sequence. In fact, procedures can be viewed as a series of rules. Unlike policies, rules do not allow discretion in their interpretation. So, while personal judgement can be used when applying policies, no such judgement is permitted with rules. The only element of discretion associated with rules concerns whether they apply to certain situations. Organisations experience problems when they fail to distinguish clearly between rules, procedures and policies, causing confusion for employees.

4.3.7 Programmes

Programmes are plans designed to accomplish specific goals usually within a fixed period of time. They can be broad in nature, such as an energy conservation programme undertaken by the organisation. Similarly, programmes can be narrow in nature focusing on particular areas within the organisation, such as a management development programme for executives.

The introduction of a programme within the organisation may lead to the development of numerous supporting programmes. Using the previous example of an energy conservation programme, supporting programmes may include the search for alternative sources of energy, better building insulation, better and more economical use of existing energy supplies and designing more efficient equipment. One of the key prerequisites for the successful implementation of a programme is that all of the various supporting programmes are well co-ordinated and contribute to the original programme's aims.

4.3.8 Budgets

A budget is a numerical expression of a plan which deals with the future allocation and utilisation of resources over a given period of time. Budgets are normally expressed in financial terms, hours worked by employees, productivity or any other measurable term. Examples of budgets include revenue and expense budgets and time, space, material and product budgets.

A budget also serves as an important control mechanism (see Chapter 7). However, for it to act as a standard of control it must reflect plans. One of the major advantages of a budget is that it forces people to plan in a precise way. Since budgets are normally developed for an entire organisation, budgeting is an important device for consolidating organisation-wide plans.

The different types of plan very clearly form a hierarchy. At the top is the organisation's mission or purpose which states in the broadest sense where the organisation is going. As one moves further down the hierarchy the plans become more specific and focused until we reach budgets, which are probably the most precise and specific form of planning in which the organisation engages.

4.4 THE CORPORATE PLANNING PROCESS

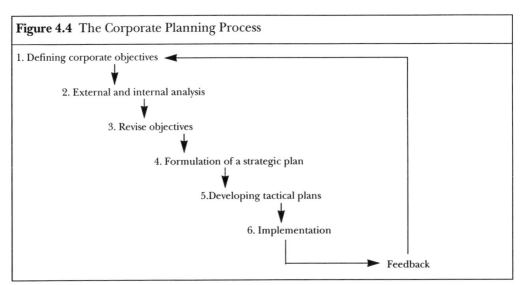

Figure 4.4 The Corporate Planning Process

1. Defining corporate objectives
2. External and internal analysis
3. Revise objectives
4. Formulation of a strategic plan
5. Developing tactical plans
6. Implementation

Feedback

Corporate planning is the process of examining all aspects of the organisation in an effort to formulate strategy, incorporating strategic, tactical and operational planning, aimed at preparing the organisation for the future. It is possible to identify certain steps that organisations typically go through in their efforts to plan. This corporate planning process is illustrated in Figure 4.4.

4.4.1 Defining corporate objectives

The first step in the corporate planning process is to establish corporate objectives. The previous section on objectives can be amplified in light of the corporate objective setting. Most organisations have just a few objectives which they hope to achieve over a long period of time. It is necessary that these objectives are clarified and documented so that they can be understood by those who are trying to further the planning process.

Economists have suggested two common types of objective found in organisations — profit maximisers and profit satisficers. The aim of a profit maximising organisation is to make the highest possible profit, and this aim is connected to all other objectives. A profit satisficing organisation, on the other hand, seeks sufficient profits to fulfil other aims such as investment in new production, enjoying a high public profile, or allowing the owner to have a good lifestyle. Many smaller businesses turn away from the chance to optimise profits in order to keep the business personal or to allow the management more free time.

Two management theories worth noting in this context are shareholder theory and stakeholder theory. Shareholder theory holds that all organisational objectives should be geared to maximising the return to shareholders. In a public enterprise the shareholders are a wide and diverse group that includes customers, employees, the government and all other interested groups whose needs have to be considered. Stakeholder theory holds that objectives have to be related to all those with a stake in the organisation which includes customers, suppliers, employees, the government and the public in general. The interests of all these groups have to be considered when setting organisational objectives. So, for example, a pharmaceutical company may be concerned with selling its products for a certain profit, providing employees with a favourable working environment, sourcing materials from local suppliers, complying with local and voluntary codes of practice and making contributions to local activities.

One well-known Irish example of objective setting is the planning system in the Electricity Supply Board (ESB). In line with the mission statement of the ESB, outlined previously, the organisation sets out nine key areas for success. Figure 4.5 outlines the ESB's corporate objectives.

Figure 4.5 The ESB's Corporate Objectives

1. Managing load growth of demand for electricity at 3 per cent per annum in the 1990s.
2. Protecting the natural environment.
3. Providing an adequate supply of quality electricity at a competitive price.
4. Good quality customer service.
5. Reducing long-term debt.
6. Developing high calibre staff in a climate of motivation and commitment.
7. Balancing a secure supply of fuel against cost and environmental considerations.
8. Increasing the availability of existing plant.

Source: Connecting With the Future: ESB Strategies for the 1990s, Dublin, March 1990.

4.4.2 External and internal analysis

When devising corporate plans the organisation must analyse its internal strengths and weaknesses in relation to its external opportunities and threats. The assessment of the organisation's strengths, weaknesses, opportunities and threats is referred to as a SWOT analysis. Every organisation has both strengths and weaknesses which it needs to be aware of and to capitalise on. Unless the organisation frequently analyses its weaknesses it may find itself unprepared to respond to unanticipated threats from the environment. As noted in Chapter 3, the organisation's ability to identify and respond to opportunities in the environment is a function of its ability to effectively manage its external environment.

According to Johnson and Scholes (1993) a typical SWOT analysis involves three related steps:

1. Identification of the current strategy/strategies that the organisation is following. Decision makers should identify current goals and strategies in order to determine whether the organisation is moving in the appropriate direction. This review should concentrate on the mission, strategic goals and corporate strategy.

2. Identification of the key changes in the organisation's external environment, using the techniques described in Chapter 3. The organisation should analyse thoroughly both its macro and task environments, focusing on the relative importance of each component and the extent to which they are changing. This process is sometimes referred to as a PEST analysis. PEST is an acronym for Political, Economic, Socio/Cultural and Technological analysis of environmental influences. In this sense it corresponds to an analysis of the primary features of the macro environment. Due to the increasingly competitive nature of the external environment, a competitive analysis of the industry within which the organisation operates has become critically important. Chapter 3 provides details of how the organisation should undertake such a task.

3. A resource profile of the organisation should be undertaken to identify the key capabilities (strengths) and key limitations (weaknesses). In order to exploit opportunities in the external environment, it is necessary to know what competencies and weaknesses exist inside the organisation. This analysis can be undertaken by considering resources under the following headings.

(i) Human resources: Human resources in this case refer to the structure and quality of the workforce. A human resource analysis might consider the age structure of employees, levels of skill, experience, staff turnover, promotion and replacement. A young, highly skilled workforce is an enormous asset, but also demands a lot from the organisation, for example, high salaries, promotion and good working conditions. The analysis should focus on future manpower requirements so that areas of scarcity and surplus can be identified.

(ii) Financial resources: A financial audit of resources includes the financial structure and current borrowing capacity of the organisation. Balance sheets, *ratio analysis*, forecasted cash flow and *working capital* have to be examined. Tools needed to facilitate this analysis will be discussed in Chapter 8.

(iii) Organisational resources: Examining organisational resources involves considering the strengths and weaknesses of each business unit and department. A critical examination of each area will reveal certain strengths and shortcomings. For example, a print firm might have a highly trained production staff, but this may be a drawback for the organisation in terms of its cost and the difficulty of introducing new technology.

(iv) Technological resources: Each organisation has to decide whether to be a leader or a follower in the area of technological capability. This has implications for the level of production costs, which has to be traded against the capital costs of acquiring new technology. Most Irish organisations are not renowned for being on the leading edge of technology, and rely on craft skills to allow them to sell high quality goods. This is in marked contrast to less developed countries like Korea, which exploited its late industrialisation to acquire the latest technology. When coupled with low wages, this gave Korea a unique advantage which has been exploited in its motor and electronics industries.

One of the main aims of an internal analysis of strengths and weaknesses is that it enables the organisation to see where it can develop a competitive advantage. In the current business environment the organisation must be able to carve out a special and distinct advantage that will endure over time.

Having conducted the above procedure, a SWOT analysis can be illustrated graphically for the organisation. A SWOT analysis of the VHI is shown in Figure 4.6.

Figure 4.6 SWOT Analysis of the VHI

Strengths	Weaknesses
1. Wide customer base of 1.3 million or 40 per cent of the Irish population	1. Little control over medical costs, consultants, hospital administration and advances in medical technology
2. Low expense to income ratio which stands at 6.2 per cent and is well below industry average of 13.5–14 per cent	2. Public perception that the VHI are constantly pushing up premiums well ahead of inflation
3. Committed workforce	3. The customer base is growing older which means the number of claims will rise
4. New CEO with vision and enthusiasm	4. No experience of dealing with competition

Opportunities	Threats
1. EU directive of 1994 opens up markets to foreign competitors, thereby providing the VHI with the opportunity to enter other markets particularly in the UK where it could target niches	1. EU directive also opens up the Irish market to foreign competition; most likely to come from the UK firm BUPA
2. Extension of the range of services provided to include an out-patients scheme and critical illness cover	2. Improvements in the Irish Public Health Service may reduce need for VHI
	3. Phased reduction in VHI tax relief from 48 per cent to 27 per cent

Source: Adapted from 'Duncan's Quiet Revolution' *Business and Finance*, 20 April 1995.

The VHI is involved in voluntary health insurance and was established in 1957. Since that date the company has enjoyed a monopoly position in the Irish market. Based on a thorough internal and external analysis, the VHI has been able to identify its current strengths and weaknesses along with specific threats and opportunities produced by the external environment. Its main strengths include a wide customer base of 1.3 million, a committed workforce, an energetic CEO and a favourable income to costs ratio. On the negative side, the VHI has little or no control over the cost of healthcare provision which is largely influenced by consultants, hospitals and advances in medical technology. The VHI also suffers from poor public perception regarding the cost of premiums which have increased by 16 per cent, well ahead of inflation. The customer base is growing older, by an average of 0.4 years every year. This means that more claims are likely to be made as older people become ill. Finally, the VHI has no experience of dealing with competition from other organisations since it has a monopoly position.

The organisation also faces a number of important opportunities. An EU directive in 1994 has opened up European markets, thereby providing the VHI with an avenue for expansion. In addition, the organisation has the opportunity to develop new services, including an option to participate in out-patients schemes that give access to private facilities in public hospitals. Another possible line of expansion includes the provision of Critical Illness Cover which provides insurance against reduced earning capacity due to long-term illness.

The VHI also faces a number of important threats to its established position in the Irish market. Firstly, the recent EU directive opens up Irish markets to foreign competitors. In the coming years, new entrants could emerge to compete directly with the VHI, particularly from the UK. The actual size of the Irish market for health insurance could decline in the future due to the improvements in the Public Health Service. Finally, the VHI has lost one of its greatest selling points — the fact that subscriptions were tax deductible at the highest rate. The 1994 budget introduced the phased reduction of VHI relief from 48 per cent to 27 per cent.

Clearly, the VHI is entering a period of great change with environmental changes presenting both threats and opportunities. By conducting a SWOT analysis the organisation will obtain a clear picture of its strengths and weaknesses, along with potential threats and opportunities. In the future, it is likely that the VHI will build on its strengths and minimise its weaknesses to grasp opportunities and manage threats. A SWOT analysis is a critically important step in any corporate planning process, providing a mechanism for systematically examining the extent to which the organisation can manage its environment.

4.4.3 Revising objectives

In the light of the foregoing external and internal analyses, it should be clear what unique competitive advantage the organisation can develop. If no distinct advantage emerges, then strategy formulation should centre on developing some competitive edge. Such advantages could include a unique product, market leadership, quality of manufacturing reputation or service back up. Developing some form of leading edge often means a complete revision of the objectives defined previously.

4.4.4 Formulating a strategic plan

At this stage the building blocks are in place, to be cemented together in the form of a strategic plan. Strategic plans are usually developed along two lines: deciding the direction of the organisation's activities (expansion, contraction, diversification or merger); and finding the resources to facilitate these activities (human and financial). The starting point for a strategic plan is the formulation of a strategy statement. This proposes how to fulfil objectives and sets the guidelines for the development of tactical plans.

4.4.5 Developing tactical plans

Tactical plans are formulated for every function or business unit within the organisation and normally have a medium-term orientation of perhaps one year, but this can vary from organisation to organisation. Tactical plans interpret the strategic plan to produce more medium-term plans for achieving strategic objectives. In this sense they are more precise formulations of plans. The ESB, for example, has formulated tactical plans to achieve its corporate objective of protecting the environment as outlined in Figure 4.7.

Figure 4.7 An Example of the ESB's Use of Tactical Plans

Corporate objective: To protect the natural environment
Tactical plans to achieve objective:

1. Foster open and co-operative dialogue with relevant governments and agencies, local authorities and environmental groups.
2. Support the environmental protection agency.
3. Actively promote national energy efficiency policies and the use of cost effective alternative energies.
4. Set up a special environmental monitoring unit for all ESB activities which will publish an annual report on its activities.
5. Carry out an independent environmental impact assessment on all proposed new ESB developments.

Source: Connecting with the Future: ESB Strategies for the 1990s, Dublin, March 1990.

4.4.6 Implementation

When tactical plans are agreed it is then necessary to formulate specific action plans to implement planning decisions. The link between tactical planning and implementation is the various operational or action plans which deal with the day to day functioning of the organisation. An example of a tactical plan for a specific functional area, in this case production, might include improving productivity and communications in the production area.

Action plans to achieve these tactical plans could include increasing productivity by 10 per cent by 1 June 1996 and issuing a three-page monthly newsletter by 30 June 1996.

Tactical plans should be flexible enough to be altered as contingencies warrant. Effective implementation means providing the necessary resources, motivating staff and holding regular (usually monthly) meetings to review how targets are being met. These meetings provide the basis for feedback to all levels of the organisation about how effective the planning process has been.

The corporate planning process is a complex and highly important process for any organisation. The process is demanding and requires that the organisation consciously determines courses of action and bases decisions on purpose, knowledge and considered estimates.

Having completed the planning process, the organisation has clearly identified objectives, strategies and various types of plan to achieve those goals. The organisation is then in a position to make decisions about other managerial functions, such as organising and controlling, which contribute to organisational efficiency.

4.5 MANAGEMENT BY OBJECTIVES

Management by Objectives (MBO) is a particular approach to setting objectives and ensuring their achievement. The technique can be used in conjunction with the planning process outlined in the previous section. It was developed by a group of management consultants, Urwick, Orr and partners and was strongly advocated by theorists such as Drucker (1954) and Humble (1972). It came to prominence in the 1960s when it was put into practice by a number of major organisations. The turbulent business environment of the last two decades has resulted in the usefulness of the approach being called into question. However, the principles of the approach remain valid.

Instead of imposing goals or objectives on employees, MBO proposes that each subordinate be free to set his/her own goals within the framework provided by the superior. The process involves the following steps:

1. The superior or manager sets performance standards which must be met by the subordinate.
2. The subordinate proposes his/her own goals depending on how he/she feels the standards can be reached or exceeded.
3. Goals are then agreed between the superior and the subordinate.
4. At agreed intervals the superior reviews the subordinate's performance.

This process assumes that individual managers are capable of assessing the goals and objectives which they can realistically expect subordinates to reach. Much depends on how MBO is communicated to those whose co-operation is required. If it is used as a 'big stick' then motivation will suffer. The objective is to improve corporate performance, and this is achieved by every individual having a part in the objective-setting process. According to Odiorne et al (1980), to be worthwhile an MBO programme needs complete support throughout the organisation. It also needs effort to monitor its implementation. The following is a list of advantages associated with MBO:

1. The employee has a clearer understanding of the goals he/she is expected to work towards.
2. Planning should improve as there is greater commitment to goals.
3. Control should be easier as performance standards now exist.
4. Motivation should improve as subordinates feel they have an input in the objective-setting process.
5. Employee appraisal is simplified by reference to each individual's objectives.

However MBO also has disadvantages associated with it which include the following:

1. If MBO is not explained properly employees may feel they are being coerced.
2. The focus on objectives can lead the business to strive towards incompatible goals. For example, a finance manager may have agreed to cut operating costs, while the marketing manager's objective is to promote the product more strongly.
3. There may be a focus on easily measurable objectives which are not always the best. For example, a business person might want to improve the quality of his/her customer service. This is difficult to measure and he/she may end up aiming for a reduction in the number of complaints, which is not necessarily the same thing.
4. Agreement on objectives can cause inflexibility when the environment changes. When time has been invested in hammering out objectives it is difficult to abandon them even when circumstances change.

4.6 DECISION MAKING

Weihrich and Koontz (1993) define decision making as 'the selection of a course of action from among alternatives'. In this sense decision making is at the heart of planning. Hundreds of decisions are made in organisations each day as they fulfil their operational requirements. Some of these decisions are small and minor and can be completed quickly, such as choosing the size and colour of envelopes. Others are more complicated and far reaching and require more detailed analysis, such as the decision to expand into foreign markets. Decision making, which takes place at all levels of the organisation is, therefore, a central part of a manager's role.

Decision making is linked closely with planning as, in order for plans to be formulated and implemented, decisions on certain courses of action have to be taken. However, despite the link with planning, decision making is a fundamental element of the entire management process.

Figure 4.8 Characteristics of Programmed and Non Programmed Decisions

Programmed	Non Programmed
Well structured	Poorly structured
Routine	New
Information available	Little information
Taken at lower levels	Taken at higher levels
Short time frame	Long time frame
Decision rules and set procedures used	Judgement and creativity used

---

4.6.1 Types of decision

Making decisions in the organisational context requires good judgement and diagnostic skills and most managers advance because of their ability to make good decisions. There are two main types of decision made by managers — programmed and non programmed. Programmed decisions tend to be well structured, routine and repetitive, and occur on a regular basis. Programmed decisions usually take place at lower levels in the organisation, have short-term consequences and readily available information. Due to the fact that the organisation is frequently presented with a decision, a decision rule can be developed which tells the organisation or decision maker which alternative to choose once the information is available. The decision rule ensures that a definite method for obtaining a solution can be found and that the decision does not have to be treated as something new each time it occurs. Frequently, simple formulae can be applied to the situation. Examples of programmed decisions include the ordering of raw materials or office supplies, and the calculation of holiday, sick pay or redundancy payments.

Non programmed decisions, in contrast, are new and unstructured and, consequently, prevent the application of a previously established decision rule. In other words, the organisation has no established procedures or records for dealing with the decision which, therefore, can appear to be highly complex. Non programmed decisions tend to occur at higher levels in the organisation, have long-term consequences and require a degree of judgement and creativity (Agor 1986). Examples include the decision to try an unproven technology or to expand into a previously unknown market.

Allegro, the Irish distribution company, took a major non programmed decision recently in deciding to launch the American snack, Pringles, on to the Irish market. This product is very different from traditional snack foods; it is marketed in a distinct tube which ensures that the product is unbroken and has a shelf life of eighteen months. The decision, however, paid off with Pringles capturing 15 per cent of the market, a figure far in excess of the targeted 5 per cent. Figure 4.8 outlines the main characteristics of each type of decision.

While these two types of decision are clearly distinguishable, they represent a continuum from programmed to non programmed rather than being exclusive categories. Many decisions will have elements of both types of decision.

4.6.2 Decision making conditions

In general, there are three different conditions under which managers take decisions (Huber 1980; Bass 1983). The first is certainty which means that the available alternatives and their costs or benefits are certain. In other words, managers are certain that particular alternatives will lead to definite outcomes and there is no element of doubt. Given the current turbulent business environment it is not surprising that very few decisions can be made under certainty. Only the most minor of decisions can be taken under a condition of complete certainty.

The second condition is risk. Under the risk condition all of the available alternatives and their potential costs and benefits are known, but the outcomes are sometimes in doubt. So, while the alternatives are known the outcomes are unknown. An example of a risk condition is the throw of a dice; the alternatives, i.e. numbers one to six are known, but the outcome is not, as there is a one in five chance of each number coming up. In today's business environment risk taking has become critically important for organisations.

The final condition is that of uncertainty when the available alternatives, the likelihood of their occurrence and the outcomes are all unknown. Decisions made under uncertainty are, consequently, the most difficult due to the lack of concrete knowledge. In the current business environment more and more decisions are taken under uncertainty (Schwenk 1984).

The various decision making conditions represent a continuum from certainty to uncertainty as shown in Figure 4.9.

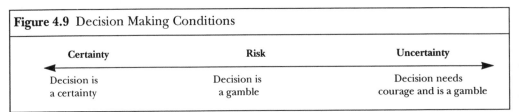

Figure 4.9 Decision Making Conditions

Certainty	Risk	Uncertainty
Decision is a certainty	Decision is a gamble	Decision needs courage and is a gamble

4.6.3 The concept of rationality

Rationality, in relation to decision making, refers to a process that is perfectly logical and objective, whereby managers gather information objectively, evaluate available evidence, consider all alternatives and eventually make choices which will lead to the best outcome for the organisation. The rational approach to decision making has its foundations in traditional economic theory which argues that managers attempt to maximise benefits and have the capacity to make complex decisions quickly. Such a rational approach to decision making assumes that the following four conditions are fulfilled.

1. There is perfect knowledge of all the available alternatives.
2. There is perfect knowledge of all the consequences of the available alternatives.
3. Managers have the capacity to evaluate objectively the consequences of the available alternatives.
4. Managers have a well-structured and definite set of procedures to allow them to make optimum decisions.

As we have seen in the previous section, decisions are made under varying conditions ranging from certainty, to risk and uncertainty. In the current environment managers seldom make decisions under conditions of certainty which would be needed to apply a completely rational model. For many managers today, although the rational approach is ideal, it is simply unattainable under current conditions of risk and uncertainty.

Given the fact that managers cannot always make decisions under certainty conditions, in a rational manner, they have to apply a less than perfect form of rationality. Simon (1976) called this bounded rationality, arguing that decisions taken by managers are bounded by limited mental capacity and emotions and by environmental factors over which they have no control. Due to these limitations managers rarely maximise or take ideal decisions with the best possible outcomes. Instead managers seek to satisfice or, in other words, settle for an alternative which is satisfactory rather than continuing to search for the optimal solution.

Therefore, the rational approach associated with traditional economic theory proposes that managers seek to maximise benefits and, in this sense, outlines how managers should behave. Bounded rationality, however, concentrates on how managers behave in practice when making decisions, and argues that due to limitations placed on managers they will seek to satisfice rather than maximise.

4.7 THE DECISION MAKING PROCESS

Although managers rarely have total control over all the factors that determine how successful decisions will be, they can ensure a degree of control over the process that they use to make decisions. In attempting to make good decisions, managers typically go through six steps as outlined in Figure 4.10. Throughout the various steps in the decision making process the recent Aer Lingus decision to lease brand new Airbus 330 aircraft for its transatlantic route is used as an example.

4.7.1 Problem identification and diagnosis

The first stage of the decision making process is recognising that a problem exists and that action has to be taken. A problem is a discrepancy between the current state of affairs and the desired state of affairs. Unless the problem is identified in precise terms, solutions are very difficult to find. In seeking to identify a problem, managers can use various sources of data, including comparing organisational performance against historical performance, the current performance of other organisations or departments, or expected future performance.

Problem identification must be followed by a willingness to do something to rectify the situation. Before taking action the problem needs to be diagnosed. This involves

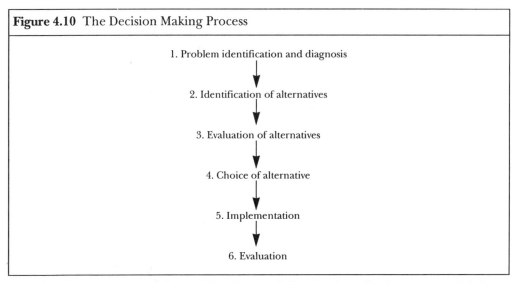

Figure 4.10 The Decision Making Process

1. Problem identification and diagnosis

2. Identification of alternatives

3. Evaluation of alternatives

4. Choice of alternative

5. Implementation

6. Evaluation

assessing the true cause of the problem by carefully selecting all relevant material about a problem and discarding irrelevant information.

For Aer Lingus the problem identification and diagnosis stage was quite simple and routine. The problem arose from the fact that the existing Boeing 747s used on the transatlantic route were starting to age. Aer Lingus had three B747s in operation, all of which had been purchased in the late 1960s and early 1970s. As the average life of a jet aircraft is between twenty and twenty-five years, these aircraft would have to be retired from service in the early 1990s. The problem did not arise suddenly, but was something of which Aer Lingus was aware from an early stage. However, as the retirement date loomed, action was needed which required a quick problem identification and diagnosis in order to place orders for new aircraft.

4.7.2 Identification of alternatives

Having identified and diagnosed the problem, the next step for the organisation is to identify a range of alternative solutions. Given that managers operate under bounded rationality, it is almost impossible to identify all alternatives. However, managers should try to identify as many as possible in order to broaden options for their organisation. In generating alternatives, the organisation may look towards ready-made solutions which have been tried before, or custom-made solutions which are designed specifically for the problem at hand. In today's business environment more and more organisations are applying custom-made solutions to enhance competitive advantage.

In seeking to solve the ageing aircraft problem, Aer Lingus identified a range of alternative solutions. The first concerned the issue of whether a new or an old aircraft should be considered. Secondly, Aer Lingus considered whether the aircraft should be purchased outright or leased. Finally, Aer Lingus considered a range of aircraft types which could be chosen, including the Boeing range of 747, 757, and 767 and the Airbus 330 and 340.

4.7.3 Evaluating alternatives

Having identified the available alternatives a manager needs to evaluate each one in order to choose the best. Each alternative should be evaluated in terms of its advantages, disadvantages, costs and benefits. Most alternatives will have varying positive and negative aspects and the manager will have to try to balance anticipated outcomes.

Depending on the situation at hand, evaluation of alternatives may be intuitive or based on scientific analysis. Most organisations try to use a combination of both approaches. When evaluating alternatives managers may consider the potential consequences under several different scenarios. In doing so they can develop contingency plans which can be implemented in the future.

In evaluating the alternatives available to Aer Lingus in relation to whether the aircraft should be purchased or leased and whether it should be old or new, the costs and benefits of each of the scenarios was examined. Aer Lingus considered numerous factors including the size of the market and the length of the routes to be served, the frequency of service, aircraft size in terms of seats and the breakdown between classes (economy and business), the design and physical performance of the aircraft, maintenance requirements, availability of spare parts and the amount of training required for cabin crew, pilots and maintenance engineers.

4.7.4 Choice of alternative

Having evaluated the various alternatives the next step is to choose the most suitable. If, for some reason, none of the alternatives discussed are suitable then the manager should revert back to step 2 of the process and begin again. Where there are suitable alternatives and steps 2 and 3 have been conducted skilfully, selecting alternatives should be relatively easy. In practice, however, alternatives may not differ significantly in terms of their outcome and, therefore, decisions will be a matter of judgement. In coming to a decision the manager will be confronted by many conflicting requirements which have to be taken into account. For example, the quality versus the acceptability of the decision and political and resource constraints.

Based on an evaluation of alternatives, Aer Lingus opted to lease a brand new aircraft as opposed to purchasing an old or new aircraft or leasing an older one. The particular aircraft type chosen was the Airbus 330 costing £70 million.

4.7.5 Implementation

Once the decision has been made it needs to be implemented. This stage of the process is critical to the success of the decision and is the key to effective decision making. The best alternative is worth nothing if it is not implemented properly. Managers must ensure that those who are implementing the decision understand fully why the choice was made and why it is being implemented and are fully committed to its success.

To ensure success, many organisations are attempting to push decision making further down in the organisation to ensure that employees have some sense of ownership in the decision.

In the case of Aer Lingus the implementation of the decision involved the lease of the aircraft from a leasing company. This required lengthy negotiations, training of staff and ensuring the availability of spare parts and putting the aircraft into service.

4.7.6 Evaluation

Having implemented the decision it then needs to be evaluated to provide feedback. This process of evaluation should take place at all managerial levels enabling managers to see the results of the decision and to identify any adjustments that need to be made.

In almost all cases, some form of adjustment is necessary.

Evaluation and feedback should form part of an on-going process. As conditions change, decisions taken should be re-evaluated to ensure that they are still the most appropriate for the organisation and to help managers make sound decisions. In the case of Aer Lingus, an evaluation of the decision will occur at regular intervals with an assessment of the costs and benefits of the choice. In doing so, Aer Lingus managers will use their experience, based on previous aircraft selection processes.

The model presented in Figure 4.10 provides a useful framework for managers when taking decisions. It must be recognised, however, that the process is seldom as neat and sequential as the one outlined. The process is subject to various biases and pressures. In line with the concept of bounded rationality, managers frequently allow their subjective biases to interfere with *objective* decision making. Pressures of time can also affect the process.

4.8 GROUP DECISION MAKING

Task forces, teams and boards are all examples of group settings where decision making occurs. The basic idea behind group decision making is that two heads are better than one. Much research (Shaw 1981; Hill 1982 and Sussman and Deep 1984) has been conducted on the subject of whether groups or individuals make better decisions. Generally, the diversity of groups facilitates better quality decisions. However, Hill (1982) found that groups can be inferior to the best individual. In some cases, groups will provide the best quality decisions and in others the individual will be better. In coming to a conclusion about the efficiency of group decision making it is necessary to consider the advantages and disadvantages.

4.8.1 Advantages
1. Group decision making allows a greater number of perspectives and approaches to be considered, thereby increasing the number of alternatives which can be drawn up.
2. Groups generally facilitate a larger pool of information to be processed. Individuals from different areas can bring varied information to the decision making setting.
3. The more people involved in the process the greater the number who will understand why the decision was made, which facilitates implementation.
4. Group decision making allows more involvement and develops a sense of ownership in the final decision which means that people will be more committed to the decision.
5. Using groups to arrive at a decision means that less co-ordination and communication is required when implementing the decision.

4.8.2 Disadvantages
1. Group decisions take longer to arrive at which can be problematic when speed of action is a key requirement.
2. Groups can be indecisive and opt for satisficing rather then maximising. Indecision can arise from lack of agreement among members. Satisficing occurs when individuals grow tired of the process and want it brought to a conclusion.
3. Groups can be dominated by individuals with either a strong personality or position. The result is that this individual exerts his/her influence, and prevents others from participating fully. The main problem with such situations is that the dominating

person need not necessarily be correct and even if he/she was, convening a group for discussion will have been a waste of time.

4. Groups inevitably have to compromise which can lead to mediocre decisions. Mediocrity results when an individual's thinking is brought into line with the average quality of a group's thinking. This is called the *levelling effect.*

5. Groups can lead to *group think.* Irving (1982) defines this as 'a mode of thinking that people engage in when they are deeply involved in a cohesive group, when members strivings for unanimity override their motivation to realistically appraise alternative courses of action.' Group think happens in situations where the need to achieve consensus among group members becomes so powerful that it takes over realistic evaluations of available alternatives. Criticism is suppressed and conflicting views are not aired for fear of breaking up a positive team spirit. Such groups become over confident and too willing to take risks.

4.8.3 Individual versus group decision making

Having considered the advantages and disadvantages, it would appear that group decision making is appropriate in certain circumstances. Sussman and Deep (1984) outline ten factors which suit individual decision making and ten which favour group decision making. Factors favouring individual decision making include:

1. short time frame
2. decision is relatively unimportant to the group
3. manager has all the data needed to make the decision
4. one or two members of the group are likely to dominate
5. conflict is likely
6. people attend too many meetings
7. data is confidential
8. group members are not sufficiently qualified
9. manager is dominant
10. decision does not directly affect the group.

Factors favouring group decision making include:

1. creativity is required
2. data is held by the group
3. acceptance of the solution by group members is important
4. understanding of the solution is important
5. problem is complex and needs a broad range of knowledge
6. manager wants to build commitment
7. more risk taking is involved
8. better understanding of group members is needed
9. group is responsible for the decision
10. manager wants feedback on ideas.

Source: Sussman, L. and Deep, S., *COMEX: The Communication Experience in Human Relations,* South Western, Cincinnati 1984.

4.8.4 Improving group decision making

In order to avoid the disadvantages and to build on the advantages, three main ways of improving group decision making have been developed (Moorehead and Griffin 1989).

1. **Brainstorming**: Brainstorming became popular in the 1950s and was developed by Alexander Osborn to facilitate the development of creative solutions and alternatives. Brainstorming is solely concerned with idea generation rather than evaluation, choice or implementation. The term effectively means using the brain creatively to storm a problem. It is based on the belief that when people interact in a more relaxed and less restrained setting they will generate more creative ideas. The acceptance of new ideas is also more likely when the decision is made by the group involved with its implementation (Summers and White 1976).

In brainstorming the group members are normally given a summary of the problem prior to the meeting. At the meeting members come up with various ideas which are recorded in full view of each other. None of the alternatives are evaluated or criticised at this stage. The introduction of new ideas and alternatives stimulates other members and, hopefully, a good solution can be identified. The concept of Bailey's Irish Cream was developed from a brainstorming session.

2. **The Delphi technique**: The Delphi technique was developed by Dalkey and Helmar in the early 1960s as a means of avoiding the undesirable affects of poor group interaction, while retaining the positive aspects. The technique got its name from Delphi which was the seat of the Greek god, Apollo, who was renowned for his wise decisions.

The Delphi technique consists of a panel of experts formed to examine a problem. However, rather than meeting together, the various members are kept apart so that they cannot be influenced by social or psychological pressures associated with group behaviour. In order to find out their views they are asked to complete a questionnaire. A co-ordinator then summarises the findings and members are asked to fill out another questionnaire to re-evaluate earlier points. The technique presumes that as repeated questionnaires are conducted the range of responses will narrow to produce a consensus. The Delphi technique is particularly useful where experts are physically dispersed, anonymity is required and where members have difficulty communicating with each other. On the negative side, however, it reduces direct interaction among group members.

3. **Nominal grouping**: This was developed by Delbecq and Van de Ven (1971) and, in contrast to brainstorming, does not allow a free association of ideas, tries to restrict verbal interaction and can be used at many other stages of the decision making process apart from just idea generation. With nominal grouping, members are given a problem and asked to think of ideas individually and without discussion. They then present these ideas on a flip chart. A period of discussion follows which builds on the ideas presented. After the discussion, members privately rate the ideas. Generation of ideas and discussion proceeds in this manner until a solution is found.

The main advantages of this approach is that it overcomes differences between members in terms of power and prestige and it can also be used at a variety of stages in the overall decision making process. Its main disadvantages are that its structure may limit creativity and it is costly and time consuming.

4.9 SUMMARY OF KEY PROPOSITIONS

• Planning has been defined as a process of establishing aims and objectives and choosing a course of action to ensure that these objectives are achieved.

• Planning takes place at various levels within the organisation and involves all managers to a greater or lesser degree. Strategic planning takes place at the top, tactical planning at the middle level and operational planning at the lower level of the organisation.

• Organisations can use a variety of different plans to guide future action, ranging from the most basic, the mission statement, to more precise and specific forms like budgets, all of which form a hierarchy of plans.

• In order to ensure that planning is effective, organisations go through a process of corporate planning, involving a sequence of stages, the success of which depends on the accuracy of the preceding stage.

• An example of one particular process for setting objectives has been outlined — MBO. This approach has many associated advantages and disadvantages.

• It was concluded that planning is a critically important function for all organisations, providing the framework for all subsequent management functions.

• Planning involves taking decisions about the future direction of the organisation, therefore, it is important to consider decision making.

• There are various types of decision which are taken by the organisation, most notably programmed and non programmed.

• Decisions are taken under different conditions ranging from complete certainty to uncertainty.

• In the current business environment more and more decisions are occurring under conditions of uncertainty. This means that managers have to apply bounded rationality, whereby decisions taken are affected by the limited mental capacity, emotions and environmental factors.

• Organisations typically go through certain stages when making organisational decisions, called the decision making process.

• Decisions can be taken by either groups or individuals depending on the nature of the decision.

• The quality of group decisions can be enhanced by three main techniques: brainstorming, the Delphi technique and nominal grouping.

DISCUSSION QUESTIONS

1. Explain why planning is one of the most important managerial functions.
2. Distinguish between strategic, tactical and operational planning.
3. Identify any four types of plans and explain their importance to the planning process.
4. Explain why corporate planning is necessary.

5. Conduct a SWOT analysis for an organisation with which you are familiar.
6. What are the main advantages and disadvantages of the Management by Objectives approach?
7. Explain, using your own examples, the differences between programmed and non programmed decisions.
8. What do you understand by the terms rationality and bounded rationality?
9. Outline the advantages and disadvantages of group decision making.
10. Explain the factors which determine that a decision should be taken by a group.
11. What methods can be used for improving group performance in decision making?
12. Apply the decision making process to a decision you have made recently.

REFERENCES

Agor, W., 'How Top Executives use their Intuition to make Important Decisions' *Business Horizons*, Vol.29, No.9, 49–53, 1986.

Bass, B., *Organisational Decision Making*, Irwin, Illinois 1983.

'VHI — Duncan's Quiet Revolution' *Business and Finance*, 22–26, 20 April 1995.

Connecting With the Future: ESB Strategies for the 1990s, Dublin, March 1990.

Dalkey, N. and Helmar, O., 'An Experimental Application of the Delphi Methods to the Use of Experts' *Managerial Science*, Vol.9, 458–467, 1963.

David, F., 'How Companies Define their Missions' *Long Range Planning*, Vol.22, No.1, 90–97, 1989.

Delbecq, A. and Van de Ven, A., 'A Group Process Model for Problem Identification and Programme Planning' *Journal of Applied Behavioural Science*, Vol.7, 466–492, 1971.

Drucker, P., *Management Tasks, Responsibilities and Practices*, Harper Row, New York 1973.

Drucker, P., *The Practice of Management*, Harper Row, New York 1954.

Hill, G.,'Group Versus Individual Performance: Are n + 1 Heads Better than One' *Psychological Bulletin*, Vol.91, 517–539, 1982.

Huber, G., *Managerial Decision Making*, Scott Foresman, Illinois 1980.

Humble, J., *Management by Objectives*, Teakfield, USA 1972.

Irving, J., *Group Think*, Houghton Mifflin, Boston 1982.

Jones, H., *Preparing Company Plans: A Workbook for Effective Corporate Planning*, Wiley, New York 1974.

Johnson, G. and Scholes, K., *Exploring Corporate Strategy*, Prentice Hall, London 1993.

Kast, F. and Rosenweig, J., *Organisation and Management: A Systems Approach*, McGraw-Hill, New York 1985.

Michiels, R., 'Planning, an Effective Management Tool or a Corporate Pastime' *Journal of Marketing Management*, Vol.1, No.3, 259–264, 1986.

Moorehead, G. and Griffin, R., *Organisational Behaviour*, Houghton Mifflin, Boston 1989.

Odiorne, G., Weihrich, H. and Mendelson, J. (eds), *Executive Skills — A Management by Objectives Approach*, Brown and Co., Iowa.

Osborn, A., *Applied Imagination: Principles and Procedures for Creative Problem Solving*, Scribner, New York 1963.

Schwenk, C., 'Cognitive Simplification Process in Strategic Decision Making' *Strategic Management Journal*, Vol.5, No.2, 111–128, 1984.

Shaw, M., *Group Dynamics: The Psychology of Small Group Behaviour*, McGraw-Hill, New York 1981.

Simon, H., *Administrative Behaviour: A Study of Decision Making Processes in Administrative Organisations*, Free Press, New York 1976.

Sisk, H., *Management and Organisation*, South Western, Cincinnati 1973.

Summers, I. and White, D., 'Creativity Techniques: Towards Improvement of the Decision Process' *Academy of Management Review*, Vol.1, No.3, 99–107, 1976.

Sussman, L. and Deep, S., *COMEX: The Communication Experience in Human Relations*, South Western, Cincinnati 1984.

Thompson, A. and Strickland, A., *Strategic Management: Concepts and Cases*, Irwin, Illinois 1990.

Weihrich, H. and Koontz, H., *Management: A Global Perspective*, McGraw-Hill, New York 1993.

5

Organising

5.1 INTRODUCTION

This chapter examines the second function of management — organising. Staffing, normally considered an integral part of organising, is discussed in Chapter 10. Organising is the process of dividing and *co-ordinating* the tasks to be achieved. The framework used for organising is called organisational structure. Organisational structure has a number of components which are examined. Also, historical approaches to structure are considered along with some more recent additions. Recent developments in structure have been triggered by changes in the business environment. As a result, three new types of structure have been developed and used by organisations, depending on their requirements. These are the network organisation, the cluster organisation and the high performance organisation.

5.2 THE NATURE AND IMPORTANCE OF ORGANISING

Organising is the process of dividing tasks between groups, individuals and departments and co-ordinating their activities to achieve organisational goals. The process usually starts with a reflection on the plans and objectives devised at the planning stage and then establishes the major tasks needed to achieve such goals. These tasks are then subdivided into sub tasks and resources are allocated to them. Finally, the outcomes of the process are evaluated and corrections made. The function of organising creates relationships between organisational areas that outline when, where and how resources are to be used.

As a result of the organising process the organisation's activities are broken down and departmentalised. Connections and means of co-ordination are then established. The pattern of dividing and then co-ordinating activities is called organisational structure. It can be defined as the system of task reporting and authority relationships within which the work of the organisation is completed (Moorehead and Griffin 1989). The purpose of any form of structure is to co-ordinate the activities of employees in order to achieve organisational goals.

In recent years organisational structure has undergone a revolution. As a result of the changes in the business environment organisations have come to realise that in order to survive their structures must be flexible and adaptable. This enables the organisation to respond to and anticipate change. Therefore, having an effective form of organisational structure has become an important source of competitive advantage. Organisations that do not adapt their structures to meet changing needs face extinction. Those that change their structure will achieve the flexibility and creativity necessary for survival. Before examining the various approaches to structure, including recent developments, it is necessary to understand the components of the organisation's structure.

5.3 COMPONENTS OF ORGANISATIONAL STRUCTURE

The main components can be divided into two main areas: structural configuration and structural operation. Structural configuration refers to the size and shape of the structure and concentrates on the size of the hierarchy, spans of control, division of labour and means of co-ordination. The structural configuration of the organisation can be clearly seen from its *organisational chart*. In contrast, structural operation concentrates on the processes and operations of organisational structure, including decision making, formalisation, responsibility and authority. Each element of the organisation's structural configuration and operation is shown in Figure 5.1.

Figure 5.1 Components of Organisational Structure

Structural Configuration	Structural Operation
Division of labour	Formalisation
Spans of control	Decision making
Hierarchical levels	Responsibility
Departmentalisation	Authority

5.3.1 Structural configuration

The division of labour within the organisation is the extent to which the work of the organisation is broken down into different tasks, to be completed by different people. It is also referred to as *job specialisation* meaning that one person is specialised in doing one particular task. A clear example of a division of labour can be found in McDonalds where staff are assigned to cleaning up the lobby areas, making fries, making burgers or serving the public. In this case, the division of labour is quite narrow. A wider division of labour could mean that each person would serve customers, prepare their food, and clean up after them.

It was hoped that narrow divisions of labour and job specialisation would lead to efficient use of labour, increased standardisation and the development of employee expertise through repetition of a task. However, narrow job specialisation can lead to reduced job satisfaction and motivation, as people have to complete the same routine task over and over again (Sherman and Smith 1984). It can also lead to absenteeism, high staff turnover and poor quality output.

Spans of control are the number of employees reporting directly to a supervisor. A narrow span means that the supervisor is in charge of a small number of employees, whereas a wide span of control means that the supervisor is in charge of a large number.

Figure 5.2 shows an example of both a wide and a narrow span of control. Supervisor A has got only three employees reporting to him/her which is a very narrow span. In contrast, supervisor B has got nine employees reporting to him/her which is a much wider span.

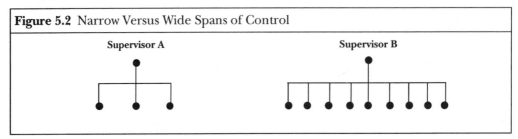

Figure 5.2 Narrow Versus Wide Spans of Control

With wider spans of control employees tend to have more freedom and discretion. In contrast, narrow spans of control usually lead to high levels of supervision, as managers watch the activities of all employees under their control. With effective spans of control, employees can be given a degree of freedom, while at the same time having some form of guidance from a supervisor should assistance be required. Many theorists have tried to identify what the optimal span of control should be. Mintzberg (1979) concludes that the size of the span depends on a number of factors not least the degree of specialisation, the similarity of tasks, the type of information available, the need for autonomy, direct access to supervisors and the abilities and experience of both supervisors and employees.

The number of levels and the extent of hierarchy outlines the reporting relationships within the organisation from top to bottom. Organisations with relatively few levels are called flat structures, while those with many levels are called tall structures. A relationship exists between the number of levels in the hierarchy and the spans of control as shown in Figure 5.3.

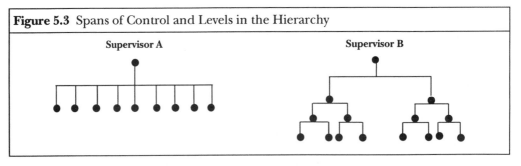

Figure 5.3 Spans of Control and Levels in the Hierarchy

The left-hand side of the figure shows that with wide spans of control less levels in the management structure are required. In this case, the span of control is fourteen and only one hierarchical level is required. However, if the spans are very narrow, as shown on the right-hand side, then more supervisors and managers are needed which increases the number of levels in the hierarchy. In this case, the span of control is two and there are three hierarchical levels in the structure. Therefore, as the span increases the hierarchy decreases and, conversely, as the span decreases the hierarchy increases.

The final element of structural configuration is concerned with co-ordinating the various activities of the organisation. Traditionally, this has been known as

departmentalisation as departments were normally set up to co-ordinate activities. In recent years, business units or even separate divisions or companies have tended to replace traditional departments as the primary co-ordinating mechanisms. However, the term departmentalisation can still be usefully applied to any means used by organisations, be it business unit or division, to co-ordinate its activities. In other words, co-ordination does not focus solely on departments within the organisation, but can include separate parts and business units. The following are the six main forms of departmentalisation that the organisation can adopt, each possessing particular strengths and weaknesses:
1. Functional departmentalisation
2. Product departmentalisation
3. Geographical departmentalisation
4. Customer departmentalisation
5. Matrix departmentalisation
6. Mixed departmentalisation

Functional departmentalisation was probably the most popular form of departmentalisation until recently. It organises the separate units of the organisation according to the functions they perform. Functional departmentalisation is usually structured around the traditional organisational functions of manufacturing, marketing, finance, engineering and personnel. Figure 5.4 provides an example of a functional approach to departmentalisation used by SDS, a subsidiary of An Post, providing courier services and the distribution of special parcels. SDS is structured around the main functions involved in its activities: finance, sales and marketing and operations.

Figure 5.4 SDS: An Example of Functional Departmentalisation

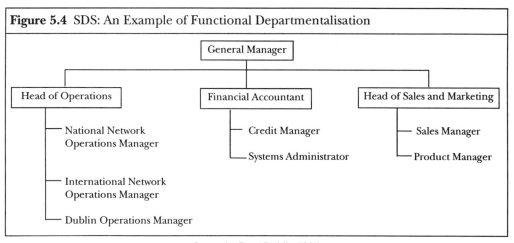

Source: An Post, Dublin 1995.

The main advantages associated with functional departmentalisation include:
1. The functions of each individual are emphasised allowing people to concentrate their efforts.
2. Resources are used efficiently by grouping the various functions and gaining economies of scale and reductions in overheads.
3. A clear and simple communication and decision making system is possible.

4. The measurement of output and performance of the various functional areas is facilitated. Consequently, performance standards are easier to maintain.
5. The training given to specialists is simplified and employees have greater opportunities for specialised training and in-depth skill development.
6. Status is given to each of the main functional areas.
7. Control by the top of the organisation is facilitated.

The disadvantages associated with this form of departmentalisation are:
1. It is difficult to co-ordinate departments if they are too big.
2. Employees tend to focus on departmental goals rather than wider organisational goals due to their limited outlook.
3. It can be quite costly to co-ordinate the activities of the various functions.
4. Such a structure makes it difficult to develop managers with experience in a wide variety of areas.
5. Competition and rivalry between departments can develop.
6. Such a structure can lower customer satisfaction when compared to alternative means of departmentalisation.

With **product departmentalisation**, the organisation is structured on the basis of the products it produces. Business units in many organisations are structured in this manner. Product departmentalisation is often used by large organisations that find functional departments too difficult to co-ordinate. An example of product departmentalisation used by Waterford Foods is shown in Figure 5.5.

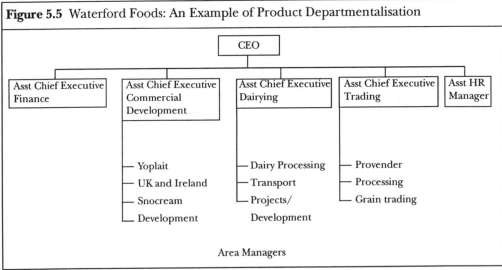

Figure 5.5 Waterford Foods: An Example of Product Departmentalisation

Source: Waterford Foods 1995.

The main products of an organisation, such as Yoplait and dairy processing, become the focus of the structure. Each product line contains the various functional activities that it requires, such as personnel and marketing. This form of structure has a number of advantages:
1. Product areas or business units can be evaluated as profit centres.

2. Additions to the product line can be easily incorporated which facilitates growth. In the same way, a product can be discontinued and resources reallocated to another product.
3. It allows quicker co-ordination and communication between functions working on a product.
4. The structure focuses on the needs of clients.
5. The structure develops managers with a wide experience of various functions.
6. Employees develop full-time commitment to a particular product line.

It also has a number of disadvantages:
1. Co-ordination among specialised product areas can be problematic.
2. There is a duplication of functional services for each product.
3. Less communication and interaction occurs between functional specialists.
4. The emphasis tends to be on product objectives rather than wider organisational objectives.

With **geographical departmentalisation**, the organisation is structured around activities in various geographical locations. An example of geographical departmentalisation used by the Smurfit Group is shown in Figure 5.6.

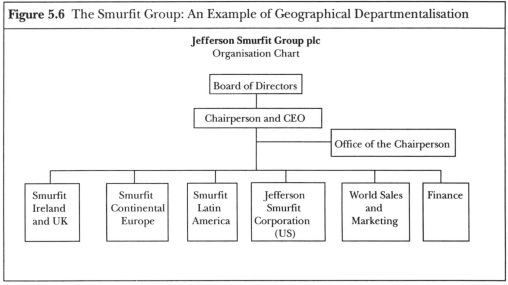

Figure 5.6 The Smurfit Group: An Example of Geographical Departmentalisation

Source: Smurfit Group 1995.

This form of structure is particularly suitable for organisations selling in many different countries where there are significant differences in markets and customer needs. The main advantages are:
1. It encourages logistical efficiency.
2. It allows divisions to adapt to local markets.
3. Legal, cultural and political difference can be minimised.
4. It provides a good training ground for managers.

The disadvantages of this form of structure are:
1. It needs a large number of general managers.
2. Top management loses a degree of control over operations.
3. A duplication of support services is inevitable.
4. Employees may focus on regional objectives at the expense of wider organisational goals.

Customer departmentalisation focuses on customers and their needs. It is found most commonly in organisations that have a few large and easily identifiable customer groups. Figure 5.7 provides an example of customer departmentalisation used by the AIB Group.

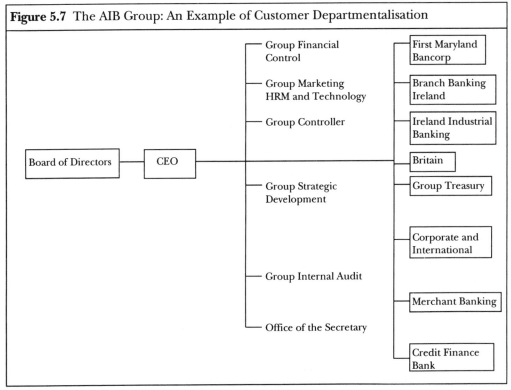

Figure 5.7 The AIB Group: An Example of Customer Departmentalisation

Source: AIB 1995.

As can be seen from the chart, AIB has clearly identified important customer groups such as branch (retail customer), corporate and international and merchant banking customer groups. The main advantages associated with this form of structure are:
1. It increases responsiveness to customers' needs.
2. It ties performance to the requirements of individual market segments.

The disadvantages are:
1. It makes it difficult to establish and implement organisation-wide practices.
2. It increases pressure for special treatment for particular customers.

A **matrix structure** is a combination of functional and product departmentalisation. It was first implemented by TRW Inc. in the USA. The company found that traditional functional departmentalisation was inadequate for managing complex technological developments. With a matrix structure employees are both members of a functional group and also a product group. So, in effect, they have two supervisors, one from their core functional area and one from the particular project area. However, when employees are involved in specific projects the Project Manager is the reporting supervisor. The most remarkable feature about the matrix structure is that functional and product lines of authority are overlaid to form a grid. This form of structure is usually found in organisations with diverse activities, or for project management. Private industry found this structure attractive particularly for projects with a high capital investment and R&D requirement.

An example of a matrix structure used by Team Aer Lingus is shown in Figure 5.8. In this case, the various maintenance operations, such as aircraft and component overhaul, and the various functional activities required for effective operation demand a matrix form of structure. Employees, therefore, may belong to a particular functional group and yet work in a particular business unit area.

Figure 5.8 Team Aer Lingus: An Example of a Matrix Structure

	Finance	Commercial	Maintenance and overhaul	Planning and engineering	Operations and resources
Business Unit 1 Aircraft overhaul					
Business Unit 2 Component overhaul					

Source: Team Aer Lingus 1995.

The advantages of this structure are:
1. The interdisciplinary nature of the project teams contributes to a high rate of new product innovation.
2. It establishes the project manager as a focal point for all matters involving a certain project.
3. It maximises the use of a limited pool of specialists.
4. It makes specialised functional assistance available to all projects.
5. It provides a good training ground for potential managers of diversified organisations.

According to Davis and Lawrence (1977) the disadvantages are:
1. It leads to interpersonal and command conflict with the existence of a dual reporting relationship.
2. It creates power struggles among project managers and functional area heads.
3. It slows down decision making.

4. It can promote narrow viewpoints associated with specific projects at the expense of wider organisational objectives.
5. It can be difficult to trace accountability and authority.

Grinnel and Apple (1975) have argued that the matrix structure is only appropriate in these circumstances.
1. When the organisation produces short-run, complex products.
2. When complicated product design needs innovation and timely completion.
3. When many kinds of sophisticated skills are needed.
4. When a rapidly changing market-place requires product changes even in the period between design and delivery.

With **mixed departmentalisation** many large organisations use a mixture of the various approaches to gain the advantages associated with the different means of departmentalisation. For example, a bank might have a geographical structure in several countries with a functional structure in each bank. An example of a mixed form of departmentalisation can be found in the organisational chart for Aer Rianta as shown in Figure 5.9.

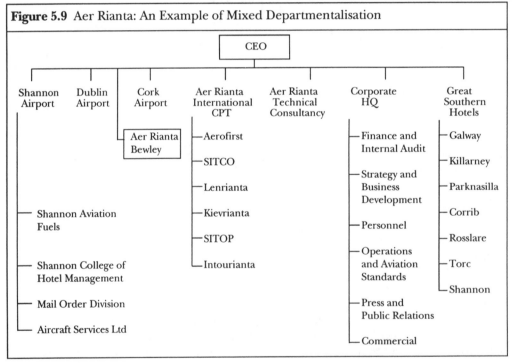

Figure 5.9 Aer Rianta: An Example of Mixed Departmentalisation

Source: Aer Rianta 1995.

The organisational chart clearly shows that the structure is a mixture of geographic, functional and product departmentalisation.

5.3.2 Structural operation
Formalisation refers to the degree to which rules and procedures shape the jobs and

tasks completed by employees. Organisations are said to be highly formalised if their work activities are governed by many rules and procedures. On the other hand, if the activities are governed by few rules and procedures then the structure is said to be lowly formalised. According to Mintzberg (1979), the main purpose of formalisation is to predict and control how employees behave on the job.

High formalisation is designed to ensure standardisation of work and also to ensure a high quality product or service. Organisations involved in the manufacture or maintenance of transport vehicles typically display high levels of formalisation due to the requirements of stringent safety and engineering standards. On the negative side, high formalisation leads to a lack of *autonomy* and freedom and initiative as people come to blindly follow rules without considering whether or not they benefit the organisation.

Decision making can either be centralised or decentralised. Centralisation refers to a decision making policy where authority resides at the top of the organisation. Decentralisation, on the other hand, means that decisions are taken at all levels of the organisation. Centralisation ensures a greater uniformity of decisions as they are all taken by the same group. Those at the top have the best knowledge and understanding of the issues facing the organisation and are, therefore, in a better position to take decisions. On the other hand, decentralisation ensures that lower level problems can be solved and decisions are taken on the spot. It also gives lower level employees the opportunity to develop decision making skills. It increases motivation and spreads the work more evenly throughout the organisation.

Responsibility can be viewed as an obligation to do something under the expectation that some act or output will be achieved. In the organisational setting managers and supervisors are responsible for achieving certain goals and also for the conduct of their subordinates. Passing on responsibility is usually referred to as *delegating*. Most organisations delegate responsibility for certain tasks to people lower down. Top managers cannot cope with the responsibility for all tasks and, consequently, delegate.

Authority is power that has been legitimised within a certain social context (Pfeffer 1981), or, in other words, the right to performance on command. In the case of organisational authority, the social context is the organisation and the authority is associated with the position in the hierarchy. This is referred to as position power or legitimate power. Specialists within organisations may also possess power arising from their expert knowledge. This is referred to as expert power. Authority and responsibility are related in that for responsibility to be truly delegated, the authority associated with such responsibility should also be passed on. However, frequently managers or supervisors pass on the responsibility for a certain task but not the authority to see it through. The end result is confusion and inefficiency.

Organisational structures, therefore, have clearly identifiable components. Structural configuration can be seen from the organisational chart and includes the division of labour, spans of control, hierarchy and departmentalisation. Structural operation focuses on the actual operation of the structure and includes formalisation, decision making, responsibility and authority.

5.4 UNIVERSAL APPROACHES TO ORGANISATIONAL STRUCTURE

The universal approaches to organisational structure maintained that there is always one best way to structure the organisation's activities. In this sense, they offered prescriptions designed to work in all situations. These approaches concentrated almost entirely on the formal organisation and its associated structure, and ignored the role of the informal organisation. Factors such as the organisation's external environment, size and technology were, therefore, largely ignored by advocates of the universal approach. The three most popular and influential universal approaches are the classic principles advocated by Fayol, Weber and Likert.

As we have seen in Chapter 2, Fayol is considered the father of modern management. He was the first person to identify what roughly corresponds to the modern five functions of management — planning, organising, commanding, co-ordinating and controlling. Fayol also identified fourteen principles of management which he considered vitally important for managers. Fayol's classical principles were widely applied in many organisations and, therefore, it is not surprising that they have had an impact on organisational structure.

Fayol's principles have served as a basis for the development of principles of organising. The application of Fayol's unity of command meant that employees should only receive instructions from one person, while unity of direction meant that tasks with the same objective should have the same supervisor. Fayol also advocated a division of labour and a clear system of responsibility. Taken together these principles have laid the foundations for both structural configuration and structural operation.

Over time, these principles have been criticised for ignoring the human element in organisations such as motivation, job satisfaction and the informal organisation. The application of these principles leads to a rather rigid, mechanical form of structure, whereby people are slotted into areas irrespective of their abilities or motivation. Fayol also neglected to outline how his principles should be put into operation to ensure success. Finally, Fayol's principles were based on his own personal experiences and not scientific analysis, which has led many people to question their general applicability.

The second universal approach and probably the most well known and enduring is that of bureaucracy. Weber used the term bureaucracy at the turn of the century to describe what he perceived as the preferred form of structure for business and government. Weber's bureaucratic organisation was designed to minimise the personal influence of individual employees in decision making, thereby co-ordinating the large number of decisions to be taken by the organisation. It was also designed to facilitate the allocation of scarce resources in an increasingly complex society. The bureaucratic structure advocated by Weber had six main characteristics which were discussed in Chapter 2 and are summarised at this point.

1. Division of labour
2. Managerial hierarchy
3. Formal selection
4. Career orientation
5. Formal rules and procedures
6. Impersonality

Organisational structures based on Weber's principles of bureaucracy developed quickly. They emphasised a narrow division of labour, narrow spans of control, many levels of hierarchy, limited responsibility and authority, centralised decision making and high formalisation. The bureaucratic structure was particularly popular in large organisations as it encouraged the performance of various routine activities needed for effective operation. It became the dominant form of structure used by the majority of organisations, as it appeared to offer an efficient form of structure and was technically superior to any other. The advantages of a bureaucratic structure are:

1. The strict division of labour advocated by Weber increased efficiency and expertise due to repetition of the task.
2. The hierarchy of authority allowed a clear chain of command to develop which permitted the orderly flow of information and communication.
3. Formal selection meant that employees were hired on merit and expertise which eliminated the nepotism associated with managerial practices in the early days of the Industrial Revolution.
4. Career orientation ensured that career professionals would give the organisation a degree of continuity.
5. Rules and procedures controlled employee performance and, therefore, increased productivity and efficiency.
6. The impersonality of the organisation ensured that rules were applied across the board, eliminating personal bias and ensuring efficiency.

Over time, bureaucracies have produced a number of unintended negative outcomes associated with individual behaviour. The main disadvantages are:

1. The behaviour of employees becomes segmented and insular, with employees focusing on their own task with little awareness of what is going on in other areas. As a result, effective co-ordination becomes very difficult.
2. The extensive rules and procedures used by the organisation can sometimes become ends in themselves. In this sense, obeying rules at all costs becomes important irrespective of whether such action is to the organisation's advantage.
3. Bureaucracy also promotes rigidity and leads to a situation where the organisation is unable to react quickly or change when necessary. Bureaucratic organisations come to believe that what has worked well in the past will continue to do so.
4. Delegation of authority and the insular nature of bureaucracy can lead to a situation where employees identify with the objectives of work groups at the expense of the objectives of the wider organisations. This is referred to as *goal displacement.*
5. The extensive hierarchy makes communications particularly difficult. Middle managers frequently become overloaded with information, and bottlenecks are created.
6. Innovation rarely occurs in a bureaucratic structure, as new ideas take so long to filter up or down the hierarchy. Each level in the hierarchy acts as a further barrier.
7. The strict division of labour can lead to routine and boring jobs where workers feel apathetic and demotivated.
8. The extensive rules and procedures provide minimum standards above which employees normally will not go. So, instead of acting as a controlling device the rules actually reduce performance.

Despite its inherent disadvantages, the bureaucratic form of organisational structure has been very successful for large organisations operating in stable and simple external environments.

The final universal approach to structure was advocated and developed by Likert with his *Human Organisation* (1967). Likert strongly criticised both Fayol and Weber for ignoring human factors. He emphasised the importance of employee participation, supportive relationships and overlapping work groups. Supportive relationships help employees to experience self worth and importance at work. Overlapping work groups are linked together by managers who belong to management groups, which facilitates co-ordination throughout the organisation. Likert believed that the most successful structure was one composed of highly cohesive groups, aligned with organisational goals by effective co-ordination and communication. To highlight his arguments, Likert developed four systems of organising:

1. Exploitative authoritarian
2. Benevolent authoritarian
3. Consultative authoritarian
4. Participative group.

Exploitative authoritarian corresponds to the classical bureaucratic structure. Managers in this system are autocratic with little trust in subordinates. Decision making is centralised and communication takes place from the top downwards. System two managers tend to have patronising confidence and trust in employees, motivating them through rewards and fear of punishment. Within this system there is limited delegation of decision making and some upward communication. System three managers have substantial trust in employees and try to use employee opinions. Motivation is achieved through rewards and occasional punishment. Decision making is somewhat decentralised and both upward and downward communication takes place. System four was the most preferred structure advocated by Likert and consisted of eight key characteristics.

1. Managers and leaders have trust in subordinates and their ideas.
2. The organisation recognises and channels employee motivations towards organisational goals.
3. Communication is both vertical and horizontal and occurs frequently.
4. Much interaction and influence occurs between work groups.
5. Decisions are made throughout the organisation in a decentralised manner.
6. Goals are set by work groups.
7. All levels are involved in the control process.
8. Top management sets high performance goals for the organisation.

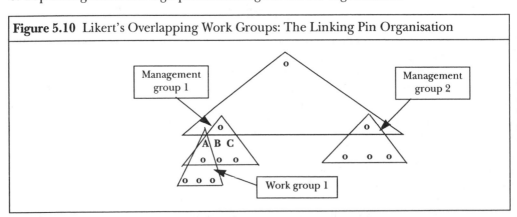

Figure 5.10 Likert's Overlapping Work Groups: The Linking Pin Organisation

Management group 1

Management group 2

A B C

Work group 1

Source: Adapted from Likert, R., *New Patterns of Management,* McGraw-Hill, New York 1961.

System four heavily contradicts both the unity of command and the hierarchical chain of command. Likert believed that work groups should overlap horizontally and vertically and he favoured a linking pin concept of overlapping groups for co-ordination, rather than the hierarchical chain of command as shown in Figure 5.10.

Managers serve as linking pins between the various workgroups. Each manager (except those at the top of the organisation) is a member of two groups — a work group which he/she manages and a management group composed of the manager's peers and colleagues. For example, manager A is both a member of workgroup 1 and management group 1. Co-ordination and communciation are facilitated by managers who perform the linking function by sharing problems and information. Likert, therefore, firmly believed that people worked best in highly cohesive work groups linked together by managers.

Although Likert focuses on human aspects, his approach has been criticised for focusing exclusively on individuals and groups and not dealing with structural factors (Katz and Kahn 1978). The cause and effect relationship between system four and positive outcomes has also been questioned. Miner (1982) has argued that the positive elements, such as high productivity and positive attitudes, could have already been present in the organisation and facilitated the introduction of the system 4 structure, rather than being outcomes of the approach.

Taken as a whole, the universal approaches to structure, while laying the foundations for further development and analysis, were heavily flawed. Both Fayol and Weber concentrated too heavily on formal aspects of the organisation which led to a rigid mechanistic type of structure. At the other extreme, Likert focused too heavily on individuals and groups to the detriment of concrete structural principles. All three approaches advocated universal principles and ignored the roles of the size, technology and external environment (contingencies) of the organisation.

5.5 CONTINGENCY APPROACHES TO ORGANISATIONAL STRUCTURE

These approaches became popular in the 1950s and 1960s and were developed to overcome many of the inadequacies associated with the universal approaches. Essentially, contingency approaches argue that there is no single best way of structuring the organisation. The most appropriate structure depends on a number of contingencies or circumstances. The three most popular contingencies are size, technology and the environment (see Figure 5.11). Each of these imperatives has been widely researched and no single theorist or researcher can be attributed with the formulation of contingency theory.

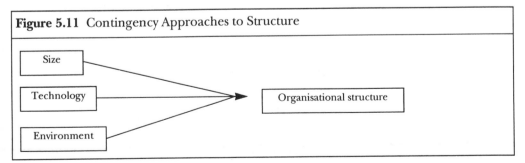

Figure 5.11 Contingency Approaches to Structure

Size

Technology → Organisational structure

Environment

5.5.1 Size

The size imperative argues that the most appropriate structure for the organisation is determined by its size. Kimberly (1976) argued that when considering this issue, the measurement of size is important and can include employees, profit, turnover and sales. Larger organisations are generally more complex and bureaucratic (Blau and Schoenherr 1971). According to Robey (1991), when compared with smaller organisations, large organisations have a number of important differences as illustrated in Figure 5.12.

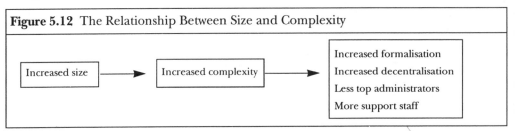

Figure 5.12 The Relationship Between Size and Complexity

Source: Adapted from Robey, D., *Designing Organisations*, Irwin, Illinois 1991.

Firstly, large organisations are more complex. There is greater specialisation of labour and speacialist groups, which makes the organisation more difficult to co-ordinate and control. As a result, more hierarchical levels are created to ensure that spans do not become too large. Secondly, large organisations have more formalisation. To handle increased complexity, organisations typically become more bureaucratic and create more rules and procedures to ensure efficiency.

Thirdly, large organisations tend to be more decentralised. Due to the size, decisions get pushed down to lower levels where appropriate information is readily available. Finally, large organisations have more top administrators arising from increased formalisation and more support staff due to the increased need for co-ordination and communication.

Increased size, therefore, leads to more complexity which, in turn, leads to more bureaucratic structures to facilitate control (Robey 1991). Size is an important contingency that determines the most appropriate type of structure. As the organisation increases in size, the original structure is simply unable to handle the complexity. Similarly, a small organisation does not need so many bureaucratic structures and controls to operate effectively. While the role of size of the organisation's structure is widely accepted, Hall et al (1967) have argued that a more accurate picture comes from an examination of both size and technology. So, while size on its own is important, other issues also need consideration.

5.5.2 Technology

The most influential work within the technology imperative was completed by Woodward (1958 and 1965). She sought to examine whether spans of control and hierarchical levels have universal application. She studied the performances and structures of 100 UK manufacturing organisations and concluded that different technologies create different kinds of demands, which are met by different types of structure. In other words, the most appropriate structure was dependent upon the technology used.

Woodward identified three different types of technology:
1. Unit production occurs where one or a small number of finished goods are produced according to customer specification. For example, tailor-made clothes or specially printed cards or invitations.
2. Mass production occurs where large batches of standardised goods are produced on an assembly line by assembling parts in a particular way; for example, car manufacturers.
3. Continuous process production occurs where raw materials are transformed into finished goods using a production system whereby the composition of the raw material changes. For example, the manufacture of pharmaceuticals.

Figure 5.13 Woodward's Relationship Between Technology and Structure

Unit production	Flat structures
	Few managerial employees
	Few policies
	Medium-sized spans of control
Mass production	Wide spans of control
	Distinctions between line and staff units
	High formalisation
Continuous process production	Tall structures
	Narrow spans of control
	High number of managers

Based on this classification, Woodward found each technology was associated with a particular form of structure as shown in Figure 5.13. For example, organisations using unit production technology had flatter structures, fewer managers and smaller spans than organisations using a continuous process technology.

Woodward concluded that successful organisations displayed an appropriate fit between the technology used and the structure. Burns and Stalker (1961) also investigated the relationship between technology and structure. They examined twenty manufacturing organisations in the UK, and came to the conclusion that the rate of technological change determined the most suitable structure for the organisation. If the rate of technological change is slow, then the most suitable form of structure is a

---

Figure 5.14 Characteristics of Mechanistic and Organic Structures

Mechanistic

Hierarchical structure

Vertical information systems

Employees instructed on work directions by supervisors

Knowledge and information resides at the top

Organic

Network Structure

Lateral communications

Work directions issued through advice and communications

Information and knowledge dispersed throughout the organisation

---

mechanistic one. On the other hand, if the rate of technological change is fast then an organic structure is more appropriate. The characteristics of both mechanistic and organic structures are shown in Figure 5.14.

The Aston Studies conducted by Hickson, Pugh and Pheysey (1969) uncovered an association between size, technology and organisational structure. They found that technology had a greater effect on the structure of small organisations. They found that in larger organisations structure depended more on size than on technology. It would appear that size and technology are both important considerations for the organisation's structure and should be considered together.

5.5.3 The environment

All organisations operate within an external environment. It is, therefore, an important area to consider when designing the organisation's structure. The environmental imperative argues that organisations face different types of environments which determine the most appropriate type of structure. Duncan (1972) identified two differences in the environment — the rate of change and *environmental complexity*.

The rate of environmental change facing the organisation can either be fast or slow. In a *dynamic environment* things change rapidly and it is difficult for managers to forecast the future and plan effectively. Static environments, on the other hand, are characterised by less rapid change. In the current business environment, very few organisations operate within a static environment.

Environments also differ depending on their degree of complexity. In a simple environment only a few factors need to be considered before a decision is made, and they are all easily identifiable. In contrast, a complex environment means that many factors have to be considered, all of which may not be easy to identify. Duncan (1972) combined both of these factors into a single framework measuring *environmental uncertainty* as shown in Figure 5.15.

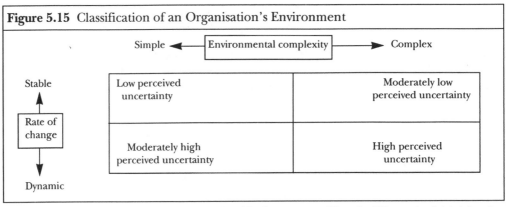

Figure 5.15 Classification of an Organisation's Environment

Source: Duncan, R., 'Characteristics of Organisational Environments and Perceived Uncertainty' *Administrative Science Quarterly*, Vol.17, No.3, 1972.

This framework, in using environmental complexity and the rate of change, allows the organisation to assess the degree of environmental uncertainty that it is facing. Environmental uncertainty exists when managers have very little information about events in the environment and their potential impact on the organisation. In this sense, it corresponds to the uncertainty condition associated with decision making. As can be seen from the diagram, organisations in which the environment is characterised by little change and is simple in nature, face a low perceived environmental uncertainty. In contrast, those facing a lot of environmental change and a complex environment face high perceived uncertainty in their external environment. The airline, computer and telecommunications industries all face high uncertainty.

It has been established that organisational environments have different characteristics. Therefore, it is important that the organisation identifies clearly what type of external environment it is operating within. It can then consider the most appropriate structure for that set of environmental conditions. The environment imperative, therefore, argues that the most suitable structure depends on the nature of the external environment. Harvard professors Lawrence and Lorsch (1969) made an important contribution to the study of the relationship between the external environment and organisational structure.

Lawrence and Lorsch examined the relationship between the external environment and two elements of the organisation's internal structure — differentiation and integration. Differentiation arises from job specialisation and the division of labour. Differentiation is high when there are many different departments, sub units and specialists all completing different tasks. Lawrence and Lorsch found that organisations with a complex uncertain environment (i.e. the plastics industry) developed a high degree of differentiation in their structures. Organisations operating within a stable environment (i.e. the container industry) used much lower levels of differentiation. Organisations operating in an environment mid way between the two had intermediate levels of differentiation.

Lawrence and Lorsch discovered the structural difference that distinguished successful organisations from those less successful. They referred to this as integration and found that in complex environments demanding high differentiation, high integration was also found in successful organisations. Integration is the degree to which differentiated units work together and co-ordinate their divided efforts. While all organisations need integration to achieve organisational goals, it becomes more difficult if a high level of differentiation is also needed in line with environmental demands. Lawrence and Lorsch found that organisations in complex environments were more likely to fail if they differentiated appropriately but neglected to integrate.

These researchers concluded that the nature of the external environment influences the most appropriate form of structure. In stable and static environments organisations need less specialisation and division of labour and, consequently, integration to achieve organisational goals is easier. On the other hand, those involved in complex and uncertain environments need more differentiation and, consequently, overall integration is more difficult.

In addition to the three main structural imperatives, another dimension needs to be examined — that of strategy and the role of strategic choice. Theorists, such as Chandler (1962), have highlighted the link between the strategy employed by the organisation and its structure. Chandler argued that structure followed strategy, observing that growth strategies are normally accompanied by decentralisation through a divisionalised structure. Managers and decision makers also effect the structure of the organisation because they assess the environment, technology and size factors before deciding on a particular strategy and, in this sense, form an intermediary stage between the imperatives and structure. Figure 5.16 shows how strategic choice follows on from an assessment of the structural imperatives and leads to a decision about which form of structure to adopt. Bobbitt and Ford (1980) have argued that managerial choice in relation to structure is determined by the organisation's purposes and goals, the imperatives and the manager's personality, value system and experience. Strategic choice theorists conclude that for organisations to be successful there must be a fit between the structure, imperatives and strategy.

Figure 5.16 The Role of Strategic Choice: An Integrated View

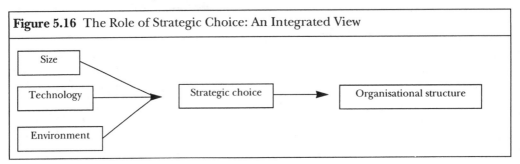

Contingency theory has been criticised for a number of reasons. It has been argued that it is impossible to identify all the contingencies facing the organisation. In addition, it is unrealistic to expect managers to observe a change in one of the contingencies and to make a rational structural change. Schoonoven (1981) has also criticised contingency theory for containing vague language which blurs the nature of the interactions being studied and makes it more difficult for researchers to test the theories. In defence of contingency theory, Donaldson (1987) has argued that it is logical and reasonable to expect that organisations will respond to poor performances caused by a change in one or more contingencies. Despite criticisms, contingency theory has remained popular.

5.6 The Mintzberg Framework

Building on contingency theory, Mintzberg (1979 and 1981) identified a range of structures and situations in which they are most commonly found. He argued that a vitally important consideration in structuring the organisation was to achieve a match or fit between the various parts. In this sense, there must be a fit between the structure, the structural imperatives (size, technology and environment), the organisation's strategy and the various components of the structure (co-ordination, division of labour, formalisation and decision making). If these various elements do not fit together, then the structure will be ineffective (Mintzberg 1981). Mintzberg identified five types of structure.

5.6.1 Simple structure
The simple structure is found in small, relatively new organisations that operate in a simple and dynamic environment. Direct supervision is the main co-ordinating mechanism, which means that a supervisor or manager co-ordinates the activities of employees. The structure is quite organic with little specialisation and little formalisation. The CEO holds most of the power and decision making authority. Due to its simple yet dynamic environment, it must react quickly to changing events. Examples are a small local shop or a garage.

5.6.2 Machine bureaucracy

A machine bureaucracy corresponds to a typical bureaucracy and can be found in large, mature organisations operating in a stable and simple environment. Standardisation of work processes is the main co-ordinating mechanism, which means that the methods employees use to transform inputs into outputs are standardised. There is a strong division of labour, high formalisation and centralised decision making. Due to its stable and simple environment the machine bureaucracy does not have to change or adapt quickly. The Civil Service or any other large, mass production organisation are examples of machine bureaucracy .

5.6.3 Professional bureaucracy

Professional bureaucracies are usually professional organisations located in complex and stable environments. The primary co-ordinating mechanism is the standardisation of employee skills. The division of labour is based on professional expertise and little formalisation exists. Decision making is decentralised and occurs where the expertise is based. Examples of professional bureaucracies are hospitals or universities.

5.6.4 Divisionalised structure

The divisionalised structure is found in old and large organisations operating in simple and stable environments with many distinct markets. It could, in fact, be a machine bureaucracy divided into the different markets that it serves. Decision making is split between headquarters (HQ) and the divisions, and standardisation of outputs is the main co-ordinating mechanism. Due to the fact that control is required by HQ, a machine bureaucracy tends to develop in each of the divisions. The most famous example of a divisionalised structure is found in General Motors, who pioneered car design in the 1920s.

5.6.5 Adhocracy

Adhocracy is found in young organisations operating in complex and dynamic environments, normally in technical areas. Co-ordination is achieved by mutual adjustment, which means that employees use informal communications to co-ordinate with each other. Decision making is spread throughout the organisation, and there is little formalisation. Specialists are placed in project teams. This form of structure is designed to encourage innovation, which is very difficult with the other structures. Examples of organisations that use adhocracies in certain areas are Johnson & Johnson and Proctor and Gamble.

Mintzberg's framework provides guidelines for the choice of an appropriate structure depending on the age of the organisation, its external environment and the nature of its employees.

5.7 RECENT TRENDS IN ORGANISATIONAL STRUCTURE

There have been two major evolutions in organisational structure to date. The first occurred in the early 1900s and involved a recognition of the independent roles and functions of management and ownership. The second evolution took place some twenty years later and introduced the command/control organisation, more commonly termed bureaucracy, with which we are so familiar today. Now organisations are coming to terms with the third evolutionary period, a shift from bureaucratic hierarchical forms to more flexible and adaptable forms. Clegg (1992) describes this as the movement from modernist to post modernist forms.

Bureaucracy has been the dominant form of organisational structure mainly because it is a rational and efficient form of structure in a simple and stable environment. However, when the external environment becomes complex and dynamic, the rigidity of the bureaucratic structure hampers its ability to be flexible and adaptive. Recent trends in organisational structure have centred on the need to achieve competitive advantage in an increasingly complex, dynamic and competitive environment.

The extent of the changes in the business environment have meant that bureaucratic and hierarchical structures are no longer effective. Such forms of structure thrive on stability and certainty, a state which characterised previous environments but not the environment within which most organisations now operate. The bureaucratic model with its extended hierarchy, narrowly segmented job design, rule bound procedures and lack of individual autonomy and responsibility, is no longer appropriate for effective organisation. The structures and systems associated with such organisational forms do not adapt readily to change and are not flexible enough to anticipate change.

Many of the developments have built on the idea advocated by contingency theory and further developed by Mintzberg, that the nature of the business environment shapes the most appropriate form of structure. Drucker (1992) has argued that, due to the nature of the current business environment, organisations are undertaking fundamental changes to their structures. Many organisations have looked to organisational structure as a means of providing the flexibility and adaptability necessary to achieve competitive advantage. As a result of the nature of the business environment and the ineffectiveness of traditional bureaucratic structure, organisations have experimented with four main structural trends as shown in Figure 5.17 (Tiernan 1993).

Figure 5.17 Recent Trends in Organisational Structure
1. Changes in job design
2. Flatter hierarchies
3. Team mechanisms
4. Increased responsibility and decision making authority

The first trend has been towards flatter, less hierarchical structures. Reducing the layers in the hierarchy is designed to lower costs, free up the flow of information, speed up communications and allow more innovative ideas to flourish. Organisations, therefore, are reducing hierarchy to more manageable levels. However, hierarchy has not been eliminated totally as this would be both impractical and in contravention of all time-tested laws of management and leadership. An example of an organisation that has reduced levels in the hierarchy is Team Aer Lingus. Team was the former Maintenance and Engineering (M&E) Department of Aer Lingus and operated with nineteen hierarchical levels in the late 1980s. After its establishment as a separate subsidiary, the number of levels was reduced to seven.

Organisations have also widened the traditional division of labour. Previously, individuals were boxed into segmented and isolated jobs with little knowledge or training in other areas. Due to the need for more flexibility, many organisations have now widened job categories and trained employees to be multi-skilled. An example of increased job scope can be seen at Dublin Bus with its introduction of driver-only buses. Previously, both a driver and a conductor were used to operate the service. Currently, the driver completes both tasks, which gives him/her a wider job design.

Changing attitudes among the workforce have led to the creation of new structures which allow individuals more responsibility and authority in their work and a larger role in decision making. In order to meet these demands, organisations have pushed responsibility downwards. For example, workers have been allowed to inspect work where previously they manufactured products only. Amdahl Ireland have introduced more participative decision making structures to ensure that employees are more involved and their skills are fully used.

The final trend has been to move away from segmented and isolated work to team-based operations. Organisations are experimenting with task forces for short-term problem solving exercises and with cross functional and cross hierarchical teams to achieve longer-term objectives. Organisations are also introducing team mechanisms for completing tasks. These *self-managed teams* and autonomous work groups complete the work of an organisation with the guidance of a supervisor. For example, Bausch and Lomb, sunglasses and contact lenses manufacturers, have begun to introduce self-managed teams to complete tasks. As organisations have experimented with these four structural trends, new types of organisational structure have emerged.

5.8 NEW FORMS OF ORGANISATIONAL STRUCTURE

A new method of managing an organisation generally evolves as a result of the actions taken by innovative organisations. In this respect, three different types of structure demand attention.

5.8.1 The network organisation

According to Baker (1992), a network organisation is a market mechanism that allocates people and resources to problems and projects in a decentralised manner. The network organisation seeks to manage complex relationships between people and departments within the organisation, and sometimes external groups such as suppliers and customers. Such relationships are established through lateral communication, decision making and goal setting. Rather than allocating responsibility and authority in line with the traditional hierarchy, the network organisation shares authority, responsibility and control among people and units that facilitate the co-operation necessary to achieve organisational goals (Powell 1990). A key element of the network organisation is its ability to redesign itself to accommodate new tasks and problems and to changing environmental circumstances. In this sense, the network organisation is designed to be flexible enough to change as tasks and goals change (McCann 1991). Organisations which have experimented with such forms of internal networks include General Motors, Saturn Corporation and Ericsson of Sweden.

The use of networks to establish relationships with external groups has also become popular. Such networks frequently include suppliers, customers, trade unions and even competitors. In some cases, these networks can be used to establish alliances with traditional competitors. An example of an external network is shown in Figure 5.18.

Figure 5.18 An Example of an External Network

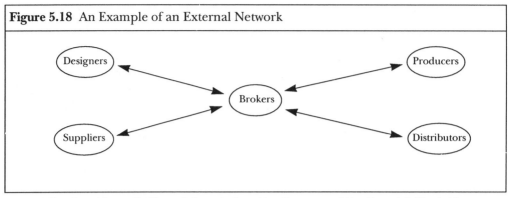

Source: Miles, C. and Snow, C., 'Network Organisations: New Concepts and New Forms' *California Management Review*, Vol.28, No.3, 62–73, 1986.

A dynamic network is arranged so that its major component parts can be assembled or reassembled to meet changing requirements. The traditional business functions such as manufacturing, marketing and distribution are no longer carried out by a single organisation but by a number of independent organisations within the network. Each part of the network is, therefore, able to pursue its distinctive competence. Because each business function is not necessarily part of the same organisation, a broker is used to assemble and co-ordinate the various contributions. The various networks are held together by contracts, which are market mechanisms, rather than hierarchy. The use of information technology, whereby networks can hook themselves together in a continually updated information system, further facilitates such developments.

5.8.2 The cluster organisation

The cluster organisation is a radical and innovative form of organisational structure in which groups of employees are arranged like grapes growing on a vine. A cluster is a group of employees from different disciplines who work together and are undifferentiated by rank or job title. No direct reporting relationships exists within the clusters and support areas have only a residual hierarchy.

Each cluster is accountable for its business results and has a customer focus. It develops its own expertise, shares information and pushes decisions towards the point of action. The central element of a cluster organisation is the business unit, which is a profit centre. A cluster organisation contains other clusters including project teams, alliance teams, change teams and staff units. In a cluster organisation, staff units run their own businesses selling to internal and external customers where possible.

Quinn Mills (1991) documents the case of British Petroleum Engineering (BPE) which he presents as a good example of a cluster organisation. BPE consists of 1000 professional engineers and support staff who provide technical support, engineering, procurement and contractual services to BP, its partners and outside organisations. Figure 5.19 illustrates the cluster structure found at BPE.

Sixteen clusters of engineers, ranging from thirty to sixty members, form the core of the organisation. These sixteen clusters are supported by three functional areas: Business Services, Engineering Resources and the Technology Development. Each cluster has a senior consultant whose responsibilities include co-ordinating and integrating between functional areas and cluster members. No direct reporting relationships exist within the cluster. Engineers, therefore, are expected to be self managing on the basis of their skills and experience. Each of the three functional areas assigns individuals to service the sixteen clusters. Engineering Resources contain resource managers who review assignments and career progress. Business Services provide people to handle contracts and to solicit business on behalf of clients, and the Technology Development assigns people to handle technical issues.

Although the cluster organisation is popular in professional organisations, it is unlikely to suit all organisations. High volume, low variance activities are poorly suited to clusters since the work cannot be made more challenging and interesting. In such situations, there is little scope for increasing responsibility and discretion. It is also difficult to see how traditional assembly line organisations could adopt such a structure, as it would involve eliminating all hierarchy and job titles.

Figure 5.19 BPE: An Example of a Cluster Organisation

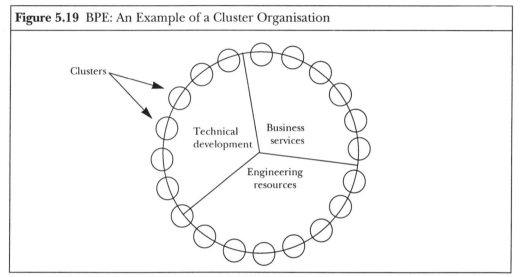

Source: Adapted from Quinn Mills, D., *The Rebirth of the Corporation*, Wiley, New York 1991.

5.8.3 The high performance organisation

The high performance organisation has a distinctive structure which is designed to provide employees with skills, incentives, information and decision making responsibilities that will lead to improved organisational performance and facilitate innovation. The trend towards high performance organisational structures is most noticeable in high technology organisations and those facing stiff international and domestic competition. The main aim of the high performance organisation is to generate high levels of commitment and involvement of employees and managers working together to achieve organisational goals (Lawler 1991).

Instead of the traditional structure of tasks, this form concentrates on teamwork by introducing self-managed teams to achieve the work of the organisation. Such teams make decisions about the tasks to be completed and deal directly with customers. In this way, the structure ensures that even lower level employees have a direct relationship with customers or suppliers and, therefore, receive feedback and are held accountable for a product/service. Employees usually work in self-managing teams where the organisational structure is flatter but some form of hierarchy still exists. The structure is decentralised and built around customers, products or services. Task forces, study groups and other techniques are used to foster participation in decisions that affect the entire organisation. Continuous feedback to participants about their performance is also fundamental to a high performance organisation.

In recent years, Bord na Mona has experimented with high performance structures. According to Magee (1991), Bord na Mona was faced with the need to increase productivity and quality, improve motivation and job satisfaction and improve overall performance. In order to meet these targets, the company introduced autonomous work groups (AWGs). Instead of working in isolation, employees became group members. Between four and six employees were selected as AWG leaders. Production and equipment were then assigned to the AWG along with the responsibility and authority to complete tasks. The AWGs were responsible for managing the seasonal workforce and were free to decide the number of hours worked, the allocation and the methods of work. Members of the AWGs were remunerated on a payment by results system. In addition to the introduction of teams, Bord na Mona also reduced the levels in the hierarchy. The AWGs were then overlaid on the delayered hierarchy as shown in Figure 5.20.

Figure 5.20 Bord na Mona: An Example of a High Performance Organisation

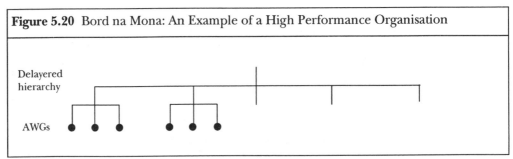

Source: Adapted from Magee, C., 'Atypical Work Forms and Organisational Flexibility'. Paper presented to the IPA Personnel Conference, 6 March 1991.

5.9 SUMMARY OF KEY PROPOSITIONS

• Organising is the process of dividing organisational tasks between groups, individuals and departments and co-ordinating their activities to achieve organisational goals. The pattern of how activities are divided and later co-ordinated is called organisational structure. Organisational structure is the system of task, reporting and authority relationships within which the work of the organisation is done.

• Organisational structure can be broken down into structural configuration and structural operation. Structural configuration is the size and shape of the structure. It includes the division of labour, spans of control, hierarchy and departmentalisation. Structural operation is the process of the structure and includes formalisation, decision making, responsibility and authority.

• Six main types of departmentalisation exist: functional, product, geographical, customer, matrix and mixed. The most suitable form of departmentalisation depends on the nature of the organisational activities.

• Traditional approaches to organisational structure were universal in that they offered principles which were designed to work in all situations. The most popular universal approaches were Fayol's classical principles of management, Weber's bureaucracy and Likert's human organisation. All three theorists argued that their particular form of structure worked well for all organisations.

• In contrast to the universal approaches to structure, contingency theory argues that there is no single best way to structure the organisation. The structure depends on a number of contingencies: size, technology and environment. Strategy and strategic choice have also recently been included in the theory. Despite its criticisms contingency theory has remained popular.

• Mintzberg identifies a range of structures: a simple structure, a machine bureaucracy, a professional bureaucracy, a divisionalised structure and an adhocracy. He concludes that there must be a fit between the structure, the structural imperatives, the organisation's strategy and components of the structure.

• Bureaucracy has been the dominant form of structure since it became popular in the 1930s and 1940s. However, it is primarily suited to stable and simple environments. The external environment is currently complex and unstable and, as a result, bureaucracies have become less effective.

• Four main trends in organisational structure have developed in response to the realisation that bureaucracy can no longer cope with a changing business environment. Hierarchical levels have been reduced, the division of labour has been widened, teams have been introduced and responsibility and decision making authority has been pushed down the organisation.

• Three different forms of organisational structure have been designed. Network organisational structures have been created which are designed to manage complex relationships. Networks can be formed between work groups and departments and are called internal networks. Networks can also be formed with outside organisations such as suppliers and customers. In this case, they are called external networks. Networks are flexible and can be redesigned as circumstances change.

• Cluster organisations have also developed. Organisational structures are arranged in clusters consisting of employees undifferentiated by job title or rank. No direct reporting relationships exist within the clusters. Clusters carry out the work of the organisation and deal directly with customers.

• Finally, organisations have experimented with high performance structures designed to provide employees with skills and responsibilities which will lead to improved performance. High performance structures typically reduce hierarchy, introduce team-based work and increase responsibility and decision making authority.

DISCUSSION QUESTIONS

1. Explain the terms organising and organisational structure.
2. Explain the terms division of labour, span of control and hierarchy.
3. Explain the elements of structural configuration.
4. Discuss the different types of departmentalisation an organisation can use. Which one do you think is most appropriate for a large organisation competing in many different markets?
5. Critically evaluate the universal approaches to the study of organisational structure.
6. Examine the contingency approach to structure. Which imperative do you think is most important in determining an organisation's structure?
7. What roles do strategy and strategic choice play in determining an organisation's structure?
8. Discuss Mintzberg's contention that effective structure arises from a fit between the structural imperatives, strategy and the components of a structure.
9. Outline the most recent trends in organisational structure. Find an example of a company that has introduced any of these changes.
10. Why have bureaucracies become less efficient in the current business environment?
11. What is the difference between a network and a cluster organisation?
12. What are the key characteristics of the high performance organisation? What is it designed to achieve?

REFERENCES

Baker, W., 'The Network Organisation: Theory and Practice' *Networks and Organisations: Structure, Form and Action*, Nohria and Eccles (eds), HBS Press, Massachussetts 1992.

Blau, P. and Schoenherr, R., *The Structure of Organisations*, Basic Books, New York 1971.

Bobbitt, H. and Ford, J., 'Decision Maker Choice as a Determinant of Organisational Structure' *Academy of Management Review*, Vol.5, No.1, 13–23, 1980.

Burns, T. and Stalker, G., *The Management of Innovation*, Tavistock, London 1961.

Clegg, R., 'Modernist and Post Modernist Organisations' *Human Resource Strategies*, Salaman, G. (ed.), Sage, London 1992.

Davis, S. and Lawrence, P., *Matrix*, Reading, Massachussetts 1977.

Donaldson, L., 'Strategy and Structural Adjustment to Regain Fit and Performance: In Defence of Contingency Theory' *Journal of Management Studies*, Vol.8, 1–24, 1987.

Drucker, Peter, 'The Coming of the New Organisation' *Harvard Business Review*, Vol.66, 33–35, 1992.

Duncan, R.,'Characteristics of Organisations' Environments and Perceived Uncertainty' *Administrative Science Quarterly*, Vol.17, 313–327, 1972.

Fayol, Henri, (1949) *General and Industrial Management*, Pitman, London 1949. Translation of *Administration Industrielle et Generale*, 1916.

Hall, R., Haas, E., and Johnson N., 'Organisational Size, Complexity and Formalisation' *American Sociological Review*, 903–912, 1967.

Hickson, D., Pugh, D. and Pheysey, D., 'Operations Technology and Organisational Structure: An Empirical Reappraisal' *Administrative Science Quarterly*, Vol.14, 378–394, 1969.

Grinnel, S. and Apple, H., 'When Two Bosses are better than One' *Machine Design*, 9 Jan 1975.

Katz, D. and Kahn, R., *The Social Psychology of Organisations*, John Wiley, New York 1978.

Kimberly, R.,'Organisational Size and the Structuralism Perspective: A Review, Critique and Proposal' *Administrative Science Quarterly*, Vol.21, No.2, 571–597, 1976.

Lawler, E., 'Executive Behaviour in High Involvement Organisation' *Making Organisations Competitive*, Kilmann, R. (ed.), Jossey Bass, California 1991.

Lawrence, R. and Lorsch, J., *Organisation and Environment: Managing Differentiation and Integration*, Irwin, Illinois 1969.

Likert, R., *The Human Organisation: Its Management and Values*, McGraw-Hill, New York 1967.

Magee, C., 'Atypical Work Forms and Organisational Flexibility'. Paper presented to the IPA Personnel Conference, 6 March 1991.

McCann, J., 'Design Principles for an Innovating Company' *Academy of Management Executive*, Vol.5, No.2, 76–93, 1991.

Miles, C. and Snow, C., 'Network Organisations: New Concepts and New Forms' *California Management Review*, Vol.28, No.3, 62–73, 1986.

Miner, J., *Theories of Organisational Structure and Process*, Dryden, Illinois 1982.

Mintzberg, H., *The Structuring of Organisations: A Synthesis of Research*, Prentice Hall, New Jersey 1979.

Mintzberg, H., 'Organisational Design: Fashion or Fit' *Harvard Business Review*, Vol.59, 103–116, 1981.

Moorehead, G. and Griffin, R., *Organisational Behaviour*, Houghton Mifflin, Massachussetts 1989.

Pfeffer, J., *Power in Organisations*, Pitman, Massachussetts 1981.

Powell, W., 'Neither Market not Hierarchy: Network Forms of Organisation' *Research in Organisational Behaviour*, Staw, B. and Cummings, L. (eds), JAI Press, California 1990.

Quinn Mills, D., *The Rebirth of the Corporation*, Wiley, New York 1991.

Robey, D., *Designing Organisations*, Irwin, Illinois 1991.

Schoonoven, C., 'Problems with Contingency Theory: Testing Assumptions Hidden Within the Language of Contingency Theory' *Administrative Science Quarterly*, Vol.26, 349–377, 1981.

Sherman, J. and Smith, H., 'The Influence of Organisational Structure on Intrinsic and Extrinsic Motivation' *Academy of Management Review*, Vol.27, No.4, 877–885, 1984.

Tiernan, S., 'Innovations in Organisational Structure' *IBAR*, Vol.14, No.2, 57–69,1993.

Woodward, J., *Management and Technology: Problems of Progress in Industry*, HMSO, London 1958.

Woodward, J., *Industrial Organisations: Theory and Practice*, Oxford University Press, London 1965.

Weber, Max, *The Theory of Social and Economic Organisation*, Henderson and Talcott translation. Free Press, New York 1947.

6

Motivation and Leadership

6.1 INTRODUCTION

This chapter discusses two concepts that are central to the management process: *motivation* and *leadership*. The two concepts are interdependent when it comes to the study of management in the sense that a good leader may well understand the principles of motivation (his/her behaviour reflects this through being all-inclusive, participatory etc), while, concomitantly, high levels of motivation may exist as a result of effective leadership (the style of leadership provided and the overall organisational direction may impact on motivation and morale). Motivation results from the drives, needs and aspirations that determine behaviour, while leadership may be viewed as a process whereby one person influences the thoughts and behaviour of others.

In this chapter we examine motivation first, as it is difficult to discuss leadership without an understanding of motivation. The importance of motivation and the ability to motivate in the workplace must be clearly understood by all managers because, as various contributions to the motivation literature demonstrate, motivation is not something that can simply be willed into existence.

6.2 THEORIES OF MOTIVATION

The study of motivation at work has been based on analysing employee behaviour. Thus, motivation theory is essentially concerned with explaining why people behave as they do, or why people choose different forms of behaviour to achieve different ends. Motivation is a psychological concept related to the direction and strengths of an individual's behaviour. However, there is no simple answer to the crucial question 'How do you motivate people?' Nevertheless, it is vital to achieve and maintain high levels of motivation, especially in competitive industry, primarily because, according to Pettinger (1994): 'There is a correlation between organisations that go to a lot of trouble to motivate their staff, and achieve profitable business performance... The ability to gain the commitment and motivation of staff in organisations has been recognised as important in certain sectors of the business sphere. It is now more universally accepted as a critical business and organisational activity, and one that has highly profitable returns and implications for the extent of the returns on investment that is made in the human resource.'

Bennet (1991) suggests that an employee's motivation to work consists of all the drives, forces and influences — conscious or unconscious — that cause him/her to want to achieve certain aims. Most of the early work on motivation was centred around getting more out of an employee, although many of the theorists were also concerned with finding an answer to the problem that was consistent with the essential dignity and independence of the individual. Motivation theory bases its analysis of employee performance on how work and its rewards satisfy individual employee needs. Numerous theories have been developed over the years to aid management in identifying employee motives and needs, the most influential of which are discussed here.

Figure 6.1. Maslow's Hierarchy of Needs

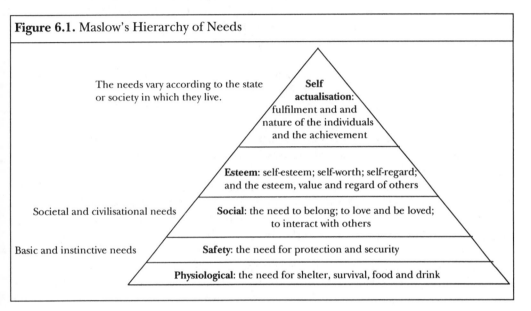

6.2.1 Maslow's hierarchy of needs

Most managers today will be familiar with the hierarchical classification of human needs first proposed by Maslow (1943). Maslow, a clinical psychologist, suggested that human motivation was dependent on the desire to satisfy various levels of needs. Maslow's hierarchy of needs is perhaps the most publicised theory of motivation. (See also, Chapter 2, page 26.) Based on the existence of a series of needs that range from basic instinctive needs for sustenance and security to higher order needs such as self-esteem and self actualisation, it seeks to explain different types and levels of motivation that are important to individuals at different times.

In all, Maslow suggests that there are five levels of needs ranked in the order in which the individual will seek to satisfy them.

1. **Physiological needs** include things such as food, shelter, clothing and heat. These basic needs must be satisfied for survival. In modern society, it is employment and the income it generates that allows the individual to satisfy such needs.
2. **Safety needs** refer to things such as security at home, tenure at work and protection against reduced living standards. Only when physiological needs have been satisfied will the individual concentrate on safety needs.
3. **Social or love needs** refer to people's desire for affection and the need to feel wanted.

Our need for association, for acceptance by others and for friendship, companionship and love would also be included here.

4. **Esteem needs** cover the desire for self esteem and self confidence and also the need for recognition, authority and influence over others.

5. **Self actualisation** refers to the need for self-fulfilment, self realisation, personal development and fulfilment of the creative faculties.

Hierarchy of needs theory states that a need that is unsatisfied activates seeking/searching behaviour. Thus, someone who is hungry will search for food or if unloved will seek to be loved. Once this seeking behaviour is fulfilled or satisfied, it no longer acts as a primary motivator. So, needs that are satisfied no longer motivate. This illustrates clearly the rationale for arranging the needs in a hierarchy. The sequential ascending order implies that it is the next unachieved level that acts as the prime motivator. However, need propensity means that higher order needs cannot become an active motivating force until the preceding lower order need is satisfied. Individuals will seek growth when it is feasible to do so and have an innate desire to ascend the hierarchy. Higher order needs will act as motivators when lower order needs have been satisfied. Self actualisation is the climax of personal growth. Maslow (1943) describes it as the desire for self-fulfilment, i.e. the desire to become everything that one is capable of becoming.

Maslow's theory has been the subject of much commentary and criticism over the years. Firstly, Maslow's work was based on general studies of human behaviour and motivation and, as such, was not directly associated with matters central to the workplace. The theory is extremely difficult to apply because of the illusive nature of the needs identified, particularly in the context of the workplace. Researchers have also found little support for the concept of exclusive pre potency. A more realistic scenario is that individuals have several active needs at the same time which implies that lower order needs are not always satisfied before higher order needs. Finally, it has also been suggested that the theory attempts to demonstrate an imputed rationality in human actions which may not necessarily exist. The conceptualisation of our needs in such a logical sequential fashion, while useful as a frame of reference to which we can all compare ourselves, has not resulted in convincing evidence among the research community.

6.2.2 ERG theory

Existence-Relatedness-Growth (ERG) theory developed by Alderfer (1969) reduces Maslow's hierarchy of needs to a three-fold taxonomy.

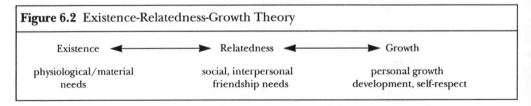

Figure 6.2 Existence-Relatedness-Growth Theory

Existence	Relatedness	Growth
physiological/material needs	social, interpersonal friendship needs	personal growth development, self-respect

Building upon Maslow's work, this theory avoids some of the issues which caused Maslow to be criticised. Here, there is no emphasis on a hierarchical structuring of needs. Instead, needs are arranged along a continuum, with equal status in terms of their abilities to induce action at a particular point in time. Another important difference is the proposition that an already satisfied need may be reactivated as a motivator when a higher order need cannot be satisfied. Furthermore, more than one needs category may be important and influential at any one time, so the notion of pre potency is rejected here.

6.2.3 McClelland's achievement theory

McClelland (1960) concentrated on developing and identifying motivational differences between individuals as a means of establishing which patterns of motivation lead to effective performance and success at work. McClelland argued that the major factor in willingness to perform is the intensity of the individual's actual need for achievement. He proposed that the organisation offers an opportunity to satisfy three sets of needs: **achievement** (nAch) which is a desire for challenging tasks and a deal of responsibility; **affiliation** (nAff) which refers to the need for developed social and personal relations; and **power** (nPow) which refers to the need for dominance. Individuals with a high need for achievement (nAch) tend to view organisational membership as a means of solving problems and providing a platform from which they can excel. Individuals with a high nAch take personal responsibility for providing solutions to problems and desire feedback on their performance. People with a high nAff wish to participate in tasks that allow them to interact frequently with others. Those who demonstrate a high nPow view the organisation as a means of providing them with status through the position they occupy. McClelland suggests that these needs are acquired throughout one's life and so may be triggered and developed through the appropriate environmental conditions.

The motivation of those with a high need for achievement is then a product of the task responsibilities, how attainable the task goals are and the nature and regularity of the feedback that they receive. Hitt et al (1989) maintain that people are often motivated by tasks that give them a feeling of competence. This, they find, is especially true of people who have a high nAch. Such individuals tend to work at tasks that lead to difficult but achievable goals. Achieving difficult goals causes them to feel competent, while goals that are too easy to achieve or that are unattainable do not. Finally McClelland maintains that individuals can actually learn to increase their nAch. This may be achieved through exposing them to human resource development programmes that place an emphasis on achievement and that are didactic with respect to the methods that can be put in place for achieving.

6.2.4 Theory X, theory Y

McGregor (1960), in his seminal writing *The Human Side of Enterprise*, attempted to focus on managerial assumptions about employees and the implications of such assumptions for subsequent managerial behaviour, particularly with respect to how they would seek to motivate their subordinates. McGregor outlined two alternative sets of assumptions concerning human nature that a manager might adopt. Labelled theory X and theory Y, McGregor suggested that autocratic managers were likely to subscribe to the assumptions of theory X, while the less bureaucratic were likely to work with the assumptions of theory Y.

This dichotomous framework is particularly useful for classifying differing managerial styles. McGregor himself maintained that, in the majority of circumstances, theory Y assumptions were the most accurate reflection of employee attitudes towards work, because work is natural to humans and those who perform it will normally devote their attention to its completion. Consequently, to the extent that these theory Y assumptions are valid they should be reflected in organisational structures, systems and practices. Thus, Bennet (1991) suggests that: 'This implies employee participation in decision making, the joint determination of subordinates' targets by the manager and the worker concerned, and relatively flexible organisational structures that allow for job enrichment, overlapping responsibilities and the motivation of junior staff.'

Figure 6.3 Theory X, Theory Y

THEORY X	THEORY Y
Employees are inherently lazy, dislike work will do as little as possible.	Employees like work and want to undertake challenging tasks.
Consequently, workers need to be corrected, controlled and directed to exert adequate effort.	If the work itself and the organisational environment is appropriate, employees will work willingly without need for coercion or control.
Most employees dislike responsibility and prefer direction.	People are motivated by needs for respect, esteem, recognition and self-fulfilment.
Employees want only security and material rewards.	People at work want responsibility. The majority of workers are imaginative and creative and can exercise ingenuity at work.

6.2.5 Two factor theory

Herzberg's (1962) research was directed at questioning people about those factors that lead to either extreme satisfaction or dissatisfaction with jobs, the environment and the workplace. His original study was based on intensive interviews with a sample of 200 engineers and accountants. Those factors which result in satisfaction Herzberg labelled motivators, while those that resulted in dissatisfaction he labelled hygiene factors.

Like McGregor, Herzberg was concerned with the impact of the job and the environment on an individual's motivation. His objective was to identify the factors at work which led to the greatest levels of satisfaction and dissatisfaction in an attempt to design work which provided job satisfaction and promoted high levels of performance. The motivators he identified were related to job content and included achievement, recognition, the work itself, responsibility, advancement and growth. The implication is that management can stimulate employee motivation by structuring work to incorporate these dimensions. The hygiene factors he identified were related to job context and included company policy, supervision, salary, peer and subordinate relationships, status and security. These, according to Herzberg, are factors that will not of themselves make people satisfied. Thus, if they are good, dissatisfaction is removed but satisfaction does not accrue. However, if these aspects of work are poor, then the result is extreme dissatisfaction. Herzberg's findings indicate that satisfaction and dissatisfaction are not at opposite ends of the same spectrum. Rather, they are on two separate spectra. Thus, the opposite of satisfaction is not dissatisfaction but rather no satisfaction and, similarly, the opposite of dissatisfaction is no dissatisfaction. Thus, pleasant or good working conditions do not actually motivate; as hygiene factors they simply prevent dissatisfaction.

The major criticisms levelled at Herzberg's work centre around the extent to which his original study was methodologically sound, i.e.the extent to which accountants and engineers are actually like all other workers.

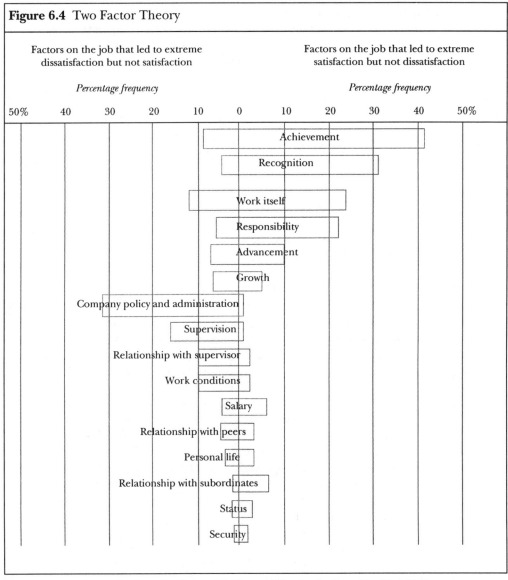

Figure 6.4 Two Factor Theory

Factors on the job that led to extreme dissatisfaction but not satisfaction

Factors on the job that led to extreme satisfaction but not dissatisfaction

Percentage frequency

Percentage frequency

50% 40 30 20 10 0 10 20 30 40 50%

Achievement

Recognition

Work itself

Responsibility

Advancement

Growth

Company policy and administration

Supervision

Relationship with supervisor

Work conditions

Salary

Relationship with peers

Personal life

Relationship with subordinates

Status

Security

Source: Herzberg, F., *Work and the Nature of Man*, Staples Press, New York 1966.

6.2.6 Expectancy theory of motivation

Associated with Vroom (1964), *expectancy theory* focuses on the relationship between the effort put into the completion of particular activities by an individual and the expectations concerning the actual reward that will accrue as a result of the effort.

Expectancy theory attempts to combine individual and organisational factors that impact on this causal effort/reward relationship. Broadly, this theory argues that individuals base decisions about their behaviour on the expectation that one or another alternate behaviour is more likely to lead to needed or desired outcomes. The relationship between behaviour and particular desired outcomes is affected by individual factors such as personality, perception, motives, skills and abilities, and by organisational factors such as culture, structure, managerial style (the context in which one is operating). Thus, expectancy theory avoids attempts to isolate a definitive set of employee motives, but rather seeks to explain individual differences in terms of goals, motives and behaviours. It postulates that employee motivation is dependent on how the employer perceives the relationship between effort, performance and outcomes.

Figure 6.5 Expectancy Theory

Motivation = Expectancy × Instrumentality × Valence

Expectancy is the probability assigned by an individual that work effort will be followed by a given level of achieved task performance (value = 0 to 1).

Instrumentality is the probability assigned by an individual that a given level of achieved task performance will lead to various work outcomes or rewards (value = 0 to 1).

Valence is the value attached by an individual to various work outcomes (rewards) (value = -1 to +1).

Thus, the motivational appeal of a given work path is drastically reduced whenever any one or more of the factors approaches the value of zero. The model suggests that the individual's level of effort (motivation) is not simply a function of rewards. Individuals must feel that they have the ability to perform the task (expectancy), that this performance will impact on the reward and that this reward is actually valued. Only if all conditions are satisfied will employees be motivated to exert greater effort. Therefore, it is critical that individuals see a connection between effort and reward and that the reward offered by the organisation will satisfy employees' needs. However, there is no simple formula since individuals possess different preferences for outcomes and have different understandings of the relationship between effort and reward. They may well be motivated in very different ways. Among the criticisms levelled at the theory are the difficulty associated with testing it empirically, and the fact that it assumes a type of rationality with respect to how the individual thinks and behaves which may not exist.

6.2.7 Job characteristics model

More recently, the characteristics of jobs have been examined to identify those which satisfy higher order needs such as self esteem and self actualisation, and which provide opportunities for satisfaction derived from the intrinsic content of the job. Hackman and Oldham (1976) identified a list of characteristics that correspond with each other and which are consistent. The *job characteristics* model combines task characteristics which the authors believed to be key factors in securing high levels of motivation. The model assumes that tasks are determined in terms of five core dimensions related to three critical psychological states and a number of personal and work outcomes.

Hackman and Oldham highlight some of the inadequacies of previous research in this area by suggesting that: 'As yet, a solid body of knowledge has not emerged from behaviour science research in this area... Neither is there abundant data available about the relative effectiveness of various strategies... There are a number of reasons for this unfortunate state of affairs. Some of them have to do with the inadequacy of existing theories about how jobs affect people... Others derive from methodological difficulties.'

Figure 6.6 The Job Characteristics Model

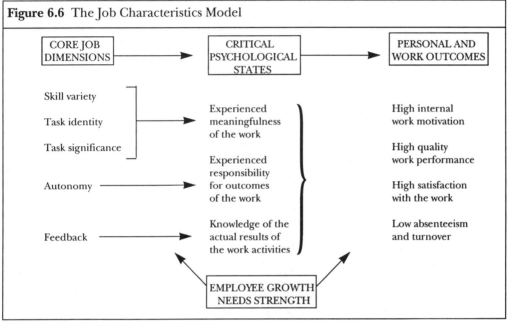

Source: Hackman, J. and Oldham, G., 'Motivation Through the Design of Work: Test of a Theory' in *Organisational Behaviour and Human Performance,* Vol.16, 1976.

The five core job dimensions identified are skill variety, task identity, task significance, autonomy and feedback. The model links these factors with motivation and subsequent performance via critical psychological states, and it explicitly acknowledges that individuals may differ in their levels of growth need. Skill variety, task identity and task significance lead to an increase in the meaningfulness of the work; work autonomy enhances experienced responsibility for work outcomes; work feedback creates an increased knowledge of results. When the three critical psychological states are present, positive personal and work outcomes, such as high intrinsic motivation, are seen to be present.

The measurement tool developed to test the job characteristics model is known as the *Job Diagnostic Survey.* It was first used by Hackman and Oldham to collect data from 658 employees about sixty-two different jobs. They argued that, above all, the survey provided valuable information on the overall motivating potential of existing jobs and highlighted those aspects of the jobs that needed to be changed in order to improve levels of motivation.

Overall, therefore, motivation theory has a role to play in assisting managers in formulating strategies and approaches for achieving high levels of performance. There is an onus on managers to begin to understand what motivates employees. If such motives can be identified and satisfied, then the first major step has been taken towards achieving effectiveness and efficiency. In order to ensure that this effort towards high performance is sustained, work must be structured appropriately and effective leadership must be provided.

Exhibit 6.1 How To Motivate Your Employees

Reversing the trend

The quest to motivate employees must be an integral part of the organisation's corporate culture. Superior companies use a variety of techniques to motivate employees and achieve their organisation goals.

Select the best. Since the source of motivation is within the individual, outstanding organisations hire only people who have the potential to be motivated in the first place. They select candidates based on more than credentials or prerequisite skills; they look for a solid system of values consistent with those of the company. All companies claim to hire superior candidates, but few actually exhibit the courage to demand — and get — the best.

Substantial time and effort must be dedicated to locating new talent. The interview process should be thorough and include assessments of personality, behaviour and management styles. Drug screening is also an imperative. Most essential of all is to identify work ethic values: discipline, desire, commitment to self-development, willingness to work hard, enthusiasm and a goal/results orientation.

The Pygmalion effect.

Outstanding managers have one thing in common: they invest psychologically in their employees. They truly believe in their people, and this confidence is irresistible. Like the teacher who puts extra effort into helping a student the teacher believes is gifted, excellent managers know their vision of an employee's performance is a self-fulfilling prophecy.

Track success. Genuine confidence and enthusiasm

create energy, and specific objectives and criteria must be established to direct that energy. At the outset of employment and at regular intervals, workers should be told what is expected of them and the criteria that will be used to evaluate their performance. Excellent companies do this positively; not in a critical or demeaning fashion. Regular performance evaluations and frequent feedback can help avoid major surprises and assist each manager to focus on ways to improve and develop.

Many managers thank that performance appraisals are an opportunity to punish or reprimand an employee, and the entire experience is viewed negatively by both parties. This should not be the case. At its best, the performance appraisal process can be a powerful motivating tool because it provides a structured way for a company to give workers what they really want — recognition and feedback, even in the contest of constructive criticism.

Recognise contributions. A pay raise alone does not have sufficient power to motivate on a long-term basis. The best way to motivate employees is to raise their level of personal and professional self-esteem. A pay increase won't do this, but public recognition will.

A manager who adopts a policy of recognising employees' outstanding contributions at every weekly staff meeting can praise them for their accomplishments in front of their peers. Those employees will respond by striving to achieve something important each week. It is a fact of human nature that

people will spare no effort to achieve the accolades of an individual or group that they are certain truly appreciates their work.

Provide incentives and rewards. This is not to say that incentives and rewards do not play an important part in motivation. But it is essential to remember that the primary motivating factor that rewards provide is the psychological effect on the individual, not the material value of the reward. Employees are motivated more by the boost in self-esteem that comes with public recognition than by monetary compensation. Nevertheless, when held out as a carrot, monetary incentives do motivate in the short term. However, once gained, they lose all motivating power.

Empower employees. One of the recent 'miracles' of business is the turnaround of the Ford Motor Co. How did it happen? Ford discovered and put into practice something fundamental to motivation: empowering employees.

Ford designers went directly to the people who were responsible for the company's product: its employees. They surveyed assembly-line workers, mechanics, dealers, sales representatives, satisfied customers — anyone who had 'stock' in the company (as opposed to those who owned stock but looked only at the bottom line). The combined input from all of these formerly fragmented pools of experience contributed to a winning team. Empowering employees does not mean trading organisational structure for chaos, but just the opposite. When people feel important, they work more

---

effectively and contentedly in any capacity, as long as they feel their contribution is meaningful. **Enhance career development**. Good companies recognise that their best people — in fact, most employees — want to improve themselves. Unfortunately, employee career development is a two-edged sword. Many 'job hoppers' will stay in a company just long enough to improve their skills, then they are off to greener pastures.

This is a social reality of our times. The only way a company can combat the loss of the most productive workers in search of career development is to provide growth opportunities. Employees cannot maintain or increase performance by staying at the same level, in the same job, preserving the status quo, indefinitely. Quality invariably suffers.

Companies must provide for career development in a variety of ways. Flexibility in scheduling can allow workers to go back to school for an advanced degree or more training. A commitment to filling positions from within the organisation provides opportunities laterally for cross-training or upwardly for promotion and advancement. Recognition and reward for workers' improvements and contributions do much to strengthen a company's reputation for caring about its employees' professional development.

Source: Extracts from Kenneth M. Dawson and Sheryl N. Dawson, 'How to Motivate Your Employees', *HR Magazine*, pp 78-80, April 1990.

6.3 Approaches to Work Structuring

The design of work is a task which requires some understanding of motivation theory, particularly when the objective is to bring about overall preformance improvements. The core of *job design* is dedicated to achieving the best 'person-environment fit' in an organisational context. While job design has waxed and waned in popularity in business and psychological literature over the years, recently there has been considerable interest in the whole area. This is reflected in the 'Excellence', 'Empowerment' and 'High Performance' literature. The motive to improve the design of work is often located in either the desire to improve the competitive position or the lot of the individual employee. Changes in work design may impact on performance measures such as productivity, absenteeism and labour turnover.

Broadly conceived, job design can be defined as the specification of the contents and methods of an employee's task-related activities, incorporating structural and interpersonal aspects of the job. The objective is to bridge the gap between the nature of work and the legitimate expectations of employees. The central argument put forward by many writers in the job design field is that the organisation of work on the basis of task fragmentation is counter productive and has consequences such as job dissatisfaction, absenteeism, decreased productivity, labour turnover and industrial conflict. It is suggested that this situation can be reversed by avoiding the narrow division of labour and attempting to meet the general expectations of employees at work as well as the economic needs of employers. According to Lupton (1976), the central issue is 'how to design for best fit', or how to design jobs to benefit both satisfaction and productivity.

It is possible to identify two distinct approaches to job design — an individualistic approach and a group/collective approach. By taking an individualistic approach, some reasearchers have examined the possibility of making individual jobs more motivating. This approach covers a wide range of models which emphasise individual dispositions and job characteristics in their analysis. The most well-known individualistic models are job enlargement and job enrichment. Other researchers took the group as their basic unit of analysis and, subsequently, advanced autonomous work groups or high performance work teams as the way forward.

6.3.1 Job enlargement

Job enlargement was dedicated to increasing the range of duties performed by the job holder through the horizontal extension of the job. Reacting against scientific management (see Chapter 2, page 18) and job specialisation, it represented an attempt to reduce boredom and alienation which had resulted from the division of labour. The employee is thus required to perform a wider job. However, the principle of performing a relatively routine series of tasks is preserved and job enlargement has been criticised on the basis that it does not go far enough. Performing a series of routine tasks is simply an extension of performing one simple task. Job enlargement has often been viewed as nothing more than an exercise in the simple addition of more meaningless tasks.

6.3.2 Job enrichment

Job enrichment is dedicated to the vertical extension of the job and involves the allocation of more interesting and challenging duties. Rather than adding more of the same, new and more difficult elements are introduced. Job enrichment has its origins in Herzberg's two factor theory of work motivation discussed earlier. Job enrichment, as defined by Herzberg, required that the job be developed or restructured to include opportunities for the psychological growth of the job holder. He established five principles central to enriching work:
1. Establish personal accountability with the job holder.
2. Provide feedback to the job holder.
3. Give the job holder control of resources.
4. Provide for the self-scheduling of work.
5. Provide for the growth and development of the job holder.

While, in principle, job enrichment allows for the psychological growth of the individual, it does not necessarily have universal applicability. Many jobs cannot be enriched in any way simply because the abandonment of the production conveyor, which remains an efficient method of production, is not feasible. Furthermore, many people do not respond well to having extra duties and responsibilities placed upon them.

6.3.3 High performance work teams

There have been numerous anecdotal accounts of high performance work teams in both academic and business literature. Recent literature almost raises the team working concept to that of an orthodoxy, calling for modest-sized, task oriented, semi-autonomous, mainly self-managing teams to be the basic building blocks of all work and organisational design.

Much like other approaches to work design, the underlying rationale for the introduction of work teams is to improve the organisation's competitive position through the more effective utilisation of human resources. The team is often the smallest identifiable element in the organisation whose members share a common set of objectives. Designed to achieve the best 'person-environment fit', high performance work teams are typically small groups of individuals (between five and twelve) who work with the same facilitator, sponsor or co-ordinator. Normally, team members undergo training and development in brainstorming, effective interpersonal skills, problem solving, conflict handling, consensus building and decision making, as well as specific training designed to increase the organisation's functional flexibility so that a team member has the ability to deploy acquired competencies across a broader range of areas. Perhaps the most famous example of this design occurred at the Volvo Motor Plant in Sweden in the 1970s. Employees at the plant were reorganised into small groups, and each group was given specific responsibility for one isolated part of the production process. Each group was self regulating, controlled its own work flow and was responsible for its own quality control inspection.

Today, high performance organisations are characterised as being built upon a socio-technical systems base with a team or group approach to production. Other prominent features of the high performance organisation include developed autonomy and control, flat, lean structures and advanced human resource practices, including the use of realistic job preview techniques, group-based employee selection and an espoused management philosophy of open communication and feedback.

Recent Irish data (Morley and Heraty 1995) casts some light on the impact of high performance work teams and supports earlier research which suggests that a team approach to work structuring can be an effective mechanism for improving job characteristics and general employee satisfaction. In the research, a series of naturally occurring groups were identified in the plant that was to be reorganised. A modified version of the Job Diagnostic Survey was used to collect data on employee perceptions of their work characteristics prior to and eight months into the reorganisation programme. Table 6.1 presents the results.

Table 6.1 Impact of High Performance Work Teams on Work Characteristics and Satisfaction

	Time 1		Time 2		
	Mean	SD	Mean	SD	
Work Variety	1.88	1.07	3.86	0.35	12.37*
Autonomy	1.72	0.74	3.25	0.34	16.04*
Suggestion/Idea Input	1.76	0.69	3.80	0.73	14.01*
Satisfaction with Work Allocation	2.24	0.57	3.40	0.83	7.90*
Satisfaction with Feedback on Performance	1.94	0.42	4.30	0.86	16.27
* $P<0.01$					

Following the introduction of the high performance work teams, work variety, work autonomy, the amount of suggestion/idea input given by employees, employee satisfaction with how the work is allocated and employee satisfaction with the amount of feedback on their performance all improved significantly. Importantly, the extant literature suggests that it is job characteristics such as these which draw out and satisfy the individual's higher needs. While the time frame for this particular study was only eight months and it is inadvisable to generalise from a single research site, the results of this work do lend support to the argument that there is a net advantage to be gained in moving towards a high performance work team approach to job structuring.

6.4 LEADERSHIP

Leadership is a widely talked about subject and, at the same time, it is somehow puzzling. The ability to provide effective leadership is one of the most important skills that a manager can possess.

Styles

'My management style is very collegial, very open-door. I have a view that facts are friendly. It doesn't matter if they're good facts or bad facts — all facts are friendly. I keep saying to my people "Tell me what the situation is."' Dr A. J. F. O'Reilly, Chairman and Chief Executive Officer, Heinz Company.

'A newspaper editor does not manage in the sense of ordering people about. It's more like being the conductor of an orchestra. In a well-run newspaper, nobody gives orders.' Douglas Gageby, former editor of *The Irish Times*. (Ivor Kenny 1987)

Manz and Sims (1991) argue that: 'When most of us think of leadership, we think of one person doing something to another person. This is "influence", and a leader is someone who has the capacity to influence another. Words like "charismatic" and "heroic" are sometimes used to describe a leader. The word "leader" itself conjures up visions of a striking figure on a rearing white horse who is crying "Follow me!" The leader is the one who has either the power or the authority to command others.'

Thus, there is little doubt that leadership is a skill that is respected and admired, but it appears rather elusive to many people. Pettinger (1994) maintains that: 'Leadership is that part of the management sphere concerned with getting results through people, and all that entails and implies — the organisation of the staff into productive teams, groups, departments; the creation of human structures; their motivation and direction; the resolution of conflicts at the workplace; creating vision and direction for the whole undertaking; and providing resources in support of this.'

Considering this, there is a strong argument to be made that leadership is a broader concept than management.

6.4.1 Leadership styles — trait theory

Among the earliest theories of leadership were those which focused on traits. Up to approximately 1950, most studies sought to identify leadership traits, principally because prominent leaders seemed to possess certain 'exceptional characteristics'. The *trait theories* argued that leadership is innate, the product of our parents given at birth. The chosen individuals are born with traits (particularly personality traits, though physical traits possibly have a role to play) which cause them to be self-selected as leaders. The findings emanating from this early work tend to disagree on what sets of traits distinguish leaders from followers. Among the characteristics identified are: intelligence, initiative, dependability, lateral thinking, self-assurance, maturity, vision and social well-being.

However, this view that leaders are born and not made is much less widely held today. There has been a fundamental shift away from this thinking for a number of reasons. Firstly, the enormous range of traits potentially affecting leadership ability is problematic and there is a difficulty associated with measuring their existence. Secondly, if birth alone was relied on to produce leaders, then, potentially, there might not be enough to go around. Thirdly, there is a growing body of evidence on the influence of nurturing and life experiences in this area. Fourthly, leadership needs are diverse and vary enormously and are commonly dispersed throughout society.

Despite their limitations, trait approaches have contributed to clarifying the nature of leadership, particularly in relation to social background traits. Many people argue that individuals with certain social backgrounds are more likely to become leaders. However, generally it is recognised that these must be combined with the personal trait of a high level of motivation to become a leader.

6.4.2 Ohio State University leadership models

Researchers at Ohio State University in the US identified two basic styles of leadership, namely *considerate style* and *initiating structure style*. According to the researchers, a considerate leadership style is one which places a strong emphasis on the status and well-being of the subordinates or followers and dedicate their time to creating an effective work climate. Such leaders innately assume that individuals will strive to do their best and thus the role of the leader should be to facilitate them in pursuing their job related goals. Considerate style leaders often downplay their formal position in the organisation hierarchy and will often seek to be a team player or facilitator rather than being viewed as a someone who is disassociated from their subordinates because of their position. Typical behaviour exhibited by such leaders include the following: open door approach to managing; frequent communication, often through the use of informal methods; providing feedback on performance; and seeking to promote a co-operative climate between the organisation and its employees.

In terms of the impact of this style, it has been shown to lead to higher levels of job satisfaction among subordinates, an increase in work motivation and decreased conflict levels in the organisation.

In contrast to the considerate leadership style, the initiating-structure leadership style focuses on process issues such as planning, organising, controlling and co-ordinating. This leader views his/her role as one of systems development and implementation. In the execution of his/her duties typical behaviours exhibited would include: scheduling work to specific employees; detailing job requirements; creating performance standards; and establishing rules and regulations to support the leadership system.

Combining these approaches to leadership results in four possible styles.

Figure 6.7 Four Leadership Styles

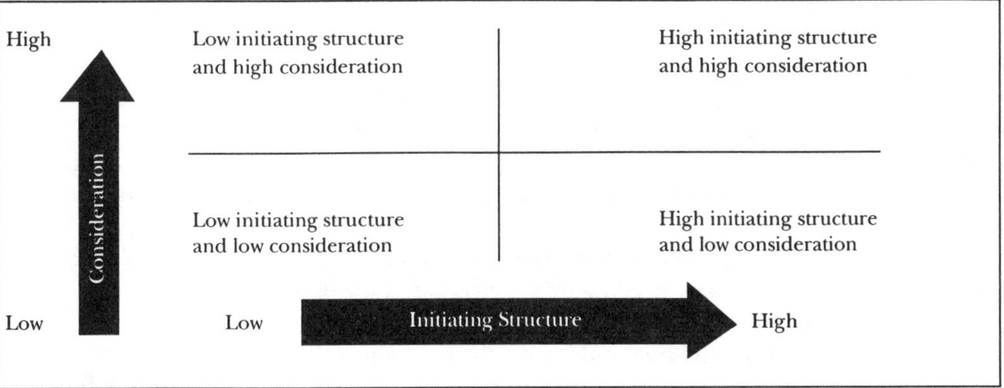

The Ohio State University research team found that leaders who rated high in consideration and low in initiating structure had low turnover rates and high job satisfaction among their employees. On the other hand, high employee grievance and turnover rates correlated with leaders who were rated high in initiating structure and low in consideration.

6.4.3 The managerial grid

One key extension of the Ohio State University work was the *managerial grid*. The managerial grid, advanced by Blake and Mouton (1962), has been particularly influential. Their writings begin with the assumption that a manager's job is to foster attitudes about behaviour which promote performance, creativity and intrapreneurship. Such managerial competence can be taught and learned. The managerial grid provides a framework for understanding and applying effective leadership.

Figure 6.8 The Blake and Mouton Grid

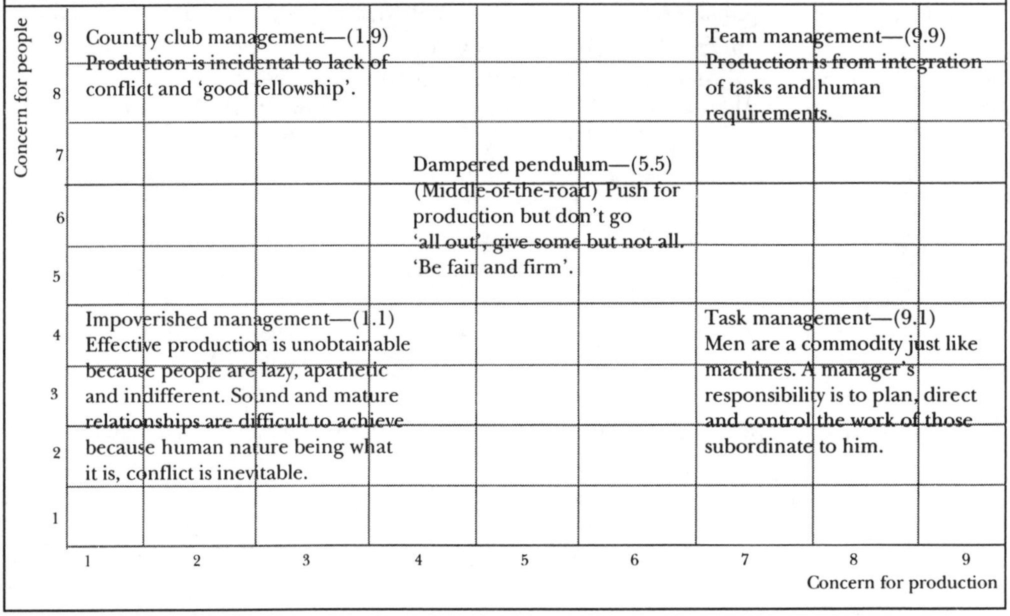

Concern for people (vertical axis, 1–9); *Concern for production* (horizontal axis, 1–9)

- Country club management—(1,9) Production is incidental to lack of conflict and 'good fellowship'.
- Team management—(9,9) Production is from integration of tasks and human requirements.
- Dampered pendulum—(5,5) (Middle-of-the-road) Push for production but don't go 'all out', give some but not all. 'Be fair and firm'.
- Impoverished management—(1,1) Effective production is unobtainable because people are lazy, apathetic and indifferent. Sound and mature relationships are difficult to achieve because human nature being what it is, conflict is inevitable.
- Task management—(9,1) Men are a commodity just like machines. A manager's responsibility is to plan, direct and control the work of those subordinate to him.

Source: Blake, R. and Mouton, J., 'The Managerial Grid' *Advanced Management Office Executive*, Vol.1, No.9, 1962.

The grid results from combining two fundamental ingredients of managerial behaviour — a concern for production and a concern for people. Any manager's approach to his/her job may show a high degree of concern for one or the other of these, or there is the possibility that they might lie in the middle with an equal concern for both. Different positions on the grid represent different typical patterns of behaviour. The grid indicates that all degrees of concern for production and concern for people are possible. Only five key styles are isolated for illustration.

The 9,1 management style focuses almost exclusively on production issues. Thus, this type expects schedules to be met and has a desire for the smooth running of production operations in a methodical way. Interruptions to this schedule are viewed as someone's mistakes. Disagreement is viewed as being dysfunctional and is seen as insubordination.

The 1,9 style or 'country club style' almost exclusively emphasises people concerns.

People are encouraged and supported in their endeavours as long as they are doing their best. Conflict and disagreement are to be avoided and even constructive criticism is not seen as helpful as it interrupts the harmonious relationship.

The 1,1 style, also known as impoverished management, signals little concern for either production or people. 1,1 managers avoid responsibility and task commitment. Leaders of this kind avoid contact and, where possible, display little commitment to problem solving.

The 5,5 manager displays the middle of the road style where he/she does enough to get acceptable levels of production, but in the techniques and skills used also demonstrates a concern for people. 5,5 managers demonstrate a firm but fair attitude and have confidence in their subordinates.

Finally, a 9,9 manager demonstrates a high concern for production and a high concern for people issues. This is a team manager whose goal is integration. He/she aims for the highest possible standard and insists on the best possible result for everyone. There is usually maximum involvement and participation and the achievement of difficult goals is viewed as a fulfilling challenge. It is accepted that conflict will occur and, when it does, it is handled in an open and frank manner and is not treated as a personal attack. This style, argue Blake and Mouton, is always the best one to adopt since it builds on long-term development and trust. In order to be truly effective, this style of leadership requires an appropriate cultural fit. The value set of the whole organisation must seek to support this style of leadership.

6.4.4 Contingency theory

In the 1970s, Fred Fiedler conducted a series of studies dedicated to the leadership of work groups. Beginning with the assumption that anyone appointed to a responsible leadership position of this kind possesses the requisite technical expertise, his research question was 'What is it about leadership behaviour which leads to effective group working?' — effective meaning how well the group performs the primary task for which it exists. Fiedler's research identified two main leadership styles — 'relationship motivated leaders' and 'task motivated leaders'. The former get their satisfaction from having good relationships with others. They usually encourage participation and involvement and are always concerned about what other team members think of them. Conversely, task motivated leaders are strongly focused on the task. The emphasis is on proceduralisation and task completion.

Fiedler subsequently developed an instrument to classify these two styles. The instrument asks leaders to review all people with whom they have ever worked and think of the one with whom they worked least well. They are then asked to rate this Least Preferred Co-worker (LPC) along a number of dimensions. Fiedler has found that relationship motivated leaders will score relationship issues high despite their problems with the LPC. Conversely, task motivated leaders were found to rate the LPC low on all dimensions. Fiedler emphasised that both these leadership styles can be useful and effective in appropriate situations. He argued that it is necessary to have a contingency perspective on leadership, because effective leadership will be contingent on the nature of the tasks to be completed and the context in which this is to be done.

6.4.5 Strong man to SuperLeadership

More recently, it has been argued that leadership style may be better interpreted as being arranged along a continuum, with leadership approaches ranging from a completely '*strong man*' approach dedicated to the issuing of strict instructions and tight supervision to one that is based on the principle of '*SuperLeadership*', the objective of which is to lead others to lead themselves. Figure 6.8 presents a perspective on different approaches to leadership.

Figure 6.9 Four Types of Leaders

	Strong Man	Transactor	Visionary Hero	SuperLeader
Focus	Commands	Rewards	Visions	Self-leadership
Type of power	Position/ authority	Rewards	Relational/ inspirational	Shared
Source of leader's wisdom and direction	Leader	Leader	Leader	Mostly followers (self-leaders) and then leaders
Followers' response	Fear based compliance	Calculative compliance	Emotional commitment based on leader's vision	Commitment based on ownership
Typical leader behaviours	Direction command	Interactive goal setting	Communication of leader's vision	Becoming an effective self-leader
	Assigned goals	Contingent personal reward	Emphasis on leader's values	Modelling self-leadership
	Intimidation	Contingent material reward	Exhortation	Creating positive thought patterns
	Reprimand	Contingent reprimand	Inspirational persuasion	Developing self-leadership through reward and constructive reprimand
				Promoting self-leading teams
				Facilitating a self-leadership culture

Source: Manz, C. and Sims, H., *SuperLeadership: Leading Others to Lead Themselves*, Prentice-Hall, New York 1989.

The authors argue that viewpoints on what constitutes successful leadership in organisations have changed over time. The strongman view of leadership is the earliest dominant form. Based on the principle of autocracy, the emphasis is on the strength of the leader. The expertise for knowing what should be done rests entirely with the leader and his/her power stems entirely from his/her position in the organisation. The second view of leadership is based on that of the transactor. The emphasis here is on the rational exchange process (exchange of rewards for work performed) in order to get employees to do their work. The focus here, according to the authors, is on goals and rewards and the leader's power stems from his/her ability to provide followers with rewards. The third type of leader they identify is that of the visionary hero. This leader is able to create highly motivating and absorbing visions. The focus in the relationship is on the leader's vision and his/her power is based on the followers' desire to relate to that vision. The final view of the leader is that of the SuperLeader. Rather than using the title to create a larger than life type of figure, the authors argue that, ironically, the emphasis in this relationship is largely on the followers. The objective of the leader is to help the followers to become self-leaders. Power is more evenly shared between the leader and the followers, the objective being to ensure that all followers experience commitment and ownership of their work.

6.5 SUMMARY OF KEY PROPOSITIONS

• Motivation theory is essentially concerned with explaining why people choose between alternate forms of behaviour in order to achieve different goals. The motivation to work consists of all the drives, forces and influences that make someone want to achieve.

• Maslow's hierarchy of needs is based on the existence of a series of needs that range from instinctive needs to the need for self actualisation.

• Achievement theory concentrates on the development and identification of motivational differences between individuals as a means of establishing which patterns of motivation lead to effective performance and success at work.

• Theory X, theory Y focuses on managerial assumptions about employees and how this impacts upon subsequent managerial behaviour.

• Two factor theory identifies motivators which result in satisfaction and hygiene factors which result in dissatisfaction.

• Expectancy theory focuses on the relationship between effort and the expectation concerning the actual reward that will accrue as a result.

• Leadership trait theory argues that leaders are born and not made.

• The managerial grid argues that leadership competence can be taught and the grid results from combining two ingredients of leadership behaviour — concern for production and concern for people.

• Fiedler's contingency theory identifies leadership styles, relationship or task motivated styles, and argues that it is necessary to have a contingency perspective on leadership.

• The SuperLeader teaches his/her followers to lead themselves.

DISCUSSION QUESTIONS

1. What lessons does motivation theory have for practising managers?
2. Outline what you see as the major sources of dissatisfaction at work. Suggest steps to help overcome them.
3. Debate to what extent Maslow's hierarchy of needs has practical relevance to effective people management.
4. A manager's perceptions of the workforce will profoundly influence his/her attitudes in dealing with people. Discuss.
5. Leaders are born, not made. Discuss.
6. What are the main problems with trait theory of leadership?
7. How might an organisation go about adopting the principle of SuperLeadership?

REFERENCES

Alderfer, C., 'An Empirical Test of a New Theory of Human Needs', *Organisational Performance and Human Behaviour*, Vol.4, 1969.

Bennet, R., *Management*, Pitman, London 1991.

Blake and Mouton, 'The Managerial Grid', *Advanced Management Office Executive*, Vol.1, No.9, 1962.

Fiedler, F., *A Theory of Leadership Effectiveness*, McGraw-Hill, New York 1967.

Hackman, J. and Oldham, G., 'Motivation Through the Design of Work: Test of a Theory' in *Organisational Behaviour and Human Performance*, Vol.16, 1976.

Herzberg, F., *Work and the Nature of Man*, Staples, New York 1966.

Hitt, M., Middlemist, R. and Mathis, R., *Management Concepts and Effective Practice*, West Publishing Company, New York 1989.

Lupton, T., 'Best Fit in the Design of Organisations' in Miller, E. (ed.), *Task and Organisation*, John Wiley, New York 1976.

Manz, C. and Sims, H., *SuperLeadership: Beyond the Myth of Heroic Leadership*, Organizational Dynamics, Summer 1991.

Manz, C. and Sims, H., *SuperLeadership: Leading Others to Lead Themselves*, Prentice Hall, New York 1989.

Maslow, A., 'A Theory of Human Motivation', *Psychological Review*, Vol.50, No.4, 1943.

McClelland, D., *The Achieving Society*, Van Nostrand, New York 1960.

McGregor, D., *The Human Side of Enterprise*, McGraw-Hill, New York 1960.

Morley, M. and Heraty, N., 'The High Performance Organisation: Developing Teamwork Where it Counts' *Management Decision*, Vol.33, No.2, 1995.

Pettinger, R., *Introduction to Management*, Macmillan, London 1994.

Vroom, V., *Work and Motivation*, Wiley, New York 1964.

7

Control

7.1 INTRODUCTION

This chapter looks at the final function of management — *control*. Control ensures the achievement of organisational objectives and goals by measuring actual performance and taking corrective action where needed. The control process and the various types of control that can be used are examined. The characteristics of effective controls are then considered. Two main methods of control exist which can be classified as financial and non financial. Financial controls include budgets, break even analysis and ratio analysis. Non financial controls include project controls, management audits and inventory, production and quality control.

7.2 THE NATURE AND IMPORTANCE OF CONTROL

Control typically involves measuring progress towards planned performance and, where necessary, applying corrective measures so that performance can be improved. Therefore, control is concerned with making sure that goals and objectives are attained. It is strongly related to planning in that for control to occur objectives and plans have to be available against which to measure performance. Similarly, planning cannot function effectively if there are no control mechanisms to correct deviations from plans. Weihrich and Koontz (1993) have likened the relationship between planning and control to that of the two blades of a pair of scissors — the scissors cannot work unless there are two blades.

Control, however, has been the most neglected and least understood function of management (Giglioni and Bedeian 1974). Its managerial role has frequently been equated with financial control. In this sense, control has been regarded as an activity associated with accountants and financial departments rather than as a management function. The word itself has also caused some confusion as it can mean the direction of others and also the evaluation of outcomes and taking corrective action. The latter provides a more accurate description of the modern control function.

In the modern organisation, control is the function of every manager. Top level managers are concerned with controlling sales and profits. Middle managers are concerned with controlling direct labour hours and production outputs. Front line supervisors are concerned with controlling quality and scrap. So, while the scope of control varies depending on the managerial level, all managers have responsibility for implementing plans and, consequently, are responsible for their control.

The control function has changed in recent years. Traditionally, the majority of organisations were involved in labour intensive industries. However, today more and more organisations are involved in the service sector where it is more difficult to measure performance. Therefore, the control function becomes more complex and, at the same time, more important.

Information technology has revolutionised control systems (Bruns and McFarlan 1987). Low cost data control systems and communications systems have made the control function a more flexible and speedy system. Computers allow organisations to speed up changes in strategies by revising financial plans, and testing changes ahead of time by quickly running and comparing various 'what if' scenarios.

Information is now available more quickly and is more accurate. As a result, information technology has revitalised the three traditional purposes that control systems serve: helping managers to use resources more effectively; aligning different parts of the organisation with organisational goals; and collecting data for strategic and operating decisions (Bruns and McFarlan 1987).

An example of the application of information technology to a control system can be found in the scanning machines in many supermarkets. The most widely known example is Quinnsworth. These electronic devices allow the organisation to:

1. identify instantly and calculate the type, quantity and price of each individual item purchased. The control of inventory is, therefore, much easier as the organisation no longer has to undertake a physical stock-take as the scanners post instant inventory records. This system also identifies slow moving products which may require a reduction in price or perhaps should not be re-ordered. The system also tracks consumer tastes and patterns which facilitates re-ordering of stock.

2. calculate employee productivity by assessing how many customers and items are dealt with per minute. For example, a slow check-out operator can lead to customer frustration. To avoid this happening the check-out operator will be sent for re-training.

3. calculate precisely how much money or revenue is generated on an hourly, daily and weekly basis from each till, store or regional area. This makes financial control more simple and accurate. It is also possible to pin-point how the organisation is deviating from budgets.

As a result of these changes, store managers have been able to lower inventory levels, boost turnover and match product mixes to consumers' changing tastes. These developments have all meant that the control function has assumed far greater importance.

7.3 THE CONTROL PROCESS

Control is a continuous process involving three steps (Daft and Macintosh 1984; Dunbar 1981; Todd 1977; Giglioni and Bedeian 1974), as shown in Figure 7.1. It is designed to ensure that employees, teams and business units meet established targets and to minimise deviations from such targets.

Figure 7.1 The Control Process

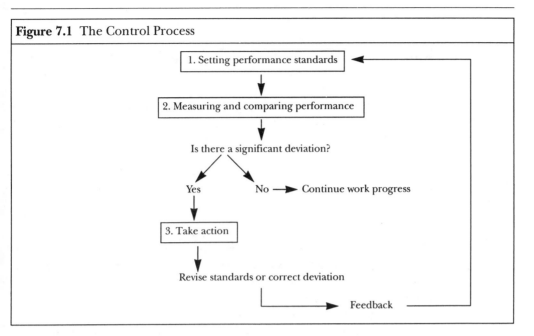

7.3.1 Setting performance standards

The first step in the control process is the establishment of performance standards. All organisations have goals and a standard can be viewed as the level of expected performance for a given goal (Flamholtz 1979). Standards are selected points in a planning programme which measure performance, so that managers can see how things are going without watching every step in the process (Weihrich and Koontz 1993). Therefore, standards are yardsticks for performance. Unless standards are established and enforced, performance across the various parts of the organisation is likely to vary. Standards of performance can be set for almost any organisational activity, as the following examples illustrate.

Market share: Increasing market share by 20 per cent.

Quality: Product deviations should not be higher than 2.5 per million.

Costs: Costs should be reduced by 15 per cent.

Innovation: 25 per cent of turnover should be generated by products less than three years old.

Employees: Turnover should not exceed 4 per cent per month.

Customers: All customer complaints should be answered within twenty-four hours.

Establishing standards of performance is a complex task, given the wide variety of standards which have to be established. In general, standards can be generated from three different sources: historical, comparative or engineering based. Historical standards are based on the organisation's past experience. In this sense, previous production, sales, profits and costs can be used as a basis from which to establish performance standards. Standards based on historical data, however, assume that the future will be the same as the past. Given the nature of the business environment, abrupt changes render historical standards useless.

Comparative standards are based on the experience of other organisations and competitors, which are used as benchmarks for generating standards. For instance, the financial performance of another organisation can be used to judge market value. Journals and trade associations provide information on sales, advertising expenditure and wages of competitor organisations, which further facilitates the establishment of comparative standards.

Engineering standards are based on technical analyses and generally apply to production methods, materials, safety and quality. Standards based on these analyses tend to be numerical and objective in nature.

7.3.2 Measuring and comparing performance

The second step in the control process is to measure actual performance and to compare it against the performance standards which were developed in step 1 of the process. In this sense, the 'what is' is compared with the 'what should be'. Data concerning performance can come from three main sources. Firstly, written reports, including computer printouts, provide data which allows performance to be measured. Secondly, oral reports from supervisors and managers provide information about levels of performance on a day to day basis. Thirdly, personal observation, which involves touring the various areas and observing activities, can provide important information about performance. However, personal observation, by its very nature, is subjective and does not generate sufficient quantitative data. Too much personal observation can be construed by employees as showing a lack of trust by management. Despite these disadvantages, many managers still believe that personal observation provides important insights which quantitative data is simply unable to do.

Actual performance can either meet, surpass or fall below the established performance standards. If performance meets the standards then no control problem exists and the progress of work can continue. Where standards have not been reached due to exceptional circumstances, such as a strike, usually no further action is taken in the control process. If performance fails to meet or exceeds expectations then further examination is required. If standards have been exceeded it is possible that standards were inappropriately set or that superior talent and effort was put in. The failure of performance to meet standards could come from inappropriate standards or, more worryingly, poor talent, lack of effort or failure to use resources efficiently.

In these instances, the critical issue facing managers is how much of a deviation is acceptable before corrective action should be taken. In reality, actual performance rarely matches established performance standards and, consequently, deviations are the norm. Managers, however, have to know when deviations are significantly different and require corrective action. Due to the fact that managers cannot react to every deviation, performance ranges are used which state both upper and lower control limits. In this sense, managers apply the principle of exception by concentrating on significant deviations or exceptions from expected results. Therefore, only exceptional cases need to be corrected. Managers can save time and money by applying effectively the principle of exception.

7.3.3 Taking action

The final step in the control process is to take action based on the comparisons made in the previous step. At this stage, control can be clearly seen as part of the management system and can be related to the other management functions of planning, organising, staffing and leading. Where a significant deviation has occurred, management should take vigorous corrective action. The organisation can either correct the deviation or revise the standards applied. When correcting deviations both positive and negative deviations should be examined as a basis for learning.

Corrective action can be taken by top managers, a specialist or by the operators themselves. Managers or supervisors, for example, could change procedures, introduce new technology, training or even disciplinary action. Further down the organisation, corrective action can be taken by specialists or operators. Traditionally, specialists corrected malfunctions. However, today operators who are multi-skilled can identify and rectify their own problems as they occur. This type of control is called operator control. Operators are closer to the problem and, therefore, can correct it closer to the source. This form of control also gives the operator more scope to use talents and skills (Wall et al 1990).

The organisation can also alter or revise standards if they are considered unacceptable or unrealistic. Standards based on historical data may no longer be appropriate due to changed environmental circumstances. Comparative standards may also prove inappropriate if based too closely on other organisations, as no two organisations are identical. Finally, engineering standards also require revision to reflect changes.

Having taken either corrective action or revised standards, the organisation will feed back lessons learned from the process into the first step, establishing standards, and the process will continue all over again.

7.4 TYPES OF CONTROL

As the control process has shown, control is necessary to identify problems, adjust plans and take action. Therefore, control is designed to regulate aspects of the organisation.

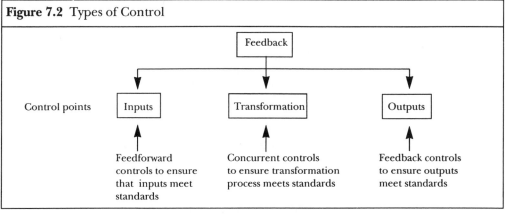

Figure 7.2 Types of Control

Source: Adapted from Bedeian, A., *Management,* page 565, Dryden Press, Fort Worth 1993.

Unlike humans, organisations are not self regulating and do not have automatic controls. As a result, their activities must be monitored to identify and adjust for deviations from established performance standards. Using the systems theory framework, the organisation's performance can be examined at three control points, before, during and after the activity has been completed. Control at each of the points corresponds to the input — transformation — output cycle associated with systems theory. Control, which occurs before the activity has been completed at the input stage, is called feedforward control (Koontz and Bradspies 1980) or preliminary control (Davis 1951; Donnelly, Gibson and Ivancevich 1981). Control exerted while the activity is being completed at the transformation stage is called concurrent control. Finally, control which occurs after the activity has been completed at the output stage is called feedback control. The various types of control points are shown in Figure 7.2.

7.4.1 Feedforward control

Feedforward control is future directed and aims to prevent problems before they occur. Due to the fact that managers need to react quickly to correct mistakes, control which prevents mistakes occurring is appealing to managers. Feedforward control carefully examines the various inputs to make sure that they meet the standards needed for successful transformation into outputs. Feedforward controls regulate the quantity and quality of financial, physical and human resources before they are transformed. For example, in order to prevent bad debts or loan defaults, banks ask for documentation about salary, other loans and credit history before granting loan approval. In this way, they are controlling the activity of giving a loan before it is sanctioned. Similarly, in the manufacture of food products, Marks & Spencer use extremely effective feedforward controls in relation to the quality of its supplies. In this way, Marks & Spencer make sure that all ingredients meet exacting quality standards. Feedforward control, therefore, strongly emphasises the anticipation of problems and preventative action at an early stage in the production process.

7.4.2 Concurrent control

Concurrent control occurs while inputs are being transformed into outputs. In this sense, they monitor the transformation to ensure that outputs meet standards by producing the right amount of the right products at a specified time. Concurrent controls ensure that materials and staff are available when needed, and that breakdowns are repaired speedily.

Because concurrent control occurs at the same time as the transformation process, it can cope with unanticipated contingencies. Concurrent controls allow adjustments to be made while the work is being done. For example, if a machine has a minor fault the manager has to decide whether to follow an alternative course or to stop and correct the situation. In this way, concurrent controls avoid waste and unacceptable outputs. Waterford Glass, Belleek China and Dublin Crystal are all examples of organisations that use particularly stringent concurrent controls to ensure the quality of the finished product.

7.4.3 Feedback control

Feedback control monitors outputs to ensure that they meet standards. This form of control takes place after the product/service has been completed. As a result, feedback control focuses on end results as opposed to inputs or transformation activities. Feedback control provides information about the return on investment, output produced, quality levels and costs, all of which are essential for planning for the future and allocating rewards for performance. Such control gives managers a basis from which to evaluate the appropriateness of organisational goals and standards, and gives insights into past performance so that important lessons can be learned.

Timing is a very important aspect of feedback control. Time lags are unavoidable because feedback control takes place after the deviation has occurred. For example, when actual spending is compared with a quarterly budget, there is a time lag between spending and any corrective action which can possibly be taken. If feedback on performance is not timely and managers fail to take immediate action, serious problems can arise. An example of a feedback control can be found in the Customer Satisfaction Surveys which Bewleys ask all customers to fill in when visiting their restaurants.

Most organisations use all three types of control to monitor their production processes. Feedforward control helps to anticipate future problems. Concurrent control allows managers to cope with unexpected contingencies. Feedback control captures defects and ensures that the organisation does not repeat mistakes.

7.5 CHARACTERISTICS OF EFFECTIVE CONTROLS

Effective controls are needed to ensure that developments conform to plans (Anthony et al 1984). According to Weihrich and Koontz (1993), effective controls must be tailored to plans, positions and individuals and the requirements of organisational efficiency and effectiveness. Irrespective of the type of control being used, effective controls have a number of important characteristics in common, as shown in Figure 7.3.

Figure 7.3 Characteristics of Effective Control
1. Appropriate
2. Cost effective
3. Acceptable
4. Emphasise exceptions at critical points
5. Flexible
6. Reliable and valid
7. Based on valid performance standards
8. Based on adequate information

7.5.1 Appropriate

Controls must be suitable and appropriate for the organisation's goals and plans. They should provide clear and concise information for managers about how well plans are progressing. Effective controls should not generate information which is irrelevant in fulfilling organisational plans.

Controls should also reflect the position in which they are used. Control used by a top level manager is very different to that used by a front line supervisor. Different areas within the organisation require different types of control. For example, controls used within a Finance Department are very different to those used in Marketing. Similarly, small and large organisations use different types of control. Controls should also be tailored to the individual manager who must clearly understand them. Controls should also reflect the organisational structure which shows responsibility for the execution of plans and any deviations from them.

While certain techniques for controlling finance and manpower planning have general application, none are completely applicable to any given situation.

Consequently, it is important to ensure that controls are tailored to the individual needs of the organisation.

7.5.2 Cost effective

The benefits achieved by control processes must offset the cost of using them. To be cost effective, the controls used must be tailored to the job and to the size of the organisation. Larger organisations can gain economies of scale and can often afford expensive and elaborate control systems. Control techniques are economical when they show up potential or actual deviations with the minimum cost. For example, the cost of inserting an electronic strip in library books which bleep when carried through an alarm system, more than offsets the cost of books lost through theft. However, employing a full-time library detective in addition to this system would probably not be cost effective, as the cost of stolen books would not cover both forms of control.

7.5.3 Acceptable

Controls must be accepted as fair and adequate by those to whom they apply. Controls that are arbitrary or unnecessary will have little impact. Similarly, controls that are harmful to an individual's social or psychological well being are also ineffective. For example, some organisations search their employees as they go home or finish shifts to make sure they have not stolen goods. This form of control is frequently considered to be unnecessary and illustrates a lack of trust in the employees. The end result is normally frustration, apathy and distrust of management and its motives. It is, therefore, important that controls are accepted by people as fair and necessary if they are to be effective.

7.5.4 Emphasise exceptions at control points

Controls should be designed to make sure that they show up significant deviations. Controls that do so allow managers to benefit from management by exception and detect those areas that require further action. However, it is not sufficient just to identify deviations. Some small deviations in certain areas may be more important than larger deviations in other areas. For example, a 10 per cent increase in labour costs is far more worrying than a 25 per cent increase in the cost of postage stamps. As a result, exceptions must be looked for at critical points, which then facilitate corrective action.

7.5.5 Flexible

Effective controls must be flexible enough to withstand changed circumstances or unforeseen developments. In the current business environment the need for flexible controls has become all the more important. For example, budgets which specify how much money is to be spent on certain resources are normally based on a predicted level of sales or profits. If, for some reason, sales fall below the expected target the budget becomes obsolete. Unless the budget is flexible, its efficiency as a control device is questionable. Over the years it has been argued that budgets are extremely inflexible and, therefore, not an effective means of control. This point will be examined in greater detail later in the chapter.

7.5.6 Reliable and valid

For controls to be effective they should be dependable (reliable) and must measure what they claim to measure (valid). If a control is unreliable and not valid there can be a lack of trust in the control process which leads to serious problems. For example, unreliable sales figures can lead to problems with inventory and future forecasts. Similarly, controls should be based on objective criteria rather than personal opinion. For example, a manager in charge of ordering materials who bases the order on how he/she thinks things are going is not as effective as one who bases the order on computerised numbers of units produced and sold.

7.5.7 Based on valid performance standards

Effective controls are always based on accurate standards of performance and incorporate all aspects of performance. However, managers should be careful not to have too many measures which can lead to over-control and potential resistance from employees. In order to avoid over-control, managers can make specific standards for a number of important areas and make satisfactory standards of performance for other areas. Managers can also prioritise certain targets or standards such as quality, costs and inventory. Finally, managers can establish tolerance ranges. For example, financial budgets often have optimistic, expected and minimum levels (Lawler and Rhode 1991).

7.5.8 Based on accurate information

Managers must effectively communicate to employees the rationale and importance of control and also provide feedback on their performances. Such feedback motivates employees and allows them to take corrective action. Operator control encourages self control and limits the need for supervision. Therefore, information about controls should be accessible and accurate. Lawler and Rhode (1991) argue that a manager designing a control system should evaluate information systems in terms of the following questions:
1. Does it provide people with data relevant to the decisions they need to take?
2. Does it provide the right amount of information to decision makers throughout the organisation?
3. Does it give sufficient information to each part of the organisation about how other related parts are functioning?

7.6 METHODS OF CONTROL

Organisations use a variety of methods of control. These can be classified as either financial or non financial. Figure 7.4 provides a summary of the most commonly used forms of both financial and non financial control which are discussed in this chapter.

Figure 7.4 The Main Methods of Control	
Financial Controls	**Non Financial Controls**
1. Budgetary control	1. Project controls
2. Break even analysis	2. Management audits
3. Ratio analysis	3. Inventory control
	4. Production control
	5. Quality control

7.7 FINANCIAL CONTROLS

The three main types of financial controls typically used by organisations are budgetary control, break even analysis and ratio analysis.

7.7.1 Budgetary control

Budgetary control is one of the most widely recognised and commonly used methods of managerial control. It ties together all three types of control, feedforward, concurrent and feedback, depending on the point at which it is applied. Budgeting involves the formulation of plans for a given period in numerical terms. Budgetary control is the process of ascertaining what has been achieved and comparing this with the projections contained in the **budget**. Most budgets use financial data, but some contain non financial terms such as sales volume or production output. However, they are predominantly financial control devices. Budgets are important because they force people to plan in a precise manner which produces a degree of order in the organisation. Budgets must reflect organisational goals and be well co-ordinated if they are to serve as an effective control instrument.

According to Weihrich and Koontz (1993) there are four main types of budget:

1. **Revenue and expense budget**: This develops projections of revenue and expenses. The most common example of a revenue and expense budget is a sales budget illustrated in Figure 7.5. Actual revenues, expenses and sales can then be compared to the expected budgetary levels.

Figure 7.5 Example of a Sales Budget

	Jan Expected	Actual	Feb Expected	Actual
Sales	1,500,000		2,000,000	
Expenses				
General	510,000		775,000	
Selling	292,000		323,000	
Production	377,000		425,000	
R&D	118,000		120,000	
Office	70,000		75,000	
Advertising	52,000		59,000	
Estimated Gross Profit	80,100		232,000	

Note: Total expenses and Gross Profit = Total Sales Expectancy

2. **Time, space, material and production budget**: This develops projections for the machine hours, space allocated, materials required and production output. Actual and expected levels can then be compared.
3. **Capital expenditure budget**: This develops projections for expenditure on items such as plant and machinery. Actual expenditure can then be compared to the projected level.
4. **Cash budget**: This develops projections about cash receipts and disbursements against which actual levels can be compared.

All budgetary control should focus on performance in what are termed *key result areas*. These are areas which are crucial to the organisation's business, such as sales of the main product, manufacturing costs, stock levels and cash position. There are also areas where problems or failures will have repercussions elsewhere, such as supplier failures, increases in material costs and strikes or stoppages. Identifying these key result areas allows performance to be reviewed in precise terms, while allowing for some leeway elsewhere.

Over time, budgetary control, in certain instances, has become inflexible and cumbersome (Stewart 1990). Over budgeting has occurred, whereby managers are constrained by budgets to such an extent that they cannot use freedom and initiative in managing their areas. Frequently, abiding by budgetary forecasts becomes the overriding objective of managers at the expense of wider organisational goals. Budgets also hide inefficiencies by establishing strong precedents, especially for capital expenditure. The fact that a capital expenditure was made in the past becomes an important justification for its inclusion in future budgets, regardless of whether or not it is needed. Finally, budgets can lead to inflexibility if they are formulated for long periods of time. As environmental conditions change so quickly, budgets become obsolete.

New approaches to budgets have been developed in order to overcome the inflexibility associated with traditional budgets. *Variable budgets* have been introduced by many organisations. These analyse expense items to work out how individual costs will vary with the volume of output. Variable budgets distinguish between fixed and variable costs. *Fixed costs* do not vary with the volume of output and include depreciation, maintenance of plant and equipment and insurance. Costs which rise and fall depending on the volume of output are called *variable costs* and include materials and labour. Variable budgets attempt to calculate the extent to which variable costs change with given levels of output. An example of a variable budget chart is provided in Figure 7.6.

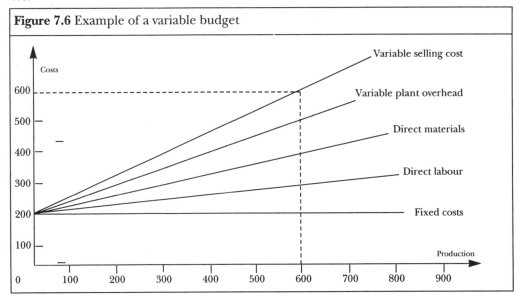

Figure 7.6 Example of a variable budget

This variable budget shows the level of costs that will be incurred for different levels of output. For example, a planned production of 300 units will cost around £400. However, if actual volume increases to 600 units, costs will increase to £600, according to the budget guideline. Variable budgets, therefore, give the organisation a good guideline of how costs will increase with increased volume. Variable budgets work well when sales or output can be reasonably well forecast in advance. Fixed budgets can work well with good plans and sales forecasts. However, the variable budget forces the organisation to examine factors that increase as production increases.

Another development in budgeting is called *zero based budgeting* and was first applied at Texas Instruments in the USA (Phyrr 1970). This approach means that managers start from zero in creating a budget each year. It is an attempt to eliminate the inefficiencies that creep in as elements are carried over from one year to the next without being questioned. Zero based budgeting is best applied to ancillary or support areas of the organisation such as R&D or marketing, rather than core areas like production, where certain expenses have to be carried forward every year. The main advantage of zero based budgeting is that it forces managers to plan each year afresh.

The final development, applicable to the areas of government and public administration, is programme planning and budgeting (PPB). This sets up budgets in terms of programmes and the costs of materials and services that are required for them. This is relatively easy to do where well established programmes exist (for example house building and defence), but is more difficult to put into action where programmes change (for example, with a change in government or policy) or where the objectives of the programme were not well understood or well received (for example, health provision which is usually a contentious issue).

Advances in information technology have improved the performance of budgets as control techniques. According to Bruns and McFarlan (1987), developments such as spreadsheets have speeded up the budgeting process and also improved the quality of budgets by allowing managers to view alternative scenarios and compare outcomes. In addition, managers can now continuously update budgets based on actual performance. Therefore, information technology has turned the budget into a meaningful set of instructions that can optimise an organisation's performance.

All budgets must be tailored to the specific task and used by all managers, not just controllers, if they are to be effective. According to Weihrich and Koontz (1993), effective budgetary control is characterised by four key elements as shown in Figure 7.7.

Figure 7.7 Characteristics of Effective Budgets

1. Top management support
2. Participation
3. Based on reliable standards
4. Accurate information available

Firstly, to be effective budgets must have the support of top management. When top management supports the budgeting process by ensuring that budgets meet plans, then the organisation as a whole becomes more alert to the process. Secondly, all managers should participate in the process in order to ensure effective implementation. Thirdly, budgets should be based on clear and valid standards. Finally, for budgets to work effectively managers need available information about forecasted and actual performance. Budgets displaying these characteristics will be effective control devices.

7.7.2 Break even analysis

The second financial control technique is called *break even analysis*. It involves the use of fixed and variable costs to analyse the point at which it becomes profitable to produce a good or service, i.e. the *break even point*. As we have seen previously, fixed costs remain constant no matter how much is produced and variable costs change. Fixed costs and variable costs, when added together, are referred to as *total costs*.

By analysing the level of both fixed and variable costs it is possible to identify the volume needed to break even, i.e. the point at which income generated from a given volume of output breaks even with total costs. Break even analysis has many applications in control and managerial decision making and is especially useful for decisions concerning dropping or adding product ranges and the choice of distribution channels. Figure 7.8 provides an example of break even analysis in graphic form.

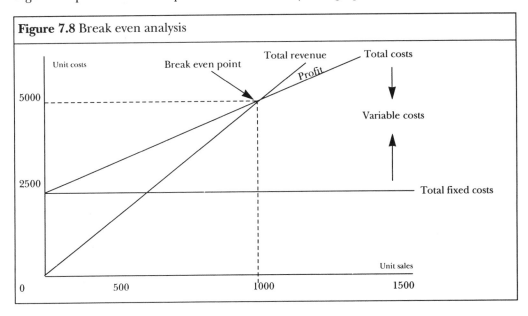

Figure 7.8 Break even analysis

In this case, the break even point at which revenues cover total expenses or costs is a volume of 1000 units which cost £5000 to produce. Producing fewer than 1000 units would mean incurring a loss, and anything higher than 1000 units means a profit can be made.

Showing the break even point in chart form highlights the relationship between costs and profit. The fixed costs have to be covered before anything is produced. It is assumed in Figure 7.8 that total costs increase in direct proportion to the units produced. Only when total costs are equal to the revenue earned can the organisation break even. In reality, the relationship between costs and output would probably not be linear. If an organisation upgrades a machine that produces 10,000 units to one, for example, that produces 25,000, it would expect to see a large bump in the cost curve. Similarly, the relationship between revenue and sales could be uneven because of bulk discounts or price cutting. On the whole, though, break even analysis provides a graphic illustration of how much needs to be produced before profits can be made. However, due to its simplistic approach break even analysis is more effective when used with other control tools than in isolation.

7.7.3 Ratio analysis

Several types of control have been developed for understanding and assessing an organisation's financial performance. Such guidelines for financial performance serve as control mechanisms in that they provide benchmarks for evaluation. These guidelines are commonly termed financial ratios and express relationships between individual or group items on an organisation's balance sheet and profit and loss account. Due to the fact that they involve ratios, this process has been called ratio analysis. Ratio analysis allows an organisation to track its performance over time and to compare it with that of competitors. Four basic types of financial ratios exist — liquidity, activity, profitability and leverage — each of which will be discussed and calculated using the balance sheet and profit and loss statement of the fictitious organisation ABC as shown in Figure 7.9.

Figure 7.9 ABC Accounts

Balance Sheet for ABC

Assets	
Current assets	
Cash	9,521
Accounts receivable	88,329
Inventory	401,273
Total current assets	499,123
Property and plant	161,000
Less depreciation	44,251
Net property and plant	116,749
Total assets	615,872
Liabilities and stockholder equity	
Notes payable	22,679
Accrued expenses	51,736
Accounts payable	9,321
Corporation tax payable	23,251
Total current liabilities	106,987
Stockholder equity	
Capital stock	358,885
Preferred stock	50,000
Retained earnings	100,000
Total stockholders equity	508,885
Total liabilities and stockholder equity	615,872

---

1. **Liquidity ratios**: An organisation's *liquidity* is its ability to pay its short-term liabilities. A commonly used indicator of an organisation's liquidity is its *current ratio*. This is a comparison of an organisation's current assets and liabilities. To obtain the current ratio

Profit and Loss Statement for ABC

Revenues	
Sales	899,000
Other income	10,000
	909,000
Costs and expenses	
Cost of goods sold	567,215
Total expenses	300,000
Total costs and expenses	867,215
Profit (net)	41,785

the current assets are divided by the current liabilities. In ABC's case the figures are as follows:

$$\text{Current ratio} \quad = \quad \frac{\text{Current assets}}{\text{Current liabilities}} \quad \frac{499,123}{106,987} \quad = \quad 4.6{:}1$$

A ratio of 4.6:1 means that for every £1 in current liabilities there is £4.6 in current assets to cover it. Most financial analysts believe that a ratio of 2:1 is desirable. A large current ratio, as found in the case of ABC, is not necessarily a good thing as it could mean that the organisation is not using its assets efficiently. Current ratios vary from industry to industry. Petrol and oil companies typically have a ratio of 1.6:1 whereas art galleries have 3.4:1.

Another method of assessing liquidity is the *quick asset ratio*. This is preferred by some financial analysts who fear that slow moving inventory can lead to a misleadingly high level of current assets under the current ratio method. Quick assets are those which are available to cover emergencies and, therefore, excludes inventory which has yet to be sold. An organisation's quick asset ratio is calculated by subtracting the value of inventory yet to be sold from the current assets and dividing that figure by the current liabilities. The larger the ratio the greater the liquidity. In the case of ABC the figures are as follows:

Quick asset ratio	=	Current assets	499,123	
		Less inventory	401,273	
	=	Quick assets	97,850	= 0.91:1
		Current liabilities	106,987	

In this case, for every £1 in current liabilities only £0.91 is available to cover liabilities. When the ratio is 1:1 the organisation is deemed liquid. So, in this case, ABC appears to be overstretched.

2. **Activity ratios**: *Activity ratios* aim to show how efficiently an organisation is using its resources. There are three main activity ratios — inventory turnover ratio, asset turnover ratio and accounts receivable turnover. *Inventory turnover ratio* measures the number of

times that an organisation's inventory has been sold during the year. It is, therefore, the ratio between an organisation's cost of goods sold and the current inventory. The ratio for ABC is as follows:

$$\text{Inventory turnover ratio} \quad = \quad \frac{\text{Cost of goods sold} \quad 567{,}215}{\text{Current inventory} \quad 401{,}273} \quad = \quad 1.4{:}1$$

ABC's inventory has, therefore, been sold 1.4 times during the last year. The *asset turnover ratio* assesses how well the organisation is using its assets. It is calculated as the ratio between an organisation's sales and the total assets. The figures for ABC are as follows:

$$\text{Asset turnover ratio} \quad = \quad \frac{\text{Sales} \quad 899{,}000}{\text{Total assets} \quad 615{,}872} \quad = \quad 1.45{:}1$$

Therefore, for each £1 invested in assets, sales have generated £1.45. Capital intensive industries tend to have small ratios. The accounts receivable turnover ratio measures an organisation's collection period on credit sales. It is calculated by dividing the sales by accounts receivable. The figures for ABC are as follows:

$$\text{Accounts receivable Turnover ratio} \quad = \quad \frac{\text{Sales} \quad 899{,}000}{\text{Accounts receivable} \quad 88{,}329} \quad = \quad 10.1{:}1$$

If we divide the 360 days by 10.1 it is possible to calculate the average collection period for accounts. For ABC the figure is 35.6 days. Greater than forty days usually indicates slow accounts receivable. However, much depends on the credit policy of the organisation.

3. **Profitability**: Profitability ratios determine how profitable an organisation's performance has been and involves the use of two ratios — net profit ratio and the rate of return on assets. The net profit ratio is a good indicator of short-term profit and is the ratio between net profit and sales. The net profit ratio for ABC is as follows:

$$\text{Net profit ratio} \quad = \quad \frac{\text{Net profit} \quad 41{,}785}{\text{Sales} \quad 899{,}000} \quad = \quad 0.04$$

This means that for every £1 in sales 0.04p is made in profit. In the region of 4 - 5 per cent is the average for successful organisations, although obviously this varies from industry to industry. The ratio of the return on assets is the ratio between an organisation's net profit and total assets and is designed to measure its efficiency in generating profit. It is calculated by dividing net profit by total assets. The figures for ABC are as follows:

$$\text{Return on assets ratio} \quad = \quad \frac{\text{Net profit} \quad 41{,}785}{\text{Total assets} \quad 615{,}872} \quad = \quad 0.06$$

This means that for every £1 invested in total assets 6p in profits is eventually made.

Organisation ABC has an average ratio as the industry norm is around 0.07 or 7 per cent.

4. **Leverage**: Leverage ratios attempt to identify the source of an organisation's capital. Leverage is the increased rate of return on stockholder equity when an investment earns a return larger than the interest paid for debt financing. The most popular measure is the *debt equity ratio* which is total liabilities divided by the total equity (i.e. liabilities plus stockholder equity). The ratio for ABC is as follows:

$$\text{Debt equity ratio} \quad = \quad \frac{\text{Total liabilities} \quad 106,987}{\text{Total equity} \quad 615,872} \quad = \quad 0.17$$

This means that for every £1 in equity 17p is borrowed capital. Total liabilities should not exceed total equities.

The best Irish example of the effective use of financial controls can be found in the Jefferson Smurfit Group. This Group is involved in the packaging business where success depends on building up relationships with customers. According to Brophy (1985), strong financial control systems have always been a central part of the Smurfit approach. In the early days, the organisation relied on profit and loss statements to control the business. However, as the organisation expanded, the control systems used became more sophisticated. Each operating unit is now treated as a profit centre and subjected to stringent financial controls, particularly budgets.

These systems are complemented by a Corporate Planning Department which develops long range and short range plans at all levels of the organisation. It performs three central functions:
1. updating and revising strategic and long range plans at all levels
2. preparing detailed actual business plans and budgets
3. reviewing actual results and changes to the plans where necessary.

Tight cash control has also been at the heart of the Smurfit approach. Each company within the Group has to buy cash (working capital) from the Group Treasury. This has encouraged careful and conscious working capital management. One final feature of the control system is the emphasis on cost control. Cost reduction targets are set on a plant by plant basis. Smurfit has been particularly successful at reducing costs in organisations which it has taken over. All in all, the Smurfit Group is a good illustration of the effective use of financial controls.

7.8 NON FINANCIAL CONTROLS

In addition to financial control, organisations employ a range of non financial controls. The most common forms of non financial control are project controls including *Gantt charts* and *Programme Evaluation and Review Technique* (PERT), management audits, inventory, production and quality control. Each of these key controls will be examined in this section.

7.8.1 Project controls
Project controls are designed to control the operation of certain projects undertaken by the organisation. The two most popular devices are Gantt charts and PERT analysis.

Gantt charts were developed by Henry Gantt who was an advocate of scientific management (see Chapter 2). A Gantt chart is a simple bar chart that portrays the time relationship between events and their outcome. In this way, the chart depicts the sequence of activities required to complete a task and allocates a time frame for each one. Figure 7.10 shows an example of a Gantt chart.

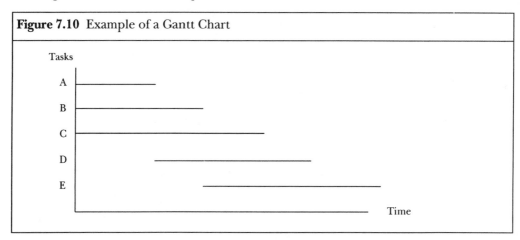

Figure 7.10 Example of a Gantt Chart

All activities which are represented by overlapping bars can be completed at the same time. In this case tasks A, B and C can all be completed concurrently. Activities represented by non overlapping bars must be undertaken in the sequence illustrated. For example, task D cannot begin until task A is finished. The Gantt chart, therefore, represents the steps of a project over time and can be used to track whether a project is ahead, behind or on schedule. An example of a Gantt chart for the development of a particular product is shown in Figure 7.11.

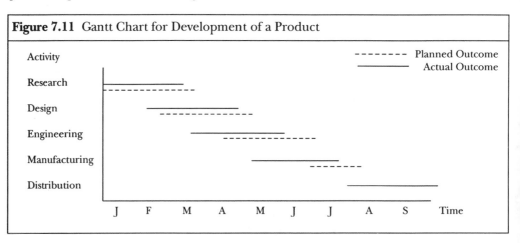

Figure 7.11 Gantt Chart for Development of a Product

As the chart illustrates, progress on the development of the new product is behind schedule at the end of the year because the product has not yet been distributed; each stage took longer than originally planned. Gantt charts help to co-ordinate activities and the scheduling of labour. They are most useful for activities that are unrelated and are less effective when dealing with many interrelated activities.

Programme Evaluation Review Technique (PERT) involves the development of a network which shows the most likely time needed to complete each task which is required to finish the product or project. Figure 7.12 provides an example of a PERT network.

Figure 7.12 Example of a PERT Network

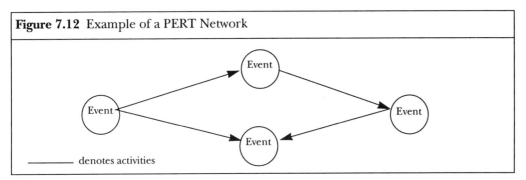

Events are circled and represent the start and end of the various activities. An event is not completed until all activities leading to it have been finished. Activities are depicted by arrows and mark the work that has to be done. An activity cannot begin until all preceding activities to which it is connected have been completed.

In developing a PERT chart the following steps should be undertaken:
1. Identify each event that must be completed and assign a time frame to it.
2. Based on the above draw a network including the various activities which need to be done and keep it in chronological order.
3. Estimate the time needed to complete each activity, usually in weeks.
4. Estimate the total time for each activity in a sequence or path of activities. The path having the longest time is the critical path. The critical path is, therefore, the earliest date that a project can be finished. Figure 7.13 illustrates a PERT network for the manufacture of a car.

Figure 7.13 A PERT Network for the Manufacture of a Car

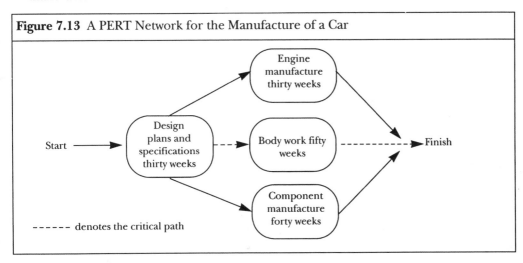

In this case the critical path is eighty weeks. Having identified the critical path, a project manager can focus on either reducing the time of the various activities or, at the very least, watch for any delays. PERT is widely used as an important control for undertaking projects. Figure 7.14 outlines the main advantages and disadvantages associated with its use.

Figure 7.14 Advantages and Disadvantages of PERT Analysis

Advantages

1. It emphasises areas where delays are most likely to occur.

2. It is a detailed means of controlling a given project.

3. It frequently stimulates alternative plans and schedules.

Disadvantages

1. Event times must be accurately calculated.

2. It can be costly.

3. It is difficult to apply stringently when outside suppliers are involved.

4. It is unsuitable for repetitive sequences of events since all events fall along a single critical path.

Source: Bedeian, A., *Management*, page 578, Dryden Press, Fort Worth 1993.

7.8.2 Management audits

According to Pomerantz (1979), management audits have developed as a means of evaluating and controlling the various elements of an organisation. Such audits can either be external or internal. With external audits managers conduct investigations of other competitor organisations. Internal audits investigate the operations of the organisation itself. The same control techniques can be used for both.

External audits involve analysing another organisation normally to aid strategic decision making. Other organisations can be investigated for possible mergers or acquisitions, to assess the strengths and weaknesses of competitors or even a possible supplier of materials. Most of the information used to assess these factors is publicly available and simply has to be located and analysed.

External audits are a useful source of control for an organisation. Such audits can be used in feedback control to discover irregularities or problems on an industry wide basis. Similarly, audits can be used for feedforward control particularly if an organisation is planning an acquisition. In this way an external audit will highlight any potential problems which could arise from an acquisition. Finally, audits can be used to learn lessons from the mistakes of other organisations. Learning where other organisations have gone wrong can lead to updated or enhanced concurrent controls.

The use of external audits as a control technique has increased rapidly in recent years. The nature of the current business environment, with its emphasis on cut throat competition, has further augmented this trend. Some organisations have even gone so far as to spy on competitors (Fuld 1986). Organisations are now developing competitor intelligence or, in other words, information about their competitors. Accountants, sales people and managers frequently collect information about opponents to aid decision making and to ensure that the organisation does not get any nasty surprises from competitors.

Internal audits concentrate on the activities of the organisation itself. Frequently, organisations undertake reviews of their planning, organising and leading functions.

Control is the essential ingredient in any internal audit. When conducting an internal·
audit a manager should concentrate on financial stability, production, sales, human
resources and social responsibility. Problems which are often uncovered by an internal
audit include duplication of resources, poor utilisation of resources or the
uneconomical use of plant and machinery. An internal audit conducted in Aer Lingus in
1994 discovered that catering suppliers had been overpaid in the region of £12 million.
As a result, the purchasing systems in Aer Lingus were reformed to ensure that the same
problem would not occur again (*Sunday Tribune* 1994).

Therefore, both internal and external management audits provide vital information
from which the organisation can evaluate its performance and take corrective action. In
addition, internal audits act as a deterrent to internal fraud.

7.8.3 Inventory control

Inventory control involves control of stock levels to ensure that the organisation has
stock when needed, yet at the same time does not have too much money tied up in stock
which is not immediately required. Up to one-third of an organisation's total costs can
be tied up in storing and handling inventory. Therefore, a control system is needed to
keep these costs to a minimum. A good inventory control system tries to answer three
questions:
1. How much of the required inventory items should be bought at a time?
2. At what point should inventory items be re-ordered?
3. What are the most economic order quantities of each item?

In the first instance, production experience and knowledge of the sources of supply
will dictate how much inventory should be bought. Some items may be seasonal or
scarce and so it may make sense to buy them in bulk. The timing of re-order depends on
two factors. Firstly, the lead time involved, that is the time between placement of the
order and its delivery. Secondly, the problem of knowing what safety stock to keep so
that production will not be disrupted because of supplier transport problems. The third
question is resolved by reference to the Economic Order Quantity (EOQ) model. The
formula for EOQ is as follows:

$$\text{EOQ} = \frac{2 \ \times \ \text{order costs} \ \times \ \text{annual consumption}}{\text{annual holding costs}}$$

This model is portrayed graphically in Figure 7.15.

Holding costs include storage space, handling and security. Ordering costs include
administration and shipping. The most economic order quantity is where the cost of
ordering the goods is not greater than the cost of holding, and the total cost curve is at
its lowest point. Models, like the EOQ model, are removed from the real world in that
they cannot take account of factors like strikes, transport problems or supplier discounts.
On the other hand, they give guidelines as to how inventory costs can be reduced.

Developments in information technology have facilitated the control of inventory.
New inventory tracking systems let organisations trace an order, update account
balances, monitor inventory and alert suppliers of upcoming requirements. Some
systems have linked their ordering function to suppliers to benefit from low inventory
without shortages. An example of this can be found in the automobile industry.

Automated order entry and inventory tracking can help organisations vary sales and pricing strategies between regions and customer types. For example, the scanning devices found in supermarkets provide an accurate picture of what has been sold and at what price.

Figure 7.15 Relationship Between Costs and Order Quantity

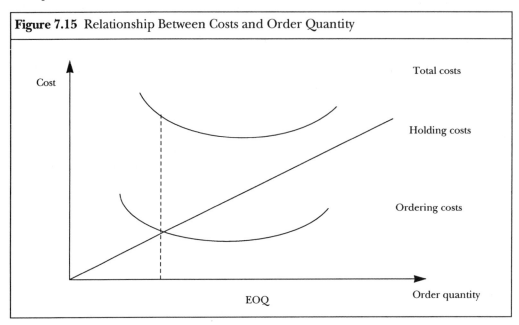

7.8.4 Production control

The aim of production control systems is to ensure that goods are produced on time at the right cost and conforming to quality standards. A good production control system should reflect the organisation's production methods and product characteristics. The type of control required in a *job shop* situation where there is an element of craft work will be different from that needed in an assembly line where *mass production* takes place. The type of product manufactured also influences the control system. An organisation that makes one-off products according to buyer specifications would have a job shop where an order control system is used. The emphasis would be on controlling each order as it passes from design through manufacture to shipment. In assembly operations, on the other hand, the flow control system would be used. This involves controlling the rate of production between one assembly point and the next so that no bottlenecks or stoppages occur. In between these two systems, where *batch production* is used, a block control system would be employed. In this case, control is concerned with the progress of the batches or blocks through the stages of production. In all three control systems activities focus on:

1. **Routing**: Determining where a required job or operation is to be done.
2. **Scheduling**: Determining when it will be done.
3. **Dispatching**: Issuing production orders at the right time.
4. **Expediting**: Ensuring that orders are being produced on schedule.

Each of these activities breaks down into a separate set of tasks. For example, routing activities involve:

(i) deciding the optimal route for product manufacture given the constraints of machinery, materials and labour

(ii) getting information about the product, the process and the time input in order to evaluate the input of labour and materials and the amount of scrap and re-work to be expected

(iii) preparing the forms for a production reporting system, including order routing sheets, process information details and timesheets.

One of the widest uses of information technology is in production control (Bruns and McFarlan 1987). Monitoring systems can track errors per hour, highlight down time, measure machine speeds and worker productivity. All of these advances allow managers to remedy production problems at an early stage. Previously, systems relied on a controller to spot variations. Early detection allows for early correction and improves the economics of manufacturing. According to Bruns and McFarlan, one cigarette manufacturer has installed automatic control systems that pull cigarettes off the line and put them through twenty tests which note even the smallest inconsistency in quality. Before this, cigarettes were only checked after problems had already occurred.

7.8.5 Quality control

Quality control and production control are intertwined in that quality control is a check on the efficiency of production. A good quality control system can offer significant cost savings due to the savings on rejected products as well as warranty and servicing costs. When Japan first entered world markets its products were cheap and of inferior quality. In the early 1950s, in a drive to increase the volume and the value of its exports, the Japanese decided to institute a set of laws which ensured that products met certain quality standards before exportation of their products. This was backed by a campaign to make employees more aware of the need for quality. That led to establishment of *quality circles*, now a standard feature of the Japanese organisation. The circle or committee is staffed by shopfloor employees and supervisors concerned with maintaining high quality and screening supplies. Another interesting facet of the Japanese system is that each employee is responsible for the quality of his/her output, reducing the need for quality control inspectors.

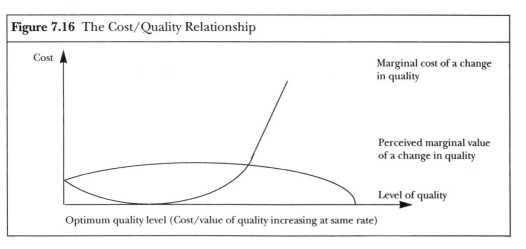

Figure 7.16 The Cost/Quality Relationship

Quality means fitness for the intended purpose and as such is a relative term. Quality standards are designed to be met at a reasonable cost by the producer, while at the same time presenting an acceptable face to the consumer. The relationship between quality levels and cost is shown in Figure 7.16.

As quality is improved the cost of producing that quality goes up and the return for higher quality declines. Any product has a most economic quality level. So, while the modern motor car may have lower quality components, it is cheaper and, therefore, has a mass market. Quality control offers the benefits of reduced costs and fewer customer complaints. It also enhances the corporate image as high quality producers are usually looked upon as leaders in the market. It must be emphasised that quality control is an ever vigilant effort, not a sporadic effort to meet standards. Both production and quality control are developed further in Chapter 9.

Irish companies have effectively used non financial controls to monitor their operations. Irish Distillers' Group combines both production controls and quality controls to ensure that production volume matches demand and that the quality of the end product meets accepted standards. Controls on both the product flow and stock turnover are also a feature of the organisation's control system. According to Brophy (1985), these systems have endured and become a competitive strength.

Two other organisations have used quality controls to their advantage. Waterford Co-op imposed stringent quality standards in response to the EU intervention system. Due to the success of its quality control systems, it became one of the first organisations to win awards from the Irish National Control Association.

Aer Lingus has also operated internal controls which satisfy both quality and safety standards. In relation to the control of safety, Aer Lingus has ensured both aircraft and staff certification and has developed sophisticated maintenance and overhaul control systems. With respect to quality Aer Lingus has introduced control systems to monitor performance in the following areas: telephone answering times, passenger queuing, baggage handling and reclaiming. Therefore, Irish organisations have widely used non financial controls. The recent financial problems at Aer Lingus, however, could indicate that more stringent financial controls were required.

7.9 SUMMARY OF KEY PROPOSITIONS

• Control is the final management function. It is the process of ensuring the efficient and effective achievement of organisational goals and objectives.

• The control process involves three steps: establishing performance standards; measuring and comparing actual performance; and taking corrective action where necessary.

• An organisation does not have automatic controls and, therefore, some form of control is needed to regulate its activities. Three types of control exist: feedforward, concurrent, and feedback control. Feedforward control monitors inputs; concurrent control monitors the transformation process; feedback control monitors the outputs.

• Effective controls have a number of important characteristics. They should be appropriate, cost effective, acceptable, emphasise exceptions at critical points, flexible, reliable and valid, based on valid performance standards and based on accurate information.

• Methods of control typically used by organisations are either financial or non financial. Financial controls include budgetary control, break even analysis and ratio analysis.

• Budgetary control is the process of ascertaining what has been achieved and comparing this with the projections contained in the budget. Common examples of budgets are revenue and expense, time, space, material and production, capital expenditure and cash. Newer approaches to budgets include variable budgets and zero based budgets.

• Break even analysis uses both fixed and variable costs to identify the point at which it becomes profitable to produce a certain product.

• Ratio analysis involves the use of financial ratios to assess the financial performance of the organisation. Ratios are used to assess liquidity, profitability, activity and leverage.

• Non financial controls include project controls, management audits and inventory, production and quality controls. Project controls most commonly used are Gantt charts and PERT analysis.

• Management audits, either internal or external, are designed to provide information about competitor organisations to aid strategic decision making and to highlight internal problems.

• Inventory, production and quality control are designed to ensure that levels of inventory are appropriate, the production process is efficient and that quality standards are high. The advances made in information technology have greatly improved these controls

DISCUSSION QUESTIONS

1. Define control and explain its importance?
2. Explain the three steps in the control process.
3. Define and explain the various types of control an organisation can use.
4. What are the characteristics of effective control?
5. Explain the concepts of variable and zero based budgeting.
6. What is break even analysis? How can it be used as a control device?
7. Using the following accounts from XYZ Co. calculate the following ratios:
   current
   quick asset
   asset turnover
   net profit
   return on assets
   debt equity.

BALANCE SHEET FOR XYZ COMPANY

Assets

Current assets

Cash	10,000
Accounts receivable	75,323
Inventory	327,421
Total current assets:	412,744
Property and plant	356,357
Less depreciation	89,462
Net property and plant	266,895
Total assets	**679,639**

Liabilities and Stockholder Equity

Current liabilities

Notes payable	53,424
Accrued expenses	87,932
Accounts payable	27,624
Corporation tax payable	56,528
Total current liabilities	255,508

Stockholder equity

Capital stock	224,131
Preferred stock	100,000
Retained earnings	100,000
Total stockholder equity	424,131
Total liabilities and stockholder equity	**679,639**

PROFIT AND LOSS STATEMENT FOR XYZ COMPANY

Revenues

Sales	1,000,000
Other income	25,000

Total 1,025,000

Costs and expenses

Cost of goods sold	775,000
Total expenses	200,000
Total costs and expenses	**975,000**
Profit	**50,000**

8. Explain what Gantt charts and PERT analysis try to achieve. What is the difference between the approaches?
9. Critically evaluate management audits as a control technique in the current business environment.
10. What three questions should a good inventory control system try to answer? How can it achieve this?
11. How have advances in information technology shaped the control function?
12. In the current business environment, what controls should an organisation focus on?

REFERENCES

Anthony, R., Dearden, J. and Bedford, N., *Management Control Systems*, Irwin, Illinois 1984.
Bedeian, A., *Management*, Dryden Press, Fort Worth 1993.
Brophy, S., *The Strategic Management of Irish Business*, Smurfit Publications, Dublin 1985.
Bruns, W. and McFarlan, F., 'Information Technology Puts Power in Control Systems' *Harvard Business Review*, Vol.65, No.5, 89–94, 1987.
Daft, R. and Macintosh, N., 'The Nature and Use of Formal Control Systems for Management Control and Strategy Implementation' *Journal of Management*, Vol.10, No.1, 43–66, 1984.
Davis, R., *The Fundamental of Top Management*, Harper Row, New York 1951.
Donnelly, J., Gibson, J. and Ivancevich, J., *Fundamentals of Management*, Business Publications, Texas 1981.
Dunbar, R., 'Designs for Organisational Control' in Nystrom, P. and Starbuck, W. (eds), *Handbook of Organisational Design*, Oxford University Press, London 1981.
Flamholtz, E., 'Behavioural Aspects of Accounting/Control Systems' in Kerr, S. (ed.), *Organisational Behaviour*, Grid, Ohio 1979.
Fuld, M., 'Cultivating Home Grown Spies' *Wall Street Journal*, 17 March 1986.
Giglioni, G. and Bedeian, A., 'A Conspectus of Management Control Theory' *Academy of Management Journal*, Vol.17, No.2, 292–305, 1974.
Koontz, H. and Bradspies, R., 'Managing Though Feedforward Control' in O'Donnell and Weihrich (eds), *Management: A Book of Readings*, McGraw-Hill, New York 1970.
Lawler, E. and Rhode, J., 'Information and Control in Organisations' in Robey, D. (ed.), *Designing Organisations*, Irwin, Illinois 1991.
Phyrr, P. 'Zero Based Budgeting' *Harvard Business Review*, Vol.60, No.6, 1970.
Pomerantz, F., 'Pre-emptive Auditing — Future Shock or Present Opportunity?' *Journal of Accounting, Auditing and Finance*, 352–356, summer.
Stewart, T., 'Why Budgets are Bad for Business' *Fortune*, 115–119, 4 June 1990.
'Aer Lingus: £12 Million in Overpayment to Suppliers' *Sunday Tribune Business Section*, 12 June 1994.
Todd, J., 'Management Control Systems: A Key Link between Strategy, Structure and Employee Performance' *Organisation Dynamics*, 65–78, Spring 1977.
Wall, T., Corbett, J. J., Martin, R., Clegg, C., and Jackson, P., 'Advanced Manufacturing Technology, Work Design and Performance; A Change Study' *Journal of Applied Psychology*, Vol.75, 691–697, 1980.
Weihrich, H. and Koontz, W., *Management: A Global Perspective*, McGraw-Hill, New York 1993.
Weiner, N., *Cybernetics or Control and Communication in Animal and Machine*, MIT Press, Massachussetts 1949.

8

Financial Management

8.1 Introduction

This chapter examines the financial management of organisations. The internationalisation of money markets has meant that the finance function has become more complicated but also far more significant. Financial management centres around two fundamental issues: the sources of finance for an organisation and how the organisation should invest spare funds. An organisation can either opt for short-, medium- or long-term sources of finance, all of which are appropriate under certain circumstances. Irish state agencies play an important role in providing finance for the development of industry in Ireland. Investment management should focus on managing working capital, inventory, cash and debts.

8.2 The Nature and Importance of Financial Management

For any organisation the appropriate use of finance is a most critical determinant of success or failure. Finance is usually a scarce resource and has to be managed carefully if it is to work to the organisation's best advantage. The financing requirements of an organisation change throughout its life cycle, with start-up costs being particularly high, further complicating the management task.

Accounting and financial management are frequently analysed together despite the fact that they are essentially different subjects. However, accounting and financial management have important linkages. Accounting is primarily concerned with processing and interpreting financial information for those inside the organisation (managerial accounting) and for those outside the organisation (financial accounting). Financial management is a functional activity concerned with the management of the financial aspects of the organisation. Financial management can be defined in terms of two broad areas:
1. Assisting in the achievement of the overall objectives of the organisation through the provision of finance, when and where required, in a manner and at a cost which provides an acceptable level of risk to the business.
2. The investigation and evaluation of investment opportunities open to the business (Kennedy, Mac Cormac and Teeling 1988).

Financial management, therefore, is concerned with the acquisition and allocation of financial resources for the organisation, and asks two central questions which provide the structure for the remainder of the chapter.
1. How should the organisation raise the necessary finance? (Sources of Finance)
2. How should an organisation choose the investments that it makes? (Investment Management)

Traditionally, financial management played a secondary role to business finance in many organisations. Business finance deals with financial institutions and the financial instruments provided by them such as loans and overdrafts. Financial management was typically viewed as a function of the manager. However, during the 1960s and 1970s, financial management assumed a central role in the management aspect of finance. *Inflation* and new technology meant that new investments were very expensive and it soon became obvious that poor investment decisions could bankrupt organisations. For this reason, sound financial management became a critically important function within the organisation.

In recent years, the financial management function has become even more important and complex. Capital or money markets have become internationalised or, in other words, crossed national boundaries. Previously, the task of the finance manager in Ireland was centred around the Irish environment only. However, today's managers must have a broader focus. Invested funds can be moved around the world easily, multi-national companies trade on stock exchanges in many countries and international financial instruments have been developed. All of these developments mean that financial management has assumed greater importance within the organisation.

8.3 SOURCES OF FINANCE

The finance function in any organisation tries to ensure that the organisation has the right type of money in the right place and at the right time (Kennedy, McCormac and Teeling 1988). In doing so, the finance manager separates the financial needs of the organisation into three main areas: short-, medium- and long-term, depending on the uses of the funds. Good management hinges on matching sources and uses for example, using an overdraft to buy more materials but negotiating a term loan to build a warehouse to store finished goods.

Each source of finance has three potential effects on the organisation. Firstly, there is a **risk** effect attached to any source of finance, in that the organisation may not be able to meet the commitments or repayments associated with the source, i.e. both *interest* and *principal*. (It is important to note that not all sources involve borrowing money.) In evaluating potential sources, a business must consider the risks involved. In Ireland, some sources are well developed while others are not in common use. For example, there is a wide network of associated banks (Bank of Ireland, Allied Irish Bank, Ulster Bank and Northern Bank), whereas the *venture capital* market remains underfunded.

Secondly, the organisation experiences an **income effect** which works in two ways. When money is borrowed there is a positive inflow of funds from the source of income, but at the same time this needs to be balanced against its cost. For example, if an organisation borrows £10,000 at 15 per cent interest, it experiences a one-off inflow of £10,000 but it also has to make repayments on the principal plus interest out of future income.

Finally, sources of finance can have a **control effect** on the organisation. The control effect is the possibility of new sources of finance affecting the management or ownership, and thereby control of the organisation. For example, the issue of new shares can bring new stakeholders to the organisation who have a degree of ownership control, and, similarly, bank borrowing may bring some control over decision making.

Finance managers seek to provide necessary finance that has a minimum risk and loss of control while generating a maximum income to the owners. A wide range of sources are available which means that sound choices have to be made by the organisation. Figure 8.1. provides a breakdown of the major sources available to organisations for the short-, medium- and long-term financial requirements which will be discussed in this chapter.

Figure 8.1 Sources of Finance Available in Ireland

Short-term	Medium-term	Long-term
1. Trade credit	1. Leasing	1. Owner's capital
2. Accrued expenses	2. Hire purchase	2. Retained profits
3. Deferred taxation	3. Term loans	3. Commercial, merchant or government bank loan
4. Bank overdraft		4. Government grant
5. Bills of Exchange and Acceptance Credit		5. Stock exchange
6. Debentures		6. Inventory financing
7. Project financing		7. Factoring
		8. Venture capital
		9. BES
		10. Sales and leaseback
		11. Commercial mortgage

Source. Adapted from Kennedy, T., MacCormac, M. and Teeling J., *Financial Management*, Gill & Macmillan, Dublin 1988.

8.4 SHORT-TERM FINANCE

There are seven main sources of finance available in Ireland to serve an organisation's short-term financial requirements.

8.4.1 Trade credit

Trade credit occurs when an organisation orders raw materials from a supplier who usually extends a period of credit to the organisation. Trade credit, therefore, refers to the utilisation of the maximum period of credit allowed by suppliers. The organisation, therefore, can retain the money due to suppliers for a period of time, consequently generating a source of short-term finance.

Trade credit would appear to be a free source of short-term finance in that the organisation can use the money that it should have paid for supplies, while at the same time gaining the benefits of the supplied materials. However, trade credit has two important consequences for the organisation. Firstly, some suppliers offer a discount of

1–2 per cent for early or on time payment in much the same way as a garage would give a discount for a cash payment by an individual customer. Taking the maximum period of credit means that the organisation loses this discount and, therefore, the finance comes at a cost. For example, if there is a discount of 1 per cent for payment within thirty days this works out at an annual interest rate of 12.7 per cent. This makes the interest as high or even higher than bank rates, so trade credit is neither free nor cheap.

Secondly, slow payment to suppliers can effect the credit rating of the organisation. Over time, suppliers become reluctant to deal with such customers, which can cause problems for organisations depending on trade credit. However, many smaller businesses have borrowed as much as they can from other sources and have no alternative but to resort to trade credit. Many organisations walk a tightrope trying to get their customers to pay them as quickly as possible while taking the longest possible credit period before paying their own suppliers. The risk is that the organisation may profit from using trade credit, but may lose out because its own customers practice the same policy.

In many industries there are standard terms of credit which have much to do with the type of product being sold. If the product is one with a small margin and high turnover, credit given is short (for example stationary for a business). Conversely, products or services where there is a long time lag between order and delivery usually have more lenient terms or phased payments (for example, plant and equipment purchase). Trade credit, therefore, is an important source of finance particularly during times of crisis where the period can be stretched. The objective of trade credit management should be to extend the payment period as far as possible without affecting the credit rating of the organisation.

8.4.2 Accrued expenses

Organisations obtain services from a wide variety of sources and the expenses associated with these services are usually paid in arrears. Wages, ESB and phone bills are all paid in arrears and, therefore, the organisation can use resources before they are paid for which can be viewed as a free source of finance. While the amounts are normally fairly small, they nevertheless account for a source of finance which gives useful leeway. Problems arise when organisations take this source for granted and are late paying bills and withhold PAYE and taxes due. Overdependency on accrued expenses to finance the day to day running of the business is a sign of poor financial health. However, if managed carefully payments can be arranged to make the best use of available cash.

8.4.3 Deferred taxation

This is a short-term source of finance similar to trade credit. It arises because tax bills (VAT, PRSI, Corporation Tax and Income Tax) only have to be paid after the revenues to which they apply have been generated. *Value Added Tax* (VAT) is charged on all invoices but is only returned every two months. Income Tax and PRSI are also deducted from employees' pay packets by the organisation, to be returned to the Revenue Commissioners at a later date. Corporation Tax is payable six months from the end of the accounting period and also provides another source of finance. No interest is charged on this form of credit, provided payments are made on time. However, the Revenue Commissioners levy interest on late payments at the rate of 1.5 per cent per month.

8.4.4 Bank overdraft

Bank overdrafts are widely used by organisations to provide short-term financial cushioning. Such overdrafts are provided by commercial banks to meet short-term capital needs. Commercial banks prefer to provide overdraft facilities for self liquidating purposes, i.e. where the overdraft is short and self financing. For example, retailers will frequently negotiate bank overdrafts before Christmas to purchase their Christmas stock, and farmers arrange overdrafts to finance purchases of fertiliser in the spring. In other, words the purpose for which the finance is required generates the funds to repay the finance.

The amount of funds available for overdrafts depends on economic conditions. If economic growth is slow or stagnant, there is little demand for such funds, but in periods of high growth the demand can exceed the supply. Lending rates for bank overdrafts vary according to current interest rates but are normally 2.5 per cent above the minimum rate. The minimum rate is also referred to as the inter bank lending rate and is the rate at which banks lend money to each other.

Banks prefer to negotiate overdrafts with organisations that are profitable and have liquid assets. If the bank has a good relationship with the management of the organisation and is familiar with its background and financial affairs, the bank will look more favourably on the overdraft request. In order to get an overdraft facility, banks require some form of security from the organisation such as a written guarantee from management or collateral.

One of the main advantages of an overdraft is its flexibility. A credit line is established which sets out the maximum that can be borrowed. Once this is agreed the organisation can borrow and repay money within that limit. Another important advantage of an overdraft is that it is a cheap source of finance. Interest is only charged on the outstanding daily balance and such interest is allowable against profits for tax purposes.

The main disadvantage of an overdraft is that it is repayable on demand, which is what differentiates it from a term loan. This places the borrower in an awkward position should the overdraft be called in, as the organisation has to have sufficient *liquid assets* available to cover it. In practice, overdrafts are not often called in, because it is not in the bank's interest to do so, but it does emphasise the importance of having contingency plans to meet overdraft repayments. Most banks are flexible enough to reconsider and extend overdrafts in the light of changing circumstances.

8.4.5 Bills of Exchange and Acceptance Credit

As these two sources of finance have similar characteristics they will be discussed together. A Bill of Exchange is an unconditional order from one person to another to pay the addressee a specified some of money at a stated date in the future. Therefore, it is similar to a post dated cheque. A Bill of Exchange is essentially a financial contract which means that the buyer can delay payment, usually for thirty, sixty, ninety or 180 days with the agreement of the seller. Figure 8.2 provides an example of a Bill of Exchange.

In this case the buyer is the Irish Export Company and the seller is Schmidt Company of Germany. As we can see, the seller has accepted a Bill of Exchange to the value of 7,256 DM payable sixty days after the date on the bill. The Irish Export Company, therefore, has sixty days of credit. Once a company has been given a Bill of Exchange it can either wait until the specified date and cash it in or cash it in at a discount rate at a bank prior to the date. In this case the bank charges a fee for cashing in the Bill of

Exchange earlier than the specified date. For example, a £1000 Bill of Exchange payable in 180 days is worth £1000 less 180 days interest when discounted. An organisation that urgently requires the money may find that the discount paid is more than offset by the cost of raising the finance elsewhere. Bills of Exchange are rarely used in domestic trade, but are popular in international trade.

Figure 8.2 Example of a Bill of Exchange

No.........   **BILL OF EXCHANGE**

Date: 24 April 1994   **Place**: Dublin   **Amount**: DM 7,256,000

At: Sixty Days....................................**Sight of this Bill of Exchange**

Pay to the order of Irish Export Company PLC

The sum of Deutsche Marks Seven thousand two hundred and fifty-six

....**value received**

To: Schmidt, AG Company   For and on behalf of
Dusseldorf Germany   Irish Export Co. PLC

                                                                ....
                                                                Drawer

---

Acceptance Credits are a form of Bill of Exchange which a company can draw from a bank, normally a merchant bank. Merchant banks are non associated, which differs from associated banks in that they rarely have branches, do not operate current accounts for personal customers and do not normally participate in the Bank Clearing House. The Bank Clearing House is the system operated by the main banks for processing cheques. Examples of Irish merchant banks include Guinness & Mahon and Investment Bank of Ireland. By accepting such a Credit, the bank promises to pay an agreed sum at a future date. The Credit itself is now valuable, as the holder can trade it in when it falls due. It can be sold to a discount house in the money market, which will pay the face value less a discount rate. Acceptance Credits are usually used by larger organisations, as they are conventionally made out for amounts of £200,000 or more. They are a form of long-term overdraft, but cheaper because the interest rate on acceptance credit does not move as quickly as the overdraft rate.

8.4.6 Inventory financing

Many Irish organisations have high levels of inventory, i.e. raw materials, work in progress and finished goods. For some organisations (jewellers and car dealers) inventory is the single largest investment they have. Inventory financing basically means that an organisation's inventory is used as security for a loan. As inventory is a liquid asset: it is viewed as a suitable form of collateral for short-term finance. Inventory finance or stock loans have become very popular in Ireland in recent years. An example of inventory finance is the grain harvest in September which is not generally sold until November. The farmer, however, needs finance in September to pay wages and to buy seed, so inventory financing of the grain harvest is frequently used to raise cash. In using inventory finance, the borrower must obtain the lender's permission before selling the inventory. This source of finance attracts interest rates about 2 per cent above the norm, but is convenient to use where inventory is the organisation's most marketable asset. There are three variations used in inventory financing:

1. **A Chattel Mortgage**: With a Chattel Mortgage a loan is granted in return for a mortgage interest in specified and itemised inventories. The inventory can only be sold with the lender's consent. This method is particularly suitable for large, slow moving goods.

2. **A Trust Receipt**: In this case the goods are itemised in a legal document and as each piece of inventory is sold the proceeds from the sale are returned to the lender. The borrower is, therefore, holding the inventory in trust for the lender.

3. **Field warehousing**: With field warehousing the inventory is stored in a specific warehouse. As the goods are sold the lender permits them to be released from the warehouse. The cash generated from the sale is then used to pay the lender.

8.4.7 Factoring

Factoring describes the situation where the organisation sells some of its debt to a factor, at up to 75 per cent of its face value. The factor, who is often a subsidiary of a bank, collects the debt and either passes on the payments minus discount to the organisation, or keeps the payments in exchange for a lump sum payment to the client. The factor reviews each of the organisation's debtors separately before agreeing to accept them. According to Kennedy, McCormac and Teeling (1988) factors offer four main services:

1. They take over the debt collection function of the client, thereby reducing the need for a credit control department.
2. They may offer insurance against *bad debts*.
3. They pay the client agreed percentages of invoices on agreed dates.
4. They pay cash to the client before payment of the invoice.

There is a mistaken belief that factors are taken on as a last resort. In fact, factors are not interested in organisations with a history of bad debts. Factors prefer to deal with organisations that have a good record and a firm growth potential. Factors are useful to organisations that have just entered business and are finding it difficult to manage debtors, or organisations pursuing high growth who want to concentrate their activities on this objective and leave debt collection to an outside agency. Many organisations do not want their customers to know that they are using a factor due to the fact that it might cause loss of confidence. In this case, the organisation sends out invoices as before, but this time acts as an agent for the factor. Payments are received and then given to the factor who deals with them as outlined above. Factoring is more costly than an overdraft but often the need for factors arises because of a difficulty in getting overdrafts. Factors tend to be of more use to smaller organisations or to those involved in export markets. Factors have a number of important benefits to offer these types of organisation as shown in Figure 8.3.

Figure 8.3 Benefits Associated with Factoring

---

1. Organisations can pay suppliers more quickly giving a good credit record.
2. Organisations can obtain cash and quantity discounts on supplies helping their bottom line.
3. Organisations are better able to cope with seasonal and peak cash demands.
4. Organisations are able to make future purchasing plans with the knowledge that cash will be available.
5. Organisations can finance a higher level of sales.
6. Organisations can obtain off balance sheet finance.
7. Organisations can improve the return on their capital without giving up equity or control.
8. Savings on sales administration can be realised.
9. Savings in management time can be achieved with more time being spent on sales and business development.
10. Cash flows can be improved and there is less risk of damaging customer relations through constant payment demands.

Source: Adapted from Kennedy, T., MacCormac, M. and Teeling, J., *Financial Management*, Gill & Macmillan, Dublin 1988.

Therefore, numerous sources of short-term finance are available to Irish organisations. The first three sources examined — trade credit, accrued expenses and deferred taxation — are termed spontaneous sources as they arise through the normal course of business. These sources are essentially unsecured and no interest is charged. The other four sources of short-term finance are termed negotiated sources in that the organisation has to negotiate with other parties to secure the funds.

Twenty to thirty years ago, trade credit and bank overdrafts were the only forms of short-term finance available to organisations. Today, however, the range of short-term sources has increased, with inventory financing becoming more popular. The key objective in raising short-term finance is to minimise the risk and control effects while maximising the income effect. Organisations need to be careful to ensure that they do not overuse short-term sources as they risk damaging the long-term reputation of the organisation.

8.5 MEDIUM-TERM FINANCE

Short-term sources of finance described in the previous section are ideally suited for investments in current assets which liquidate themselves in time to pay back the capital raised. However, not all investments are of this nature. Some have intermediate lives of between three and seven years, such as plant and machinery. Short-term finance would be of little use to an organisation seeking to make a medium-term investment in, for example, machinery. Therefore, a series of medium-term sources of finance exist to cater for such financial demands. The three main sources of medium-term finance discussed below are leasing, hire purchase and term loans.

8.5.1 Leasing

Leasing is a form of finance where an organisation can take out a lease on an asset and use the asset for a period of time without actually owning it or gaining title to it. The most common items leased by organisations include motor vehicles, office equipment, plant and earthmoving equipment. Where organisations are content to have the use of the asset without owning it then leasing is an important source of medium-term finance.

Leasing generally involves two parties, the lessor who provides the asset and the lessee who leases it. Lessors are normally finance companies who purchase the asset and lease it to the lessee for a fixed term in return for making agreed payments. (Sale and leaseback is where the organisation owns an asset, sells it to a finance company and then leases it back. It can be viewed as a source of long-term finance and will be discussed later.) At the end of the lease agreement ownership remains with the lessor. However, once the primary lease has expired the lessee may be given the option of a secondary lease, usually for much reduced payments.

According to Kennedy, MacCormac and Teeling (1988), two main types of lease agreement are commonplace: an operating lease and a financial lease. An operating lease can be cancelled by the lessee before expiration of the agreed period. The sum of all payments does not necessarily cover the full cost of the asset so subsequent leases or the lease sale are needed to recover the investment. The lessor in an operating lease is responsible for service, maintenance and insurance.

With a financial lease the lease cannot be cancelled by the lessee before the specified date. The lessor is not necessarily responsible for the service, maintenance and insurance of the asset. A financial lease allows the asset to be fully *amortised* over the life of the asset. Therefore, the key difference between operating and financial leases is the cancellability of the lease. Leasing agreements typically cover four main areas:
1. The period of time covered by the lease.
2. The frequency and the amount of payments to be made.
3. Options of renewing the lease or purchasing the asset upon expiration of the lease.
4. Arrangements concerning insurance, service and maintenance.

Leasing offers the organisation a number of important advantages:
1. It allows the use of assets which the organisation could not afford to purchase.
2. Scarce financial resources are not used.
3. It provides tax advantages for the organisation.
4. Some assets are not worth purchasing due to the fact that they become obsolete, therefore, leasing is a sensible option.
5. Leasing is traditionally seen as a form of 'off the balance sheet' financing. Leased items are not recorded as assets on the balance sheet, yet the organisation enjoys their use. Leasing, therefore, does not interfere with the organisation's borrowing capacity.

In deciding whether to lease or purchase an asset, the organisation should assess the costs and benefits that are associated with each option. The costs associated with leasing depend on the value of the asset being leased, the period of the lease, current interest rates and the credit rating of the organisation. The costs of leasing an asset can be deducted against tax. However, the organisation loses out on depreciation allowances against tax. The organisation should also consider the availability of Government grants, cash discounts and annual allowances provided by the Government for purchasing assets.

Leasing as a form of medium-term finance has become increasingly popular in recent years rising from less than £12 million in 1972 to £200 million in 1986. Specialist companies have entered the market in Ireland and are cheaper, quicker and more flexible than the traditional banks. Examples include Leasepack, AIB Finance and

Leasing and Bank of Ireland Finance. Due to the increased competition in this sector costs have been reduced which means that an organisation can often lease an asset at a cheaper rate than purchasing it.

8.5.2 Hire purchase

Hire purchase (HP) involves an organisation hiring equipment or machinery from a hire purchase company, making a series of payments of both the principal and interest over a fixed period of time. At the end of that period of time ownership of the asset is transferred from the HP company to the hiree. A slightly different form of HP has become popular in recent years — credit sales. Credit sales allow the transfer of ownership to occur immediately after the purchaser has agreed to pay for the goods over a specific period of time. Examples include credit sales offered by the ESB for washing machines and cookers. Credit sales tend to be more popular in the consumer market.

The advantages of HP are similar to those associated with leasing:
1. The organisation has the use of the asset without large capital outlay.
2. Scarce organisational resources are not used.
3. Costs are tax deductible.
4. *Depreciation* allowances and initial allowances can, in some cases, be obtained.

However, hire purchase is very expensive. Interest rates charged for HP are very high and unlike all other forms of lending, interest is charged on the original sum until the termination of the agreement. The HP company also has the right to repossess the goods should the hiree default on payments. Under these circumstances the hiree cannot reclaim any payments that have previously been made.

HP is popular in Ireland but tends to be used when other sources are not available or for the occasional purchase of office equipment. HP can be viewed as a convenient source of medium-term finance, in that, like a lease agreement, the terms are fixed and will not change throughout the course of the agreement. The asset also acts as security since it is assumed to have a market value even after the agreement has expired. Therefore, an organisation having difficulty borrowing elsewhere might consider HP as an option. Otherwise, the high interest rates and lack of ownership cause organisations to look elsewhere.

8.5.3 Term loans

Bank overdrafts are not appropriate for investments in fixed assets and as a result term loans have been developed by the banks to cater for the demand for capital for investment in fixed assets. A term loan is a loan negotiated for a fixed period of time with repayments payable on both the principal and interest at agreed intervals. The average time span for a term loan is between three and five years.

Term lending has increased enormously in Ireland. One of the main advantages is its inherent flexibility. As well as medium-term loans most banks will listen to lending proposals with terms up to twenty years. The repayments can be geared to suit the borrower's needs. Some loans incorporate rest periods, usually at the start of the loan, where only the interest is repayable. Payments are then accelerated towards the end of the loan period to repay the capital sum.

Term loans make sense for an organisation borrowing to meet medium-term requirements, for example, buying more machinery. The bank will look carefully at the previous borrowing history, the company's reputation and future prospects. The Government assists borrowing to certain sectors of the economy through the Agricultural Credit Corporation (ACC) and the Industrial Credit Corporation (ICC). Disadvantages of term loans include the rate of interest payable which is normally 2 - 5 per cent above the bank's minimum lending rate, depending on the organisation's credit rating. The bank may also dictate certain conditions such as the prescribed level of interest cover or *current assets* cover.

The use of medium-term financial instruments has grown rapidly in Ireland. HP is widely used, but is very expensive and ownership does not transfer until the final payment has been made. Term loans, while useful, are also very expensive. Leasing has become very popular particularly due to the fact that technological change means that much equipment becomes obsolete quickly. In terms of the risk effect, lease and HP have contractual obligations, i.e. repayments which if defaulted upon can lead to repossession and, therefore, loss of business. Term loans have a restrictive control effect in that the banks can dilute the control of the owners by imposing certain terms and conditions.

8.6 LONG-TERM FINANCE

In addition to short- and medium-term finance, organisations also require finance which is stretched over a longer period of time. For example, long-term sources of finance are required to fund new product development. In order to meet this need, eleven main sources of long-term finance are available to organisations in Ireland.

8.6.1 Owner's capital

Owner's capital, also called equity, represents the seed capital which is the foundation of the organisation, although it can be used at any stage in the organisation's life cycle. By law, certain types of business must have a certain proportion of owner's equity made known. The reason for this requirement is that equity capital represents the commitment, without which the business is more likely to fail. The equity shareholders, known as ordinary shareholders, bear the greatest risk in a limited liability company. If the business fairs badly the ordinary shareholders suffer in terms of a small dividend or possibly none at all. If the business fails the ordinary shareholders also have the last call on the remaining assets, as creditors have to be paid first of all. However, if the business is successful ordinary share holders stand to make a more than proportionate return on their investment.

Equity is by far the most popular method of raising long-term finance for organisations. As the organisation grows, the original owner may opt to bring in some more shareholders and widen the equity base. For example, if the requirement is to raise £10,000 this could be fulfilled by two shares of £5000 each or 10,000 shares of £1 each or any of an infinite number of combinations. *Fiacla*, the Irish toothpaste manufacturer, used this method to raise long-term finance. Fiacla was established in 1984 with a £15,000 capital investment by its founder. In 1989, to fund large capital expenditures associated with expansion the founder sold 51 per cent of the company to raise funds (*Business and Finance* 1994). When issuing equity capital the organisation should consider the following factors:

1. The cost of the issue, which depends on whether it is a rights issue (i.e. available to

existing shareholders only) or a public issue. In 1994, the Smurfit Group, James Crean and Anglo Irish Bank Corp all made rights issues.

2. The cost of paying out *dividends*.

3. The potential loss of control. If new shareholders come in, voting patterns may change to the detriment of the original owners and directors. This can be overcome by restricting the fund raising to a rights issue. It also explains why so many organisations prefer retained profits rather than additional equity as a long-term source of finance. An Irish example of a company using retained profits as a source of finance is Lake Electronics.

8.6.2 Retained profits

Retained profits represent a surplus which is ploughed back into the business rather than being distributed as dividends. It is normal practice for an organisation to retain profits in the first few years of its existence, to act as a buffer against financial difficulties. Retained profits also act as a form of insurance for the organisation's future.

Retained profits initially appear to be a free source of finance in that there are no interest costs. However, investors denied a return in the early years will have higher expectations in the future. Also, from an investor's point of view, there is the opportunity cost of the dividend foregone as it could have been invested to provide a further income stream. Retained profits also presume that such profits will continue into the future. In other words, an organisation ploughing back profits assumes that it will generate a higher profit in the future. In competitive climates such an assumption is built on dubious foundations. However, retained profit saves costs associated with a share issue. The main advantages associated with retained profits are similar to those of equity, except that there is no loss of control which is inevitable with new shareholders.

8.6.3 Commercial, merchant and government banks

Due to the fact that Ireland is a relatively small country there is less specialisation in the banking sector than in other countries, such as Germany and the UK. Therefore, while it is possible to discuss in general terms the role of each type of bank in providing finance, under certain circumstances a bank may be willing to lend outside its traditional sphere of activity.

The commercial or associated banks provide long-term finance to every sector of business. Larger clients are serviced through the merchant banking arm of the bank, for example Ulster Investment Bank and the Investment Bank of Ireland. Associated banks can also offer a complete financial package, for example medium-term loans and insurance. Merchant banks are often mistakenly assumed to only have an interest in dealing with larger organisations. Though the loans sought must be of a significant amount before a merchant bank will express an interest. Many banks in this sector were originally established to serve foreign organisations in Ireland, but are now an integral part of the lending economy.

The two Government banks, the Industrial Credit Corporation (ICC) and the Agricultural Credit Corporation (ACC), were established to serve both industry and agriculture respectively. The ICC lends to the retail sector of Irish industry, whereas the ACC lends to the farming community. In recent years both banks have increased the range of services provided in order to broaden their customer base. The role of these two banks will be further developed when discussing state financial aid to industry.

Banks distinguish between three categories of risk in their lending activities. **AAA** categorises a negligible risk, an example of which is lending to the Government. **AA** categorises a moderate risk, an example of which is lending to an established organisation. **A** categorises a significant or high risk, an example of which is start-up finance where the organisation or founder has no financial track record. In the past, the banks have been reluctant lenders to the **A** category of borrower as a result of their bad debt experiences. It could be the case that banks would be more willing to lend to this category if they were offered a share of equity in the proposed venture. Small businesses often find that a personal guarantee is necessary before funds are made available. Taken as a whole, the Irish banking sector is now a more flexible source of finance, but the guarantee requirement and higher interest rates attached to category **A** loans are clear disadvantages.

8.6.4 Government grants

Government grants are an attractive source of finance from a business point of view. However, such financial incentives are granted with conditions attached. The conditions or strings mean that the project must be perceived as a worthwhile venture which will create jobs and remain viable in the long run. By far the largest amount of financial aid is available through the auspices of the former IDA, now called Forfas, which is divided into Forbairt and IDA Ireland. However, a number of other state agencies also provide financial support including ICC, FAS and Bord Failte among others. Due to the importance of the grant aid provided by State agencies, the next section (8.7) of the chapter focuses on the role of these agencies and the financial packages that they supply to Irish industry.

8.6.5 The stock exchange

Most Irish organisations formerly discounted the possibility of raising funds on the stock exchange due to the stringent requirements and continuing obligations it involved. The opening up of new sectors including the Smaller Companies Market and the Unlisted Securities Market has resulted in many organisations taking the opportunity to raise funds. A recent example of an organisation obtaining a stock exchange quotation is the Irish Permanent Building Society. The main advantages of obtaining a stock market quotation to raise funds include:
1. It helps to raise equity capital.
2. It helps growth by the use of the organisation's shares in the acquisition of other businesses.
3. It enables existing shareholders to realise part of their investment.
4. It enhances the status of the organisation.
5. It can motivate staff by introducing share option schemes.

However, there are a number of disadvantages associated with the stock exchange as a means of raising finance:
1. The effort required to bring an organisation to market. This requires discipline in the areas of finance and administration.
2. The costs involved.
3. The obligation in regard to disclosure.

Figure 8.4 lists the top ten companies listed on the Irish stock exchange along with details concerning price and share performance.

Figure 8.4 Top Ten Companies Listed on the Irish Stock Exchange May 1995

	Price P	% Change WK	% Change YTD	1995 P/E	1995 High	1995 Low
Smurfit	356	-1.1	-5.3	7.2	415	345
AIB	284	-1.4	5.2	8.6	290	253
Bank of Ireland	335	-2.0	11.7	7.0	342	290
CRH	382	-3.3	7.0	11.1	395	338
Elan Corporation	2103	-3.8	-8.9	3.8	2389	2103
Kerry Group	388	-0.5	17.6	13.5	390	322
Irish Life	194	-4.0	1.6	7.7	202	179
Waterford Wedgewood	56	-0.9	-4.3	16.8	60	51
Greencore	443	-0.4	9.4	10.4	445	400
Fyffes	105	0.0	1.0	13.0	113	100

Source: 'Dublin Closing Prices' *Sunday Tribune*, 21 May 1995.

The price of each share is indicated in pence, along with the percentage change in that share price for the week and the year to date. As can be seen from the chart, the share price of most of the listed companies declined that week. The price/earnings ratio is a widely used measure of investment worth and is calculated as follows:

$$\text{P/E ratio} \quad = \quad \frac{\text{Market price of the share}}{\text{Earnings per share}}$$

The price/earnings ratio represents the period of time required to recover the purchase price assuming that earnings per share remain constant. Earnings per share (EPS) is the annual profit of the business divided by the number of shares outstanding. It is that portion of the annual profit attributable to one share. The highest and lowest prices of each company share are also indicated.

8.6.6 Debentures

A debenture is a fixed interest loan made to an organisation. It differs from other loans in that it is available on the stock exchange. Debentures are issued with specific terms regarding capital repayments, interest and security and are normally redeemable on a set date. They are securities that bear a fixed interest rate and are redeemable at a predefined date. These are normally issued for a period of ten to twenty years, though it is possible to come across perpetual loan stock. Debentures vary in popularity generally in line with economic prosperity. A fixed interest stock is more attractive in times of economic uncertainty. Since a debenture has to be repaid it is really a long-term loan. The collateral for such a loan is some specified asset or else all the assets of the organisation. If there is no collateral the stock is described as an unsecured debenture.

From an organisation's point of view, debentures cost relatively little to issue. This type of investment is especially advantageous for financial institutions guaranteeing their clients a fixed rate of return, for example pension funds. The interest requirement will affect control of the organisation since failure to pay can lead to liquidation or bankruptcy. The organisation also has a requirement to repay the capital sum which imposes a future obligation.

While a fixed rate loan stock may initially seem attractive to an organisation there is an opportunity cost to be considered. If interest rates rise then the cost of debenture stocks falls as other sources of finance are charging a higher rate of interest. Similarly, if interest rates fall a debenture becomes a relatively expensive source of finance.

8.6.7 Project finance

Project finance is a form of long-term borrowing specially designed to finance the completion of a particular project, so large that no one bank is willing to finance it. Examples include the construction of the natural gas pipeline from Kinsale and the building of a new power station by the ESB at Moneypoint. The security offered in project financing is the project itself, as opposed to the credit rating of the actual borrower. The lender provides funds and the long-term payoff is the completion of the project or the generation of output, for example the gas or oil.

Project finance can be assembled in a number of different ways. It may be that one organisation is responsible for the entire project, for instance when the ESB was building Moneypoint power station (though arranging subcontracts was necessary). It is now more common to see a consortium of organisations come together to take on a project such as the Custom House Docks development in Dublin. On the lending side, different financing arrangements apply depending on who takes the risk. At one end, the borrower may take no risk at all and let the lender take the risk. This is unusual but might occur if a bank buys a site, commissions a construction firm to build property and lends the money to see the project through. A second type of situation is where the borrower takes some risk until the project comes on stream. Examples would be gas pipelines or oil exploration. A third possibility is that the borrower takes the commercial risk and the lender takes the political risk, for instance lending to less developed regions. Finally, the borrower may be a Government or State agency. For example, An Bord Trachtala's (ABT) market entry scheme gives finance to small- and medium-sized organisations entering export markets. If they succeed they repay the loans at a commercial rate of interest, and if not they repay what they can and the rest is covered by a contingency fund.

The largest provider of project finance is the *World Bank*, but the merchant and commercial banks are the usual participants in Irish projects. Due to the risk associated with certain projects, the banks may seek a higher than average return and perhaps an equity participation.

8.6.8 Venture capital

Venture capital is provided by financial institutions specialising in new ventures. The home of the venture capital market is undoubtedly the USA. In Ireland venture capital has grown as a source of long-term finance since the mid 1970s. Initial investment only took place in established organisations. However, the venture capital market now includes start-up ventures. In 1985, the Irish Venture Capital Association was established and by the end of the decade it had equity shares in over 200 organisations. In Ireland venture capital is provided by Forbairt which inherited the role from the former National Development Corporation (NAD Corp) and the ICC. In the private sector a number of banking subsidiaries and organisations set up specially for the purpose exist such as ACT Venture Capital, Riada Corporate Finance and Allied Irish Investment Bank to name but a few. Venture capital is suitable as start-up finance, development capital, expansion finance, buy out finance and rescue.

There is only one specialist Irish venture capital fund — Food Venture Fund — which specialises in the food and agribusiness sectors. Venture capitalists are looking for a high rate of return due to the high risk they are taking, and, therefore, are more supportive of projects in growth markets with good export prospects. In recent years health care, food processing, financial services, the film industry and biotechnology have been good examples.

Venture capital funds are generally only interested in lending amounts of over £50,000. The investment is usually made by taking part of the equity of the organisation concerned. Ultimately, the venture capitalist seeks to realise a gain on the equity invested instead of being locked in indefinitely. Realisation can take place in a number of ways:
1. floatation on the stock exchange
2. sale of the shares back to the promoters
3. sale of the shares to another corporate investor.

8.6.9 Business Expansion Scheme
This is a particular form of venture funding but deserves separate attention because of the opportunities it offers to private investors to become involved with small, high risk ventures. The Business Expansion Scheme (BES) has been in operation since 1985 and offers individuals total relief from income tax on amounts up to £25,000 invested in any one year, in qualifying companies. With the higher rates of tax reaching 58 per cent, the net cost of investing £25,000 is only £10,500. The investment must be for a minimum of five years. Qualifying organisations can be manufacturing or service companies receiving aid from the IDA. Many of the organisations receiving funding have been in high risk areas such as electronics. In 1994, the BES scheme raised £25 million (Coonan 1995). In 1993, the Seed Capital Scheme (SCS) was introduced which is a sub set of the BES. It is designed to enable entrepreneurs to claim back tax paid for investment in new ventures.

8.6.10 Sale and leaseback
Sale and leaseback occur when an organisation sells an asset and then leases it back from the purchaser. The organisation has the benefit of a large cash inflow and the buyer gains an asset for which a lease is already created. The organisation can deduct the lease payment for tax purposes, though it could be subject to *Capital Gains Tax* if the sale price is in excess of the value agreed by the Revenue Commissioners. This option is an attractive one for many organisations with substantial assets who require cash for expansion purposes. The payments for the lease are negotiated in advance, though with long-term leases there is a provision for regular reviews. The drawback is that the organisation loses an asset and has to make regular payments for its continued use. The organisation also loses the depreciation allowance for the asset which could have been written off against tax. If the value of such an asset starts to appreciate (for example rising property values) the organisation will have lost valuable security to offer against

future borrowings. All of these consequences have to be measured against the extra amount of working capital which is created.

Sale and leaseback is advantageous where the organisation has an asset that is in short supply, such as a city centre office property. Likely investors in such an arrangement are property and pension funds. In the long term, though, the organisation using such an option has to consider the consequences of rent reviews and whether re-purchase of such an asset will be necessary in the long term. For example, what happens when the lease ends?

8.6.11 Commercial mortgage

The advantage of mortgaging rather than sale and leaseback is that the ownership option remains with the mortgagee. An organisation can borrow money on a mortgage basis from insurance companies, building societies, investment companies and pension funds. A mortgage on a business property involves the lenders advancing a cash sum which the borrower agrees to repay in instalments of the principal plus interest. The rate charged fluctuates and is usually higher than the base lending rate. The interest paid is tax deductible and, over time, inflation may diminish the cost of repayments. At one time a commercial mortgage cost more than the sale and leaseback option, however, the trend has been reversed in recent years.

Therefore, in Ireland there are eleven main sources of long-term finance for organisations. Owners capital, Government grants, venture capital and the BES are most commonly associated with start-up finance. The remaining sources can be used at any stage of an organisation's development.

8.7 IRISH AGENCIES PROVIDING STATE AID

State aid to Irish industry has developed since the 1950s when it was realised that the best way to attract technology, access to markets, management and capital was to encourage overseas companies to invest in Ireland. During the 1960s and 1970s, the range of assistance and incentives provided to overseas investors increased. The emphasis of the aid provided has changed somewhat over the years. In the late 1970s, as unemployment rose the focus turned to employment grants. In the 1980s, the focus has been on developing Irish-owned business and encouraging Irish entrepreneurs. Figure 8.5 outlines the main forms of assistance provided by State agencies which will be discussed.

Figure 8.5 Financial Assistance Provided by Irish State Agencies

Employment grants
Capital grants
Training grants
R&D grants
Feasibility grants
Rent subsidies
Corporation tax rate of 10 per cent
Loan guarantees
Leasing grants
Interest subsidies

8.7.1 The Industrial Development Authority (IDA)

The IDA was established in 1949 to promote industrial development. Its success in this regard can be gauged from the fact that in 1994 total employment in IDA-backed organisations rose to 82,600 marking a 6.8 per cent increase on the previous year. Overseas companies spent £3.3 billion in the Irish economy which represented 34 per cent of their total sales (Forfas 1995). In 1994, the IDA and Eolas (previously responsible for developing science and technology) were restructured into a new agency, Forfas. Forfas has overall responsibility for industrial development policy in Ireland. It has two subsidiaries — Forbairt, which is responsible for creating indigenous Irish industry and IDA Ireland, which is responsible for attracting overseas companies. IDA Ireland assists manufacturing, internationally traded services and financial service companies to set up facilities in Ireland (O'Kane 1993). In some cases the IDA may take an equity investment of between 5–15 per cent in the new venture.

The following is a selection of some of the many financial packages that are provided by Forfas to promote industry.

1. **Feasibility grant**: Forfas will assist and partially fund (50 per cent) a feasibility study of a manufacturing or international services venture. Examples include market research studies, negotiation with joint venture partners and costings and projections.
2. **Employment grant**: A one-off payment of £5000 is available for every job created for start-up companies employing more than fifteen people.
3. **Corporation tax**: A 10 per cent tax rate has been guaranteed until the year 2000 for all manufacturing organisations.
4. **Rent subsidies**: Rent subsidies of 45 per cent are provided for five years rental and up to 60 per cent in designated areas. Advance factories on IDA industrial estates are also available.
5. **Training grants**: These grants are jointly administered with FAS and include up to 50 per cent of the total training costs, including management development programmes.
6. **Interest subsidy**: Forfas offers grants to reduce the interest on loans raised to finance the business. Forfas will also act as a guarantor for loans required.
7. **Capital grants**: Non repayable capital grants are available for the capital cost of machinery and equipment. The normal figure is 60 per cent in designated areas and 45 per cent in non designated areas.
8. **Leasing grants**: Grants are provided for the lease of machinery up to 45 per cent in non designated areas and 60 per cent in designated areas.
9. **Product and process development grants**: Up to 50 per cent of the cost of developing or improving a product or process can be obtained.
10. **Small business programme**: This programme provides a range of employment and capital grants for small industry including 60 per cent of the costs of fixed assets in designated areas and 45 per cent in others.

Source: Forfas 1995.

In addition, Forfas also makes equity investments in organisations which receive its backing.

8.7.2 Shannon Development

Shannon Development was established in the Shannon region in the 1950s as a result of the free port status assigned to Shannon Airport. Shannon Development offers similar grants and incentives to Forfas, but concentrates on the Shannon region and has particular responsibility for developing small Irish-owned businesses. Like Forfas, Shannon Development offers non repayable capital grants, training grants, product and process development grants, employment grants (£4000 for each job created in companies with less than fifteen employees and £9000 for more than fifteen employees), interest subsidies, loan guarantees and rent reductions. Shannon Development is also starting to take up to 30 per cent equity in some organisations which have received its backing (Flynn 1994).

8.7.3 Udaras na Gaeltachta
Udaras was established in 1979 to promote the economic, social and cultural development of the Gaeltacht region. In relation to economic and industrial development, Udaras tries to promote overseas investors and indigenous industry to the Gaeltacht regions. Like Forfas it provides employment grants (ranging between £3000–£9000), capital, training and feasibility study grants along with interest and rent subsidies.

8.7.4 The Industrial Credit Corporation
The ICC was established in 1933 to provide capital for the development of Irish industry. It offers a range of services to Irish industry including special term loans for up to twenty years, underwriting services, equity investment, HP facilities, leasing facilities and finance for under-capitalised organisations.

8.7.5 Bord Failte
Bord Failte was established in 1952 to promote the tourism industry in Ireland. It seeks to develop the potential job creation from tourism, to enhance and preserve the quality of life and to develop the nation's cultural heritage. In order to promote the Irish tourist industry, Bord Failte offers grants for accommodation improvements, including providing new rooms or improving them, and for the development of supplementary holiday accommodation in the form of town and country homes. Bord Failte also offer a Hotel and Guest House Improvement Scheme which gives grants for improvements in B and C grade hotels in Donegal, Monaghan, Louth, Leitrim, Cavan and Sligo. In addition, a Tourist Amenity Scheme is provided for the same areas which offers grants to develop amenities.

8.7.6 Bord Iascaigh Mhara (BIM)
BIM was established in 1952 to promote the development of sea fisheries. In order to promote this industry, BIM offers a number of grant packages to organisations involved in the sector. The packages include capital grants for expanding and modernising production facilities ranging from 25 per cent to 50 per cent, an Aquaculture Grant Scheme of up to 50 per cent for pilot projects, a Co-operative and Small Business Development Grant Scheme which provides capital grants, a Marine Credit Plan for the purchase of boats and Mariculture Training Education Grants.

8.7.7 FAS
FAS was established in 1988 to co-ordinate the activities of the former AnCo, the Youth Employment Agency and the National Manpower Service. It has responsibility for

training and job placement. FAS provides company-based training, apprentice training, management and supervisory training and a range of employment programmes for school leavers. The FAS Training Support Scheme helps companies to improve existing skills and provides training grants of up to 65 per cent for organisations employing less than fifty people and 25 per cent for those employing between 201 and 500 people. Under the Levy Grant Scheme a company is levied 1–1.5 per cent of payroll costs. The company is then entitled to 80–90 per cent of the amount levied in the form of a Training Activity Grant. Apprenticeship Grants provide £59 per week for attendance at approved courses. An Employment Incentive Scheme offers grants for companies that employ people who were previously unemployed.

8.7.8 An Bord Trachtala (ABT)

ABT (formerly Coras Trachtala) was established in 1959 and provides a range of support and advisory services and grant aid to exporters. ABT offers grants for overseas advertising, participation in trade fairs and exhibitions, costs associated with designers to upgrade products, to assist foreign buyers to come to Ireland and overseas market research projects. For example, the Financial Incentive Scheme provides up to £5000 a year to help companies achieve marketing initiatives overseas. The Sales Performance Incentive Scheme allows ABT to share the financial risk with companies involved in overseas marketing investment.

8.7.9 County Enterprise Boards

In the period 1993–1994, County Enterprise Boards were established to promote local initiatives. Such boards give local areas the power to obtain local funding for new and existing initiatives. Thirty-five boards have been established and are supported by local authorities. The County Enterprise Boards are intended to assume responsibility for business areas not covered by the existing State bodies. The main area of responsibility for the County Enterprise Boards is the development of new and existing small businesses in the local areas. To facilitate such a development, capital grants of up to 50 per cent and feasibility grants of up to 75 per cent are offered.

These are the main State agencies that offer industry grants and financial aid to further develop and promote their activities. European funds are also available for numerous programmes as well as the International Fund for Ireland and the Leader Programme.

8.8 INVESTMENT MANAGEMENT

Every business has to manage its current assets in order to maximise the return, a process generally known as investment management. This section covers the management of *working capital*, inventory, cash and debtors. These are the broad headings under which day to day and long-term financial decisions are taken.

8.8.1 Working capital

In simple terms, working capital can be defined as the excess of current assets over *current liabilities*. This excess represents net current assets, which are a measure of the liquidity of the organisation or, in other words, the ability of the organisation to meet its current obligations. Two common ratios are referred to frequently in the context of liquidity, namely the current ratio and the acid test ratio. (The use of these ratios as a control technique was discussed in Chapter 7 and is summarised at this point. For a more indepth discussion the reader is referred to section 7.7.3.)

$$\text{(A) The current ratio} \quad = \quad \frac{\text{Current assets}}{\text{Current liabilities}}$$

$$\text{(B) The acid test ratio} \quad = \quad \frac{\text{Quick assets}}{\text{Current liabilities}}$$

Quick assets can be defined as current assets minus inventories, since inventory is held to be an asset that will rarely be sold for its book value. There is also the risk that inventory will deteriorate or become obsolete. The general norm for the current ratio is 2:1, though careful management of stock and creditors can reduce it to levels which are still acceptable. More stringent control of receivables also pushes down the acid test ratio.

Every organisation balances on a knife edge in trying to have enough working capital available to meet day to day needs without tying up assets that could be committed to long-term investments. Regarding the liquidity ratios, there are no levels which are considered to be universally correct, and judgement is made by each business according to its objectives and by its creditors. In general, the lower the ratios the more pressure is imposed by creditors, and the organisation will experience more difficulty in maintaining a good credit rating. Ratios which are too high mean that too much cash is tied up in working capital and could indicate that the organisation should make more use of its borrowing capacity. Tying up current assets in a high level of working capital makes an organisation liable to a take-over from another organisation looking for a cash-rich purchase. Working capital could be reduced by lowering the investment in inventory, calling in debts faster and leaving minimal cash balances.

Interpretation of liquidity ratios in individual cases deserves caution. While the ratios may look poor, the organisation may be holding off from borrowing or stock-piling inventories for a particular reason. Also, conditions change, so analysts charting progress over time always look at the number of days which would be needed to pay off current debt, using the following formula which provides a much better indicator of current liquidity:

$$\text{Current assets} \quad - \quad \text{Quick liabilities} \quad \times \quad 365 \quad = \quad \text{Revenues for one year}$$

8.8.2 Inventory

Control of inventory tries to reconcile two objectives, namely to have sufficient inventory to fill orders and to hold a minimum amount of inventory. The financial manager has to balance the cost of investing in inventory against the risk involved in carrying none at all. The level of risk varies according to the nature of the industry and the goods and services provided. The theoretical optimum level of stock has already been discussed in section 7.8.3 of Chapter 7 and at this point the financial costs of holding stock and the problems associated with insufficient levels of stock are considered. The costs of holding inventory include the following:

1. **Lost interest**: If the finance used to buy stock was invested elsewhere it could earn interest.

2. **Storage costs**: Storing inventory gives rise to costs including warehousing, transport, handling and security.
3. **Insurance costs**: If an organisation invests in substantial inventories these have to be insured against the risk of damage or loss.
4. **Obsolescence**: Some stocks go out of style or out of date. The residual value of such inventory is virtually zero.

On the opposite side there are certain risks in having no inventory:
1. **Production difficulties**: Low levels of inventories cause problems for production of goods and services due to unavailability of raw materials. The *just-in-time (JIT)* inventory system breaks down when any supplier fails to deliver. The risk depends on the stage of the production involved. It may be that the material is a critical input to the process, or that it is a part which can be added on at the end. This disruption has financial implications in terms of the cost of overtime and loss of revenue from delayed orders.
2. **Loss of goodwill**: Customers may not necessarily tolerate a delayed order and in this situation may seek other more reliable vendors.
3. **Loss of flexibility**: An organisation holding no stocks is leaving a very short lead time between receipt of an order and the ordering of stock. This policy means piecemeal purchasing, loss of quantity discounts and more demanding relationships with suppliers. If a really large order comes in the organisation might have to reject it if it cannot assemble the stocks required. If a customer wants to bring the delivery date closer the organisation will also find this difficult to do.
4. **Re-order costs**: Small, frequent orders cost far more than periodic orders of sizeable quantity. All the costs already mentioned are magnified in a zero stock situation. Another expense is the regular passing and payment of invoices for small amounts.

8.8.3 Cash

Every organisation has to try to balance the need to hold a certain amount of cash against the investments to which that cash could be committed with a greater return. In a sense cash is dead money, as it does not earn any interest and, therefore, should be kept to minimal amounts. Against that the organisation needs a certain amount of liquid assets to take advantage of opportunities for discounts and purchases. There is no formula for deciding the ideal cash balance, each manager must make judgements based on available information. Cash is required for three reasons:
1. **Transactions**: Cash is needed to purchase materials and equipment and to pay wages.
2. **Safety**: A reserve of cash is a useful contingency fund.
3. **Speculation**: Opportunities for speculative gains can be financed from cash holdings.

The key to forecasting the right amount of cash to hold is to draw up a cash budget detailing the sources and uses of cash. If done on a monthly basis this offers a guideline as to how shortfalls and excesses of cash can be managed. Figure 8.6 provides an example of a small organisation which has only been in business for three months.

'StartUp PLC' has the usual problems associated with a new business. Collections from sales are low at this stage while the organisation is burdened with running expenses and repayments. Management could consider the following options in meeting the cash shortfall of £1000: bank overdraft; prompt collection from debtors; lengthening the time taken to pay creditors; and postponing some material or equipment purchases.

Figure 8.6 Cash Budget for StartUp PLC, Month 3

Cash sources	£ IR
Collections from debtors	5,000
Equipment grant	1,000
Total Sources:	6,000
Cash uses	
Materials	2,000
Wages	1,000
Creditors	900
Equipment	2,000
Loan repayment	1,000
Overheads	100
Total uses	**7,000**
Total sources	**6,000**
Cash shortfall	**1,000**

Realistically, the first option is the only feasible one for a small organisation trying to become established. The overdraft might have a ceiling of £2,000 to provide a cushion against unforeseen events. When developing its forecasts, StartUp PLC would be well advised to budget for a number of alternatives so that it will not be unprepared. A computer can be used to generate the answers to all the 'what if' questions that need to be asked.

Once an organisation has been in business for some time it needs to look at ways of improving its cash management procedures. Two alternatives already mentioned are to speed up receivables and stretch payables as far as it is acceptable. An organisation might try to reduce the size of its float, that is the money which is being transferred (but not yet received) as accounts receivable. If a buyer in Donegal posts a payment to a Dublin company today it could be six to seven days before payment is received (up to three days in the post and then a further three days for the cheque to be cleared by the bank). More efficient transfer methods are to use local banks, credit transfers and electronic funds transfers. Deposits could also be made daily rather than weekly.

If a business finds it has a surplus of cash it might use short-term investments to improve the situation. The investment type will depend on the amount available, the time horizon and the degree of liquidity sought. In Ireland the most common short-term investments are:

1. **Exchequer bonds**: These are issued by the Government with a life-span of ninety days. They can be re-sold before the due date if required.
2. **Commercial paper**: These are commercial IOUs (I Owe Unto) issued by larger organisations which can be resold in the money markets.
3. **Government lending**: This is done by purchasing stock with a fixed interest rate loan that can be liquidated easily.
4. **Short-term bank deposits**: A fixed rate is negotiated for these deposits before investment.

8.8.4 Debtors

At any time, a significant proportion of total assets are tied up in accounts receivable, and so the financial manager or entrepreneur must know how to manage this asset effectively. In Ireland there is a long-standing tradition of taking sixty or ninety days to pay, and, quite frequently, the biggest customers cause the longest delays. Another Irish problem is that there are fewer sources of reliable credit information when compared to other countries, making it difficult to ascertain who are the most creditworthy customers. An Irish attitude exists whereby most people are unwilling to give unfavourable reports about someone's credit worthiness, fearing that it reflects badly upon themselves and that the report could cause legal action. In other countries there is a greater desire to keep credit records up to date for everyone's benefit.

In considering the problem of debtors' management an organisation must answer four main questions:

1. What information is available on the potential credit buyer?
2. What terms of sale should be offered?
3. What is the organisation's policy on the collection of outstanding debts?
4. Should the organisation take out credit insurance?

In Ireland credit information is available through a number of sources outlined in Figure 8.7.

Figure 8.7 Sources of Credit Information in Ireland

1. Credit agencies such as Dun and Bradstreet and the Irish Trade Protection Agency give a credit rating to every registered company.
2. Bankers will give a reference or opinion based on their experience.
3. Other published sources such as the Companies Office, business journals and trade journals provide credit information.
4. Salespeople can offer opinions based on personal experience.
5. Other creditors may provide information about the payments record of a particular customer. In many sectors of industry there is a blacklist of creditors compiled from credit agencies (for example *Stubbs Gazette*) and bank references.

Having established that a customer is creditworthy the terms of sale can be agreed. The terms are normally common to the industry but the most frequently used terms are thirty days. For example, cash discounts could be offered for payment within ten days and these discounts are usually up to 3 per cent. When considering a discount the selling organisation must evaluate the cost to the organisation as well as the attraction of the discount for the buyer. A discount makes it more difficult to process invoices. Some organisations have found that all their customers took advantage of the discount whether or not they paid early. This has led to cash discounts being replaced by quantity discounts which are easier to operate.

In cases where a customer fails to pay within the agreed thirty days the organisation can take a number of steps to recover the debt. The first step is to send one or several reminders followed by telephone calls and personal visits. Alternatively, the debts could be handed over to a factor or debt collection agency. It is important to call these agencies in time as older debts are much harder to collect. If letters and reminders do not work, a solicitor's letter threatening legal action might have some effect. Most organisations never resort to court action unless the debt is substantial because of the legal costs involved.

At each stage in the process the cost of pursuing debtors has to be balanced against the potential revenue. Smaller organisations with a number of small debtors find it harder to collect outstanding accounts. Organisations typically find that, on average, 5 per cent of total sales result in bad debts. Consequently, when establishing prices organisations should take this factor into account. To encourage customers to pay, interest could be charged on accounts overdue. This is common in Europe but is rare in Ireland, except in the case of late payments to the Revenue Commissioners.

Credit insurance can be used as a safety net against the threat of non payment. An organisation can choose to insure all of its debts for a charge based on a percentage of turnover. Alternatively, a particular credit account could be insured against at a premium rate.

8.9 SUMMARY OF KEY PROPOSITIONS

• The appropriate use of finance is an important contributor to an organisation's success or failure. Financial managment tries to achieve organisational objectives through the provision of finance and investment in opportunities open to the business. Financial management concentrates on providing finance when needed and choosing suitable investments.

• Every source of finance can affect the organisation in three ways. Firstly there is a risk affect in that the organisation might not be able to repay the money. Secondly, there is an income affect in that there will be a positive inflow of money. Thirdly, there is a control affect in that new sources of finance can affect the management structure of the organisation.

• The short-term sources of finance available to Irish organisations are: trade credit; accrued expenses; deferred taxation; bank overdraft; Bills of Exchange and Acceptance Credit; inventory financing; and factoring. The first three are spontaneous as they arise through the normal course of business. The last four are negotiated sources.

• There are three main sources of medium-term finance available to Irish organisations. Leasing and HP both allow the organisation to use the asset without large capital outlay or scarce resources being used. The costs associated with both sources of finance are also tax deductible. Term loans are given by banks for a fixed term usually for investment in fixed assets.

• There are eleven main sources of long-term finance available in Ireland: owners capital; retained profits; commercial, merchant and Government banks; Government grants; stock exchange; debentures; project finance; venture capital; BES; sale and leaseback; and commercial mortgage.

• State aid is also given to assist and promote industrial development. Assistance provided includes employment grants, training grants, cash grants for fixed assets, a 10 per cent corporation tax, rent subsidies, advance factories, loan guarantees and R&D grants.

• Investment management involves managing current assets to ensure a maximum return. It involves four main areas: working capital, inventory, cash and debtors.

DISCUSSION QUESTIONS

1. What is financial managment? Why is it important for an organisation to consider?
2. Explain the three potential effects that sources of finance can have on the organisation.
3. Explain four of the short-term sources of finance that are available to organisations.
4. Explain with examples the differences between a merchant bank and an associated bank.
5. What is the key objective in raising short-term finance?
6. Explain how leasing is a source of medium-term finance.
7. What are the advantages and disadvantages associated with term loans and hire purchase?
8. Critically evaluate the stock exchange as a source of long-term finance.
9. How do venture capital and the BES scheme contribute to the financing of Irish industry?
10. Examine the advantages and disadvantages of holding inventory.
11. What steps should an organisation take to make sure that it keeps the amount owed by debtors to a minimum?
12. A potential overseas investor has approached you about establishing a facility in Ireland. Explain the grants and incentives available.

REFERENCES

'Business With a Bite' *Business and Finance*, 28–29, 1 December 1994.

'The IDA's Achievement' *Business and Finance*, 22 December 1994.

Coonan, C., 'BES Heads for £300 million' *Business and Finance*, 5 January 1995.

Dunne, M., 'The Year of the Deal' *Business and Finance*, 40–41, 15 December 1994.

Flynn, G., 'Shannon to Take up to 30% Equity Stakes' *Business and Finance*, 15 December 1994.

'Documents Outlining Grants and Financial Aid Available' IDA, Dublin 1994.

Kennedy, T., MacCormac, M. and Teeling, J., *Financial Management*, Gill & Macmillan, Dublin 1988.

McLaney, E., *Business Finance, Theory and Practice*, Pitman Publishing, London 1986.

O'Toole, A., *The Pace Setters*, Gill & Macmillan, Dublin 1987.

'Dublin Closing Prices' *Sunday Tribune Business Section*, 31 May 1995.

Teeling, J. and Lynch, A., *Modern Irish Business*, ETA Publications, Dublin 1985.

9

Production Management

9.1 INTRODUCTION

Today's environment is uncertain, dynamic and complex. Economic circumstances change, technology advances, markets evolve and competitors respond. The organisation that does not respond will almost surely decline. The dynamism of the 1980s symbolised a new stark reality for manufacturing — the impact of industrial competition, yet, for the most part, according to Hill (1993), production decision making in manufacturing industry has not changed dramatically to meet this new challenge. *Production management* refers to the transformation of material resource inputs into outputs of goods and services. The title 'production management' implies that the process is confined to physical products, but production management principles are being widely applied in the service sector where the problems of producing an output are similar. In this case, though, the output is less tangible. The main purpose is to identify the range and complexity of activities and the combinations of concepts, techniques and knowledge that are necessary to direct and organise productive efforts (Pettinger 1994). It is, however, normally associated with manufacturing.

Figure 9.1 The Production Process

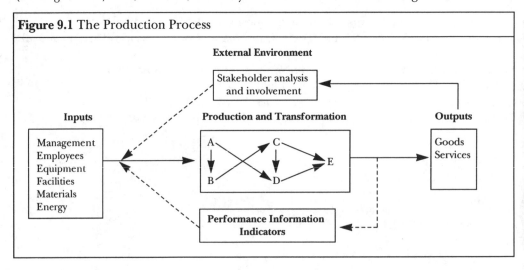

This chapter begins by looking briefly at the productivity changes that have occurred in Irish manufacturing industry in recent years. Production and technological advancements that have impacted upon the production process are discussed. Just-in-time manufacturing as an approach to production and the notion of quality management are considered. Aspects of innovation and creativity are examined and the regulatory framework for health and safety management is presented.

9.2 THE PERFORMANCE OF IRISH MANUFACTURING

Manufacturing industry in Ireland falls into two broad categories; newer, largely foreign-owned, highly export-oriented firms; and traditional, smaller Irish-owned firms in older sectors supplying the domestic market (EIU 1995).

Between 1953 and 1989, the volume of goods produced by the manufacturing sector increased by a factor of 7.03, a large increase even allowing for the relatively low volume of output in the immediate post war era (Turner and Morley 1995). More impressively, net output, or value, added after fixed costs are deducted, increased by almost a factor of ten at constant prices. However, overall employment in manufacturing only increased by 30 per cent. As we would expect, the pattern of change over this period (1953–1989) varies considerably.

Table 9.1 Changes in Net Output, Employment and Assets in the Manufacturing Sector, 1953–1989

	NET OUTPUT		EMPLOYMENT		NET OUTPUT PER WORKER	ASSETS ADDED
	% increase in decade (000)	% yearly increase	% increase in decade	% yearly increase	% increase in decade	% yearly increase £(000)
1953–1960	27 % (23,216)	3.4 %	5.4 %	0.7 %	20.6 % (123)	2.6 % 63,070
1960–1970	121 % (131,853)	12.1%	31 %	3.1 %	69.0 % (497)	6.9 % 236,425
1970–1980	89 % (213,546)	8.9%	13.7 %	1.4 %	66.1 % (804)	6.6 % 532,955
1980–1989	86 % (390,571)	8.6%	-15.5 %	-1.7 %	120.0 % (2429)	12.0 % 584,147

Source: Turner, T. and Morley, M., *Industrial Relations and the New Order: Case Studies in Conflict and Co-Operation*, Department of Enterprise and Employment, Dublin 1995.

After the stagnation of the 1950s, net output rose rapidly in the three succeeding decades. Although the yearly rate of increase was highest in the 1960s, the actual increase in net output added in constant prices in the 1980s was three times that added in the 1960s. Despite the less buoyant economic climate in the 1980s, the average yearly rate of increase in net output was maintained at similar levels to the previous decade. During the same decade, employment in manufacturing fell by 15.5 per cent, or an average yearly decline of 1.7 per cent. It was only during the 1960s that employment increased at a relatively high yearly average of 3.1 per cent. The period between 1970 and 1989, when net output rose fastest in real terms, had an overall net decrease in employment of 3.9 per cent. The higher net output of this period is mainly a result of increased investment in capital assets which increased the productivity of labour.

However, the phenomenon of transfer pricing associated with foreign multinationals may have exaggerated net output. In 1974, foreign industry accounted for 25 per cent of gross output, by 1985 this had grown to 50.2 per cent (Foley 1991). The aggregate assets added each year more than doubled (2.7 times) in the 1960s, increased again by a factor of 1.25 in the 1970s (See Table 9.1), and remained constant in the following decade. (See Turner et al 1995.)

Table 9.2 Employment in Manufacturing Industry by Ownership, 1992

	Employees in Irish-owned firms		Employees in foreign-owned firms		Total
	No	%	No	%	No
Food	26,924	25.9	7,826	8.7	34,750
Electronics and engineering	24, 060	23.1	39,951	44.5	64,011
Paper and printing	11,422	11.0	1,848	2.1	13,270
Timber and furniture	7,704	7.4	437	0.5	8,141
Clothing, footwear	7,559	7.3	3,693	4.1	11,252
Grant-aided services	5,053	4.9	6,926	7.7	11,979
Non-metallic minerals	6,749	6.5	1,878	2.1	8,627
Health-care, chemicals	3,246	3.1	12,083	13.5	15,329
Textiles	2,737	2.6	6,399	7.1	9,136
Drink and tobacco	1,857	1.8	4,380	4.9	6,237
Miscellaneous industries	6,829	6.6	4,278	4.8	11,107
Total	**104,140**	**100.00**	**89,699**	**100.00**	**193,839**

Source: Gill 1995.

Table 9.3 Indices of Production in Major Industrial Groups (1985 = 100)

	1987	1988	1989	1990	1991	1992
Non-metallic mineral products	92.9	94.0	111.1	116.5	109.5	113.8
Chemicals	104.0	120.7	144.8	149.0	181.5	212.9
Metals and engineering	126.0	153.7	178.1	189.8	185.1	205.7
Food	117.4	123.5	126.2	130.9	136.0	149.1
Drink and tobacco	100.1	105.5	116.8	117.2	122.9	122.4
Textiles	102.1	106.3	111.1	119.1	119.0	125.5
Clothing, footwear and leather	98.6	91.7	87. 0	87.9	77.2	73.6
Timber and wooden furniture	96.3	105.8	111.1	117.5	117.5	120.4
Paper and printing	116.8	127.7	137.4	139.4	151.1	165.1
Miscellaneous industries	110.3	113.2	120.6	129.2	127.5	133.1
Total manufacturing industries	**113.6**	**127.6**	**142.5**	**149.2**	**154.3**	**169.6**

Source: EIU 1995.

The fastest-growing sectors of Irish manufacturing industry over recent years have been chemicals and metals and engineering — predominantly foreign-owned — while most of the other sectors have declined somewhat, particularly clothing, footwear and leather.

Overall, the 1980s was a decade of significant change in Irish manufacturing. There was an enormous leap in productivity per worker and, at the same time, considerable reductions in the numbers employed in manufacturing. The average size of foreign firms declined from 106.4 employees in 1978 to 90.9 in 1988, and from 32.2 to 17.5 in Irish firms (Ruane and McGibney 1991). The majority of firms shed employees during this decade. Increasing international competition, company down sizing and the introduction of new forms of technology generated a need for greater flexibility in production operations, which often demanded new skills or the amalgamation of old skills in new combinations.

9.3 PRODUCTION PLANNING AND CONTROL

In the production area, planning and control systems are intertwined because the outputs of the planning system are the inputs of the control system, and vice-versa. It is therefore appropriate to consider the two elements together.

The planning element of production can be considered at two levels: strategic and tactical. Strategic production planning is concerned with long-term decisions, for example, what to produce and what plant capacity to choose. In the short term, tactical production planning concerns itself with operational problems, for example, how to schedule production and what size inventory to hold. Table 9.4 shows what production planning decisions have to be taken at the strategic and the tactical levels.

Table 9.4 Time-scale for Production Planning Decisions		
	Time horizon	**Decision**
Strategic	Long term (2 years +)	Introduction of new products Number and location of facilities Type of technology to be used
	Medium term (1 - 2 years)	Relative mix of products Changes in capacity
Tactical	Medium term (1 year)	Size of workforce Subcontracting Overtime working Stockholding policy
	Short term (3 months)	Production schedule Output targets

Source: Mapes, J. and New, C. C., 'Planning for Production' in Lock, D. and Farrow, N., *The Gower Handbook of Management*, Gower Press, Hampshire 1992.

The objective of a *production planning and control system* (PPC) is to ensure that the correct quantity of the product is manufactured at the right time, at the right quality, and at the most acceptable cost (see also Chapter 7, page 155). Production planning and control are required in any type of manufacturing situation, whether it be a continuous flow system (typical of the beer industry), or a batch system (for example, a bakery).

The production planning and control process is shown in Figure 9.2.

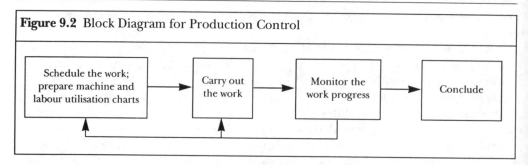

Figure 9.2 Block Diagram for Production Control

The planning element is crucial if the following problems are to be avoided:
1. material shortages
2. machinery breakdowns
3. delays in producing orders
4. shortages of manpower
5. high rejection rates
6. inadequate stock control.

Production control then involves identifying whatever problems have arisen under the headings above, and proposing solutions to them. The four main elements involved in the process are outlined below.

1. **Loading and scheduling**: Loading involves assigning the work to fill the available capacity. Scheduling is the determination of the actual tasks needed to complete the job, and the sequence in which they must operate. When an order is received, the production manager needs the following information to prepare a schedule for completion:
   i. the required quantity and quality
   ii. the due delivery date
   iii. the product specification
   iv. details of parts, components and special tools required.

Figure 9.3 Gantt Chart Schedule for a Small Workshop

Job No.	Monday	Tuesday	Wednesday	Thursday	Friday	Note
107						
108						
109						* requires
110						special jig
111						
112						
113*						
114						

When the Bill of Materials and the labour input have been clarified, a production scheduler then places the activities in the necessary sequence. The third step in the sequence is routing the job from section to section. Figure 9.3 shows a Gantt chart representing the work of an engineering workshop during one week. (For more details on Gantt charts see Chapter 2, page 19 and Chapter 7, page 150.) In this case, two jobs (107 and 108) have been carried over from the previous week, and two jobs (113 and 114) will be carried forward into the following week.

Loading then involves deciding what percentage of capacity will be utilised and what machines will be used. Firms do not rely on 100 per cent capacity utilisation, except for very short periods.

2. **Provisioning materials and parts**: Provisioning involves making sure that the right inputs are available at the right time and in the right place to enable the final product to be produced.

The first decision in securing supplies is whether to make or to buy them. A decision to make them may be taken if suppliers are unreliable or difficult to find, if the input is a crucial one, if sufficiently large quantities are demanded, and if the cost of manufacture is economic.

A second issue is what quantities to order. To reduce stockholding costs, many firms are changing over to a just-in-time production system which is discussed later in this chapter. This places the onus on suppliers to hold stocks until one week or even one day before they are required. It involves a search for reliable suppliers and the establishment of close relationships which will enable the system to work.

Once all the materials and parts are in-house, the final aspect of the provisioning task is making up kits of the items necessary to complete a job. A production planner may issue requisitions in advance to check if all required materials are available. A more modern version of the task is to use the computer to do the kitting.

3. **Monitoring and expediting work**: Up-to-date information must be available to allow effective monitoring to take place. This information can be collected by using job cards or tickets to update the master schedule, or the same data can be entered into computer terminals.

Monitoring should be related to the 'management by exception' principle, paying attention to jobs that are running late, or problems arising in the process of manufacturing. Progress meetings are often used to clarify the status and problems of each job. Specialists, known as expeditors, may be employed to chase key orders through the factory and ensure they get production priority. Some of this activity can be self-defeating if it means that non-priority jobs fall behind schedule, and thus become urgent jobs in their turn. The solution is to have an upper limit on the number of jobs that can be treated as urgent. If this does not work, investment in extra capacity should be considered.

4. **Production management information**: Much of the information gathered in the production department is relevant to the management task. The main types of information sought are: orders received and processed, total factory production, rate of breakdown, delivery lead times, spoilage rate, stocks of materials, work in progress and finished goods. This information must be presented in an up-to-date summary form to higher management. It should plot trends over time, so that the reader will

be able to compare figures with previous periods and learn if the situation is better, worse or the same.

Typical forms required to collect this information are requisitions, job orders, progress cards and store receipts. These can be completed manually or printed out by the computer.

9.4 PRODUCTION TYPES AND CATEGORIES

The production process is concerned with the conversion of raw materials into finished products. Production can be one of three types: job production, batch production or continuous flow production.

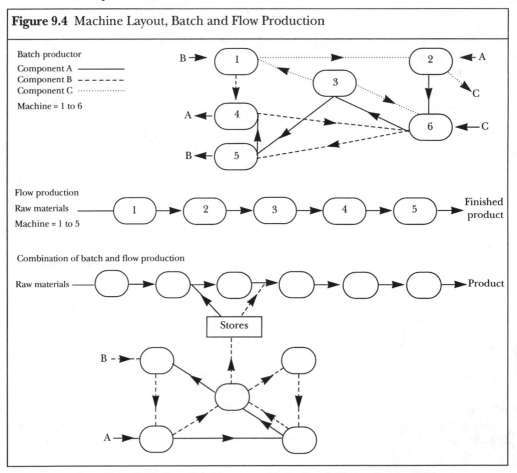

Figure 9.4 Machine Layout, Batch and Flow Production

Source: Betts, P. W., *Supervisory Management* (sixth edition), Pitman, London 1993.

Job production relates to the production of one-off type products such as a house. Usually completed under contract, there is little scope for standardisation as the production should occur to the customer's precise needs. *Batch production* refers to the manufacturing of a range of products on the basis of a predetermined run or quantity that does not justify continuous flow. A batch is defined as 'being a quantity large enough to require a measure of technology and investment and capital output and yet small enough to have its own distinctive identity' (Pettinger 1994). This mode is also used where a product's specifications are periodically altered. Thus, batch production is, essentially, an attempt to combine standardisation with the need to meet customer requirements in a cost effective way. To produce an economic batch size, the amount is often increased above the demand level with the surplus being placed in stock. *Continuous flow production* is the production of commodities in a continuous flow. Each piece of work is manufactured in a strict standardised operational sequence. It is appropriate for standardised homogenous products. Because of the capital intensive nature of flow production, to be viable the plant and equipment must be utilised all the time. Heavy losses quickly accumulate when the plant is not operational.

9.5 PLANT LAYOUT

This refers to the physical arrangement of production facilities: machines, stores, handling equipment, receiving and despatch areas, and circulation areas. Eventually, every manufacturer finds his/her process is more suited to a certain layout. Planning a layout only begins after decisions have been made about:
1. the product(s)
2. what inputs to make or buy
3. what production process is to be used
4. what materials handling methods to use
5. forecast demand levels.
   Four main types of layout can be distinguished:

1. **Fixed position layout**: The product being made remains in a fixed position while manufacturing operations are completed. Such a situation arises when a product is bulky or delicate, for example, shipbuilding, or aircraft engine overhaul. Materials and labour must be transported to the product.
2. **Process layout**: Similar process capabilities are placed close together. Each order follows its own path through the various processes. Such a layout is used in batch production, where the volume is not sufficient to have a special process for each product being made. Instead, the batches are put through processes which have some common and some customised elements. Figure 9.5 illustrates this.
3. **Product layout**: In a mass production situation an assembly line is dedicated to a particular product. Each item on the line goes through the same routine of production operations, so the flow of materials through production dictates the layout of machines. Throughput will then determine the exact form each operation takes. For example, a high throughput makes more severe demands on machinery and manpower. Therefore, the layout of a plant producing 9,000 cars per week is very different to one turning out 900. Where the plants differ is not so much in the manpower area, but in the type of machinery and work standards demanded.
4. **Group technology:** This represents an effort to gain some of the advantages of line production in a batch situation. Group technology starts by trying to find similarities of feature and design between batches. Larger batches can then be built up with assemblies or parts in common. The outcome is that large batches are used at as many stages of production as possible, and this is a criterion to bear in mind in the order/processing delivery cycle.

197

Group technology flow lines are really batch flow lines. Each operation can be performed in a cell, with conveyors or forklift trucks moving products from one cell to the next.

The operation is best suited to a firm with a stable product mix, where demand forecasts are reasonably reliable. It requires a significant investment, because even if all that is involved is a redesign of the layout of existing machines, links between cells must be arranged properly. The main gains in using group technology are higher productivity, shorter set-up times, lower inspection costs, and shorter lead times.

Figure 9.5 Example of a Process Layout

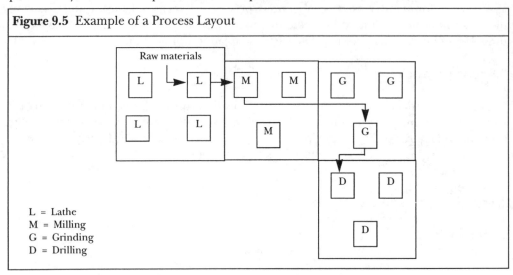

L = Lathe
M = Milling
G = Grinding
D = Drilling

Source: Foley, E., *Irish Business Management,* Gill & Macmillan, Dublin 1989.

9.6 TECHNOLOGICAL ADVANCEMENTS AND AUTOMATION

As mature markets demand greater product diversification and new products, and as competitive rivalry intensifies, increasingly organisations face the need to employ more advanced technologies. Broadly conceived, technology can be seen as a set of processes and systems used by organisations to convert resources into products or services. Technology is a central source of competitive advantage provided organisations take advantage of the newest, most efficient ways of operating. Technological development in manufacturing centres around three key areas: automation, computer integration and robotics. Automation can be defined as a process of designing work so that it can be performed completely or almost completely by machines. In this respect, automation relies on feedback, information sensors and strong control mechanisms. Feedback relates to the flow of information from the machine to the sensor while the sensor gathers information and compares it with predetermined standards.

The whole automation process has been considerably extended in recent years through the use of computers in manufacturing. It is possible to identify at least four variations. Computer aided design (CAD) relates to the use of computer technology in the design of parts and products, and also in the stipulation of performance so that prototypes need not necessarily be constructed. Computer aided manufacturing (CAM) refers to the use of computers to plan and control manufacturing processes. Computer integrated manufacturing (CIM) is the integration of CAD and CAM. The computer that controls production shares the design computer's information and is able to have machines with the exact settings ready when production is needed. Thus, all design, testing and manufacturing activities are computer controlled.

A flexible manufacturing system (FMS) consists of a collection of computer-controlled machine tools and transport systems. Here, robotic work units, work stations, robotic carts or some other form of computer-controlled transportation system work in synchronisation. Most flexible manufacturing systems rely on robots for the completion of routine production. A robot is defined as any artificial device that has the ability to perform functions indirectly on behalf of human beings. Robotics refers to the science and technology of the construction, maintenance and use of robots. The use of robots in manufacturing has increased steadily in recent years and is expected to continue as more and more organisations recognise the benefits. Among the key advantages are a reduction in headcount, a reduction in spans of control, decreased human resource development and training costs and a possible reduction in work-in-progress inventories. However, there are possible disadvantages, too. Automation of this kind is expensive and it raises a comapny's break even. The organisation which converts to any of these systems requires fundamental structural and workforce changes, which often leads to large-scale resistance. Furthermore, robotic technology can be inflexible as it is designed and programmed for the completion of a specific set of tasks. Any significant changes in tasks or assembly procedures may require the robot to be completely reprogrammed or perhaps even replaced.

9.7 JUST-IN-TIME MANUFACTURING

Just-in-time manufacturing refers to a sophisticated production control system. Originating in Japan, its main purpose is to ensure that goods are available precisely as their input is required, whether they are parts, sub-assemblies or complete products. JIT is based on three key principles: waste elimination, total quality control and employee involvement. With respect to waste, in a JIT environment any non value added is viewed as waste. Such activities are costly to the company and do not contribute to the increase of value of a product. One of the key ways to eliminate such waste is to eliminate defects, work in progress and over-production requiring stock space. With respect to quality control, the aim is not simply to detect defects but to prevent them occurring by tracing any problems back to their source. The emphasis within the manufacturing area is on statistical process control and in-process costing, rather than inspection after processing. This ensures that processes can satisfy actual specifications. In relation to employee involvement in the process, management seek to provide leadership which results in employees wanting to be involved. There must be clear opportunities for cross functional teamwork, education and human resource development.

JIT uses two key tools for levelling production: KANBAN and 'pull manufacture'. KANBAN systems are statistical techniques which form an integral part of JIT and are used to reduce the amount of in-process inventory to the minimum level needed to prevent any break in the production process. In relation to 'pull manufacturing', the linkage of machines, the development of KANBAN inventory control systems and the quest for uniform plant load produce mechanisms for converting from a traditional form of push manufacturing. Where the push system was concerned with maintaining large stocks, pull manufacturing is dedicated to just-in-time. Push manufacturing is closely linked with KANBAN because it serves as a signalling device for up stream suppliers.

Figure 9.6 JIT Cycle of Success

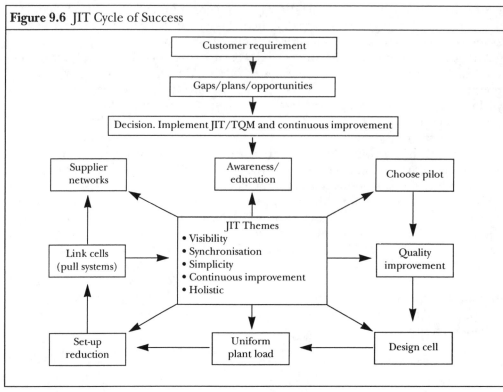

Source: Adapted from Stasey, R. and McNall, C., *Crossroads: A JIT Success Storey*, H. Irwin, Homewood 1990.

Exhibit 9.1 Microsoft Ireland

Turnaround: the Road to World Class Manufacturing, 1988-90

In 1988, Brian Reynolds, the general manager of Microsoft Ireland, attended a conference where the keynote contributor was Richard Schonberger. With top-selling management books such as *Japanese Manufacturing Techniques: Nine Hidden Lessons in Simplicity, World Class Manufacturing and Building a Chain of Customers*, Schonberger had espoused the need to reform the traditional practices of western mass production and introduce the leaner customer-driven manufacturing operations that had been a major feature of Japan's emergence as a major economic power. Emphasising the contribution of just-in-time

(JIT) techniques, total quality management (TQM) strategies and employee involvement (EI), he was acknowledged as being one of the most influential proponents of the argument that western industry urgently needed to confront the issues of simplifying manufacturing, managing the supply chain and ensuring that operations should be customer-driven.

Reynolds was impressed with what he heard. Confronted with problems of working capital tied up in inventory, quality and product availability, he decided to apply the approaches suggested by Schonberger in his plant. He commissioned a consultancy study which highlighted that on average, Microsoft's process leadtime was 151 days — 60 days in raw material, one day in work-

in-progress and 90 days in finished goods. On the other hand the product received value for only four minutes (the time it took the package to be assembled on the line) during a normal production run. Faced with a value-added to non value-added ratio of four minutes:151 days, his response was immediate. He transferred his materials manager to the role of project manager with responsibility for implementing world class manufacturing on the factory floor. Emphasising throughput, a policy was taken to manufacture smaller lots more frequently. The objective was to receive supplies daily and build (assemble) daily. The company identified the four following critical dimensions in the implementation process.

Supplier Reduction

The company's supplier base included indigenous printing companies (manuals), packaging manufacturers, disk manufacturers and freight forwarders. Microsoft decided to initiate a process of selecting strategic partners. In return for providing their suppliers with a long term commitment, standardisation of product design and rolling sales forecasts, Microsoft received assurances with regard to mutual cost reduction and daily deliveries. These commitments were not based on legally binding contractual agreements but rather on the basis of 'gentlemen's agreements' coupled with quarterly reviews. The result of cutting its supplier base by 70% led to a significant reduction in transaction and communication costs. In addition, the enhancement of supplier capability that resulted from the financial stability of a partnership agreement provided the springboard for improved product design. In fact, suppliers began to apply JIT techniques to their own production process and supplier base further down the value chain.

Production Batch Sizes Were Cut in Half

To facilitate shorter production runs, lower inventories and the assembly of all products on a JIT basis, set-up times had to be dramatically reduced. Set-up involved ensuring that all the disks, manuals and packaging were available at the appropriate work-station for assembly. The company came up with an imaginative and novel approach to eliminating lengthy set-up times. While many exponents of JIT suggested that U-shaped production lines facilitated the process, Microsoft replaced the traditional assembly lines with fifteen dual-level carousels or 'round-tables' (see Figure 1).

While operatives assembled from one level of the carousel, individuals who had completed their tasks for that run set-up the other carousel for the next production run.

Employee Involvement

The solution to overcoming resistance to change on the shop floor required a radical change in the way individuals were managed. The company identified employees who were felt to be suitable facilitators in the training of operatives in JIT/TQM techniques. Employees were now to be paid on the basis of the number of new skills they acquired by way of in-coming training. Considerable resources were devoted to education and a library containing the works of Schonberger and other management strategists was opened for all employees. Quality focused teams were introduced to brainstorm on how the manufacturing process could be improved. The Japanese concept of *kaizen* or continuous improvement was seen as critical to the success of such teams. The impact of such changes were immediately noticeable: employees wanted to be flexible and champion the production process. A measure of this change was the 3,700 suggestions forwarded to the company's suggestion scheme in the first two years of operation. Richard Schonberger, on a visit to the plant, was later to remark that this was the highest rate of contribution he had observed in any western manufacturing plant.

Focused Factories

Wickham Skinner pioneered the concept of focus in manufacturing in the 1970s. He argued that a plant would perform better if it limited itself to a focused number of tasks, processes or products. Brian Reynolds was intrigued with this approach and considered how it might apply in the case of Microsoft. He concluded that a customer-driven approach must form the basis of organising 'factories within the factory'. The requirements of the marketplace were now to have an impact on the manufacturing process. Since the geographic destinations of the software packages were language-related, four factories within the plant were introduced — Britain and English language produces (Euro), Germany, France and the Rest of Europe (multilingual). Each focused factory was now charged with dealing with specific geographic markets and had its own independent manufacturing cells, production equipment (duplicating machines and carousels) and work teams. In addition the possibility of extra paperwork and administration was eliminated by extended the concept of focus to suppliers. A printing supplier would now typically deliver to only one focused factory. The national flags of the destination markets were in evidence at each focused factory, highlighting the market-driven nature of the approach. Under the revamped rate-based manufacturing approach, orders were now placed by customers on a Wednesday for the forthcoming week. This weekly order could then be allocated evenly to each of the new five days with MRP used only for capacity planning, e.g., for a weekly order of 1,000 units, a daily production rate of 200 units would be assembled on each of the five days of production. Within months, cost of goods sold had been reduced by 25%, while inventory levels in the plant had been cut by 70%. There was also a significant improvement in lead times as a result of the changes introduced by Brian Reynolds.

Source: Extracts from Fynes, B. and Ennis, S., 'Beyond World Class manufacturing: Microsoft Ireland', *Irish Marketing Review*, Vol.7, 1994, pp. 8-15.

9.8 QUALITY MANAGEMENT

The goal of industry over the last decade, as far as product quality is concerned, has been to provide a product in which quality is designed, built, marketed and maintained at the most economical cost which allows for full customer satisfaction. Quality has become crucial for business success or failure. The Japanese influence on total quality has been considerable. Japanese companies now account for over 50 per cent of total trade in more than thirty distinct product areas. This increased emphasis on quality has lead many organisations to adopt a Total Quality Management approach. Feigenbaum (1983) defines quality as 'the total composite product and service characteristics of marketing, engineering, manufacture, and maintenance through which the product in use will meet the expectations of the customer.' Thus, the organisation's total quality system will have a number of sub-systems.

Figure 9.7 Six Key Principles of TQ

1. People will produce quality goods and services when the meaning of quality is expressed daily in the quality of their relations with their work, colleagues and organisation.
2. Myron Tribus said it best: 'Workers work in the system; managers should work on the system, to improve it with their help'.
3. TQC is a strategic choice made by top management and consistently translated in guidelines for the functioning of the whole organisation.
4. Each system with a certain degree of complexity has a probability of deviation, which can be understood by scientific methods.
5. Inspection of the process (or process control) is as important as inspection of the product. It can best be achieved by the workers closest to the process.
6. Envisage what you want to be as an organisation, but start working from where you actually are.

Source: Vansina, L. S., 'Total Quality Control: An Overall Organisational Improvement Strategy', National Productivity Review, Vol.9, No.1 1990.

The approach must be management led. Successful *TQM* requires the continuous commitment of the top management team. This commitment must be translated into action and embedded in attitudes and behaviour. The approach must also be company-wide. Quality must be the responsibility of all departments and people who constitute the business. The underlying philosophy must be one of prevention. This integrates detection into the production process and directs attention towards the process rather than the outputs of the process. The theme should be one of continuous improvement and the methodology must be scientific. TQM needs to be rooted in an understanding and application of scientific principles and statistical tools. Developing and enhancing these sub systems is the real key to TQM.

Successful TQM can lead to the achievement of internationally recognised quality standards, which certify that a company's systems are firmly in place and highly effective. For example, companies trading internationally will strive to achieve ISO9000. This has legal status and world-wide recognition. In May 1987, a new version of the British Standard for Quality Systems (BS 5750) was introduced. In 1982, the Irish Quality Association introduced the Quality Mark Scheme which is applicable to all industries, regardless of company size, and, if awarded, can provide partial exemption when applying for accreditation under the IS or BS systems.

In terms of the benefits of a TQM approach, those organisations that have traversed this route have proven the value of the approach. Some of the most notable benefits to have occurred as a result of successful TQM implementation include improved/enhanced company image, improved productivity, increased certainty in operations, cost reductions, increased customer satisfaction, increased job satisfaction and an enhanced competitive position. However, this impressive array of benefits does not come easily. Many organisations fail to appreciate that it is a total effort and that a whole gamut of issues must be addressed including culture change, management behaviour, planning and strategy development for successful implementation. As a result, TQM as an approach has suffered because of its demanding nature.

Figure 9.8 Four Levels in the Evolution of Total Quality Management

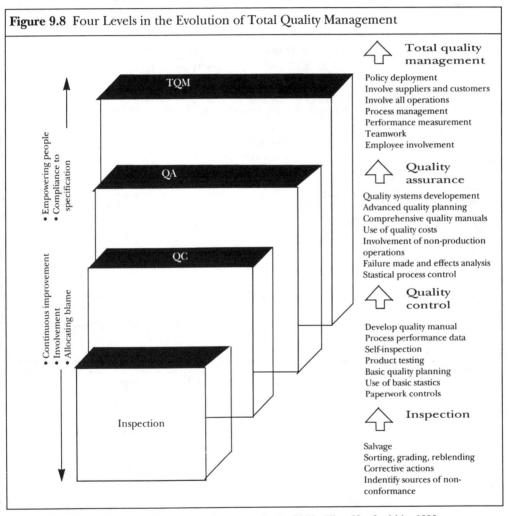

Source: Dale, B. and Plunkett, J., *Managing Quality,* Philip Allan, Hertfordshire 1990.

9.9 INNOVATION IN ORGANISATIONS

Part of the function of production and operations management is ensuring that a flow of new ideas and products is available. It is essential that creative and innovative attributes are present if organisations and their employees are to develop. The overall concern must be to foster energy, enthusiasm and drive and a personal as well as a professional commitment to the work in hand and its development (Pettinger 1994). Innovation in organisations can take many forms: it can be radical or incremental; it can be technological or management focused or indeed product or process focused. Radical innovations are new products or technologies that replace completely existing products or technologies. Incremental innovations, on the other hand, are new products or processes that modify existing products or technologies. Radical innovations will usually fundamentally shift the nature of competition in an industry, while often incremental innovations will not fundamentally alter the prevailing competitive situation. Product innovations usually refer to changes in the physical characteristics or performance capacity of existing products or services or the creation of brand new ones. Conversely, process innovations impact on the way products or services are manufactured, created or distributed. Figure 9.9 illustrates the effect of product and process innovations on economic return.

Figure 9.9 Effects of Product and Process Innovation on Economic Return

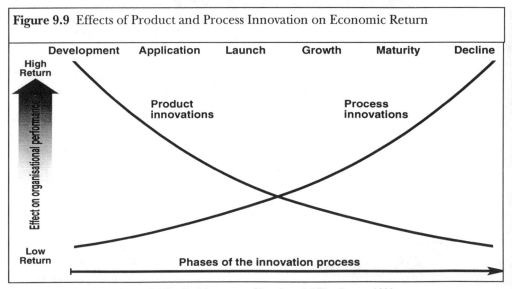

Source: Griffin, R., *Management,* Houghton Mifflin, Boston 1992.

The level of return clearly depends on the stage of the innovation process. In this respect, three key stages can be identified. Broadly it consists of development, application and launch phases. Clearly the majority of ideas that emerge from the individual creative process are not ready to be transformed into new products or services. They need development which usually involves some type of evaluation (usually organisational), possible modification and improvement. The application phase consists of the organisation taking a developed idea and using it in the design, manufacture or delivery of new products, services etc. The idea is thus transformed into a tangible good. The final launch stage refers to the organisation introducing the product on to the market-place. Ironically, it is at this stage that most products fail often because the fundamental question of whether customers will actually want the product has not been properly addressed.

Garavan et al (1994) highlight three key ways in which organisations can actively promote innovation in organisations: rewards, intrapreneurship and cultural fit. Organisations can use rewards to encourage and discourage certain behaviour in employees. In this respect, rewards can be used to promote creativity and innovation by providing financial and non-financial rewards to individuals and groups who directly innovate ideas. If employees perceive a link between new ideas and rewards they are more likely to be creative. Concomitantly, it is also important that organisations do not resort to punishment when creativity results in failure to produce highly successful innovations. Intrapreneurship is a strong mechanism for helping organisations to be innovative. It can be defined as a process where individuals or groups develop a new product or business within the context of a larger organisation. This, according to Garavan et al (1994), involves the performance of a number of different roles. The inventor must actually conceive and develop the new idea by means of the creative process. The product champion, who is usually a middle manager committed to the product, helps overcome organisational resistance and convinces others to take the innovation seriously. A product champion's greatest skill is in understanding exactly how the organisation ticks. Finally, the sponsor is usually the member of the top management team who approves of and supports the project. The sponsor will commit to finding the budget to develop the idea. With respect to organisation culture as a means of assisting innovation, there is general agreement in the extant literature of the value of having a strong, appropriately focused culture to support creative and innovative activity. A well-managed culture can communicate a sense that innovation is valued and will be rewarded and that failure is accepted as an outcome of this natural selection type process. Thus, supportive cultures should value individual creativity, risk taking and inventiveness.

9.10 HEALTH AND SAFETY MANAGEMENT

Health and safety at work is a complex issue in Ireland. Gunnigle et al (1993) point out that there are some twenty acts that have some bearing on safety and health at work as well as almost 200 regulations. Two key sources of legislation are considered: common law and some aspects of statute law.

Under common law in Ireland, employers must exercise reasonable care towards employees and protect them against any likely injury. The Irish courts have determined that, in this respect, employers must provide a safe system of work, ensure that fellow workers are competent, provide safe equipment and effective supervision, and a safe place of work.

In relation to statute law, Figure 9.10 summarises the legislation in Ireland concerning health, safety and welfare at work.

The Health, Safety & Welfare at Work Act of 1989 and the Safety, Health & Welfare at Work Regulations of 1993 are arguably the most significant pieces of legislation within the employment sphere in the recent years. The 1989 Act is a comprehensive piece of legislation with sixty-one provisions organised into a number of larger sections. Part I deals with definitional aspects. Part II sets out a number of general duties, including the duties of an employer in relation to his/her employees, duties of employees and duties of persons in control of the workplace. Garavan (1989) suggests 'that these duties are in the main statutory enactment of the common law principles of providing a safe place of work, a safe system of work, proper tools and equipment and competent staff. The act provides a basis for the issuing of codes of practice and regulations on all of these general duties.' Parts III, IV & V deal with the establishment of a national authority, the regulation and enforcement of the legislation and the need to review all health and safety legislation. The Act firmly recognises the role of the employee in health and safety management. There is an obligation on employees to co-operate with their employers on health and safety issues.

Figure 9.10 Health and Safety Legislation in Ireland

Summary of Employment Legislation in Ireland (Health and Safety at Work)

Act	Date	Subject
Safety in Industry Acts	1955–1980	Minimum health and safety standards Safety committees
Mines and Quarries Act	1965	Safety rules and procedures in mines/quarries
Fire Service Act	1981	Responsibilities of local authorities for fire
Safety, Health and Welfare at Work Act	1989	Duties on employers, employees and others
Office Premises Act	1958	Minimum health and safety standards for offices
Dangerous Substances Acts	1972/1979	Safety in handling certain substances
Safety, Health and Welfare at Work Regulations	1993	Specific procedures and regulations for at work employers

Source: Gunnigle, P., Garavan, T. and Fitzgerald, G., *Employee Relations and Employment Law in Ireland,* Plassey Management and Technology Centre, Limerick 1992.

The 1993 regulations are designed to support the key duties set out in the 1989 Act and their central aim is to help employers focus on matters which need to be addressed for the purpose of controlling risks. Under the 1993 regulations, employers in the management of safety are required to take the following issues into account: the evaluation of unavoidable risks; the combating of risks at source; the replacement of dangerous articles or substances; the drawing up of a prevention policy; the adoption of work to suit the individual employee; and the provision of adequate training and instruction to employees. Detailed requirements are specified in relation to a safe place of work, health surveillance, visual display units, electricity and the notification of accidents.

9.11 SUMMARY OF KEY PROPOSITIONS

• Between 1953 and 1989, the volume of goods produced by the manufacturing sector in Ireland increased dramatically, yet overall employment in manufacturing only increased by approximately 30 per cent.

• While in the same period labour costs increased by a factor of four, the lowest percentage increase in labour costs has come about in the 1980s. While output per worker increased substantially, labour costs were tightly controlled.

• In terms of changes in the employment structure of Irish manufacturing, in recent years manual operatives have declined as a proportion of all employees in manufacturing.

• There are three major types of production: job, batch or continuous flow production.

• The major technological advancements in manufacturing in recent years include computer aided design, computer aided manufacturing, computer integrated manufacturing and flexible manufacturing systems.

• Just-in-time manufacturing is a sophisticated production control system which uses KANBAN and pull manufacturing as key tools for levelling production.

• Total Quality Management has become crucial for business success. The approach must be organisation-wide and management led and the underlying philosophy must be one of prevention.

• Innovation in organisations can be radical or incremental and can be actively promoted through appropriate reward management, intrapreneurship and good cultural fit.

• Health and safety management in Ireland has two sources of legislation: common law and statute law. The Health, Safety and Welfare at Work Act of 1989 and the Safety, Health and Welfare at Work Regulations of 1993 are the two most recent pieces of legislation in this area.

DISCUSSION QUESTIONS

1. Discuss the significance of the manufacturing sector to the Irish economy.
2. Define the following terms: job production; batch production; and continuous flow production. Give an example of each.
3. Outline the advantages and disadvantages of a flexible manufacturing system.
4. How would you go about introducing a just-in-time manufacturing system?
5. Total Quality Management can be a major source of competitive advantage. Discuss.
6. Define innovation and highlight ways of promoting it in organisations.
7. Examine the provisions of the recent health and safety legislation. How well do you think the legislation achieves its aims?

REFERENCES

Betts, P., *Supervisory Management*, Pitman, London 1993.
Dale, B. and Plunkett, J., *Managing Quality*, Philip Allan, Hertfordshire 1990.
Foley, E., *Irish Business Management*, Gill & Macmillan, Dublin 1989.
Garavan, T., Fitzgerald, G. and Morley, M., *Business Analysis: Books 1 and 2*, Certified Accountants Educational Trust, London 1994.
Griggin, R., *Management*, Houghton Mifflin, Boston 1992.
Gunnigle, P., Garavan, T. and Fitzgerald, G., *Employee Relations and Employment Law in Ireland*, PMTC Open Business School, Limerick 1993.
Mapes, J. and New, C. C., 'Planning for Production' in Lock, D. and Farrow, N., *The Gower Handbook of Management*, Gower Press, Hampshire 1992.
Pettinger, R., *Introduction to Management*, Macmillan, London 1994.
Stasey, R. and McNall, C., *Crossroads: A JIT Success Storey*, H. Irwin, Homewood 1990.
Turner, T. and Morley, M., *Industrial Relations and the New Order: Case Studies in Conflict and Co-Operation*, Department of Enterprise and Employment, Dublin 1995.

Personnel Management

10.1 INTRODUCTION

An organisation's workforce represents, possibly, one of its most valuable resources. However, human resources are also potentially the most difficult to manage, principally because of individual differences. The extent to which a workforce is managed effectively is a critical factor in improving and sustaining organisational effectiveness and efficiency. The management of human resources is one of those pivotal factors that distinguishes a high performance organisation from an average performer (Hanna 1988, Buchanan and McCalman 1989).

The expression *personnel management* may be interpreted in specific or in general terms. In its specific or narrow interpretation, the expression refers to the professional specialist function performed by personnel managers. The head of personnel is responsible for devising and executing his/her organisation's policies and strategies relating to employment (Tyson and York 1992). More generally, the term may refer to all those who have responsibility for people matters — a responsibility that most managers, across all functions, have to fulfil (Torrington and Hall 1987). However, for the purpose of this chapter, it is necessary to take a narrow interpretation and to concentrate on the specialist personnel function and its activities.

This chapter provides a short historical overview of the development of the specialist function in Ireland and discusses the main activities of the personnel function, incorporating recent Irish research data where available.

10.2 HISTORICAL DEVELOPMENT OF THE PERSONNEL FUNCTION

In order to understand properly the current nature of personnel management, it is necessary to sketch its historical development. This overview will highlight the major transitions that personnel management has gone through and give some indications of its development as a specialist management function.

10.2.1 The early 1900s
Prior to the 1930s, two key traditions can be identified which represent the first prominent influences on managerial practice relating to human resources and, as such, lay the foundations for the development of personnel management as we now

understand it (Foley and Gunnigle 1994). The two traditions are Welfarism and Taylorism.

Welfarism: The origins of personnel management lay in the Protestant work ethic and a concern, amongst a few enlightened employers, for the alleviation of the abhorrent working conditions that followed the Industrial Revolution. In Britain, the first recorded appointment of a welfare worker in 1896 was formal recognition of the need for specialist individuals to deal with people management issues.

The early years of the twentieth century saw the appointment of a number of welfare workers among Irish employers. Prominent Irish examples include Jacobs and Maguire and Paterson in Dublin. However, the depression that followed the First World War, coupled with large-scale unemployment, led to the abandonment of much of this work.

Taylorism: As welfarism was increasingly becoming a victim of the depression, Taylorism and its associated notions of labour efficiency became a popular alternative (see Chapter 2). The quest for efficiency and profitability among employers led to the standardisation of work systems and a more systematic approach to a wide range of managerial activities.

10.2.2 The mid 1900s

If some developments in Taylorism caused personnel practitioners to develop a more calculative approach to managing employees, this was partially redressed by a growth in the behavioural sciences (Gunnigle and Flood 1990). This period was marked by a trend towards increasing organisational size and complexity and the application of personnel management practices to wide areas of management. The emerging behavioural sciences established a body of knowledge that underpinned many aspects of personnel work, such as selection, training, motivation, industrial relations and payment systems. The increasing complexity during this period led to the emergence of two different traditions: Bureaucrats and Consensus Negotiators (Foley and Gunnigle, 1994).

Bureaucrats: As organisations became more complex, the range of personnel activities widened, which, in turn, led to the need to formalise procedures. Under this tradition, personnel management included areas of employment, wages, joint consultation, health and safety, welfare and education/training. Personnel functions largely became custodians of the procedures which regulated the operation of these activities within the organisation.

Consensus negotiators: Following the lifting of the Emergency Powers Order in 1946, trade union density in Ireland accelerated sharply, as money and real wages began to rise for the first time since 1939 (Roche and Larragy 1986). Foley and Gunnigle (1994) argue that this 'new unionism' was to have a large impact on both the organisational environment and on the functioning of specialist personnel departments. Firstly, trade unions enjoyed a period of legitimacy in the eyes of employers and governments, highlighted best, perhaps, by the establishment of the Labour Court in 1946. Secondly, with increasing union density came an enhanced ability to engage in industrial action in the pursuit of collective objectives.

10.2.3 Centralised pay bargaining — the 1970s

The return to centralised pay bargaining in 1970 did not result in a decline in the importance of the personnel specialist, as union negotiators switched their focus to other issues in the workplace, such as employment conditions and productivity. This resulted in the necessity for the personnel specialist to become a legal expert.

The 1970s brought with them an unprecedented wave of legislation which sought to protect employees and provide for redress in cases where rights had been infringed. In turn, this required that personnel functions had a high level of expertise in all aspects of employment law. This development, in particular, added a strong impetus to the drive for greater professionalism in the field of personnel management. Clearly, interest in greater professionalism in personnel management cannot be absolutely confined to this period, but it did receive a much stronger impetus at this time. The Donovan Commission on industrial relations (1968) highlighted the need for greater expertise in the operation of the employer/employee relationship and, in 1970, the IPM developed an exam only scheme in an attempt to regulate and improve standards within the personnel management profession.

10.2.4 The 1980s — the transformation of personnel management?

The 1980s was a decade of change. It was also a period of reappraisal for personnel management. A depressed economic climate since the beginning of the decade, together with increased competitive pressures, led to a slump in business activity. These developments helped to change both the focus of personnel management and the nature of personnel activities. Internationalisation, Japanisation, excellence theories, new technology and economic pressures combined to set new priorities, forcing the personnel function to act under strict cost controls and to accommodate a greater range of work with few extra resources (Berridge 1992, Lawler 1988, Tyson 1987, Foley and Gunnigle 1993). As Gunnigle and Flood put it: 'The onset of recession lessened the need for some of these core activities, such as selection and recruit training. At the same time, organisations were looking for ways of establishing competitive advantage through improvements in quality, service and performance. One source of such improvements lay in the better utilisation of human resources. Some organisations began to investigate different approaches to workforce management. These led to changes in personnel management, particularly in areas such as work organisation and job design, remuneration systems, management-employee relations and employee development.'

The personnel function turned increasingly to more innovative practices, the most important being *human resource management* (HRM).

10.2.5 Recent developments — HRM

One of the most significant developments in personnel management has been the emergence of HRM, which, as Guest (1989) argues, is slowly, but inevitably, replacing personnel management. HRM refers to the development of a strategic corporate approach to workforce management. It has its roots in US industry which has been receptive to the application of organisational psychology and behavioural science principles in an attempt to improve organisational performance. The central contention is that organisations incorporate human resource considerations into strategic decision making, establish a corporate human resource philosophy and develop personnel strategies and policies to improve human resource utilisation (Gunnigle and Flood 1990, Guest 1987, Beer et al 1985).

The implications for personnel management are unclear. Some contributors argue that HRM as a development merely involves a retitling exercise (Keenoy 1990, Horwitz 1990), while others feel it may involve a complete reorientation of the personnel function, depending on how strategic it actually is (Storey 1992, Gunnigle and Flood 1990).

10.3 ACTIVITY AREAS IN PERSONNEL MANAGEMENT

The variety of personnel management activities which may be undertaken by the organisation is extensive, and, as a result, the role of the specialist personnel function clearly may vary between organisations. As Gunnigle and Flood (1990) suggest: 'Many are basic activities common to all types of organisation, such as recruitment. Others may be appropriate in certain organisational contexts (for example, collective bargaining in unionised firms), while still others are optional in character and their use related to managerial perspectives on personnel management (such as an emphasis on personal career development).'

10.3.1 Human resource planning

Before launching into more mainstream personnel activities, such as recruitment or training, the organisation must decide on a human resource strategy which fits with its present and future needs. The importance of planning the material resources of the organisation has never been called into question. However, planning for people as a resource — the human resource — has not been accorded the same status. Because people are, arguably, the single most important resource, it is important that sufficient numbers of the appropriate calibre are available to an organisation in pursuit of its objectives. In other words, it is crucial to plan for people, much like any other resource.

Bowey (1974) defines *human resource planning* as: 'an effort to anticipate future business and environmental demands upon an organisation and to provide the personnel to fulfil that business and satisfy those demands.'

The major objectives of human resource planning are: to ensure that the organisation finds and retains the quantity and quality of human resources that it requires; to ensure that the organisation makes the best possible use of its human resources; and human resource planning attempts to ensure that the organisation can manage the human resource implications of employee surpluses or deficits. Thus, human resource planning is not simply about numbers of people, but also, as Cole (1986) points out, about the quality of personnel and how they are deployed in an attempt to ensure organisational effectiveness and efficiency. It is a process which affects every aspect of personnel management (recruitment, selection, performance appraisal, training and development etc), and one which must be aligned with the corporate objectives/mission and strategic plans.

Tyson and York (1992) suggest that sound human resource planning needs to be based on the following six principles and actions which are necessary pre-requisites for any organisation:
1. The human resource plan has to be fully integrated into the other areas of the organisation's strategy and planning.
2. Senior management must give a lead in stressing its importance throughout the organisation.
3. In larger organisations, a central human resource planning unit responsible to senior management needs to be established, the objective of which is to co-ordinate and reconcile the demands for human resources from different departments.
4. The time-span to be covered by the plan needs to be defined.
5. The scope and details of the plan need to be determined.
6. Human resource planning must be based on the most comprehensive and accurate information that is available.

The major stages in the process are:
1. demand analysis
2. supply analysis
3. estimating deficits/surpluses
4. developing action plans.

Figure 10.1 The Human Resource Planning Process

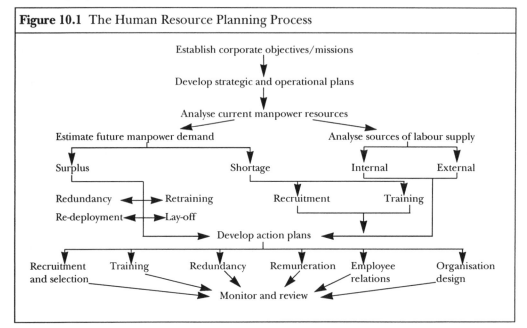

Source: Gunnigle, P. and Flood, P., *Personnel Management in Ireland: Practice, Trends and Developments*, page 46, Gill & Macmillan, Dublin 1990.

Stage 1 Demand Analysis: This stage of the process estimates the quantity and quality of human resources needed to meet the objectives of the organisation. It is based on a thorough understanding of the organisation's strategy and its implications for the workforce, planned technological changes, a detailed inventory of employee characteristics (age, sex, marital status, tenure, skills, qualifications, promotion potential and performance levels) and the attrition rate among current stock. The most common techniques employed when conducting a demand analysis are managerial estimates/judgements, statistical methods/techniques and work study methods/techniques (Cole 1986, Torrington and Hall).

Managerial estimates are the most straightforward method and are often the most commonly used. Typically, individual managers, based upon their knowledge of the situation, draw up estimates of human resource requirements. Managerial estimates are often collected at different levels in the organisation's hierarchy, with managers at lower levels submitting estimates that are passed up through the hierarchy for discussion and consideration. Clearly, since these estimates rely entirely upon personal judgements, their major weakness is one of subjectivity.

Statistical techniques are now more commonly used for making estimates. However, techniques such as regression analysis or econometric models are often only employed by larger organisations that have particular difficulties with human resource planning.

Work study is the systematic analysis of work in terms of people, skills, materials and machines and, in particular, the man-hours needed per output unit to achieve maximum productivity (Tyson and York 1992). Work study is a particularly useful form of analysis for tasks that lend themselves to measurement and, consequently, work study methods are often employed for estimating the demand for 'direct' employees.

Stage 2 Supply Analysis: Supply analysis is concerned with estimating the quantity and quality of human resources that are likely to be available to the organisation. In this instance, there are two major sources: the internal labour market (existing employees) and the external labour market (the potential supply of manpower that is available outside the organisation). The following table summarises the issues on which a typical supply analysis might focus.

Table 10.1 Supply Analysis: The Areas to be Considered

Existing	Staff Potential	Staff Leavers
Numbers	Location	Retirements
Categories	Categories	Wastage rates
Skills	Skills	Redundancies
Performance	Trainability	Dismissals
Flexibility	Attitudes	
Promotability	Competition	

Source: Cole, G. A., *Personnel Management: Theory and Practice*, page 46, DP Publications, Hampshire 1986.

One of the most common factors which complicates the task of human resource planning is labour wastage. Both planned and unplanned losses need to be taken into account. Planned losses might be those that relate to retirements, for example. Unplanned losses are more difficult to deal with. The most typical source of unplanned loss is through voluntary wastage, i.e. when employees leave of their own accord. Useful indices for calculating wastage are provided in Figure 10.2.

Table 10.2 Indices used in Human Resource Planning

Labour turnover index	Number of employees leaving in period Average number employed in period × 100
Labour stability index (Extent to which experienced employees are being retained)	Number of employees with more than one year's service Number employed one year ago × 100

Finally, with respect to supply analysis, there are external factors that need to be taken into account. Factors such as the nature of the competition for labour, population trends, education/training opportunities, government policies etc will all have an impact on the external labour market.

Stage 3 Estimating Deficits/Surpluses: As a result of conducting both a demand and supply analysis, it is now possible to compare the results in order to determine whether the supply of labour available matches the demand for labour. Equally, it is possible that the supply of labour will exceed or fall short of the estimates required. Depending on the result achieved at this stage of the process, an action plan will be prepared.

Stage 4 Preparing an Action Plan: This last stage is based on the information that the preceding stages have yielded. The purpose of an action plan is to ensure that the day-to-day human resource needs of the organisation are satisfied. Plans should include what the organisation must do and how it will manage recruitment, selection, training and development, promotions etc.

10.3.2 Recruitment

Information arising from the process of human resource planning will be used to make decisions about the planned level of recruitment. *Recruitment* is concerned with attracting a group of potential candidates to apply for the vacancy that the organisation has available. Effective recruitment procedures are a prerequisite to the development of an effective workforce. Clearly, in recent years, there has been an ever increasing emphasis on the recruitment of employees that are committed to the goals of the organisation. Influential contributors, such as Plumbley (1985), suggest that the profitability and even the survival of an enterprise usually depends upon the calibre of the workforce, while Pettigrew, Hendry and Sparrow (1988) indicate that human resources represent a critical means of achieving competitive advantage.

The key choice in relation to recruitment is whether to recruit internally or externally. There are advantages and disadvantages associated with both and the choice largely depends on the position being filled. Smith, Gregg and Andrews (1989) suggest that the benefits of recruiting internally are that it is good personnel practice, there is a reduction of induction time and the costs and uncertainties of recruiting from outside are reduced. However, there are also drawbacks as it limits the potential range of candidates and may lead to employee frustration should employees feel that they have been overlooked for promotion. Gunnigle (1992) feels that the apparent desire among some Irish organisations to focus on the internal labour market may be linked to 'soft' human resource management (HRM) practices such as career planning, counselling and employee development.

Two key stages can be identified in the recruitment process: the background stage; and the actual recruitment stage.

Stage 1 Background: This stage involves the conducting of what is termed a 'job analysis'. This may be defined simply as 'specifying the job and defining what the job demands in terms of employee behaviour'. Typically, two major products are derived from the process of job analysis: a *job description* and a *person specification.*

A job description is a statement of the main tasks and responsibilities of the job. It is clearly an important aspect of the background stage of recruitment, because the ideal individual is specified based on this job description. If an inaccurate description is prepared, then the individual characteristics subsequently specified may also be inaccurate or inappropriate. Organisations may take different approaches to the preparation of this job description; some ask current employees to keep diaries of their daily job activities and draw up a job description accordingly, while in other instances this task may be reserved for managers and supervisors.

The person specification details the skills, qualifications, knowledge, and experience an individual should possess in order to best match the job. The specification may often distinguish between what are considered essential and desirable characteristics. In order to aid the process of preparing a person specification, two frameworks are frequently cited in the extant literature. These are Rodger's Seven Point Plan and the Munro-Fraser Five Fold Grading System.

Rodger's (1952) Seven Point Plan suggests that the following characteristics may need to be examined:
1. physical make-up; health, physique, appearance
2. attainments; education, qualifications, experience
3. general intelligence
4. special aptitudes
5. interests
6. disposition
7. circumstances.

Munro-Fraser's (1954) Five Fold Grading System details the following characteristics:
1. impact on others; physical make-up, appearance, speech
2. acquired qualifications; education, training, experience
3. innate abilities
4. motivation
5. adjustment.

Both frameworks focus on the desired characteristics of potential employees that may need to be specified in the background phase, and also serve as useful tools in the preparation for, and conducting of, interviews in the subsequent selection phase.

Stage 2 Recruitment: Armed with a job description and a person specification, the task now becomes one of attracting a pool of potential candidates. In considering possible sources of labour, it is in some ways easy to assume that these are inevitably external. However, as mentioned earlier, they may be either internal or external. Internal sources may come about through transfers, promotions or, indeed, demotions. Potential external sources include schools, regional technical colleges, universities and other educational establishments, FAS, employment agencies, unsolicited applications received previously, advertising (local/national media, professional/technical journals) and management consultants/executive search agencies. Each of these sources should be evaluated, particularly with respect to their suitability to yield the right candidate and the costs involved. The following table highlights the major costs associated with different sources of recruitment.

Table 10.3 Costs Associated with Different Sources of Recruitment

SOURCES	DIRECT COSTS
INTERNAL	
Transfer	
Promotion	
Demotion	None

continued next page

SOURCES	DIRECT COSTS
EXTERNAL	
Existing workforce: recommendations from friends, relatives etc	Very low
Casual applications: unrequested CVs	Very low
Advertising: local, national media, professional/technical journals etc	Expensive (dependent on media used)
Schools and colleges: contacts, careers officers, 'milk round'	Low (except for travel costs)
FAS	None (can receive financial benefits for employing some categories of workers)
Employment agencies	Expensive (10 per cent to 25 per cent of starting salary)
Management consultants/ executive search agencies	Very expensive (25 per cent plus of starting salary)

Source: Gunnigle, P. and Flood, P., *Personnel Management in Ireland: Practice, Trends and Developments*, page 46, Gill & Macmillan, Dublin 1990.

In the Irish context, recent research data emanating from the Price Waterhouse Cranfield Project (see Note 1), suggests that a broad spectrum of recruitment methods are being utilised by organisations and what is currently happening in Irish recruitment is, for the most part, relatively unsurprising. Table 10.4 highlights the recruitment methods used to fill vacancies for four different grades of employees.

Table 10.4 Recruitment Methods used to Fill Vacancies in Irish Organisations

(N=269)	Managerial	Professional/ Technical	Clerical	Manual
From among current employees	53 %	35 %	46 %	29 %
Advertise internally	42 %	39 %	57 %	41 %
Advertise externally	65 %	69 %	46 %	36 %
Word of mouth	9 %	12 %	22 %	37 %
Recruitment agencies	41 %	42 %	28 %	6 %
Search/Selection consultants	35 %	24 %	1 %	0.5 %
Job centres	0.4 %	1 %	15 %	26 %
Apprentices	–	9 %	4 %	15 %

Source: Price Waterhouse Cranfield Project (Ireland), University of Limerick 1992.

The data suggests that the external labour market is preferred when recruiting both managerial and professional/technical employees. Conversely, the internal labour market is utilised more in the recruitment of clerical and manual employees. Organisations, when filling managerial and/or professional vacancies, favour external advertising above all other methods — 64 per cent of respondents advertise managerial posts externally, while 68 per cent advertise externally for professional/technical employees. Internal advertising is preferred for the recruitment of personnel at clerical and manual levels. At these levels it is often cheaper and quicker to avail of this recruitment method as the necessary expertise may already be present in the organisation. Utilising the internal labour market for recruitment purposes is not limited to internal advertising, and may occur on a much more informal basis. Word of mouth is an important method in this respect. This method of recruitment appears more popular for clerical and manual positions than for vacancies at higher levels. Thus, while only 9 per cent of managerial positions are filled through word of mouth, 37 per cent of manual vacancies are filled this way. As might be expected, the use of recruitment agents and search and selection consultants is confined mainly to the recruitment of higher level positions. One of the key influencing factors here is the cost associated with engaging such consultants. Consequently, they are often restricted to posts where the necessary skills are in short supply (Heraty, Gunnigle and Crowley 1993).

Regardless of the method of recruitment used, the organisation requires details on the skills, abilities, aptitudes etc of all the candidates. Typically, the choice here is between asking the applicants to submit their own curriculum vitae (CV) or to have all applicants complete a standard application form. From the point of view of getting standardised information and assessing candidates on the same parameters, application forms are to be preferred. Individual curriculum vitae give scope for creativity, but may also include some irrelevant information, whilst excluding some essential facts. A compromise situation lies between both of these alternatives: design an application form specific to the job, but allow some blank space for supporting information.

10.3.3 Selection

The selection process effectively begins when application forms are received. *Selection tools* available to organisations range from the more traditional methods of interviews and references, through to the more sophisticated techniques such as biographical data, aptitude tests and psychological tests. The degree to which a selection technique is perceived as effective is determined by its reliability and validity. Reliability is generally synonymous with consistency, while validity refers to what is being measured, and the extent to which those measures are correct (Muchinski 1986).

The interview is widely held to be the most commonly used selection technique. For example, McMahon (1988), researching in Ireland, found that over 90 per cent of job categories were filled with the assistance of an interview. Often described as a 'conversation with a purpose', the interview can take a number of different forms. The three most common types are one-on-one interviews, panel interviews and group interviews/assessments.

In a one-on-one situation, there will be one interviewer and one interviewee/ candidate. This type of interview tends to be less formal than panel interviews and facilitates the development of rapport between interviewer and interviewee. It also makes a lower demand on management time. Perhaps its biggest weakness is the potential for subjectivity and bias.

In a panel interview, there will normally be a number of interviewers (often up to seven people) and one interviewee. The key advantage here is that it is more objective than the one-on-one interview and reduces the opportunity for bias. However, it may prove difficult to co-ordinate from the organisation's perspective and it clearly increases the demand on management time.

Finally, a group interview/assessment attempts to assess a group of interviewees/candidates together. A relatively informal process, in some respects, it attempts to observe and assess the individuals' behaviour in a group situation. It is often used as a preliminary selection tool.

Regardless of the type of interview being conducted, the interviewer/s should have three constant objectives:

1. To get enough information about the candidate to determine how he/she will fit the job.
2. To ensure that the applicant has enough information about the vacancy and the organisation.
3. To leave the applicant with the impression that he/she has been treated fairly.

It is important to prepare for an interview and to have a set plan when interviewing. The interview has a poor track record in predicting job performance. Most managers have little interview training, and yet they rely on the process to turn up the most suitable person for the job. Table 10.5 highlights the interviewing errors that most frequently occur.

Table 10.5 Common Interviewing Errors
Inadequate preparation: little job analysis; inadequate interview preparation; poor planning and administration.
Absence of interview structure.
Premature judgement: arriving at early decisions on candidate suitability and using interview to justify such decisions.
Interviewer dominance: interviewer talking too much, not listening, observing or analysing.
No rapport: atmosphere too intimidating; being overly critical and judgmental.
Horns/halo effect: allowing favourable/unfavourable characteristics or reports to influence final decision.
Interviewer bias: allowing prejudices or subjective opinions to influence selection decisions.
Structural rigidity: adhering slavishly to a pre-planned structure and not adapting to the needs of each candidate.

Source: Gunnigle, P. and Flood, P., *Personnel Management in Ireland: Practice, Trends and Developments*, page 46, Gill & Macmillan, Dublin 1990.

The whole objective of the exercise is to establish a rapport with the interviewee, and to obtain all the information relevant to the post. The interviewer must be wary of allowing his/her own biases and interests to influence the decision. Clearly, since the interview is likely to be an important role in employee selection, management should make every effort to gain the best possible results from its use.

A number of tests are available to assist in selection decisions. Owing to the subjective nature of the interview, such tests are sometimes used to give a more objective rating. The most common types of tests are:

1. **Intelligence tests**: These measure mental capacity and potential. They are particularly useful for giving an insight into a candidate's ability to learn. However, they are not a good indicator of subsequent job performance.

2. **Aptitude tests**: These are generally used to predict areas of special aptitude and to examine a candidate's suitability for particular types of work. However, as with intelligence tests, they cannot predict subsequent job performance.

3. **Proficiency tests**: Otherwise known as ability tests of achievement, they can be a good measure of specific knowledge or skills.

4. **Personality tests**: These tests strive to ensure that the successful candidate has the best personality to suit the particular job. While these tests do give a measure of the individual's suitability for certain jobs, their reliability and validity is rather low.

Reference checking typically forms a part of most selection processes. Indeed, McMahon (1988) found that, after interviewing, reference checking is the next most popular selection technique. The reference check helps to validate information already obtained and establishes a picture of the individual's previous performance. References may be sought in different ways:

1. by writing a standard business letter, detailing the position and asking the referee to give his/her opinion of the candidate's suitability;
2. by forwarding a standard form, asking the referee to give details of the candidate's past experience and character;
3. by requesting information over the telephone about the candidate's past performance.

Regardless of the method used, the object is the same — to seek independent corroboration of the facts as presented by the applicant. Typically, the reference is used as a 'rubber stamp' in approving the final decision (McMahon 1988).

With respect to the selection tools most common in Irish organisations, the data generated by the Price Waterhouse Cranfield Project indicates that relatively little use is being made of what are considered the more 'sophisticated' selection techniques. The picture that emerges from the data suggests that the interview panel and the reference check are the most commonly used selection methods, while more sophisticated and reliable techniques, such as biodata, testing and assessment centres, are used only in a small percentage of cases.

Table 10.6 Selection Methods Used by Irish Organisations

	N	%
References	234	88
Interview panel	227	86
Aptitude tests	82	31
Psychometric testing	49	19
Group selection methods	19	7
Assessment centres	13	5
Biodata	13	5
Graphology	3	1
		N=267

Source: Price Waterhouse Cranfield Project (Ireland), University of Limerick 1992.

The high level of usage of both the interview and the reference check found by McMahon (1988) is confirmed by the Price Waterhouse Cranfield Project research, yet the research in the extant literature highlights that these remain selection tools with low validity and reliability (Makin and Robertson 1986, Attwood 1989).

Biodata, assessment centres and testing are increasingly being viewed as valid predictors and, while their usage remains rather low in Ireland, the feeling is that they may become more widespread in the future.

Group selection methods and graphology remain the least utilised techniques in Ireland. Graphology has been criticised on the grounds of low reliability and validity and there is some difficulty associated with assessing the performance of an individual in a group context during the selection stage (Arnold et al 1991, Smith and Robertson 1986). McMahon (1988) found little evidence of the use of either method in Ireland, and the more recent research data confirms this (Heraty, Gunnigle and Crowley 1993).

10.3.4 Pay and benefits

The organisation's *reward system* is a powerful indicator of its philosophy and approach to workforce management. High or low pay and the range of fringe benefits in existence provide a valuable insight into the corporate approach to workforce management.

The design and implementation of an effective reward system has proven a difficult task for many organisations. Beer et al (1985) suggest that many employee grievances and criticisms of reward systems may actually mask more fundamental problems. Dissatisfaction with aspects of the employment relationship, such as the supervisory style or opportunities for personal development, may manifest themselves in dissatisfaction with aspects of the reward system. Consequently, organisations experiencing problems with their reward system should examine decisions taken on other personnel issues, such as selection or work design, rather than making piecemeal changes to the compensation system (Gunnigle and Flood 1990).

Employee rewards are usually classified under two broad headings: intrinsic rewards and extrinsic rewards. Intrinsic rewards spring from the job itself and include such things as autonomy, responsibility and challenge. Extrinsic rewards are more tangible in nature and include pay, job security and working conditions. The relative importance of intrinsic over extrinsic rewards and vice versa is a much debated issue, rooted in the various theories of motivation. (For a full discussion see Motivation and Leadership, Chapter 6.)

The organisation's reward system may attempt to incorporate the motivational principles underlying the various motivation theories in an attempt to improve or reinforce performance. Actual reward satisfaction will be one of the key determinants of performance improvements. Lawler (1977) concluded that the following five key factors influence satisfaction with a reward:

1. Satisfaction with a reward depends on the amount received versus the amount the individual feels he/she should receive.
2. Comparisons with what happens to others influence an individual's feelings of satisfaction.
3. Employees' satisfaction with both the intrinsic and extrinsic rewards received from their jobs affects overall job satisfaction; individuals who are dissatisfied with the reward system are likely to express dissatisfaction with their jobs.
4. People differ widely in the rewards they desire and in what value they attach to those rewards; effective reward systems should meet workers needs.

5. Many extrinsic rewards satisfy workers only because they lead to other rewards; for example, increased pay may only satisfy because of what it can buy.

Turning specifically to payment systems, the choice of a payment system is an important consideration for the organisation. The money which a person receives for carrying out work can be a major source of motivation and, therefore, it is imperative that the organisation maintains an appropriate and equitable payment system. The particular package offered will be determined by a variety of factors, not least the organisation's ability to pay, labour market conditions, comparable rates/levels elsewhere and, possibly, the bargaining strength of the trade union. There are numerous options in the type of payment system the organisation might adopt. The more common types of payment systems utilised in Irish organisations are as follows:

1. **Flat rate only**: Flat rate schemes are by far the most popular and simply involve a fixed hourly, weekly or monthly rate. Such schemes are simple, easy to administer, are easily understood and provide stability of earnings for the employee. Flat rate schemes are typically used in jobs where specific performance criteria are difficult to establish.

2. **Flat rate plus individual, group or company-wide payment by results**: Schemes of this kind are becoming more popular. It is estimated that over one-third of manufacturing establishments in Ireland operate some type of wage incentive scheme for direct manual employees. While schemes of this kind often act as good motivators due to the immediacy of the reward, they are often difficult to establish and administer and indeed may be a source of conflict due to perceived inequities.

3. **Merit rating**: Under merit rating schemes employees receive bonus payments based on a systematic assessment of their performance. Thus, performance is evaluated against specified objectives, and, on the basis of this, an employee gets a merit payment. While such systems are positive from the point of view of rewarding good performers, it is clearly difficult to find an accurate measure of overall performance.

4. **Profit/gain sharing**: Under schemes of this kind, employees receive a bonus related to improved company performance. That bonus/reward may take the form of money or company shares. While schemes of this nature create greater employee awareness of the organisation's overall performance, and may go some way towards increasing the employees' commitment, their take up in Ireland has been low.

5. **Piecework**: In this instance, employees are only paid for the work that they have completed. Payment is based solely on performance. As a payment system it may be a major source of conflict as it does not guarantee any minimum income.

Mooney (1980), in a study of wage payment systems in Ireland, found that the flat rate system was by far the most popular, particularly for indirect employees.

Table 10.7 Payment Systems in Ireland

Payment system	% Utilisation	Direct manual employees	Indirect employees
Flat rate only	70.5	53.4	66.3
Flat rate plus individual PBR	15.3	27.4	6.2
Flat rate plus group PBR	8.6	12	15.8
Flat rate plus company PBR	2.6	3.9	6.0
Piecework	3.0	3.3	0.2

Source: Mooney, P., *An Inquiry into Wage Payment Systems in Ireland*, ESRI/European Foundation for the Improvement of Living and Working Conditions, Dublin 1980.

More recent research evidence suggests that incentive schemes seem to be experiencing increased popularity in many Irish organisations.

Table 10.8 Use of Incentive Schemes in Ireland

	Managerial	Professional/ Technical	Clerical	Manual
	%	%	%	%
Employee share options	20.4	11.9	8.2	7.8
Profit sharing	15.2	11.5	10	8.9
Group bonus schemes	13	11.5	9.7	12.6
Individual bonus/commission	30.1	22.2	13.8	11.5
Merit/performance related pay	46.1	39	28.6	13.4
N=269				

Source: Price Waterhouse Cranfield Project (Ireland), University of Limerick 1992.

The growth of incentive schemes in Ireland has been linked to the trend towards relating pay more closely to performance. However, the take up of incentive schemes is correlated with the organisational ownership. Thus, in the Irish context, American-owned organisations, on the whole, appear far more likely to utilise incentives than their counterparts, particularly Irish indigenous organisations which demonstrate a low take up across the range of incentives (Gunnigle, Foley and Morley 1994).

When planning pay systems, an approach which takes account of all the benefits and their interrelations is to be preferred (Tyson and York 1992). Pay should not, therefore, be examined without some consideration at least being given to the other benefits that may apply. The nature of voluntary fringe benefits provided to employees varies between organisations. In general, it is estimated that fringe benefits (both statutory and voluntary) constitute an additional 25 per cent–30 per cent on top of basic weekly pay for manual grades. For clerical, administrative and managerial grades, a figure of 15 per cent–30 per cent should be added (Gunnigle, Foley and Morley 1993). The following table lists a range of benefits, some of which are common in Irish organisations.

Table 10.9 Employee Benefits (Statutory and Voluntary)

Maternity leave	Child care facilities	Career breaks
Holidays (above the statutory minimum)	Additional holiday pay	Sick pay
Sports/recreation facilities	Health insurance	Company cars
	Pension schemes	

10.3.5 Performance appraisal

Assessing the work of employees is a key function in personnel management and, indeed, a central aspect of all managerial work. The objective is to achieve and sustain high performance standards in an attempt to ensure organisational survival and success. Designed to complement the continuous evaluation and reward of people at work, *performance appraisal* has been defined as 'a procedure and process which assists in the collection, checking, sharing and use of information collected from and about people at work for the evaluation of their performance and potential for such purposes as staff development and the improvement of that work performance' (McMahon and Gunnigle 1994).

It can, therefore, be seen as a periodic assesment of an individual's performance dedicated to reviewing his/her past performance, as well as examining the individal's future potential. This review and examination will allow decisions to be made with respect to the training/development of the individual and when salary increments, bonuses etc are awarded on the basis of the individual's performance.

Tyson and York (1992) identify six major objectives of the performance appraisal process.

1. To determine how far people are meeting the requirements of their jobs and whether any changes or action are indicated for the future.
2. To determine developmental needs in terms of work experience and training.
3. To identify people who have potential to take on wider responsibilities.
4. To provide a basis for assessing and allocating pay increments and similar rewards.
5. Generally to improve communication between managers and their staff.
6. Generally to develop motivation and commitment by providing regular and scheduled opportunities for feedback on performance and discussions of work, problems, sugestions for improvement, prospects etc.

In their recent study, McMahon and Gunnigle (1994) identified a number of central objectives of performace appraisal in Irish organisations.

Table 10.10 Objectives of Performance Appraisal in the Republic of Ireland

Objectives	%
Improve future performance	98
Provide feedback on performance	96
Agree key objectives	95
Identify training needs	95
Strengthen appraisee commitment and motivation	89
Improve communication	84
Assess promotion potential	82
Career counselling	77
Assist personnel decisions	70
Aid salary review	64
Secure feedback on supervisory/managerial effectiveness	63

Source: McMahon, G. and Gunnigle, P., *Performance Appraisal: How to Get it Right*, Productive Personnel Limited in association with IPM (Ireland).

The results reveal that in the Irish context there are, on average, more than eight objectives for each appraisal system, which, as the authors point out, is somewhat ambitious, given that some of the objectives may not be compatable, for example appraisor playing judge and counsellor.

Accompanying the large number of objectives which performance appraisal may attempt to fulfil is an equally large number of appraisal methods. The method/s selected will be a major determinant of the success or otherwise of the process. Selection of a particular method should be based upon a stringent assessment of the strengths and weaknesses of the methods and the relevance of the methods for the organisation's circumstances. The following table summarises the characteristics of the more common appraisal methods and highlights some of the strengths and weaknesses associated with each method.

Table 10.11 Appraisal Techniques

Method	Characteristics	Strengths	Weaknesses
Ranking	Appraiser ranks workers from best to worst based on specific characteristics or overall job performance	Simple, facilitates comparisons	Little basis for decisions, degrees of difference not specified, subjective
Paired comparison	Two workers compared at a time and decisions made on which is superior resulting in final ranking order for full group	Ease of decison making, simple	Difficult with large numbers plus weaknesses attributed to ranking
Critical incident	Appraiser/supervisor observes incidents of good/bad performance; used as a basis for judging and assessing/discussing performance	Job related; more objective	Needs good observation skills; time consuming
Free-form/ narrative	General free-written evaluation by appraiser	Flexible	Subjective; difficulty of comparison
Self-assessment	Appraisees evaluate themselves using a particular format/ structure	Participative; facilitates discussion; promotes self-analysis	Danger of lenient tendency; potential source of conflict between appraiser and appraisee
Assessment centre	Appraisees undergo a series of assessments (interviews, tests etc) undertaken by trained assessors	Range of dimensions examined; objective	Expensive; not necessarily job specific
Performance/ objectives — job targets/ standards oriented systems	Appraiser evaluates degree to which specific objectives have been achieved	Job related; objective; participative	Needs measurable targets; danger of collusion
Rating	Appraiser specifies on a scale to what degree relevant characteristics (normally related to job-related behaviour or personality) are possessed by appraisee	Ease of comparison; range in complexity from very simple to very involved using descriptions of behaviour/performance	Subjective; personality/ behavioural traits difficult to measure

Source: Gunnigle, P. and Flood, P., *Personnel Management in Ireland: Practices, Trends and Developements,* Gill & Macmillan, 1990.

With respect to the methods of appraisal used in Irish organisations, research by MacMahon and Gunnigle (1994) suggest that the performance/objective or results-oriented appraisal method is the most widely used. Rating on the basis of traits that the appraisee possesses and the free form descriptive essay also feature prominently.

Table 10.12 Performance Appraisal Scheme Types Used in the Republic of Ireland

Scheme	%
Results-oriented	62 (45)
Trait rating scales	51 (37)
Descriptive essay	44 (32)
Critical incidents	22 (16)
Ranking	10 (7)
Other (e.g. peer and group appraisal, assessment centre)	21 (15)

Source: McMahon, G. and Gunnigle, P., *Performance Appraisal: How to Get it Right,* Productive Personnel Limited in association with IPM (Ireland).

Finally, the research suggests that many organisations opt to combine the key features of different appraisal schemes, using self-appraisal, in particular, as a component of most other appraisal techniques.

10.3.6 Training and development

Helping employees to become effective in their jobs is one of the most important aspects of personnel management (Tyson and York 1992). The initiative for providing this help lies in *training* and *development*. Garavan, Costine and Heraty (1995), in their recent text on training and development in Ireland, draw a clear distinction between the two concepts. They define training as a planned, systematic effort to modify or develop knowledge, skills and attitudes through learning experiences, to achieve effective performance in an activity or range of activities. They view development as a broader concept referring to the general enhancement and growth of the individual's skills and abilities, through conscious and unconscious learning, with a view to enabling him/her to take up a future role in the organisation. In some quarters training and development was often seen as an optional extra, something to be indulged in when times were good, but one of the first areas to suffer cutbacks. However, it is becoming more generally recognised that there is a strong correlation between organisational success and investment in training and development. In recent times, academic literature has witnessed a resurgence in the whole area of training and development, with much of the literature, according to Heraty (1992), focusing on the strategic development of human resources as a means of increasing the effectiveness of organisations. Much of this interest has perhaps occurred through the popularisation of Porter's (1980) notion of competitive advantage, and the emergence of the 'excellence' literature (Peters and Waterman 1982). This notion of excellence has been expanded into an analysis of the management of human resources generally and, more specifically, into the development of human resources in an attempt to achieve competitive advantage. (Heraty, Morley and Turner 1993) In the Irish context, the Advisory Committee on Management Training (1988) documented case histories of Allied Irish Bank, Howmedica Inc., Blarney Woollen Mills, the Department of Social Welfare, the Electricity Supply Board and Guinness to demonstrate and highlight the relationship between investment in training and development and improved performance.

A number of factors external to the organisation are also partly responsible for the increased interest in training and development. These include the pervasive spread of new technologies (Walton 1985), increasing global competition resulting in the need for greater flexibility (Barrow and Loughlin 1992), and the emergence of gaps in skill in certain industries (Collins and Sinclaire 1991). Unfortunately, over the past decades, Ireland has been the focus of much debate concerning the uncompetitiveness of indigenous firms in the traded area, and the overall consequences for economic growth, employment and the balance of payments. While explanations have included the country's resource deficiency, peripheral location, population growth and unhappy history, they have also included '...poorly trained managers . . . inadequate investment in technology, marketing, equipment and human resources' (Heraty 1992).

At national level, responsibility for training in Ireland currently lies with FAS which has as its primary objectives the co-ordination, promotion, and the provision of training activities in Ireland. Table 10.13 provides a historical overview of training in Ireland.

Table 10.13 Historical Overview of Training in Ireland

1098 Norman Invasion	Introduction of the Guild System of operation
1879 Industrial Revolution	Evolution of factory system of production
1896 Agricultural and Technical	First form of regulated apprenticeship in Ireland Instruction (Irl) Act
1930 Vocational Education Act	Established VECs to provide a nation-wide system of continuing education
1931 Apprenticeship Act	Set up Apprenticeship Committees to regulate apprenticeship training
1959 Apprenticeship Act	Established An Cheard Chomhairle to co-ordinate and regulate the apprenticeship system
1967 Industrial Training Act	Set up AnCO to assume full responsibility for all industrial and commercial training, including apprenticeships. Also to promote training at all levels in industry
1987 Labour Services Act	Established FAS — the amalgamation of AnCO, NMS and the YEA to provide, co-ordinate and promote training activities in Ireland.

Source: Heraty, N., *Training and Development — A Study of Practices in Irish-Based Companies*, Unpublished MBS thesis, University of Limerick, 1992.

Clearly, training and development is an issue that has to be faced by every organisation. At this juncture it is necessary to distinguish between what is meant by training and development. For the purposes of this discussion, training is taken to be that activity which is concerned with the development of knowledge, skills and attitudes that are required by the individual in order for him/her to execute his/her job effectively and efficiently.

Development, on the other hand, is seen as a broader concept relating to an individual and his/her future career in the organisation, as well as the organisation's own future. It is not concerned with immediate performance, but rather future potential.

In practice, process distinctions are rarely made between training and development except when it comes to choosing the particular interventions.

The process of training and development should be thought of as a logical sequence of events, beginning with the establishment of a policy, followed by the identification of training needs, planning and conducting the training and, finally, evaluating the process.

The objective in formulating a training policy is that those responsible for training and development in the organisation, in conjunction with other managers, agree a definite policy. The policy should clearly establish clearly what the organisation is prepared to do with respect to the training and development of its employees. The policy should ensure that employees can find solutions to their training and development needs and that training and development is put into action through the creation of a facilitative atmosphere backed up with the necessary resources.

An accurate identification of training needs is vital for the development of effective, relevant, timely training and development interventions. It should aim to identify what is currently happening and what should actually be happening. It is, in some ways, a rather subjective area as training needs for a particular job are open to different interpretations. The most common method used to identify training needs is a survey which would examine key questions such as the following:
1. Who needs to be trained — numbers and types of employees?
2. What standards of performance is the training expected to achieve?
3. What are the present training arrangements?
4. What are the suggestions for improvements?

Planning and conducting the training refers to the actual planning of the training to take place and deciding on the most appropriate methods. There is a whole range of training methods from which a suitable selection can be made: on-the-job; coaching; counselling; secondment; project work; formal lectures; group discussions; case studies; computer-assisted training. When choosing a particular intervention, the guiding principle should be the facilitation of high learning transfer. In other words, seeking activities/interventions which focus as closely as possible on the job to be performed.

Evaluation of training and development activities ensures that control is maintained over the total process and allows a considered assessment of the outcomes, methods and overall impact of any particular training and development programme (Gunnigle and Flood 1990). Training evaluation can take place at a relatively informal level (e.g. by simply asking participants how they felt about the programme and judging their reactions), or at a more formal level (e.g. using questionnaires or tests to assess what the participant has learned).

In her study of training and development practices in Ireland, Heraty (1992) found that on-the-job training was the most frequently used strategy. Internal and external formal training and development programmes and part-time professional training were also used regularly by respondent organisations. However, more long-term developmental methods, such as secondment and special projects, were used in a much smaller number of cases.

Table 10.14 Training and Development Methods used in Irish Organisations

Methods	%
On-the-job training and development	91
External formal training and development programmes	83
In-house formal training and development programmes	7
Part-time professional training programmes	74
Open/Distance learning	45
Special projects/task force participation	36
Secondment	19
	N=58

Source: Heraty, N., *Training and Development: A Study of Practices in Irish-Based Companies*. Unpublished MBS thesis, University of Limerick 1992.

Heraty (1992) also sought to identify the activities undertaken by those responsible for training and development in the organisation.

Table 10.15 Activities Undertaken by Those Responsible for Training in Irish Organisations

Activity	% Used
Formulation of training and development policies	74
Identification of training needs	85
Securing physical resources for training and development	69
Evaluation of training and development programmes	83
	N=58

Source: Heraty, N., *Training and Development: A Study of Practices in Irish-Based Companies*. Unpublished MBS thesis, University of Limerick 1992.

From a sample of fifty-eight companies, the data suggests that critical activities are being undertaken by a majority of respondents. The results confirm earlier research by Shivanath (1987) of a sample of seventy-one companies which indicated that over 80 per cent of respondents assessed training needs, and approximately 85 per cent evaluated the effectiveness of this training.

10.4 SUMMARY OF KEY PROPOSITIONS

• The expression 'personnel management' may be interpreted in general or specific terms. In its general interpretation, it refers to all those who have responsibility for people matters. In specific terms, it refers to the specialist function performed by personnel managers.

• Historically, personnel management has gone through a number of major transitions, the most prominent being the Welfarist and Taylorist phases in the early 1900s, the move towards bureaucracy and negotiators in the mid 1900s, the increased legislation in the 1970s, and the move towards a more strategic role in more recent years, culminating in the emergence of HRM.

• Manpower planning is concerned with the quantity and quality of manpower available to the organisation and how this manpower is deployed throughout the organisation in an attempt to ensure effectiveness and efficiency. The major stages in the manpower planning process are demand analysis, supply analysis, estimating deficits/surpluses and developing action plans.

• Recruitment is concerned with attracting a group of potential candidates to apply for the position that the organisation has available. Two key stages can be identified in the recruitment process. Firstly, the background stage which is concerned with the conducting of a job analysis. Secondly, there is the actual recruitment stage which is concerned with attracting a pool of potential candidates from either the internal or the external labour market.

• Selection is concerned with choosing the most suitable candidate from the pool that has been attracted during the recruitment phase. The most common methods of selection include the interview, the reference and the aptitude test.

• The choice of payment system is an important consideration for organisations as the money a person receives for carrying out work can be a source of motivation. The most common types of payment systems used in Irish organisations include flat rate only, flat rate plus bonus, merit rating, profit sharing and piecework.

• Performance appraisal is the process of reviewing an individual's performance and progress in a job and assessing his/her potential for future promotion. The results-oriented appraisal method is the most commonly used in Irish organisations. Rating and free form are also used frequently.

• Training and development is aimed at helping employees to become more effective on the job and developing their potential. Good training practices should begin with the development of a policy, followed by the identification of needs, then planning and conducting the training and, finally, evaluating the process. On-the-job training is the most commonly used training method in Ireland.

DISCUSSION QUESTIONS

1. What are the main phases in the history of personnel management in Ireland?
2. Define manpower planning and give reasons why it should be linked to an organisation's overall strategic plan.
3. Identify and describe the main phases in producing a manpower plan.
4. What should be included in a job description and person specification?
5. What are the major sources of recruitment available to an organisation?

6. Describe the different types of selection interview with which you are familiar and highlight the advantages and disadvantages associated with each.
7. What factors will influence an employee's satisfaction with the rewards he/she receives?
8. Describe the different types of payment systems that an organisation could adopt. What factors will influence the choice of payment system?
9. Define performance appraisal and identify some of the major objectives of the performance appraisal process.
10. Describe the methods of performance appraisal with which you are familiar including their advantages and disadvantages.
11. Distinguish between training and development and identify the factors that are responsible for the increased interest in training and development in recent years.
12. Describe each of the major stages involved in systematic training and development.

NOTES

The Price Waterhouse Cranfield Project on International Strategic Human Resource Management was established in 1989 and is designed to analyse the nature of Human Resource Management practices at enterprise level in Europe. The project is co-ordinated by Professor Chris Brewster and Ariane Hegewish at Cranfield University School of Management in the United Kingdom. The Republic of Ireland participated in the survey for the first time in 1992. The Irish component of the study is located at the Department of Management at the University of Limerick and is co-ordinated by Patrick Gunnigle, Michael Morley and Thomas Turner.

REFERENCES

Advisory Committee on Management Training, *Managers for Ireland: The Case of the Development of Irish Managers*, Government Publications Office, Dublin 1988.
Arnold, J., Robertson, I. and Cooper, C., *Work Psychology: Understanding Human Behaviour in the Workplace*, Pitman, London 1991.
Attwood, M., *Personnel Management*, Macmillan, London 1989.
Barrow, M. and Loughlin, H., 'Towards a Learning Organisation: 1, The Rationale', *Industrial and Commercial Training*, Vol.24, No.1, 1992.
Beer, M. et al, *Human Resource Management: A General Managers Perspective*, The Free Press/Macmillan, New York 1985.
Berridge, J., 'Human Resource Management in Britain' *Employee Relations*, Vol.14, No.5, 1992.
Bowey, A., *Manpower Planning*, Heinemann, London 1974.
Buchanan, D. and McCalman, J., *High Performance Work Systems: The Digital Experience*, Routledge, London 1989.
Cole, G., *Personnel Management: Theory and Practice*, DP Publications, Hampshire 1986.
Collins, D. and Sinclaire, J., 'The Skills Time Bomb: Part 1' *Leadership and Organisation Development Journal*, Vol.12, No.1, 1991.
Foley, K. and Gunnigle, P., (1994), 'The Personnel/Human Resource Function and Workplace Employee Relations' in Gunnigle, P., Flood, P., Morley, M. and Turner, T., *Continuity and Change in Irish Employee Relations*, Oak Tree Press, Dublin 1993.

Garavan, T., Costine, P. and Heraty, N., *Training and Development in Ireland: Context, Policy and Practice*, Oak Tree Press, Dublin 1995.

Guest, D., 'Personnel and HRM: Can You Tell the Difference?' *Personnel Management*, January 1989.

Guest, D., 'Human Resource Management and Industrial Relations' *Journal of Management Studies*, May 1987.

Gunnigle, P., 'Human Resource Management in Ireland' *Employee Relations*, Vol.14, No.5, 1992.

Gunnigle, P. and Flood, P., *Personnel Management in Ireland: Practice, Trends and Developments*, Gill & Macmillan, Dublin 1990.

Gunnigle, P., Foley, K. and Morley, M., 'A Review of Organisational Reward Practices in Ireland' in Gunnigle, P., Flood, P., Morley, M. and Turner, T., *Continuity and Change in Irish Employee Relations*, Oak Tree Press, Dublin 1993.

Hanna, D., *Designing Organisations for High Performance*, Addison-Wesley, New York 1988.

Heraty, N., *Training and Development: A Study of Practices in Irish-Based Companies*, unpublished MBS thesis, University of Limerick 1992.

Heraty, N., Morley, M. and Turner, T., 'Trends and Developments in the Organisation of the Employment Relationship' in Gunnigle, P., Flood, P., Morley, M. and Turner, T., *Continuity and Change in Irish Employee Relations*, Oak Tree Press, Dublin 1993.

Horwitz, F., 'HRM: An Ideological Perspective', *Personnel Review*, Vol.19, No.2, 1990.

Keenoy, T., 'Human Resource Management: A Case of the Wolf in Sheep's Clothing?' *Personnel Review*, Vol.19, No.2, 1990.

Lawler, E., 'Human Resource Management: Meeting the New Challenge' *Personnel*, January 1988.

Lawler, E., 'Reward Systems', in Hackman, J. and Suttle, J. (eds), *Improving Life at Work: Behavioural Science Approaches to Organisational Change*, Goodyear 1977.

Makin, P. and Robertson, I., 'Selecting the Best Selection Technique' *Personnel Management*, November 1986.

McMahon, G. and Gunnigle, P., *Performance Appraisal: How to Get it Right*, Productive Personnel Limited in association with IPM (Ireland), Dublin 1994.

McMahon, G., 'Personnel Selection in Ireland: Scientific Prediction or Crystal Ball Gazing?' *IPM News*, Vol.3, No.3, October 1988.

Mooney, P., *An Inquiry into Wage Payment Systems in Ireland*, ESRI/European Foundation for the Improvement of Living and Working Conditions, Dublin 1980.

Morley, M. and Garavan, T., 'The New Organisation: Its Implications for Training and Development', paper read to the Irish Institute of Training and Development Twenty-fourth National Conference, *The Emerging Organisation*, Galway, April 1993.

Muchinski, P., 'Personnel Selection Methods' in Cooper, C. and Robertson, I. (eds), *International Review of Industrial and Organisational Psychology*, John Wiley, New York 1986.

Munro Fraser, J., *A Handbook of Employment Interviewing*, MacDonald & Evans 1954.

Peters, T. and Waterman, R., *In Search of Excellence*, Harper & Row, New York 1982.

Pettigrew, P., Hendry, C. and Sparrow, P., 'Linking Strategic Change, Competitive Performance and Human Resource Management', results of a UK-based Empirical Study, University of Warwick.

Plumbley, P., *Recruitment and Selection*, Institute of Personnel Management, London 1985.

Porter, M., 'How Competitive Forces Shape Strategy', *Harvard Business Review*, March/April 1979.

Purcell, J., 'Macho Managers and the New Industrial Relations' *Employee Relations,* Vol.4, No.1, 1982.

Roche, W. and Larragy, J., 'The Trend of Unionisation in the Irish Republic' in *Industrial Relations in Ireland: Contemporary Issues and Developments,* University College Dublin 1986.

Rodger, A., *The Seven Point Plan,* National Institute of Psychology, UK 1952.

Shivanath, G., *Personnel Practitioners 1986: Their Role and Status in Irish Industry,* unpublished MBS thesis, University of Limerick 1987.

Smith, M., Gregg, M. and Andrews, D., (1989), *Selection and Assessment: A New Appraisal,* Pitman, London 1989.

Smith, M. and Robertson, I., *The Theory and Practice of Systematic Staff Selection,* Macmillan, London 1986.

Storey, J., *Developments in the Management of Human Resources,* Blackwell 1992.

Torrington, D. and Hall, L., *Personnel Management: A New Approach,* Prentice Hall International, London 1987.

Torrington, D., 'Will Consultants Take Over the Personnel Function?' *Personnel Management,* September 1986.

Tyson, S. and York, A., *Personnel Management,* Butterworth-Heinemann, London 1992.

Tyson, S., 'The Management of the Personnel Function' *Journal of Management Studies,* September 1987.

11

Employee Relations

11.1 Introduction

In recent years, many organisations have tried to establish a competitive edge through improvements in quality, service and performance. One key source of competitive improvement has been an increased emphasis on the more optimal utilisation of human resources. A critical factor in influencing success or failure in this area is the relationship between the parties in the labour process. It is to this relationship, encompassing the spectrum of employee, employer and State interactions that we now turn. The way in which this relationship is set up and managed defines the climate of employee relations in an organisation.

This chapter reviews the nature of employee relations in Ireland. Firstly, the expressions industrial relations and employee relations are discussed. Secondly, the nature and context of employee relations is sketched briefly. A short historical background is provided and more recent developments are highlighted. The focus then moves to the structure of employee relations and the parties in the process. Trade unions, employer organisations and State institutions in employee relations are examined. Where research data is available on trends and developments in these areas, they are incorporated into the body of the chapter.

11.2 Industrial Relations or Employee Relations?

It is important to clarify what is meant by employee relations as the term itself is a source of some confusion. There are, as Salaman (1987), observed almost as many definitions of the concept as there are writers on employee relations' issues. The majority of classical definitions of industrial/employee relations emphasise the rules, or job regulations mechanisms that govern the employment relationship in the workplace. For example, Dunlop (1958) defines industrial relations as 'the study of employment rules and their variation over time'. This early perspective set a broad and integrated agenda for the discipline of industrial relations. Accordingly, the parties in the labour process — management, trade unions and government agencies — establish a network of rules for the workplace and the work community. The central task of industrial relations is, therefore, to explain why these particular rules are established and how they are administered. These rules are divided into procedural rules and substantive rules. Procedural rules refer to methods for formally handling specific issues that might arise, such as trade union recognition, disciplinary issues or dispute resolution. Substantive rules refer to detailed outcomes of negotiations such as percentage pay increases and extra holidays.

The traditional management focus has been on the pluralist concept of industrial relations, encompassing the premise that a basic conflict of interest exists between management and labour, and that this conflict can be handled through collective bargaining between employers and trade unions over divisive issues, particularly pay and working conditions (Roche 1990; Gunnigle 1992). Collective bargaining refers to the process through which agreement on negotiable issues is reached between organised employees and management representatives. The pluralist approach recognises that a coalition of various interests exists and, therefore, management's role is to achieve a balance between these differing interests. Because of the existence of this coalition of interests, conflict is likely to arise and management's role is to plan for the reconciliation of the conflicting interests. During the 1980s, it was suggested that although this concept aptly described management/worker relations in many organisations, it did not encapsulate organisations where the focus was more unitarist in perspective (Gunnigle 1992). *Unitarism*, as a philosophy of industrial relations, is based on the existence of a mutuality of interests between the parties in the labour process (Marchington 1982). The organisation's goals are fundamental and it is management's prerogative to manage. Consequently, this latter approach placed the emphasis on dealings with the individual employee, using various mechanisms such as elaborate communications, career development, quality circles and merit pay. In this chapter, employee relations is seen in generic terms as incorporating all employer, employee and State interactions on employment matters.

11.3 HISTORICAL OVERVIEW OF EMPLOYEE RELATIONS

Despite Ireland's relatively recent history of industrialisation, trade unions and collective bargaining were well established by the early 1900s (Gunnigle et al 1995). The development of trade unionism in Britain profoundly influenced events in Ireland. The passing of the Trade Disputes Act of 1906, often referred to as a 'Bill of Rights for Workers', provided legal immunity for unions involved in strike activity and authorised peaceful picketing. By the turn of the century, the trade union movement successfully organised many industries in Dublin, Belfast and Cork (Gunnigle and Flood 1990). After turbulent disputes in Dublin in 1913, industrial relations moved towards a more conciliatory approach based upon negotiations and mutual agreement. The union movement was accepted reluctantly and employers began to put employee relations machinery in place to deal with trade unions. Traditionally, the Irish system of employee relations has been described as voluntary. This is generally taken to mean an approach in which employers and trade unions are largely free to regulate the substantive and procedural terms of their relationship without State interference. The State's role is restricted to legislating on peripheral aspects and providing institutions of last resort for dispute resolution. This strategy has been termed one of 'auxiliary State control' and had been the dominant approach of Irish Governments towards employee relations up to the 1970s (Roche 1989). The major characteristic of this strategy is the general abstention of the law from the conduct of collective bargaining and particularly for matters relating to pay determination, trade union affairs and industrial conflict. State intervention through legislation, where it does occur, tends to focus on the provision of various conciliation services and arbitration facilities, and enacting individual employment legislation in areas where unions see little interference with their traditional bargaining freedom (Hillery 1989; 1995).

As in the UK, the 1980s in Ireland was a period of considerable change in the environment and practice of employee relations. Two major developments have contributed to a marked difference in the conduct of employee relations (Gunnigle and Morley 1992). At State level, public policy has caused the Irish system to move towards a more corporatist model, involving greater State intervention in the conduct of industrial relations. This departure is particularly manifest in the greater integration of the social partners, particularly the trade union movement, in policy making. The Programme for National Recovery (1987), the Programme for Economic and Social Progress (1991) and, currently, the Programme for Competitiveness and Work (1994) reflect this approach and incorporate centralised agreements on wages and other aspects of social and economic policies. Key developments have also occurred at organisational level.

11.3.1 Recent organisational level developments

At the workplace level, employee relations practice in the great majority of medium and large organisations in Ireland has traditionally been associated with a strong collectivist emphasis (Roche 1990). In this model, it is argued that employee relations is rarely a consideration of strategic decision makers and relations between management and employees are grounded in the pluralist tradition with a primary reliance on adversarial collective bargaining (Gunnigle 1992). This pluralist tradition is manifested in high levels of union density, highly developed collective bargaining institutions at establishment level and employee relations as the key concern of the specialist personnel function (Gunnigle 1992).

However, the period since the 1980s has witnessed considerable change in the context and practice of employee relations in Ireland (see Gunnigle and Roche 1995). The onset of recession lessened the emphasis on many core workforce management activities, such as recruitment and industrial relations. Trade union membership fell in the period between 1980 and 1987, and industrial unrest also declined significantly over the decade (Brannick and Doyle 1995). At the same time, many organisations tried to establish a competitive edge through improvements in quality, service and performance. One key source of such improvements has been an increased emphasis on the more optimal utilisation of human resources. At the organisational level, there has been a tendency, recently, to link employee relations with employee-oriented approaches to workforce management, which often incorporate a preference for non union status (Gunnigle 1994). Within this approach, preferential emphasis is placed upon dealing with employees as individuals as opposed to dealing with trade unions under the collectivist framework.

A second area that has arguably changed at organisational level is communications. Communications has grown in importance as part of the move towards greater individualism and in an attempt to improve the trust climate between the individual and the organisation. Recent Irish research casts some light on the changes that have been occurring in communications. In a survey of some 300 organisations, respondents were asked to indicate whether employees were briefed on company strategy and finances. This is a central question. In most larger organisations, the lines of communication have tended to be vertical, linked closely to the management hierarchy. The emphasis in these situations is on downward communication and, typically, both the flow and the weight of communication is biased in favour of management.

Table 11.1 Provision of Information on Business Strategy to Employees

GRADE OF EMPLOYEE	LEVEL OF COMMUNICATIONS/BRIEFING ON BUSINESS STRATEGY
Management	94 %
Professional/technical	65 %
Clerical	42 %
Manual	41 %
N = 267	

Source: Price Waterhouse Cranfield Project (Ireland), University of Limerick 1992.

Table 11.2 Provision of Information on Financial Performance to Employees

GRADE OF EMPLOYEE	LEVEL OF COMMUNICATIONS/BRIEFING ON FINANCIAL INFORMATION
Management	94 %
Professional/technical	65 %
Clerical	41 %
Manual	36 %
N = 267	

Source: Price Waterhouse Cranfield Project (Ireland), University of Limerick 1992.

The evidence suggests a trend towards a greater management emphasis on communication, particularly at lower levels in the organisation. This indicates a more direct relationship with employees in many organisations that includes briefing on strategic and financial matters. Whether this creates a more co-operative climate between management and employees is a moot question and will depend, among other things, on the nature and extent of the information provided to employees.

11.4 TRADE UNIONS

The Webbs, who wrote the first comprehensive history of trade unions and early collective bargaining, arrived at what is generally accepted as one of the most comprehensive definitions of a *trade union*, i.e. 'a continuous association of wage earners with the objective of improving or maintaining conditions of employment'. Essentially, therefore, unions are organisations that aim to unite workers with common interests. They seek to define those interests, express them and collectively advance them.

(Gunnigle et al 1992) Their basic strength lies in their ability to organise and unite. While employees join trade unions for a host of reasons, among the most common are a desire to influence pay claims, to have protection against arbitrary management actions and because they fundamentally believe in the function and the role of trade unions in society. By joining unions, employees provide themselves with the collective means and the strength to redress the imbalance in bargaining power which normally exists between an individual employee and his/her employer. In Ireland, there is a constitutional guarantee of freedom of association which gives individuals the right to join trade unions. This guarantee, embodied in article 40.6.1 of the Constitution, confers on workers the right to form or associate/disassociate with unions or other associations. However, while the Constitution supports the freedom of workers to organise, there is no statutory or constitutional provision for trade union recognition. Consequently, there is no obligation on employers to recognise or bargain with trade unions. Historically, this did not seem to cause many difficulties as most larger employers seemed happy to recognise and conclude collective agreements with trade unions. However, with the declining membership and power of Irish trade unions, the issue of recognition became contentious in the 1980s with some evidence of increased opposition to unionisation in recent years, particularly among some multinational organisations and indigenous small firms (Gunnigle and Brady 1984; McGovern 1989; Gunnigle 1992).

A major piece of legislation governing employee relations in Ireland was introduced in 1990 in the form of the Industrial Relations Act. The act deals with trade disputes, immunities, picketing, secret ballots, injunctions and trade union mergers and rationalisation. The act provides for the protection of persons who organise or engage in trade disputes from civil liability. The act further provides for the protection of trade union funds against actions for damages and the legalisation of peaceful picketing in trade dispute situations. It requires that trade unions conduct secret ballots prior to engaging in industrial action.

Table 11.3 highlights the major objectives of trade unions in Ireland.

Table 11.3 Trade Union Objectives in Ireland
1. Achieving satisfactory levels of pay and conditions of employment and providing members with a range of services.
2. Replacing individual bargaining with collective bargaining, thereby redressing the balance of bargaining power in favour of employees and reducing management prerogative in employment-related matters.
3. Facilitating the development of a political system where workers have a greater degree of influence on political decisions resulting in an economic and social framework which reflects employee needs rather than those of employers/management.

Source: Gunnigle, P., Garavan, T. and Fitzgerald, G., *Employment Relations and Law in Ireland*, PMTC Open Business School, Limerick 1992.

11.4.1 Types of trade union

Irish trade unions are normally organised on an occupational basis and may be loosely grouped into three broad categories: craft unions, general unions and white collar unions.

Craft unions cater for workers with a particular skill in a trade where entry is restricted through apprenticeship or otherwise. Craft unions have traditionally been protective of their trade by ensuring that only people holding union cards carry out certain types of skilled work. This has often led to criticisms of restrictive and inefficient work practices and, sometimes, to demarcation disputes. Increased mechanisation and consequent deskilling has had a detrimental impact on the membership and power of craft unions, as reflected in the reduction of their share of union members from a high of 17 per cent in 1940 to approximately 11 per cent in the 1980s. Examples of craft unions in Ireland are the Electrical Trade Union (ETU), and the National Union of Sheet Metal Workers of Ireland (NUSMWI)

General unions cater for all workers, regardless of skill or industry. However, they have traditionally centred on semi-skilled and unskilled workers. They form the largest unions and account for approximately half of all trade union members. General unions are common in all types of organisation and in all industrial sectors. The best known is the Services, Industrial, Professional and Technical Union (SIPTU), which is by far the largest union in Ireland.

White collar unions normally cater for professional, supervisory, clerical and managerial grades. Unions of this type experienced significant growth in membership in the 1980s, as reflected in their increased share of membership from 24 per cent in 1940 to over 35 per cent in the late 1980s. The Manufacturing, Service and Finance Union (MSF) and the Association of Secondary School Teachers of Ireland (ASTI) are examples of white collar unions.

Table 11.4 Trade Union Membership 1945–1990

YEAR	MEMBERSHIP	EMPLOYMENT DENSITY*	WORKFORCE DENSITY**
1945	172300	27.7	25.4
1960	312600	49.6	45.4
1975	448800	59.3	52.3
1980	527200	61.8	55.2
1981	524400	61.5	53.5
1982	519900	60.3	51.4
1983	513300	61.1	49.7
1984	500200	60.7	48.2
1985	483300	59.9	46.6
1986	471000	58.0	45
1987	457300	56.2	43.1
1988***	470644	57.1	44.2
1989	458690	55.6	43.4
1990	462451	54.6	43.2

*   Employment density = Trade union membership/civilian employees at work × 100
** Workforce density = Trade union membership/civilian employee workforce × 100
*** Figures for 1988–1990 are estimates and are derived from the annual affiliated membership of unions affiliated to the Irish Congress of Trade Unions

Source: Roche, Dues Project UCD 1992.

11.4.2 Trade union membership

The total number of trade unions in Ireland numbers some sixty-five, catering for a total membership of around 460,000 or 44 per cent of the workforce (Gunnigle et al 1995) (see Table 11.4). The period since 1980 has witnessed the most serious decline in trade union density in the post-war period. In the period between 1980 and 1987, trade union membership in Ireland fell by almost 10 per cent (Roche and Larragy 1989). However, this decline is principally attributed to macro-economic factors, most notably economic depression, increased levels of unemployment and changes in employment structure, characterised by a decline in highly unionised sectors (typical employment forms in manufacturing industry and the public sector), and a growth in sectors which have posed difficulties for union penetration, particularly private services (see Roche and Larragy 1989, 1992; Roche 1992). A study by Mc Govern (1989) points to increasing opposition to union recognition in the 1980s, suggesting that management approaches to unionisation have either hardened in line with the 'anti-union' style or become 'more subtle' in attempting to avoid unionisation.

The organisational level data emanating from the Price Waterhouse Cranfield Project reveals that the levels of trade union density in the surveyed companies is high, with almost two-thirds of respondent firms reporting that more than 50 per cent of their staff are trade union members (see Table 11.5.). Average union density across the companies is approximately 55.9 per cent. This compares closely with a union density of 56.2 per cent for the employed national labour force (i.e. the number of union members as a percentage of the employed labour force).

Table 11.5 Trade Union Density: Organisational Level

Proportion of employees in trade unions	%
1–25 %	6.4
26–50 %	10.9
51–75 %	18.0
76–100 %	2.3
Don't know/missing	4.1
N = 269	

Source: Price Waterhouse Cranfield Project (Ireland), University of Limerick 1992.

A large proportion (63 per cent) of the companies sampled have union levels in excess of 50 per cent of their workforce. The level of unionisation does appear to be related to the size of the organisation (in terms of number of employees), with large employers more likely to have higher levels of union density. This finding is supported by most of the empirical research on the determinants of unionisation.

11.4.3 Trade union structure

Essentially, there are three different levels at which trade unions operate: workplace level; branch level; and national level. Figure 11.1 illustrates this structure.

At the workplace level, shop stewards are the main trade union representatives. A shop steward is an employee who is accepted by both management and the union as a

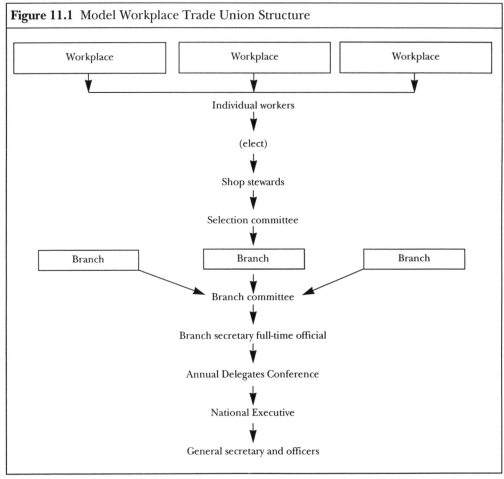

Figure 11.1 Model Workplace Trade Union Structure

Workplace | Workplace | Workplace

Individual workers

(elect)

Shop stewards

Selection committee

Branch | Branch | Branch

Branch committee

Branch secretary full-time official

Annual Delegates Conference

National Executive

General secretary and officers

Source: Gunnigle, P., McMahon, G. and Fitzgerald, G., *Industrial Relations in Ireland: Theory and Practice*, Gill & Macmillan, Dublin 1995.

lay representative of the union and its members. A steward is charged with the responsibility of acting on the membership's behalf in industrial relations matters at the organisational level. He/she is elected by fellow trade union members at annual elections. A steward must also perform his/her job like all other employees. In this respect, shop stewards are given reasonable time off work for union business. The major functions of the shop steward are as follows:

1. recruit new members into the union
2. collect union subscriptions from members
3. negotiate with management on behalf of the members
4. liaise with the unions central office
5. represent workers in grievance and disciplinary situations.

The section committee is a group of trade union members elected by fellow union members who work in a specific section of the organisation. The section committee's main activity is to help shop stewards to perform their tasks effectively. On a committee of this kind all of the stewards are from the same trade union. If they are members of different trade unions, the committee is known as a joint shop stewards committee. Such a committee can regulate conflict between unions and support individual stewards. It also constitutes a more powerful body for negotiating with management.

A trade union branch is typically made up of employees from different organisations located in the same geographical area. The branch manages the internal affairs of the union and strives for improvements in the terms and conditions of branch members. The affairs of the branch are managed by the branch committee.This committee is elected at an Annual General Meeting, which is also the forum for electing delegates from the branch to attend the Annual Delegate Conference of the union.

Both the branch committee and the branch members are served by a branch secretary. In larger unions, this individual may be a permanent employee of the union. If so, he/she is described as a full-time branch official, whose role is to administer the affairs of the branch and negotiate terms and conditions for all branch members with management.

At national level, the election of union officers takes place at the Annual Delegate Conference. Motions concerning the union and its policies are discussed and voted upon. These motions are usually branch resolutions and a motion that is approved at the Annual Delegate Conference becomes a resolution of the conference and, ultimately, union policy. The Annual Delegate Conference is made up of branch delegates and the union's National Executive, responsible for carrying out the decisions of the Conference. In particular, it appoints the union's full-time branch officials and appoints staff employed by the union.

The general officers of the union are usually full-time employees of the union who do not have other jobs. In some unions, they are appointed to their position by the National Executive, while in others they are elected at the Annual Delegate Conference or by a ballot of union members. The general officers usually consist of a General President, a General Secretary, a General Vice President and a General Treasurer.

11.4.4 The Irish Congress of Trade Unions

The *Irish Congress of Trade Unions* (ICTU) is the central co-ordinating body for the Irish trade union movement, with over 95 per cent of trade unionists in membership of unions affiliated to Congress. Individual unions maintain a large degree of autonomy and the ICTU relies on the co-operation of affiliated unions in promoting its overall goals. However, Congress does seek to represent the collective interests of the Irish trade union movement. The annual conference of the ICTU comprises delegates from affiliated unions. The ICTU plays a critical role at national level, representing union views to Government. Along with the other social partners (Government, employer representatives, farmer federations), it is party to national negotiations on pay and other aspects of social and economic policy. It is a vehicle through which trade unions decide whether or not to participate in centralised agreeements (such as the Programme for Competitiveness and Work). Various committees operate under the auspices of Congress to deal with internal union issues such as transfer of membership.

11.5 EMPLOYER ORGANISATIONS

The major driving force for the development of *employer organisations* was the perceived need for employers to organise collectively in order to counter balance and deal effectively with the emerging trade unions. Employer organisations in Ireland are of two types: Employer Associations and Trade Associations. Employer Associations were established to aid in the conduct of employee relations, whereas Trade Associations were established for trade and commercial reasons.

Gunnigle et al (1995) highlight that Employer Associations have the following broad objectives:

1. To effectively represent employer's views to Government and to other appropriate bodies so as to preserve and develop a political, economic, social and cultural climate in which business objectives can be achieved.
2. To create an environment/climate which supports free enterprise and enshrines managerial prerogative in decision making.
3. To ensure the existence of a legislative and procedural environment which supports and co-ordinates employer's views on employee relations matters and provides assistance to affiliated employers.

The largest Employer Association in Ireland is the Irish Business and Employers Confederation (IBEC), which was formed in 1993 through an amalgamation of two previously separate institutions — the Federation of Irish Employers (FIE) and the Confederation of Irish Industry (CII). IBEC represents the alliance of some 4,000 companies and organisations which recognised the need for a single cohesive force capable of providing effective leadership and representation in the current turbulent business environment. IBEC is dedicated to promoting a favourable climate for economic growth, investment and employee/industrial relations. IBEC has offices in Dublin, Cork, Limerick, Waterford, Galway, Donegal Town and Brussels. Among its services are:

1. representation in relations with Government, trade unions and EU institutions on commercial, economic and industrial and employee relations issues
2. membership of an appropriate sector organisation with direct links to the corresponding European association; conferences, seminars, specialist publications, statistics, business sector profiles and customised research
3. a range of additional consultancy services, such as human resource management, health, safety and environment, training and development.

At national level, IBEC has a strong regional membership structure through which the views of members are co-ordinated and representation can be made on matters of regional interest. At European level, through its Brussels office, IBEC seeks to influence EU economic and social policy, represent Irish interests in the Union of Industry and Employer Confederations in Europe (UNICE), and produce a range of specialist publications, including *EU Business Opportunities* and *EU Monthly Report*. The Confederation also represents members' interests in many international organisations, such as the International Labour Office and the International Organisation of Employers.

11.6 THE ROLE OF STATE INSTITUTIONS IN EMPLOYEE RELATIONS

Traditionally, the role of the State in employee relations in Ireland has been restricted to the establishment of legislative ground rules and the provision of mediation and arbitration machinery, leaving employers and employees relatively free to develop work rules and the procedures to suit particular organisational contexts. In more recent years, the role of the State in employee relations has increased, particularly through a process of reforming the system of employee relations and also acting as a party to national agreements such as the PNR, PESP and the PCW (see Roche 1995).

The State provides a number of specific institutions — the *Labour Relations Commission*, the *Labour Court, Rights Commissioners, Equality Officers* and the *Employment Appeals Tribunal* — all charged with various responsibilities for employee relations matters.

11.6.1 The Labour Relations Commission

Formally established by the then Minister for Labour in January 1991, the Labour Relations Commission's statutory authority and functions derive from Section 24 and Section 25 of the Industrial Relations Act 1990. It is a tripartite body with employer, trade union and independent representation and has been charged with the general responsibility of promoting good industrial relations. The Commission provides a comprehensive range of services designed to prevent the occurrence of disputes and, where they do occur, some mechanisms for resolution. The key services provided by the Labour Relations Commission are as follows:

1. conciliation service
2. industrial relations advisory service
3. preparation of codes of practice relevant to industrial relations after consultation with unions and employers' organisations
4. providing guidance on codes of practice
4. appointment of Equality Officers and the provision of an equality service
5. selection and nomination of persons for appointment as Rights Commissioners
6. commissioning of research into matters relevant to industrial relations
7. review and monitoring of developments in the area of industrial relations
8. assisting joint labour committees and joint industrial councils in the exercise of their functions.

The conciliation service was formally provided by the Labour Court. The service can be seen as a proactive measure to resolve disputes before they require full Labour Court investigation. The focus of the conciliation service is on the dispute at hand. In 1992, the work of the conciliation service was undertaken by an average of ten Industrial Relations Officers. As the following Table highlights, activity levels in the conciliation service were high during 1992.

Table 11.6 Conciliation Service Activities 1992					
Year	No. of disputes		Total	Meetings settled	
	Private sector	*Public sector*			
1991	1303	577	1880	2485	85 %
1992	1388	547	1935	2450	75 %

Source: Labour Relations Commission Annual Report 1992.

An analysis of the cases dealt with in 1992 shows that conditions of employment, special pay increases and basic pay claims were the main issues dealt with by the conciliation service.

The role of the advisory service is broader than that of the conciliation service and is designed to help in the identification of general problems which may give rise to employee relations difficulties. The advisory service brings with it a new dimension to the services available to Irish employers and trade unions. It has as its central brief the task of preventing industrial disputes by encouraging good industrial relations policies, practices and procedures in the workplace. The service becomes involved in assignments either on the basis of union/management agreement or on the initiative of the Labour Relations Commission, with the agreement of the parties concerned. In 1992, the advisory service undertook eight projects of which two involved private sector companies and six involved private sector employments.

11.6.2 The Labour Court

Established in 1946 by the Industrial Relations Act, the Labour Court is a central institution in the Irish system of employee relations. Its role has changed significantly as a result of the 1990 Industrial Relations Act. The Court's central role is investigating and making recommendations on cases referred to it by parties in dispute. If the conciliation service provided by the Labour Relations Commission fails to resolve a dispute, both parties can ask the Labour Court to hear their case. The 1990 Industrial Relations Act provides that the Labour Court may investigate a dispute only in the following situations:
1. If it receives a report from the Labour Relations Commission that no further efforts on its part will help resolve the dispute.
2. If it is notified by the chairperson of the Commission that the Commission has waived its function of conciliation in the dispute.
3. If it is hearing an appeal in relation to a recommendation of a Rights Commissioner or an Equality Officer.
4. If it decides after consultation with the Commission that exceptional circumstances of the case warrant a Labour Court investigation.
5. If it is referred to under Section 20 of the Industrial Relations Act 1969.
6. If it requested by the Minister for Enterprise and Employment to do so.

A Labour Court hearing normally consists of an independent chairperson, an employer and a trade union representative. Hearings typically involve both written and oral submissions and some element of cross examination. When the Court has fully investigated the case it will issue a recommendation which is not legally binding.

11.6.3 The Rights Commissioner

Rights Commissioners are appointed by the Minister for Labour under the auspices of the Industrial Relations Act 1969. They deal with disputes concerning individual employees. Originally established under the operation of the Labour Court, the Rights Commissioner Service now operates as part of the Labour Relations Commission. Commissioners remain completely independent in the performance of their functions. They investigate disputes under the Industrial Relations Act 1969, the Unfair Dismissals Act 1977, the Maternity Protection Act 1981 and the Payment of Wages Act 1991. A Rights Commissioner will only deal with a dispute if:

1. it is not connected with the pay and conditions of a collective group of workers
2. it has been or is not already being investigated by the Labour Court
3. a party to the dispute does not object in writing.

Generally, a Rights Commissioner will investigate disputes concerning individual employees only. Recent legislation in the form of the Industrial Relations Act 1990 provides that an objection to an investigation by a Rights Commissioner must be notified in writing to the Commissioner within three weeks. An appeal against a recommendation from a Rights Commissioner must be notified in writing to the Labour Court within six weeks from the date of the recommendation.

The number and category of disputes investigated by Rights Commissioners in 1992 are shown in Table 11.7.

Table 11.7 Rights Commissioner Investigations 1992					
YEAR	INDUSTRIAL RELATIONS ACT 1969	UNFAIR DISMISSALS ACT 1977	MATERNITY PROTECTION ACT 1981	PAYMENT OF WAGES ACT 1991	TOTAL
1992	965	110	1	115	1191

Source: The Labour Relations Commission Annual Report 1992.

The figures here represent an increase of 7.5 per cent from 1991. Stemming from recommendations made by Rights Commissioners in 1992, there were 125 appeals to the Labour Court. In seventy-four cases the Rights Commissioner recommendation was upheld, thirty-nine were amended and twelve were overturned.

11.6.4 Equality Officers

Equality Officers deal with issues relating to discrimination on the grounds of sex or marital status arising under the Anti-Discrimination Pay Act 1974 and the Employment Equality Act 1977. Employers are obliged to abide by the terms of both acts and claims under the acts are referred to an Equality Officer. Such officers operate under the auspices of the Labour Relations Commission, but are independent in the performance of their duties. When a dispute is referred to an Equality Officer, he/she will carry out an investigation and issue a recommendation. If either party is dissatisfied with the recommendation, they may appeal to the Labour Court within forty-two days. In such circumstances the Court's determination is legally binding.

In 1992, a total of fifty-seven cases were referred for investigation by an Equality Officer, twenty under the Anti-Discrimination Pay Act 1974 and thirty-seven under the Employment Equality Act 1977. The Equality Officers issued thirty-six recommendations during 1992, twenty-two under the 1974 Act and fourteen under the 1977 Act (Labour Relations Commission Annual Report 1992). During 1992, the recommendations of Equality Officers dealt with disputes in a wide range of employments in both the public and private sectors. In the case of the 1974 Act, in addition to disputes involving claims for equal basic rates of pay, the recommendations covered disputes relating to claims for marriage gratuities, voluntary redundancy benefits and overtime/call-out payments. Recommendations under the 1977 Act dealt with disputes in relation to access to employment, promotion, alleged discriminatory advertisements, alleged sexual harassment, reduction of working hours and alleged discrimination in relation to conditions of employment. A number of recommendations under the 1977 Act also dealt with alleged discrimination relating to pregnancy or maternity leave.

11.6.5 Employment Appeals Tribunal

The current Employment Appeals Tribunal (EAT) was initially established as the Redundancy Appeals Tribunal under the terms of the Redundancy Payments Act 1969, and was later renamed the Employment Appeals Tribunal under the Unfair Dismissals Act 1977.

The Employment Appeals Tribunal consists of a chairperson, who must be a practising barrister or solicitor, seven vice-chairpersons and a panel of ordinary members drawn equally from employer associations and the Irish Congress of Trade Unions. The Tribunal operates in divisions consisting of a chairperson or vice-chairperson and two other members, one from the employer's side and one from the trade union side.

The EAT adjudicates upon a number of Acts, including the Redundancy Payments Acts 1967 - 89, the Terms of Employment Act 1994 (replacing the Minimum Notice and Terms of Employment Act 1973), the Unfair Dismissals (Amendment) Act 1993 and the Unfair Dismissals Act 1977, and the Maternity (Protection of Employees) Act 1981.

At the beginning of 1993, there were 2,678 cases awaiting hearing, including 1,623 under the Minimum Notice Acts and 435 under the Unfair Dismissals Acts. During 1993, the Tribunal disposed of 5,789 cases compared with 5,761 cases in 1992. At the end of 1993, there were 1,496 cases waiting to be heard. A breakdown of the cases referred to and disposed of under the various Acts during 1993 is given in the following Table.

Table 11.8 Employment Appeals Tribunal: Cases in 1993

Act	No. of appeals referred	Allowed	Dismissed	Withdrawn during hearing	Withdrawn prior to hearing	Total number of appeals
Redundancy Payments	967	444	202	162	142	950
Minimum Notice and Terms of Employment	3,425	2,609	368	174	329	3,480
Unfair Dismissals	1,145	223	199	239	275	936
Maternity Protection of Employees	23	0	8	9	9	26
Protection of Employees (employers' insolvency)	100	266	6	1	4	277
Worker Protection (regular part-time employees)	50	3	21	8	9	41
TOTAL	5,710	3,545	804	593	768	5,710

Source: Department of Enterprise and Employment Annual Report 1993.

Overall, State institutions play a major role in employee relations in Ireland.

Operating within the framework of the Industrial Relations Act 1990 and earlier legislation, State institutions are largely concerned with conciliation and arbitration.

11.7 SUMMARY OF KEY PROPOSITIONS

• Classical definitions of employee relations emphasise the rules or job regulation mechanisms which govern the employment relationship in the workplace. These rules are divided into procedural rules and substantive rules.

• Pluralism in employee relations refers to the existence of a conflict of interest between management and labour which can best be handled through collective bargaining. Unitarism refers to the existence of a mutuality of interests between the parties in the labour process.

• Traditionally, the Irish system of employee relations has been described as voluntary which refers to an approach in which employers and trade unions are largely free to regulate their relationship without state interference.

• Recent years have brought major changes which are evident at two levels: the State and the organisational levels. At the State level, the voluntarist tradition has been diluted in favour of a consensus approach to employee relations. Secondly, the absence of a constitutional provision for trade union recognition has become contentious. At the organisational level, there has been a tendency to link employee relations with employee-oriented approaches to workforce management and communication has grown as a part of the move towards greater individualism in employee relations.

• A trade union can be defined as a continuous association of wage earners with the objective of improving or maintaining conditions of employment. There are three major types of trade union in Ireland: craft unions, general unions and white collar unions. Currently, the total number of trade unions in Ireland is around sixty-five, catering for a total membership of 460,000, or 44 per cent of the workforce.

• There are two types of employer organisation in Ireland: Employer Associations and Trade Associations. The largest Employer Association is IBEC which represents an alliance of some 4,000 companies

• The major State institutions involved in employee relations in Ireland are the Labour Relations Commission, the Labour Court, Rights Commissioners, Equality Officers and the Employment Appeals Tribunal.

DISCUSSION QUESTIONS

1. Define the following terms:
    employee relations
    procedural rules in employee relations
    substantive rules in employee relations
    pluralism in employee relations

unitarism in employee relations

voluntarism in employee relations.

2. Describe the major changes that have taken place in Irish employee relations in recent years, giving reasons for the changes.

3. Outline the major aims of trade unions and discuss the key strategies that are employed to achieve these aims

4. Discuss the changes that have occurred in trade union membership in Ireland since 1945.

5. There are too many trade unions in Ireland relative to the total membership. Discuss.

6. Write a note on the Irish Business and Employer's Confederation, focusing on its role and the advantages and disadvantages of membership from the organisation's perspective.

7. Discuss the role of both the Labour Court and the Labour Relations Commission in Irish employee relations.

REFERENCES

Brannick, T. and Doyle, L., 'Industrial Conflict' in Murphy, T. and Roche, W. (eds), *Irish Industrial Relations in Practice*, Oak Tree Press, Dublin 1995.

Breen, R., Haman, D., Rottman, D. and Whelan, C., *Understanding Contemporary Ireland*, Gill & Macmillan, Dublin 1990.

Dunlop, J., *Industrial Relations Systems*, Carbondale, Southern Illinois University Press, Carbondale 1959.

Gunnigle, P., Garavan, T. and Fitzgerald, G., *Employee Relations and Employment Law in Ireland*, PMTC Open Business School, Limerick 1992.

Gunnigle, P. and Brady, T., 'The Management of Industrial Relations in the Small Firm' *Employee Relations*, Vol.6, No.5, 1984.

Gunnigle, P. and Flood, P., *Personnel Management in Ireland*, Gill & Macmillan, Dublin 1990.

Gunnigle, P. and Morley, M., 'Something Old, Something New: A Perspective on Industrial Relations in the Republic of Ireland' *Review of Employment Topics*, Vol.1, No.1, 1992.

Gunnigle, P. and Roche, W., *New Challenges to Irish Industrial Relations*, Oak Tree Press, Dublin 1995.

Gunnigle, P., 'Changing Management Approaches to Employee Relations in Ireland' *Employee Relations*, Vol.14, No.1, 1992.

Gunnigle, P., McMahon, G. and Fitzgerald, G., *Industrial Relations in Ireland: Theory and Practice*, Gill & Macmillan, Dublin 1995.

Hillery, B., 'An Overview of the Irish Industrial Relations System' in *Industrial Relations in Ireland*, UCD, Dublin 1989.

Marchington, M., *Managing Industrial Relations*, McGraw-Hill, New York 1982.

McGovern, P., 'Union Recognition and Union Avoidance in the 1980s', in *Industrial Relations in Ireland*, UCD, Dublin 1989.

Roche, W. and Larragy, J., 'The Trend of Unionisation in the Irish Republic' in *Industrial Relations in Ireland*, UCD, Dublin 1989.

Roche, W., 'State Strategies and the Politics of Industrial Relations in Ireland' in *Industrial Relations in Ireland*, UCD, Dublin 1989.

Marketing Management

12.1 INTRODUCTION

Marketing has emerged as a recognised and separate discipline in Ireland during the last thirty years. The early successes of Irish brands such as Guinness, Kerrygold and Waterford are the results of good marketing. Marketing awareness has been heightened since Ireland's entry into the European Union in 1973, making business more conscious of the need to compete on equal terms with other member states. Membership has brought about a significant change in exporting patterns, as dependence on the UK market has gradually been replaced by a focus on mainland European countries. The Irish market has itself become more competitive and indigenous firms have to fight harder to maintain market share.

Irish companies are keenly aware of the need to be market-led in their choice of *products* and services to sell. Ireland exports about 71 per cent of its Gross National Product, making it one of the most trade dependent nations in the world. Ireland's advantage as a competitive country — ranked nineteenth in the 1994 world league of competitiveness (*The Irish Times*, 1994) — offers companies a strong incentive to produce goods and services that can be marketed world-wide.

12.2 THE MARKETING CONCEPT

Marketing existed from the time man carried out the earliest exchanges. These exchanges increased as formal markets emerged where buyers and sellers could trade goods and services. The development of a monetary system allowed exchanges to be valued on a more objective basis. From these earliest concepts, Kotler (1993) was able to define marketing as: 'a social and managerial process by which individuals obtain what they need and want through creating, offering and exchanging products of value with others'.

As discretionary income grew, people could exercise more choice in their purchasing behaviour. Certain products acquired a status or scarcity value and, therefore, could command a higher price. Marketers began to recognise different segments, or buyer groups, based on criteria such as age or income. Henry Ford's old adage that the car buyer could have 'any colour he wanted so long as it was black', was gradually replaced by promises such as that offered by Texaco, '100 % satisfaction guaranteed — or your money back'.

Marketing, as it is understood today, has evolved through several stages, each of which reflected the prevailing business environment.

Figure 12.1 Phases of Marketing Development

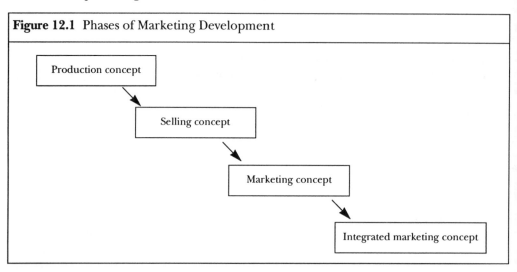

In the early days of mass manufacturing, firms were production-orientated in their approach. The emphasis was on selling whatever the firm could make, and this focus on manufacturing is still evident in many cases today. As the scale of output increased, and consumer demand boomed from the late 1940s, firms became more sales-oriented in their approach. The emphasis was on making whatever products would sell, in order to use capacity and achieve sales targets. By the late 1950s, booming demand and a recognition of customer needs were responsible for the development of a marketing orientation. Researching customer needs, developing better products and planning marketing activity became more important. By the late 1980s, mixed experiences of boom and recession had reinforced the marketing message. The success of the Japanese in world markets caused many firms to re-examine their marketing strategies. Porter's (1980, 1985) analyses of competition and the sources of competitive advantage (see Chapter 3) suggested that businesses should develop a market-focused approach. This means putting marketing at the centre of business activities in order to build a more concrete and long-term relationship with customers. The level of service offered and the company's interest in doing business with its customers determine whether buyers remain loyal or decide to take their business elsewhere.

These trends have led to the development of another widely accepted definition of marketing, proposed by the UK Chartered Institute of Marketing: 'Marketing is the management process responsible for identifying, anticipating and satisfying consumers' requirements profitably' (Dibb et al 1994).

Currently, the unceasing demand for innovation and ever shortening *product life cycles*, mean that marketing is high on most business agendas. The marketing function is becoming more closely integrated with other functions within the firm, in order to build and maintain a more sustainable competitive advantage. As the scale of world trade increases, and markets become more exposed to international as well as domestic competitors, it is evident that a marketing focus is the key to survival.

12.2.1 Marketing as an attitude

A firm will only survive as long as it can find groups of customers willing to buy its products at a price sufficient to ensure an acceptable profit. To have a 'marketing attitude' a company must meet these requirements:

1. It must listen to its customers. This means conducting *market research*, bearing in mind customer needs when designing and pricing the product, and using buyers as a source of new product ideas.
2. It must integrate its efforts. The marketing function must be integrated with other functions of the company, rather than acting in isolation. Finance, R&D and manufacturing departments must all be aware that their survival depends on serving the customer.
3. It must be profit conscious. A company or an entrepreneur can be so taken with the idea for a new product that the cost and profit considerations are put to one side. For example, John de Lorean's dream of producing a new concept in sports cars went ahead, even though it became apparent at an early stage that the venture was a loss maker. Therefore, a marketer needs a good understanding of financial aspects, such as costs, margins and variances.
4. It must obtain high visibility in the market-place: A well-known brand or company name is a valuable asset in the marketplace. When Glen Dimplex took over Morphy Richards, a consumer survey was conducted to test brand awareness. Knowledge of the brand name was so strong that people associated Morphy Richards with a whole range of appliances apart from the irons and toasters which were their staple products. This led Dimplex to decide to capitalise on the brand name by broadening the product range.

12.2.2 The role of the marketing manager

The job of the marketing manager evolved from the sales function described in Section 12.2. The marketing manager is responsible for anticipating and serving customer needs in a way that will best profit the company. The activity of marketing management ranges across consumer, business-to-business and non profit *enterprises*. In many small firms no one is exclusively responsible for marketing, but a marketing awareness is still necessary if the venture is to succeed.

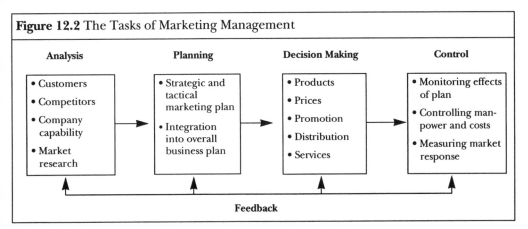

Figure 12.2 The Tasks of Marketing Management

Analysis	Planning	Decision Making	Control
• Customers • Competitors • Company capability • Market research	• Strategic and tactical marketing plan • Integration into overall business plan	• Products • Prices • Promotion • Distribution • Services	• Monitoring effects of plan • Controlling man-power and costs • Measuring market response

Feedback

As Figure 12.2 illustrates, the task of marketing management spans four areas of responsibility: market analysis, marketing planning, *marketing mix* decisions and marketing control.

12.3 MARKET ANALYSIS

The starting point for market analysis is usually customer analysis, whether the customers are individuals, couples, households, individual firms or buying groups. The second dimension is competitor analysis, the extent of which depends on how broadly competition is defined. With a knowledge of both customers and competitors, the firm is better equipped to analyse its own capability to compete. Market research can then be used to explore and test these ideas in the market-place.

12.3.1 Customers

A customer may buy goods or services while acting in his/her capacity as an individual, a parent buying on behalf of a child, as part of a household or as part of a corporate buying committee. The nature of the goods being purchased may be simple and routine, often described as a limited problem-solving situation. For example, the purchase of most grocery products is routinised, and consumers rely on display and promotions to trigger their actual choice. For more expensive or infrequent purchases, the buyer is involved in extensive problem solving. Because he/she is less knowledgeable and more likely to be acting as part of a group, he/she is likely to take more time and to collect information before making a decision.

The stages in the buying decision making process are illustrated in Figure 12.3. The buying process may be quick and impulsive, as with a chocolate bar, and in such a case the buyer moves quickly from need perception to purchase. In more complex buying situations the process is formalised and takes more time, as with a hospital buying new X-ray equipment.

Figure 12.3 Steps in the Buying Process

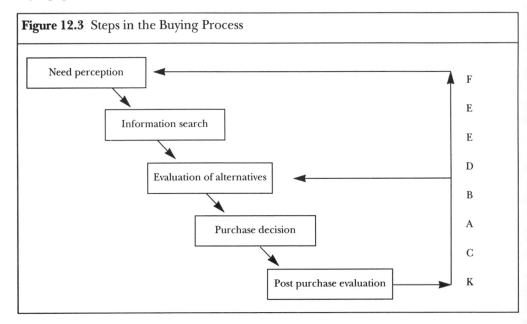

In any type of buying situation, the initial stage is the perception of a need or a want, which may be absolute or discretionary. One of the main purposes of advertising is to heighten perceived needs, which the advertiser then suggests can be satisfied through purchasing certain goods and services.

Next, the buyer gathers information. For low-cost items, this is done passively through absorption of advertising and other information. If the purchase is more involved, the buyer will be active in seeking information from personal sources (family, friends, colleagues), as well as the mass media.

Now that the buyer is aware of some options (not necessarily all those that exist), he/she has to evaluate the alternatives. With routine purchases, this will be done informally by switching brands or sampling new products. In complex situations, the buyer will develop a range of criteria against which to rate his/her options.

At this point, he/she decides on a course of action. The decision may be to do nothing, to postpone a decision, to make an enquiry, or to make a purchase. Much marketing effort is designed to encourage buying now rather than later, and eases the buyer into purchasing through reduced prices, loans or no-interest repayments.

The actual purchase represents the beginning of a formal relationship between the buyer and seller. The buyer evaluates the product he/she has bought, either formally or informally, and wants to be reassured that it was right decision. The seller can use advertising or direct marketing techniques to talk to existing as well as prospective buyers, and offer a level of service that will encourage the buyer to return.

Having developed an understanding of how customers buy, the second stage in customer analysis is the identification of the segments in the market. A market segment is defined as 'a group of customers whose needs and consumption patterns are very similar to each other while being different in some significant way from the other groups in the same general market.' (Murray and O'Driscoll, 1993). For example, in the bicycle market there are key differences between buyers who use bicycles for recreation, for sport or for transport. Each segment can have sub-segments, for example, customers using bicycles for recreation may be looking for high or average performance machines in the price bracket £150 to £350.

The main approaches to defining market segments are shown in Figure 12.4.

Figure 12.4 Approaches to Market Segmentation

Customer Characteristics

• Geographic	• Population within a mile radius of a new shopping centre
• Type of Organisation	• Computer needs of small firms versus large firms
• Lifestyle	• The family station wagon buyer versus the recreational vehicle customer
• Sex	• Female buyers of mobile phones
• Age	• Cereals for children versus adults
• Social Class	• Newspapers aimed at specific social class groupings

Product Related Approaches

• User Type	• Users of electric drills — builders, home owners, DIY enthusiasts
• Usage	• Heavy users of convenience foods
• Benefits Sought	• Dairy spreads: difference between the calorie conscious and the taste conscious
• Price Sensitivity	• The Ford Fiesta buyer versus the Jaguar buyer
• Competitor	• Software users committed to Microsoft
• Application	• Home computer users versus business users
• Brand Loyalty	• Heinz beans buyers versus the rest

Source: Adapted from Aaker, D. A., *Startegic Market Management,* John Wiley, New York 1995.

A breakdown of the key segments in the market is vital to an understanding of how the market works. It also signals how resources should be allocated to effectively target the chosen segments.

12.3.2 Competitors

Every firm has to be aware of its rivals, both immediate and potential. It is probably easy enough to identify one's direct competitors; the greater difficulties are encountered when quantifying all the existing players in the market and the potential entrants. For example, it is a straightforward exercise to identify all the manufacturers of branded frozen pizza products sold in Ireland. More work is needed to identify the makers of *own-branded products*. Additionally, there are potentially hundreds of food firms who could enter the market (recent examples include McCain and McVities).

The next step is to identify the positions of the competitors — that is, the market segment that they are addressing and the particular needs they claim to serve. New competitors usually try to address a different set of needs and hence build a unique market position. For example, Sony took a tape player and headphones, redesigned them around the concept of portability, and came up with the Walkman. It is also important to analyse exactly how competitors compete and react to moves by rivals. Aer Lingus has often reacted to new competitors on the Dublin - London route by cutting its fares and stepping up advertising. New entrants have sometimes complained to the European Commission about these practices.

Analysis of competitors' strengths and weaknesses will reveal possible angles for attack. For example, in the ice-cream market, Mars identified a new niche through the development of ice-cream bars, targeted towards the teenage/adult market. A more recent entrant, Haagan Daaz, is developing the super premium end of the market and has pioneered new distribution outlets, such as cinemas and video stores.

With these concepts in mind, the firm can develop its own competitive strategy. To develop a complete picture of the competitive structure of an industry, Porter (1980) has suggested that competitors and competitive rivalry are only one of five forces to be considered. The other forces to be analysed are the threat of new entrants, the bargaining power of suppliers, the threat of substitutes and the power of buyers (see Chapter 3).

Taking the Irish telecommunications market as an example, the Single European Market has opened up the market to new entrants. A new competitor, Esat Telecom, has targeted large companies and offered them guaranteed reductions on international calls. Business customers are using their buying power to keep call rates down. Pressure groups have lobbied government on behalf of the individual consumer. Many *substitute products* are potentially available, both locally and internationally, e.g. a second licence for the mobile telephone market is expected to be announced in 1996. Telecom Eireann is being pressurised to keep costs down, and is currently engaged in a search for a strategic partner.

12.3.3 Company capability

The 'insiders' within a company often experience extreme difficulty in putting forward an objective definition of capabilities. Personal and internal political reasons can also override the desire to be objective. For these reasons, outside consultants or auditors are often helpful.

The objective of a *capability analysis* is to reach an understanding of the firm's core competences — areas in which it has a strong or unique ability. Murray and O'Driscoll (1993) have summarised the process by which a firm reaches an understanding of its strengths, weaknesses, opportunities and threats — a *SWOT analysis.*

Even the smallest firm operating in a commodity business must develop some core skills and assets that will enable it to compete in the long term.

Figure 12.5 SWOT Analysis

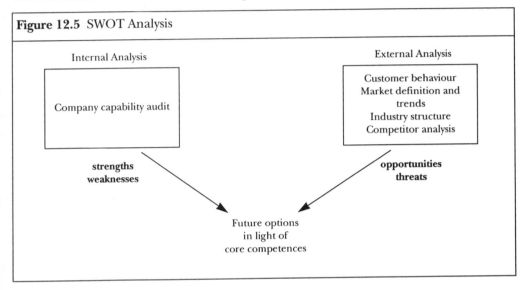

12.3.4 Marketing information and research

As markets have become more complex and more segmented, the demand for *marketing information* has exploded. Irish companies generally seek information in relation to the following questions:

1. At the start-up stage, is there a market for the planned product or service?
2. As the company develops, how can products be improved and competitors countered?
3. As the company considers new markets, what are the key differentiating factors between the export market and the home market?

Marketing information is generally classified as any information that is relevant to making marketing decisions. This includes information about legal regulations, customers and competitors, as well as information directly related to the product or service concerned. A market-focused firm will be keen to develop a marketing *information system* — a channel through which marketing information can be collected and disseminated in a timely fashion. Such a system enables a firm to better manage and anticipate the external anvironment, so that it is less likely to be surprised by unforeseen events. It also facilitates the organisation in contingency planning.

Marketing information is collected from two sources:

1. Internal data: Company records of sales volume, profits, production and shipping schedules, sales per customer, delivery times and customer turnover, are important indicators of how well the business is performing.
2. External data: This comes from two different sources:
   (i) *Secondary data* — information which is already available, usually through third

party sources. Examples include research reports, government and trade statistics, the media, books, directories and commercial *databases*. While much of this information is useful and available at a low cost, it may be incomplete or out of date. Appendix 1 gives a description of the main sources of secondary data relevant to Irish business. Exhibit 12.1 gives an example of the relevance and availability of secondary data.

Exhibit 12.1 Secondary data sources

Danielle O'Donnell has worked for seven years in a bridal wear outlet and is now hoping to set up her own bridal wear boutique in her native town of Castlebar. Her first step in putting together a business plan is to gather relevant secondary data. After two months research she has accumulated the following secondary information:

Data	Source
Population of catchment area Age structure of population Number of marriages Average age of marriage	Central Statistics Office
Listing of bridal firms in the region	*Golden Pages, Kompass,* directories Bridal magazines
Number of marriages and seasonality of the business	Local churches
Start-up capital required	Existing outlets
Average bridal spend	Franchisors Bridal wear distributors Published surveys Trade magazines
Future market trends	Economic and Social
(See Appendix 1)	Research Institute and CSO projections

Primary data is new information which is collected for the specific purposes of the research in hand. This data is collected through direct observation, the collection of survey data, or by setting up an experimental situation. Primary data collection can be expensive and time consuming, but its objective is to present a more complete and up to date picture of the situation. It is particularly important when studying new markets or export markets.

The market research process (i.e. the process of collecting and analysing the information required to address marketing problems) is carried out in five steps:

1. **Defining research objectives**: To be successful, the aims of the research must be agreed from the outset. If the project is to explore a new market, the information needed will be of a general and descriptive nature. If the aim is to resolve a particular issue, such as why the product is not selling well in a particular area, the need is for specific, conclusive information.

2. **Developing a research plan**: This involves deciding on the extent of the information search, how it is to be conducted and the cost. Many projects limit themselves to secondary data, which can be quite adequate in established, well-documented industries. For new markets and new products, both primary and secondary data can

be used in order to develop a more detailed picture.

3. **Collecting data**: This refers to the time-consuming work involved in actually acquiring the information. The availability of databases has speeded up the acquisition of secondary data, but the information still has to be sifted through, analysed and re-presented. With primary data collection adequate time must be allowed for the completion of interviews or questionnaires.

4. **Analysing data**: Without proper information analysis, much of the effort put into data collection would be wasted. Information must be tabulated and graphed. Statistical techniques such as correlation and regression are used to test the reliability of the information collected.

5. **Preparing a research report**: This enables the raw data to be represented to management in a more understandable format. Such a report usually starts with a summary of the main findings, followed by a more detailed report and statistical analysis. The idea is that the report should contain enough information for all the target audiences, and should also summarise the data in such a way as to highlight the main findings.

Exhibit 12.2 Ballygowan Kisqua

In 1988, Ballygowan Spring Water Company considered launching a new fruit-flavoured soft drink. Once a product had been formulated, the first step in researching the market was to test a range of flavours. The next step was to test a range of brand names and pack designs. From the findings produced by the research company, the brand name 'Kisqua' was chosen as best to represent a natural orange-based soft drink. The findings also recommended that the drink be aimed at the middle to higher income groups of both sexes in the eighteen to thirty age group. The product was then tested extensively in the market-place before being launched in 1991.

Source: Cullen, B., *Ballygowan: Kisqua,* case study, The Marketing Institute, Dublin 1993.

12.4 MARKETING PLANNING

Having researched its marketing environment, the company is then in a position to plan how to go forward with that environment. Strategic marketing planning involves the company taking a long-term view of the market. The crucial questions to be answered in devising a marketing strategy are:
1. Where are we now (markets, products, competitors)?
2. Where do we want to be (marketing mission)?
3. How do we get there (gap analysis, resource analysis, marketing tactics)?

Many companies have learned from the Japanese approach to markets, where firms enter with a committment to the long term, rather than focusing on short-term objectives. Japanese firms are willing to plan ahead for up to 100 years, knowing that while their predictions will never be completely accurate, the planning process itself helps to reduce risk.

In order to implement its strategy, the enterprise must devise a tactical marketing plan. This sets out the most immediate decisions which must be taken within a specific time horizon (typically one year), for example:

1. Which segment of the market to aim at?
2. How can the product or service be targeted, or aimed, towards this market? In the case of Ballygowan's Kisqua proposal, one of the problems encountered in research was that consumers perceived the product as being very similar to Club Orange, the market leader in the orange soft drinks sector. The proposal had to be re-worked to clarify how Kisqua would be differentiated in terms of taste, product communication and packaging.
3. How will the product be positioned against competing products in the marketplace? Buyers will always make comparisons with similar or related products. For example, when the compact disc was launched, the mass market was reluctant to accept that the claimed superior sound quality justified the price premium over vinyl and cassette. As the compact disc price was lowered, it won greater market acceptance.

The actual process of developing a marketing plan can be broken down into seven steps:

1. **Situation analysis**: This presents the background to the marketing situation faced by the firm, in terms of the macro environment, products, markets, competition and distribution.

2. **Analysis of strengths, weaknesses, opportunities and threats** (SWOT): This looks at the internal strengths and weaknesses of the firm's performance, and the opportunities and threats presented by the outside environment.

3. **Marketing objectives**: The aim of this section is to set down and, where possible, quantify the targets to be reached in terms of sales volume and value, market share and profits.

4. **Marketing strategy**: This sets out the approach proposed to achieve the objectives already outlined. It also serves a useful purpose as a way of re-examining objectives to see how viable they are.

5. **Action programmes**: This section spells out specific plans of action and deadlines, under such headings as product, pricing, promotion and distribution.

6. **Financial projections**: This involves quantifying plans in terms of profit and loss, cash flows and working capital requirements.

7. **Controls**: It is important to set up control systems at the outset, so that marketing performance and costs can be evaluated and adjusted if necessary.

Exhibit 12.3 Irish Seafood Producers Group

ISPG was formed in 1986 by six salmon producers, and is located in Kilkieran, Connemara, Co. Galway. The company now represents twelve producers as a sales and marketing co-operative, employing fifteen people directly and 250 through producers. It markets salmon, seatrout and shellfish under the trade name 'Bia Mara'. In 1992, turnover was £17 million, and exports accounted for 70 per cent of sales.

ISPG's main objectives are to:
1. maximise sales prices for suppliers, who are required to sell exclusively through the company
2. provide consistent sales outlets for the fish farms' output, fifty-two weeks of the year
3. realise a profitable investment for its producers, who are also the shareholders.

These objectives are underpinned by a three-pronged strategy. Firstly, the company has developed co-operative working relationships with its suppliers. This leads to consistent supplies of a product which can command better prices and strengthen the company's marketing position. Secondly, the firm seeks to build strong relationships with distributors and the retail/catering trades. Thirdly, ISPG operates as a tightly-run, flexible operation, organised around four teams responsible for product supply, sales, market development and administration.

Source: Garvey, S. and Torres, A., 'Winning Success in Aquaculture Marketing' *Irish Marketing Review*, Vol.6, 1993.

The development of the marketing plan must be set in the context of the overall business planning process. The marketing plan is a core part of any business plan, since it defines the products to be offered and the planned sales targets. Increasingly, marketing planning and business planning are part of a continuous process. This is in contrast to the more traditional approach, where marketing and business plans were a once a year event. The current team approach encourages marketing planning to be seen as an integrative force throughout the organisation. This heightened level of awareness should lead to a more focused approach, and greater co-operation in implementation and control processes.

12.5 THE MARKETING MIX

The marketing mix comprises four elements: the product itself; the price at which it is offered; the promotion used to attract buyers; and the channels of distribution (McCarthy and Perreault 1990). A fifth element, also worthy of inclusion, is the service offered with the product (Lovelock 1984).

Describing these five elements as the 'marketing mix' captures the idea that each element can be examined separately, and then combined in a particular marketing strategy. The following sections examine the decisions to be considered in each element of the marketing mix.

12.5.1 Product decisions

A product represents a bundle of features, both tangible and intangible, which are presented to a prospective consumer. A product can be a tangible good such as a pen, a service such as education, an idea such as a no smoking campaign, or part good and part service such as a car with an extensive warranty.

A number of different approaches have been proposed to classify the various types of goods available in a market, and two of these approaches are discussed below.

The first approach defines goods according to how much search effort the consumer is willing to invest. Using this approach, goods can be divided into three categories:

1. **Durable goods**: products which are relatively expensive and bought infrequently, for instance, houses, cars, washing machines. Because of the higher cost, buyers are willing to invest time in searching for information and evaluating alternative purchases.

2. **Non-durable goods**: products which only endure for one or a few uses and are low in cost, for example, grocery items or disposable items. The purchasing of such goods becomes routine, or happens on impulse, because of the low cost of a trial purchase.

3. **Services**: products which are intangible and often inseparable from the person producing the service, for example, medical services or hairdressing. Because of the intangible nature of the product, the consumer may be willing to search a lot and rely on word of mouth or informed opinion when making a choice.

The second approach involves an initial distinction between consumer goods — that is, goods bought for use by an individual or a household, and industrial goods which are purchased as inputs to *finished goods*. Consumer goods can be subdivided into:
1. **Convenience goods**: items that are bought easily and frequently, for example, newspapers.
2. **Shopping goods**: goods for which the buyer is willing to search to some extent, e.g. a camera.
3. **Specialty goods**: goods with some unique features which involve the buyer making more effort in the purchase, for example, custom built furniture.

With industrial goods, a distinction is made between:
1. **Materials and parts**: goods which enter the production process completely, for example, a speedometer in a car.
2. **Capital items**: goods that are required in order to produce or to manage production, such as factory equipment or delivery vehicles.
3. **Supplies and services**: supporting products which may have a relatively short life, such as typing paper or machine oil.

Having clarified the general range of products to be produced, the next decision for the firm is what mix of products it will offer. A firm can have a range of closely related or very diverse products. For example, Waterford Glass sells crystal glass, bone china and table linen, whereas the Smurfit Group has interests in print, packaging and leisure.

Further, the *product mix* will have a certain width, depth and consistency. The width refers to how many seperate product lines are offered — for example, a dairy co-op might sell milk, cheese, butter and yoghurt. The depth refers to how many variations of each line are offered — full cream, low fat, skimmed and vitamin enriched milk for instance. Consistency refers to how closely related the lines are to each other. For example, the producers of Bailey's Irish Cream decided to capitalise on its success by developing Sheridan's Cream Liqueur, aimed at a closely related segment of the market. This decision offered the company significant savings in marketing and distribution costs.

The firm's *branding* policy will also be a key issue in product policy. Three general approaches to branding can be distinguished:
1. **Manufacturer's brands**: produced and marketed under a brand name owned by the manufacturer, for example, Jacobs' biscuits. The firm may have a range of brands to cover different market segments and price brackets — for example, Jacobs also owns the Bolands brand which is positioned in a different price bracket.
2. **Private brands**: marketed by private organisations of retailers or distributors, such as Superquinn's Thrift brand. These brands can themselves grow in stature and international recognition, for example, The Body Shop or Marks and Spencer's brand St Michael.
3. **Generic brands**: the brand is of secondary importance to the pricing strategy. Here,

the brand is presented as being good value for money rather than as a unique product. For example, Quinnsworth's Five Star range of products are marketed as being good products at reasonable prices and all the advertising is price based.

Exhibit 12.4 Brand names

Although balance sheets don't reveal it, brand names and consumer recognition are the key factors in the marketing mix, which create added value and, hence, basic profit. For example: Where would Carroll's cigarettes be without the brand name? Where would Phillip Morris be without 'the Marlboro Man'? Where would ketchup be without the prefix Heinz or the famous '57 varieties'? Where would Schweppes be without its 'effervescence'? Where would American Express be if we all 'left home without it'?

Source: O'Reilly, A. J. F., 'Building Ireland's Brands' speech to the National Management Conference, Killarney 1988.

12.5.2 Product development and planning

New products are the life blood of any enterprise. In a world of intense competitive rivalry, there is an ever increasing appetite for new products. Not all new products are absolute *innovations*. Indeed, most innovation is incremental and builds on existing products and concepts. The majority of innovations, therefore, fall into the categories of product improvements (a new model of car), or process innovations (the catalytic convertor). (See Chapter 13.)

The whole process of developing a new product or service moves through a cycle illustrated in Figure 12.6.

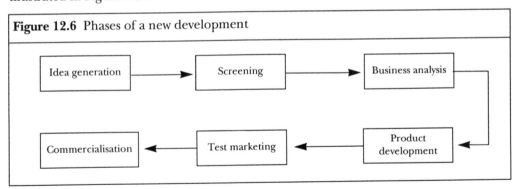

Figure 12.6 Phases of a new development

Idea generation → Screening → Business analysis

Commercialisation ← Test marketing ← Product development

In order to reduce the time taken to get a product to market, a range of products may be at different stages of the development process. The aim is to achieve continuous innovation, rather than just a one-off effort.

Old product development, according to Nilson (1992), is just as important as new product development, in the sense that existing products also need to be revitalised and re-presented. Products such as washing powder have been relaunched many times in order to revive consumer interest or present a new selling point.

A business's concern with a product does not cease when the product has been introduced to the target market. Like people, goods have a life cycle, each stage of which warrants a different style of product management.

Figure 12.7 The Product Life Cycle

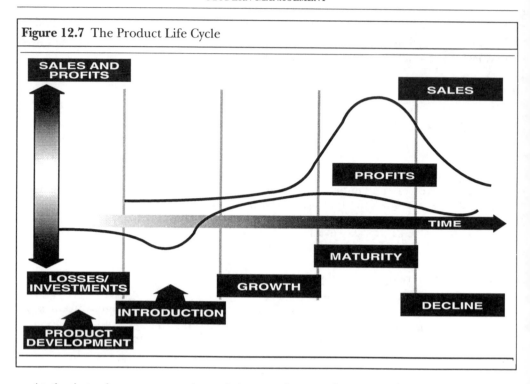

At the introductory stage, the task is to make people aware of the product. Large investments are made in promotion in order to catch the attention of the trade and the consumer. Prices may be pitched high to recoup initial costs, or low to gain market share and reach the break even point (see Chapter 7).

As consumers become more aware of the product, sales grow. Increased usage and visibility cause further growth. Production increases in response to demand, and competition enters the market as other companies recognise a profit opportunity. Because of scale economies and competition, prices stabilise or decrease. Promotional efforts may be increased in order to maintain the momentum of growth.

Over a certain period of time, which is often difficult to forecast, sales peak. Now, the objective is to keep existing customers loyal and encourage increased usage, for example, persuading computer users to stay with their existing supplier and increase the number of applications in use. Marketing effort concentrates on keeping consumers interested in what is by now a well-known product.

Eventually sales decline, either suddenly, as with fashion, or gradually, as with the change over from black and white to colour television. Every business must anticipate a decline in sales and profits. New products must be planned to plug the gap, so that as one line reaches the decline stage another is introduced.

12.6 PRICING DECISIONS

Price is the only element of the marketing mix that generates revenue. Because of its strategic importance to the organisation, the pricing decision is often made by a multi-disciplinary team.

Price represents the *perceived value* of the product or service in the market-place. In the short term, many firms compete on the basis of price, or, alternatively, they may have to accept the going rate as the price they charge. In the longer term, firms are more interested in adding value while still maintaining a competitive price, or improving quality in order to increase the price.

The consumer will consider price not just in absolute terms, but also with respect to product life, guarantees and services, the cost of competing products and relevant time savings or *opportunity costs*. For example, today's consumer has a wide range of choices in the preparation of meals. The cheapest alternative in monetary terms is to buy the basic ingredients and cook a meal from scratch, though this involves a significant time investment. Prepared ingredients and sauces cost more, but save time. Precooked convenience meals are higher again in price, but only require reheating. Takeaway meals or eating out offer other convenience/price tradeoffs. The consumer's perception of these alternatives will be determined by his/her financial resources and willingness to spend time cooking.

12.6.1 Key determinants of price

1. **Market structure**: How many sellers and buyers are there? How easy is it to enter the market? How do competing firms compare in terms of their market share and position?
2. **Economic conditions**: In a recession, sellers will hold down prices and be willing to cut margins, whereas in a buoyant situation, increases may go unnoticed by buyers. Interest rates and fiscal policy shifts may lead to rapid movements in prices.
3. **Competitive behaviour**: Is there a monopoly or cartel in operation? Do competitors match each other's price increases? Is there a history of price cutting or price wars?
4. **The product itself**: Is it perishable or long lasting? What are the costs of production and distribution that have to be covered? Are there any substitutes whose pricing should be monitored? What unique features are offered? How strong is the 'added value' element?
5. **Customers**: Do they perceive the product as a need or a want? Where are they located and what type of disposable incomes have they? What beliefs and attitudes have they about each brand in the market? How do advertising and sales promotion influence their decisions?
6. **Goals of the seller**: What is the key objective for the product: market share, profit, or break even? What is the target *rate of return* on capital investment? Is the product a core or a marginal one? Does the producer want to exploit his/her monopoly power or become the market leader?
7. **Legal restrictions**: The product may be in a category subject to price controls. Price increases may be dependent on government approval, e.g. electricity. The product may be in a category which attracts duties or taxes such as VAT, as is the case shown in Table 12.1.
8. **Distribution channels**: The number of intermediaries and the margins expected by each will account for much of the difference between the factory price and the price on the retailer's shelf.
9. **Exchange rates**: Currency prices will affect the prices of components and supplies, and the prices of both exports and imports. The exchange rate of the punt in 1993 and 1995 caused Irish exporters to increase their prices by an average of 10 per cent.

Table 12.1 The Cost of a Bottle of Wine

Wine	£1.44
Cork, label, carton	£0.35
Bottle	£0.10
Bond, transport, distribution	£0.30
Excise duty (1994 rates)	£1.61
VAT at 21 %	£1.00
Retailer's mark-up at 20 %	£1.20
Retail price	£6.00

Source: Irish Vintners Federation 1994.

12.6.2 Pricing policies

Pricing policies are the management guidelines set up to determine the day to day pricing structures. If a company has spent significant money on research and development and is anxious to recoup this investment quickly, it may adopt a policy of market skimming, which means it charges a high price in order to skim the top of the market. For instance, pharmaceutical companies set high prices on new products during the life of the patent in order to gain a return on the high investment in research and development.

If the objective is to gain high visibility or high market share, penetration pricing may be used. This involves setting a low price to win market share early and, consequently, benefit from economies of scale. Software producers often use this approach in order to convert a greater number of users to a new package.

A third policy is price discrimination. A seller charges different prices according to the elasticities he/she perceives in different market segments. For example, a grocery multiple may charge different prices for the same item in different outlets, depending on local competition.

12.6.3 Pricing tactics

In practice, most pricing is pragmatic and reacts to the most urgent demands in the market-place. The most commonly used pricing methods are:

1. **Cost-plus pricing**: Price is decided by reference to product costs, plus a variable mark-up which tends to be standard in a particular industry, for example 6 per cent on grocery items or 50 per cent on clothing. This is the most widely practised approach to pricing, although it takes no account of customer attitudes to price.

2. **Target pricing**: The firm decides the target profit or rate of return, and then works out the price to be charged to achieve it. It is used by firms with a significant investment in research and development, or firms whch have offered their shareholders a certain rate of return. It works well in industries where there is a captive or passive market.

3. **Perceived-value pricing**: Here, the producer looks at the product in terms of the value or performance it offers to the buyer. This may suggest a policy of competitive prices or a premium price strategy. Dell Computers allows buyers to custom design the machines they order for a small additional price.

4. **Competition-oriented pricing**: In this situation, the driving force in pricing is the competition and what they are charging. This is particularly the case in a mature or declining market, where firms are battling it out to survive.

264

5. **Bid pricing**: In markets where business is done on a project or contract basis, each supplier submits a bid or tender to the firm or agency offering the contract. Prices are set by reference to competitors and the customer's sensitivity to price.

6. **Price bundling**: Two or more products may be grouped together and offered at a price that is less than what the items would cost individually. This is often used to deliver extra value to the customer, while at the same time offering the manufacturer additional profits through the additional sales generated. Many computer hardware firms have teamed up with software suppliers to offer machines with pre-installed software.

12.7 PROMOTION

Promotion represents any effort, apart from price, made by the marketer to communicate with a prospective, actual, or past customer.

Before a sale takes place, a firm will use advertising, personal selling and public relations to communicate an image and a position in the market-place. During the purchasing phase, personal selling, sales promotion and advertising may be used to convince the buyer that he/she is making the right choice. After the transaction, sales follow-up, public relations, and servicing will influence the customer in his/her decision about a repeat purchase.

Marketing communications efforts have become more complex, in response to more fragmented markets and more demanding consumers. Mass communications are being replaced with an increasing emphasis on direct response, value for money and evaluation. The choice of communications media has increased, and many media are now available on a European or a global basis. Personal selling relies heavily on technology to provide customer information and evaluate sales performance. The rapid acceptance of *direct marketing* results from the need to generate a faster and more direct response from buyers. Most countries use a combination of legal and voluntary restraints on marketing communications, and the European Union is pressing for more regulation of activities. All of these developments pose new challenges for the marketer in designing a communications package that will reach the right person, at the right time, in the right place and at the right cost.

12.7.1 The marketing communications process
At a given time, any organisation is trying to communicate with a range of stakeholders — customers, prospective customers, past buyers, competitors, distributors, suppliers, government, key interest groups, or the general public. In each case, a planned approach is required, as is illustrated in Figure 12.8.

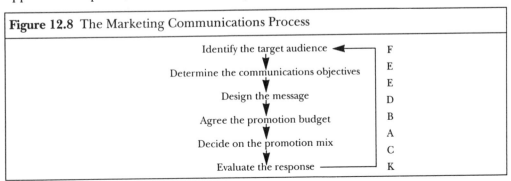

Figure 12.8 The Marketing Communications Process

265

The target audience is the starting point in any communications effort. A clear description of the desired audience leads on to a definition of the objectives that marketing communication is expected to achieve. A simple hierarchy of objectives is outlined in Figure 12.9.

Figure 12.9 Hierarchy of Effects

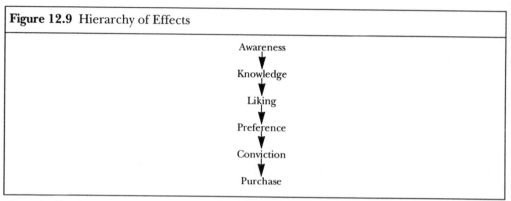

Source: Lavidge, R. and Steiner, G., 'A Model for Predictive Measurements of Advertising Effectiveness' *Journal of Marketing,* October 1961.

The next step involves the design of a promotional message to achieve the desired objective. For example, with the National Lottery, the objective was to generate loyal repeat purchasers. The message generated expressed the concept 'If they could see me now!' showing in a humorous way how people might spend their lottery winnings.

The range of communications channels represents a choice between personal sources, such as word of mouth and referrals, or impersonal sources such as the mass media. The cost of these decisions will largely determine the amount allocated to the promotional budget. This budget will be split among the various elements in the promotional mix — advertising, personal selling, sales promotion, public relations and direct marketing. Finally, consideration must be given to methods of evaluation, such as measuring the change in awareness levels or the additional sales generated by a campaign.

12.7.2 The promotional mix

Promotional efforts make use of five main tools — advertising, sales promotion, personal selling, public relations and direct marketing. Other elements include packaging, sponsorship, trade exhibitions and special events. Every seller makes a decision as to which combination of elements is most suitable for his/her product. For example, Premier Banking was launched using advertising and direct marketing, and Ballygowan Spring Water was launched by spending the entire promotion budget of £1,000 on publicity.

12.7.3 Advertising

Advertising is defined as 'any paid form of nonpersonal presentation and promotion of ideas, goods or services by an identified sponsor' (Kotler 1993). Advertising is particularly relevant in achieving the following communications objectives:
1. Information about products, usage, image.
2. Persuasion about the virtues of one brand over another, or about why you should buy now.

3. Reinforcing brand loyalty, reducing seasonality, or reminding buyers of the nearest outlet.

The main advertising media are described in Table 12.2.

Table 12.2 Advertising Media in Ireland

Television (RTE 1, Network 2)	Thirty seconds at peak time: £200–£4,000	Broad reach of mass audience
National radio (RTE 1, 2FM)	Thirty seconds at peak time: £750	Flexibility; specific audiences
Local radio 98 FM	Thirty seconds at peak time: £75	Segmented and/or local listenership
Newspapers (daily, evening, Sundays)	Daily, one page black and white: £13,000	Wide and timely coverage
Magazines	*Woman's Way* one page colour: £2,800	More specialised target audience
Cinema	Weekly coverage of ROI screens: £6,238	Mainly under-25s
Posters	Forty-eight sheet site: £400 per month	Covers urban and commuter audiences

Source: Foley, E., *The Irish Market: A Profile,* The Marketing Institute, Dublin 1994.

In 1993, the amount spent on advertising media in Ireland was £235 million.

12.7.4 Sales promotion

Sales promotions are short-term incentives to encourage product trial, shift brand loyalty, or increase product usage. Therefore, you might choose a certain brand of shampoo because it is offered at '20p off', or stock up on cornflakes in order to collect the tokens to qualify for the 'special offer'. Sales promotion can be a very effective way of increasing sales, while at the same time adding value and maintaining brand interest and loyalty.

The most common types of consumer sales promotion are:

1. **Reduced price offers**: These offer money off, sometimes in combination with extra product free. They are the single most effective type of sales promotion, but if over used can damage a brand's reputation.

2. **Sampling**: This means giving samples of the product to people in the hope that they will make a purchase. It is the most effective way of introducing a new product but can be very costly. It is often tied in with some other promotion, such as money off or a competition.

3. **Demonstrations**: These are used as a way of stimulating interest in a product, for example electrical appliances or cosmetics. Demonstrations are useful in arousing interest and desire, and are often used in conjunction with interest-free or money off deals.

4. **Coupons**: These offer price reductions on current or future purchases. They can be distributed in-store, on the pack, door-to-door, or as part of print advertising.

Redemption rates have increased as consumers have become more value conscious.

5. **Premiums**: These invoive offering some additional item with a product, either free or at less than the full price. The objective is that the additional sales generated should more than balance the cost of the premium.

6. **Games, contests and lotteries**: Competitions of all sorts are widely used, and traditionally well received by the Irish consumer. The area is regulated by the Gaming and Lotteries Act of 1958.

7. **Merchandising**: Since consumers use displays to trigger purchase, the management of shelf space and display has become very important to any company in the area of fast moving consumer goods. Merchandisers are responsible for negotiating shelf space and positions with the retailer, arranging displays and maintaining stocks. The objective is to maximise market coverage, since many sales can be lost because the product is out of stock or inadequately displayed.

Sales promotion is also used extensively to generate a response from the trade or sales force.

12.7.5 Personal selling

Advertising can create interest and awareness, but the salesperson's role is to convert interest into an actual purchase.

The salesperson has a variety of tasks:

1. **Prospecting**: Searching out potential new business.
2. **Communicating**: Telling customers about the product and its benefits.
3. **Selling**: Persuading people to buy the product.
4. **Servicing**: Maintaining customer relationships. The salesperson may also be responsible for co-ordinating finance, training and after sales service.
5. **Information gathering**: The salesperson is a valuable source of customer information and marketing intelligence.

Salespeople can work in a variety of situations: telephone selling, new business development, customer support, selling to key accounts, preparing specifications, or acting as part of a multi-disciplinary team. The selling process is intricate and demanding. The salesperson must research the prospective customer's business, and then approach him/her for an appointment. Next, he/she must prepare a sales presentation, based on an understanding of the customer's needs. A good salesperson will be able to counter objections by stressing benefits or offering a customised solution. Finally, he/she must close the sale, by persuading the customer to place an order. A significant part of the salesperson's time may be spent progressing the order, to ensure the customer is supplied on time and at the agreed price.

12.7.6 Public relations

'Public relations (PR) is the management function of planning and sustaining two-way communications between an organisation and the audiences critical to its success.' (PRII 1994) Each business has an image in the market-place. It is in its own interest to work at creating a positive image and be seen as a worthy company with which to do business. Public relations is not to be confused with the narrower activity of publicity, which describes the firm's efforts to get exposure in the media. While this is an important activity, increasingly the focus of public relations is on establishing long-term relationships which will work in the firm's best interest.

PR is a cost-effective weapon, though it can be difficult to quantify the benefits. The key emphasis is on establishing credibility, a long-term objective achieved using a variety of tools. The main activities of the PR officer or consultant include:

1. **Media relations**: Creating interesting news stories and establishing links with the relevant editors and journalists.
2. **Event management**: Designing and managing corporate events such as press conferences or product launches.
3. **Organising exhibitions and conferences.**
4. **Community relations**: Forging links with local communities or special interest groups.
5. **Sponsorship of personalities or events**. Opel's sponsorship of the Irish soccer team has built a unique platform for their advertising and PR efforts.
6. **Crisis management**: Minimising the firm's exposure in adverse situations such as an air crash or a pollution problem.

It is interesting to note that Irish firms were among the earliest in Europe to recognise the need for good public relations. The ESB was the first firm in Ireland to set up a full-time public relations department.

12.7.7 Direct marketing

Direct marketing is an interactive system of marketing that uses one or more media to effect a measureable response and/or transaction (Baier, 1983). The objective of a direct marketing campaign is to communicate directly and personally with the potential buyer in a way that facilitates a direct response. Interactivity means that direct marketing encourages two-way communication, something which is lacking in conventional advertising. This, in turn, facilitates the measurement of response, making direct marketing a very cost-effective weapon.

The need for direct marketing arose as markets became more fragmented, leading to a greater demand for customisation and personalisation. Modern computer technology has greatly assisted the development of the area, allowing for the creation of a database and the preparation of mailshots at low cost. The tools of direct marketing are:

1. **Direct mail**: The use of mailshots which can be delivered addressed or unaddressed. Replies are facilitated through the use of An Post's Freepost or Business Reply services. The volume of direct mail in Ireland is one of the lowest in Europe, at eighteen items per household in 1992, so there is still vast scope for expansion.
2. **Telemarketing**: This involves using the telephone for inbound sales enquiries or customer support, or as an outbound medium to help in securing leads or orders. Freephone (1-800) and local charge (1-850) numbers are used to encourage usage. For example, Dell Computers uses the telephone as the medium for its direct selling operation. Telemarketing offers ease of access, anonymity, and longer opening hours for the user.
3. **Advertising**: Print or broadcast advertising increasingly incorporates a direct marketing element through the use of freephone numbers, enquiry cards, or bar-coded coupons. These tools also make it easy to measure the response to a campaign.
4. **Catalogues**: These are increasingly targeting niche markets, and using telephone ordering and faster delivery to expand their appeal. While the Irish market is still small, in Germany, for example, 20 per cent of clothing is purchased through this medium.

Irish consumers still have a positive attitude to direct marketing, and are, as yet, underexposed to the medium. As newer communications media such as the Internet and interactive television become more popular, they offer further potential for the development of direct marketing efforts.

12.8 DISTRIBUTION

Distribution represents all the efforts made by the producer to have the product available for sale in the right place, at the right time and at the right price. For many firms, in particular small and start-up firms, securing good distribution is the single biggest barrier to success. Many manufacturers see strong distribution as the key to their market, for example Levi's strength in Europe is mainly attributed to its decision to establish specialist Levi's stores and concessions. Making the goods available at the right time presents another set of problems, both in terms of securing distribution agreements and ensuring the resources are in place to service the distributor's requirements. The final part of the challenge is measuring the costs of distribution — both the cost of physical distribution and the margins sought by intermediaries — and ensuring there is still a satisfactory profit for the supplier.

Distributors have different names and functions:

1. Wholesalers take full title to the goods and perform a range of services for suppliers and customers.
2. Agents and brokers do not take title to the goods. They act to bring buyer and seller together, but do not handle the physical transfer of the merchandise.
3. Retailers carry out similar functions to wholesalers, except on a smaller scale. Discount warehouses seek to combine the advantages of the two.

12.8.1 Distribution policy
In selecting channels of distribution, a manufacturer can go through several levels, as seen in Figure 12.10.

Figure 12.10 Distribution Systems

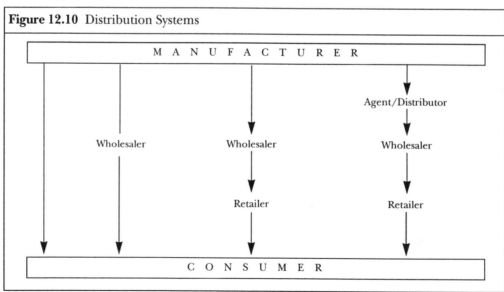

The simplest approach is for the producer to sell direct to the consumer. This has always been the practice for many commodity items, but more and more firms see direct marketing as an option which gives them greater control over the distribution channel. The use of the wholesaler is another link in the distribution chain. A wholesaler serves the functions of breaking bulk, providing storage, passing on market information, giving credit and offering buyers a wide range of goods. Retailers carry out similar functions, but on a smaller scale. Wholesaling and retailing functions are being merged in the development of discount warehouses, covering such areas as hardware, electrical and grocery items.

In selecting a channel, the producer has to consider what distribution policy is most suitable for his/her product. He may choose intensive distribution, where the objective is to get as many stockists as possible for the product. Another option is selective distribution, where the most suitable outlets are chosen using some prejudged criteria. A final choice might be exclusive distribution, where one or a few middlemen are awarded exclusive rights to serve the market. The policy chosen usually relates to the product.

Exhibit 12.5 An Bord Bainne

An Bord Bainne, the Irish Dairy Board, has enjoyed remarkable success throughout Europe with the Kerrygold brand of dairy products. One of the keys to success in the Benelux countries has been access to the distribution network. In 1989, it acquired two distribution companies, Primus and Dela, making it the largest food distributor in Belgium.

'This has given us access to all the different retailing levels', says Oliver McQuillan, managing director of Bord Bainne in Belgium. Both Primus and Dela distribute for a number of other European manufacturers, and they are also keen to take on more business from Irish food companies. 'While we sell Belgian salads and quiches, we would like to sell more food products that are Irish', says McQuillan.

Source: McGee, J., 'Hoisting the Green Flag' *Business and Finance*, 13 May 1993.

12.9 SERVICES

As economies become more affluent, the service sector takes on a more significant role. As incomes rise, people spend more money on services such as education, entertainment and travel. In Ireland, for example, every ten jobs in manufacturing support nine others in the service sector (O'Malley, 1993).

It is important to distingush between goods which have tangible physical features, such as a washing machine, and services which are mainly intangible, such as education. However, as goods have become more similar in terms of their tangible features, the services offered with the goods are increasingly emphasised as the key points of differentiation. Therefore, one can say that, today, most products are part good and part service, and firms are becoming more service conscious in response to customer and competitor pressures. The service elements that can be offered with either a good or a service are depicted in Figure 12.11.

Figure 12.11 Dimensions of Customer Care

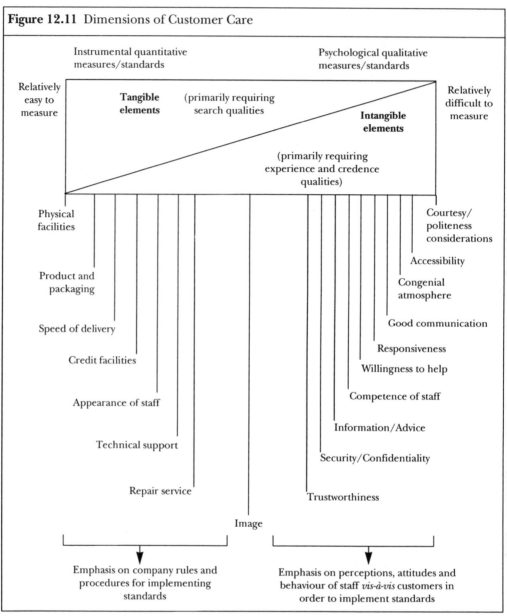

Source: Carson, D. and Gilmore, A., 'Customer Care: The Neglected Domain' *Irish Marketing Review*, Vol.4, No.3, 1989/90.

From this, it can be seen that service is an important element before, during and after the sales transaction. For example, in searching for a new car, the customer may visit several dealers and enquire about guarantees and finance. His/her actual choice of product is influenced by image and word of mouth. His/her evaluation of the quality of service will determine whether to remain loyal to the same dealer.

As evidence of their committment to service, firms are conscious of the need to obtain certified service standards, such as the Q-Mark for services or ISO 9004-2. These standards offer the customer the reassurance that the firm has attained a recognised standard of service quality, and are often emphasised as a requirement when businesses are seeking suppliers.

In summary, the motivation for good service is in customer retention. Research shows that it is five times more expensive to recruit a new customer than to retain an existing one. Furthermore, the most common reason for customer defection is poor service, rather than any inherent fault of the product itself. The service element is a vital part of selling any product and good management of service is at the heart of any customer-driven organisation.

12.10 MARKETING CONTROL

Marketing results seldom go according to plan. Changes in the environment, in competitors' behaviour and in buyers' ability to buy mean that marketing plans must be revised. The marketing plan also defines the control measures to be used during the period of the plan.

The marketing control process starts with the selection of the performance measures to be monitored. Typical measures include sales volume and value, market share, marketing costs, distributor penetration and production costs. Each business will have its own particular list of priorities in regard to these measures. The next step is to compare actual and planned performance at regular intervals, usually weekly or monthly. The marketing manager will need to specify the acceptable degree of deviation, so that attention can be focused on the important variances. Thirdly, the implications of a deviation must be analysed to see if it is attributable to controllable or uncontrollable factors. For instance, if sales targets are not being achieved, is this due to a lack of selling effort, or economic conditions, or more intense competitor activity? The end result of this analysis will be some modifications to the plan; either of a minor nature, involving a change of marketing tactics, or more extensive, calling for a re-drafting of the entire marketing strategy. Good controls should make the marketing organisation more flexible and adaptable to change in the marketing environment.

The State has also recognised the need for better marketing and offers support through such organisations as An Bord Trachtala, Forbairt, Bord Failte and other state bodies. The Culliton Report (1992), highlighted the need to focus on European markets and to generate more products with a high 'value added' input. Government policy has responded by encouraging firms to be more export-oriented from the start-up point.

Marketing strategies currently emphasise *segmentation*, customisation and service. New developments in technology are now offering the possibility of establishing more direct, interactive links with customers. This new era of marketing should spawn a fresh spirit of enterprise and competitiveness among Irish firms, who have to date demonstrated their ability to compete, and win, in global markets.

12.11 SUMMARY OF KEY PROPOSITIONS

• The marketing concept has developed through a number of distinct stages: the production orientation, the sales orientation, the marketing orientation, and, more recently, the integrated marketing orientation. The marketing concept will continue to evolve as markets themselves change.

• The activity of marketing management ranges across all types of business-consumer, business-to-business and non profit enterprises.

• Market analysis involves analysis of customers and competitors, in order to create a picture of the present and future markets.

• A marketing plan describes the strategy and tactics that are proposed to enable the firm to achieve its marketing objectives.

• The marketing mix consists of five elements: product, price, promotion, distribution and service.

• Price represents the perceived value of the firm's product in the market-place. It is the only revenue-generating element of the marketing mix.

• Promotion represents any effort, apart from price, made by the marketer to communicate with a prospective, actual or past customer. Marketing communications efforts have today become more complex, in response to more fragmented markets and more sophisticated consumers.

• Promotional efforts make use of five different tools: advertising, sales promotion, personal selling, public relations and direct marketing. Every seller makes a decision as to whch combination of elements is most suitable for his/her product.

• Distribution represents the effort made by the seller to have the product available to the buyer in the right place, at the right time and at the right price. Many manufacturers see strong distribution as the key to success.

• Services are goods which are strong on intangible features. The services offered with physical goods are also a key point of differentiation amongst rival products.

DISCUSSION QUESTIONS

1. What do you understand by the terms:
   (i) production concept?
   (ii) marketing concept?
   (iii) integrated marketing concept?
2. Distinguish between durable goods, non durable goods and services. Give an example of a good in each category.
3. Analyse the steps in the buying process for the following situations:
   (i) A parent selecting a birthday present for his/her ten-year-old son.
   (ii) A gardener choosing a new lawnmower.
   (iii) A factory buying committee upgrading the packaging machinery on the shopfloor.
4. Outline the sources of secondary data that might be used by a person considering setting up an enterprise to manufacture industrial workwear.
5. Write a short profile of all the firms competing in the branded pizza market in Ireland.
6. The survey is the most popular device for collecting primary data. Why is this so?

7. Why do producers consider brand names to be important?

8. Distinguish between the various levels of product innovation. Give examples of each level.

9. Research the mark-up on various types of consumer goods. Were the margins what you expected?

10. What type of firms spend most on media advertising in Ireland? Why?

11. What channels of distribution are available to:

(i) a manufacturer of men's ties?

(ii) an insurance company?

(iii) a photo processing laboratory?

12. Outline the differences between a marketing plan and a business plan.

REFERENCES

Aaker, D. A., *Strategic Market Management*, John Wiley, New York 1995.

Baier, M., *The Elements of Direct Marketing*, McGraw-Hill, New York 1983.

Carson, D., and Gilmore, A., 'Customer Care: The Neglected Domain' *Irish Marketing Review*, Vol.4, No.3, 1989/90.

Cullen, B., 'Ballygowan: Kisqua', case study, The Marketing Institute, Dublin 1993.

Culliton, J., et al, 'A Time for Change: Industrial Policy for the 1990s', report of the Industrial Policy Review Group, Government Publications, Dublin 1992.

Dibb, S., Simkin, L., Pride, W. M. and Ferrell, O. C., *Marketing: Concepts and Strategies*, second European edition, Houghton Mifflin, Boston 1994.

Foley, E., *The Irish Market: A Profile*, The Marketing Institute, Dublin 1994.

Garvey, S., and Torres, A., 'Winning Success in Aquaculture Marketing' *Irish Marketing Review*, Vol.6, 1993.

'Ireland "Less Competitive"' *The Irish Times*, 7 September 1994.

Kotler, P., *Marketing Management: Analysis, Planning, Implementation, and Control*, Prentice-Hall, Englewood Cliffs, New Jersey 1993.

Lavidge, R., and Steiner, G., 'A Model for Predictive Measurements of Advertising Effectiveness' *Journal of Marketing*, October 1961.

Lovelock, C. H., *Services Marketing*, Prentice-Hall, Englewood Cliffs, New Jersey 1984.

McCarthy, E. J., and Perreault, W.D., *Basic Marketing*, Irwin, Homewood, Illinois 1990.

McGee, J., 'Hoisting the Green Flag' *Business and Finance*, 13 May 1993.

Murray, J. A. and O'Driscoll, A., *Managing Marketing: Concepts and Irish Cases*, Gill & Macmillan, Dublin 1993.

Nilson, T., *Value Added Marketing*, McGraw-Hill, London 1992.

O'Malley, E., *The Employment Effects of Manufacturing Industry*, Economic and Social Research Institute, Dublin 1993.

O'Reilly, A. J. F., 'Building Ireland's Brands', speech to the National Management Conference, Killarney 1988.

Porter, M. E., *Competitive Advantage: Creating and Sustaining Superior Performance*, Free Press, New York 1985.

Porter, M. E., *Competitive Strategy: Techniques for Analyzing Industries and Competitors*, Free Press, New York 1980.

'The Business of Public Relations', information bulletin of Public Relations Institute of Ireland (PRII), Dublin 1994.

13

Entrepreneurship and Small Business

13.1 INTRODUCTION

The term '*entrepreneurship*' has become very fashionable over the last decade. It is associated with enterprise, small businesses and job creation. High profile *entrepreneurs* such as Richard Branson or Gillian Bowler have become well-known media personalities. Small business has become an important engine of job creation, and the European Union has taken a particular interest in encouraging a higher rate of small business start-ups. The general work climate has become less secure, leading more people to consider the option of self-employment or contract work. Within Ireland, attitudes towards enterprise are changing, and government policy is now geared towards giving more *incentives* to would-be entrepreneurs.

In this chapter, the entrepreneurship process is analysed by looking at the traits of the entrepreneur and the reasons why people 'go it alone'. Having defined the concept of entrepreneurship, the business culture and climate in Ireland are described, along with the possible sources of finance. Guidelines for putting together a *feasibility study* and business plan are offered. There are suggestions about the various modes of entry to business, and how to build up the business once it is established. A list of agencies offering help for entrepreneurs is contained in Appendix 2.

13.2 ENTERPRISE: THE ECONOMIST'S PERSPECTIVE

Economists have traditionally viewed enterprise as one of the factors of production, along with land, labour and capital. Wilken (1979) viewed enterprise as the intervening element between other factors of production and economic growth. However, there is much debate in the literature as to whether enterprise is a causal factor in economic growth, or whether it is an effect, the occurrence of which is dependent on how favourable the other factors of production are. Supporters of the causal argument point to the rapid emergence of newly industrialised countries such as Korea as evidence that enterprise sparks off economic growth. Economists who view enterprise as an effect refer to nations such as Japan, poorly endowed with natural resources or capital and having to compensate by offering a higher input of enterprise. Similarly, countries well endowed with land, labour and capital, such as Germany, can harness these factors for economic growth, without having to rely so much on the entrepreneurial function.

The term 'entrepreneur' has its origins in the French verb 'entreprendre', meaning to undertake something. Entrepreneurs were viewed as people undertaking risk. Cantillon (1755), an Irish businessman living in France, was the first economic commentator to identify an entrepreneur as a person who takes on uncertainty in the hope of making a profit. He observed that some traders 'buy at a certain price and sell at an uncertain price', and those who cope with this risk are the true entrepreneurs.

Another French writer, Say (1845), who himself ran a spinning factory, made the distinction between the interest payable on capital and the profit from enterprise. His view of the entrepreneur was of someone who was able to organise the factors of production to best advantage, and in return receive a wage for his input of enterprise — a scarce factor of production. This vision saw enterprise as a balancing element to achieve equilibrium within the factors of production. There was no mention of *dynamism*, uncertainty, or innovation.

In Britain, Smith (1776), in his *Inquiry into the Nature and Causes of the Wealth of Nations*, made no distinction between profit gained through risk and interest gained on capital invested. His concept was that the *capitalist* employer accumulated capital as a return for his/her efforts and also made it available to be used by his/her workers. By failing to distinguish between enterprise and pure capital accumulation, Smith ignored the risk bearing element of the business.

John Stewart Mill (1862) described the entrepreneur as a bearer of risk and supervisor of a business enterprise. He introduced the word 'entrepreneur' to the English language, using it to refer to an individual who founded a business.

Austrian economist Menger (1871) proposed that economic change does not result merely from circumstances, but from the individual's understanding and interpretation of those circumstances. For instance, a stock market crash occurs not just because the price of some stocks starts to fall, but because individuals interpret some event as a cause for concern and in turn decide to sell their stocks. The entrepreneur had particular calculating abilities and decision making skills which enabled him/her to deal with uncertainty more successfully than others.

Marshall (1920) added the dimension of leadership to the list of entrepreneurial tasks. But it was Schumpeter (1939) who made the link between enterprise and innovation. He considered enterprise as a creative force: creating new markets and waves of innovation. In Schumpeter's opinion, the entrepreneur played a key role in economic development. Hayek (1949) viewed the process of innovation as something continuous and incremental, rather than sporadic bursts of major discoveries. More recently, Keynes (1964) placed the entrepreneur in the role of decision maker, making investment decisions in the face of uncertainty.

The theory of X-efficiency proposed by Leibenstein (1979) suggests that inefficient use of resources is the norm within firms. In this imperfect situation, enterprise is seen as having two roles. First of all it is a 'gap filler', compensating for the inadequacies of factor utilisation. Its second role is more creative and expansive, helping the firm to connect with different markets and to grow.

To summarise, economists have viewed enterprise as a factor of production, or as the 'glue' or enabling resource which binds the other factors together. To obtain some insights into the behavioural aspects of enterprise, other elements such as personality traits and motivation need to be examined.

13.3 TRAITS OF THE ENTREPRENEUR

Many studies have attempted to analyse the psychological make up and personality of the entrepreneur. It is certainly true that many prominent entrepreneurs appear to share a common personality type. However, entrepreneurship is also a function of an individual's background and personal situation, and there are many potential entrepreneurs who lack the education or opportunities to bring their ideas and instincts to fruition.

The most widely known psychological theory is that of McClelland (1961). He suggested that entrepreneurial behaviour is the result of a need for achievement — n Ach for short. (see Chapter 6)

In the context of McClelland's theory, money has two functions: a means of achieving the objective and a method of assessing performance. An entrepreneur will take high profits as an indication that he/she is doing well, but may just as easily want to inject those profits back into the business. McClelland also suggested that if a society could lift the level of need for achievement, the amount of entrepreneurial activity would increase, stimulating economic growth.

In the Irish context, O'Connor and Lyons (1983) found that the most common personal traits among the entrepreneurs they surveyed were:
1. need for control and independence
2. need for achievement, typically seen as personal satisfaction in doing a job properly
3. calculated risk taking, where risk covered such areas as finance, property, or a loss of reputation
4 seeing money as a tool — to achieve aims and as a means of keeping score — not as an end in itself
5. strong sense of social responsibility and responsibility to employees
6. major emphasis on feedback on, and measurement of, performance
7. self-confidence and a positive self image.

Many new ventures are born out of an individual's frustration with a lack of recognition or independence within an organisation. This has the effect of driving the individual out to 'go it alone'.

O'Farrell (1986) identified the following types of new firm founders, based on an Irish sample:
1. **The graduate entrepreneur**: Typically a graduate of engineering or business, he/she is usually involved in high value added technology based goods with export or import substitution potential.
2. **The opportunist entrepreneur**: Usually of a lower middle class background and educated to Leaving Certificate level, this person has typically held a variety of jobs and may have a family background in small business. He/she tends to have nursed an ambition to found his/her own business for a long time.
3. **The craftsman entrepreneur**: Generally of a semi-skilled or skilled working class background with a technical education or apprenticeship. He/she often starts a business on a part-time basis with little capital. He/she may have little business or management experience and is more likely to be limited to one or two products or services.

Exhibit 13.1 'Out on Their Own'

'If I don't achieve my goal instantly, that doesn't mean that I will give up. I will always have it in the back of my mind and work patiently towards it. I am extremely persistent, single-minded, determined. If I don't get what I want in year one, I won't have forgotten it in year five. I never stop trying.'

Gillian Bowler, Budget Travel

'When I looked at all those grey faces crammed into the railway compartments, I decided I was never going to live like that, that I was never going to work for anybody else. If I ever made a conscious decision about my life, that was probably it. While I will never work for anybody else, funnily enough, I don't find working in *partnerships* any way difficult.'

Mark Kavanagh, Hardwicke Ltd

'Risk is the greatest of all aphrodisiacs. I like the feeling that you can be wrong but I like the odds to be in my favour even if ever so slightly. Once the risk goes out of a project, I lose interest. Risk is not a philosophy, it's an addiction.'

John Teeling, Countyglen plc, Cooley Distillery

Source: Kenny, I., *Out on Their Own: Conversations with Irish Entrepreneurs*, Gill & Macmillan, Dublin 1991.

This description of psychological traits is not meant to imply that the possession of such traits is a recipe for success. The right product and the availabilty of finance are also key factors. What does appear to be true is that successful self-proprietors share some or all of these traits, and that *lending agencies* and government bodies look carefully at the personality of the prospective entrepreneur. If notable traits are absent, they may be compensated for by the addition of partners and shareholders to the business, which is why *joint ventures* and partnerships are such popular structures.

Entrepreneurs come from the whole range of social classes, but many have a self-employed background, or come from families where both parents worked. Most have a strong work ethic and come from stable homes where education and self-achievement were encouraged. All share a strong desire to learn, but the learning does not necessarily have to be done within the academic system of education.

Most business owners find their responsibilities can disrupt their home life. The venturer must be relieved of domestic responsibilities and available to work the long hours needed to get the business off the ground. They have little time for social life or leisure interests that are outside of their business responsibilities. The entrepreneur's lifestyle invariably introduces an element of stress which most find difficult to cope with, but see as a necessary evil. A supportive partner and stable home background are seen as important elements of success.

13.4 DEFINING ENTREPRENEURSHIP

Entrepreneurs posess two qualities: the willingness to take risks and the ability to identify opportunities and to capitalise on them.

Notice that a business background is not a prerequisite — many successful businesses have been established by technologists or craftspeople. The decision to become self-employed is itself a risk, and there is also the opportunity cost of an alternative career foregone.

Defining entrepreneurship has also proved problematic — in practice the terms entrepreneur, founder, owner, innovator, inventor and marketeer are used interchangeably. A starting point is to view entrepreneurship as the process of wealth creation. Hisrich (1986) puts it like this: 'Entrepreneurship is the dynamic process of creating increased wealth. This wealth is created by individuals who assume the major risks in terms of equity, time and/or career commitment, of providing value for some product or service. The product or service itself may or may not be new or unique but value must somehow be infused by the entrepreneur by securing and allocating the necessary skills and resources.'

Drucker (1985), who has written widely on management and enterprise, offers a very succinct definition of the entrepreneur as someone 'who starts his own, new and small business.'

Another approach, suggested by Meredith et al (1982), is to emphasise the personal abilities of the entrepreneur. 'Entrepreneurs are people who have the ability to see and evaluate business opportunities; to gather the necessary resources to take advantage of them, and to initiate appropiate action to ensure success.'

Not all entrepreneurs are successful. As new enterprises start up, others close down or struggle to survive. There is also the luck factor — a business opportunity rejected by one person may be seized on and exploited elsewhere or years later.

It is worth making a distinction between entrepreneurship and innovation. An entrepreneur, in founding a new business, may not offer anything new in the nature of the goods or services he/she produces. The majority of new firms founded simply add to the quantity of goods produced, using existing technology and marketing appeals. The risk that they undertake is in the foundation of the enterprise and the efforts to ensure its survival. Many of those self employed in Ireland are from the professions or the farming community. Innovation, on the other hand, involves an individual behaving in a creative way; bringing in new products or processes, or changing labour or capital structures. So, innovation can involve employees as well as the owners of the firm.

To summarise, there is agreement in the literature that the entrepreneur has the following distingushing characteristics:
1. ability to recognise an opportunity
2. ability to marshal resources in response to an opportunity
3. ability to undertake risk, which by its nature implies being willing to live with the consequences of failure.

13.4.1 Intrapreneurship

The term *intrapreneurship* refers to intra-company enterprise: the ability of a business organisation to create a climate that encourages innovation. This presents a challenge to companies both large and small. In the larger firm, there may be many levels of decision making, stifling efforts at innovation percolating from the bottom up. Smaller firms face a different problem: because *demarcation lines* are fuzzy, employees find themselves faced with a range of responsibilities that leave little time for creative thinking.

Frustration with an organisation's inability to acknowledge innovation may in itself be the spur to enterprise. Lack of interest in creative ideas may force the individual out of this restrictive environment in an effort to make the concept a reality. Other factors such as poor working conditions, low pay and lack of promotion also play a part.

Within an organisation, most innovation has to be incremental if it is to be acted on. Business entities, by their nature, prefer to keep 'doing more of much the same' rather than embark upon completely new ventures. The employee who floats a proposal for a completely new area of activity is likely to be perceived as a maverick or a time-waster. In other instances, good ideas are dropped because there is no incentive to continue to champion them. To counter these difficulties, firms are recognising the need to foster a climate that encourages innovation. The current trend for delayering the organisation hopes to unlock some of that untapped creativity.

Rosenfeldt and Servo (1990) suggest that the most common places for an idea to be dropped within an organisation are with the idea originator, by middle management and across organisational boundaries. Kanter's study (1983) of successful corporate entrepreneurs shows how these problems can be overcome. She found that creative organisations facilitated people in crossing boundaries and finding possibilities for change. Leadership is an important skill at this juncture: managers must be encouraged to put their weight behind ideas and give acknowledgement for trying, even if failure is the eventual outcome. Japanese companies often succeed because of their willingness to try out a range of new ideas rather than put all their eggs in one basket. *Team building* is important: a coalition of interests is more likely to get a result than a lone explorer. Finally, there must be a willingness to share the credit and the spoils of success. Rewards and acknowledgement make people feel recognised as individuals who have left their mark on an organisation. Most individuals are, by nature, creative, it is just that some organisations, in their efforts to organise, shut out that creativity.

13.5 THE CLIMATE FOR ENTERPRISE

Contrary to popular opinion, the level of enterprise in Ireland is similiar to other European countries. According to the Task Force on Small Business (1994), the number of start-ups and the number of businesses overall is proportionate to the European average. However, Ireland is above average in the number of business failures, for example, 56 per cent of grant-aided businesses set up in 1983 were not in existence ten years later. The country is also behind in the number of fast growth firms it generates. In other countries, for example, the USA, these firms have made a significant impact on job creation.

Historically, Ireland's colonial influence spawned a dependency mentality. One manifestation of this mentality was the pressure put on governments to establish and maintain a range of financial and advisory incentives for industry. The incentives were geared towards attracting multi-nationals, and Ireland's marketability as a location was enhanced by EU membership. The result is a two-tier system: multi-nationals which account for 40 per cent of employment (Task Force on Small Business, 1994) and two-thirds of exports (An Bord Trachtala, 1995) and indigenous industry which tends to be more labour intensive, less productive and has limited access to capital.

The education system has been widely criticised as encouraging passive learning and not acknowledging efforts at initiative or creativity. It is certainly true that the 'points race' has emphasised academic learning and fostered an employee culture. The lack of a large-scale, formalised apprenticeship scheme means that a potential route to self employment for young people has been closed off. Many entrepreneurs have found their experiences with the education system unsatisfactory. However, attitudes are changing and enterprise is being incorporated into the curriculum at second and third levels. Universities and colleges have developed enterprise programmes, campus companies and innovation centres. Many young graduates, after gaining some experience, have turned to self-employment with success. There is a range of schemes, both publicly and privately funded, to ease the transition from employment to enterprise creation.

Culturally, the Irish have a reputation for criticising the rich and successful and rejoicing in failure. According to Dr Anthony Clare (1994), the Irish label risk takers as 'chancers' and put them down accordingly. 'As a people', he says, 'the Irish are wary of change, and risk taking is all about change. It is all about the unpredictable and the unpredictable is something we are not very fond of here. People by and large do not like the idea that those who influence or lead us are actually involved in the business of the unpredictable.' Dr Clare also points to a lack of self confidence as a nation which militates against ventures into the unknown. These attitudes discourage failed entrepreneurs from trying again, even if the failure itself was a valuable learning experience.

Interesting comparisons can be drawn between the track record of Irish-owned firms and foreign-owned firms operating in Ireland, in the area of innovation. A survey by the Henley Centre (1994) shows a dangerous gap. Fewer than one-fifth of Irish-owned firms are truly innovative, compared to one-third of foreign owned firms in Ireland. Irish firms' response to competition tends to be price focused, whereas foreign firms are more innovation focused. The survey also points out that innovation is not limited to new products or services, but covers production, distribution and organisational changes.

The rate of new firm formation shows interesting variations throughout the Republic of Ireland. A 1994 survey (McEnaney 1994) analysing the net number of company formations during 1980–90 found that Monaghan and Clare had the highest rates of *indigenous company* formation in the country, with rates of 20.6 and 19.5 per thousand firms. These rates are almost double the national average of 11.5. Kildare, Dublin, Carlow and Laois have a formation rate of 75 per cent of the national average. The study also showed an *inverse correlation* between a high proportion of people attending higher education and the level of enterprise in the area.

The rewards to entrepreneurs in Ireland are not always tangible. New business owners find a web of complex bureaucracy and form filling stands in their way. High taxation rates, particularly for service companies, reduce the financial rewards. New businesses are constantly plagued by the 'equity gap' — the shortage of venture capital available to start-up firms with no track record and little collateral. The organisers of management buyouts in Ireland have been known to resort to UK finance houses because of the unwillingness of local banks to underwrite the venture.

On a more positive note, awareness of the need for enterprise is growing. Increased international competition has forced indigenous firms to be more entrepreneurial in their outlook. EU policy is emphasising the importance of small firms. The media have also played a part. The Forbairt 'Student Enterprise Awards' help to raise the level of interest in enterprise amongst third level students. RTE's 'Up and Running' series has increased the awareness of small firms and highlighted success stories. Entrepreneurs are receiving more formal recognition of their efforts and the contribution they can make to revitalizing local communities.

13.6 STATE INDUSTRIAL POLICY

Since the foundation of the State, wealth creation and the generation of employment have been key strands of industrial policy. As the economy developed, the focus of industrial policy was on attracting foreign firms to locate in Ireland. This policy fulfilled a dual role: it created employment and it improved the level of technology within the country. As time went on, this policy proved to be less effective. During the 1970s and 1980s, multi-nationals became more inclined to locate in the lower cost economies of the Far East. The State's response was to increase the package of grants and tax incentives on offer, as a way of continuing the relationship with the multi-nationals. The policy of attracting foreign companies was re-examined with the publication of the Telesis Report (NESC, 1982). This report, commissioned by the Government, showed that while foreign companies had a strong export performance, the products they manufactured had a high import content, so that their net contribution to the economy was not as significant as had been thought. It also pointed out that indigenous firms had not been as successful as had been hoped in establishing linkages with foreign firms. The report called for greater selectivity in the attraction of foreign firms, and a more directed approach towards the support of local firms. The Telesis Report forced policy makers to give more recognition to indigenous industry and resulted in some re-organisation of State agencies. The intervening forces of recession in the 1980s meant, however, that governments felt obliged to continue policies supporting foreign industry, because of their net contribution to jobs and the economy.

13.6.1 The Culliton Report and response

A further re-examination of policy was co-ordinated with the Report of the Industrial Policy Review Group in 1992. Commissioned by the Ministry for Industry and Commerce, the Group, chaired by Mr Jim Culliton, set out to recommend policy changes for the 1990s. The aim of the Culliton Report (1992) was to formulate and evaluate policy for industry and employment, and it made the following recommendations:

1. The barriers to Irish industry achieving its maximum potential lie in the areas of national industrial policy, competitiveness and productivity. Policy formulation needs to be broadened to take account of taxation, *infrastructure*, education and training in order that industry can progress.
2. The role of industrial promotion agencies needs to be kept under constant review. There is potential to rationalise State aid and to force greater selectivity in the projects being supported.
3. Industrial promotion agencies should try to support clusters of related industries, building up leverage points of national advantage. The food sector is clearly a priority area in this respect.
4. There should be a decisive shift away from grants for indigenous industry, in favour of an expansion of equity and venture capital activities by the State agencies.

283

5. The supports for indigenous industry need to be integrated into a single new agency. They also need to be underpinned by a stronger regional structure. A single agency should be given responsibility for promoting internationally mobile investment in Ireland.

The response by the Government to the Culliton Report was the establishment of a Task Force, which published recommendations for operational changes. The changes to date have included:

1. The establishment of the Department of Enterprise and Employment, giving acknowledgement to the pivotal role of enterprise in the economy.
2. The establishment of County Enterprise Boards.
3. The re-organisation of the Industrial Development Authority (IDA) and EOLAS, the state R&D agency. Under the new system, there are three agencies responsible for industrial development:
   (i) The IDA is responsible for supporting international investment in Ireland.
   (ii) Forfas is responsible for developing industrial policy.
   (iii) Forbairt is responsible for indigenous industry development and technological R&D.
4. The setting-up of An Bord Bia, responsible for the development of the food industry.
5. A re-evaluation of industrial training and apprenticeship schemes co-ordinated by FAS, the national training agency.
6. Greater emphasis to be placed on the links between enterprise and education, and on the need for training to be industry-focused.

The Culliton report and the recommendations of the Task Force are expected to act as a continuing reference point for policy makers throughout the rest of the 1990s.

13.7 SUPPORT AGENCIES FOR ENTERPRISE

A significant number of agencies, both publicly and privately funded, offer advice, grants, workspace and ongoing support. For the would-be entrepreneur, it can often be difficult to judge which of these agencies is the most appropriate to his/her needs. As the business is established and developed, the type of support needed changes from day to day handholding to a requirement for planning strategy, raising capital and developing exports. Geographic location is also a factor in the level of support available. The border counties and Gaeltacht areas benefit from a number of special schemes (see Chapter 8) and certain areas of high unemployment have been singled out for community enterprise schemes and local area partnerships.

The Department of Enterprise and Employment is responsible for overseeing the activities of the various Government-funded agencies responsible for enterprise. The Minister and the Department carry out the functions of policy development and review. EU funding in the areas of training, enterprise and employment initiatives is also channelled though this Department. The 1994 round of Structural Funds rated training as the second most important priority after infrastructure.

13.7.1 Government supported agencies

Forbairt is the government agency responsible for the development of indigenous industry. Its objective is to assist Irish firms in becoming more competitive and achieve growth, and to encourage the establishment of more firms. Services and support facilities are offered under the following headings:

1. **Small Business Development**: Small businesses are classified as those employing not more than fifty people. Financial support is available to assist with feasibility studies, employment creation, *management development*, capital grants, product and process development and technology acquisition and training. Assistance is available with the installation of management systems, and the recruitment of specialist business skills. The Mentor Programme assigns an experienced business executive as a counsellor at no cost to the company. The Enterprise Development Programme assists experienced managers and professionals who are planning to establish a business.

2. **International Services**: Financial support, consultancy and advice are available to existing and potential businesses in the internationally traded services sector. Software, computing and financial services are the biggest areas of activity.

3. **Development of Medium and Large Firms**: Financial incentives offered are similar to those for small firms. Medium to large firms are given particular assistance in enhancing their capabilities in all functional areas and in becoming more export-oriented in their outlook. The National Linkage Programme aims to maximize the amount of raw materials, parts and services sourced in Ireland by both the public and private sectors.

4. **Development of Food and Agribusiness**: As this is the largest element of exports from indigenous firms, it has been singled out for special attention. Finance offered includes capital grants, equity and revenue grants to assist in training, management development, and R&D. Services include sectoral information, industry contacts, advice on EU grant programmes, and assistance in searching for international business partners.

5. **Technology Support**: These programmes assist firms in achieving quality standards, improving production efficiency, raising technological skills, protecting the environment, and sourcing funds for technology development and implementation. Technical consultancy is available to help increase competitiveness and to access new technology. Laboratory and test services offer facilities which enable firms to keep pace with international competition.

Forbairt operates a walk-in or freephone enquiry service and library. Workspace for start-up companies is available in a range of craft and enterprise centres.

FAS — the Training and Employment Authority — is responsible for industrial training. Its network of regional offices provide training and employment services relevant to the needs of small businesses. The Training Support Scheme assists SMEs in improving the level of skills in areas such as production, planning, marketing, languages, quality, technology etc. Apprenticeship grants are available in some sectors to assist with the cost of training craftspeople. The Job Training Scheme facilitates an employer in providing training for people who were previously unemployed. The Small Business Management Development Programme provides training on a one-to-one basis to the owner or manager of the business. FAS also operates a wide range of industry-related training courses, including a 'Start Your Own Business' course. One successful graduate of this course was Geoff Read, founder of Ballygowan Spring Water.

The County Enterprise Boards, set up in 1993, represent an effort to place enterprise at the heart of community affairs, following criticism that administration was purely at a national or regional level. There are thirty-six Boards, one for each county or county borough area. The aim of the Boards is to plan and develop enterprise at local level. Each Board is allocated a grant budget, and works closely with other State agencies.

An Bord Trachtala — the Irish Trade Board — is the agency responsible for the promotion of sales in the international and domestic markets. Through a network of offices in Ireland and overseas, it assists with market identification and development. Grants are available to help meet the cost of research and promotional activities.

An Bord Bia, the Food Board commenced operations on 1 January 1995. It is responsible for the market development of the food and drink industries, and offers similar services to An Bord Trachtala in this area.

The Business Innovation Centres are an initiative co-financed by the government and the EU. The four centres provide advice, support and assistance with seed capital to existing and potential small businesses. Each BIC operates as an independent private company.

Other agencies relevant to the entrepeneur include:

1. **The National Food Centre** is responsible for R&D activities in the food area.
2. **University and College Enterprise and Innovation Centres**.
3. **Bord Failte** is responsible for the tourism sector.
4. **Bord Iascaigh Mhara** is responsible for the fisheries industry.
5. **The Offices of the European Union** provide information about EU programmes and sources of funding.
6. **The National Microelectronics Centre** provides R&D and training facilities in the electronics field.
7. **The Bolton Trust**, established by the Dublin Institute of Technology, offers a tailored project development programme and workspace with support services.
8. **The International Fund for Ireland** administers funds provided by the US and Irish Governments, and other public and private interests. Firms operating in the border regions and in Northern Ireland have benefited from this source.
9. **Community Enterprise** projects and initiatives. Certain areas of high unemployment or rural depopulation have been singled out for assistance. Local enterprise offices and higher than average grant support may be available.

13.7.2 Privately funded agencies

Private enterprise has acted to support several initiatives through the provision of workspace and finance.

First Step raises funds through the private sector to assist entrepreneurs who would otherwise have difficulty raising capital. It works through existing community service groups and also provides a mentoring service. **The Liffey Trust** is a voluntary, privately-funded body that operates its own enterprise centre. It provides consultancy and support services at no charge, while the business is getting off the ground. The **Society of St Vincent de Paul** operates an Enterprise Support Scheme which offers seed capital and support. Other privately funded agencies of relevance to the entrepreneur include:

The Chambers of Commerce
The Small Firms Association
The Irish Small and Medium Enterprise Association (ISME)
Small Business Units of the commercial banks
Business and financial consultants.

13.8 THE SMALL BUSINESS SECTOR

The Task Force on Small Business (1994) defined a small business as one employing fifty people or less or where annual turnover is less than £3 million. Small firms in Ireland number approximately 160,000, a little over half of which employ at least one person, and a little under half of which are run solely by their owners. Most businesses are small, and most small businesses are very small. About 98 per cent of non-farm businesses are classified as small, while 90 per cent of all companies employ less than ten people. Since there is no particular agency registering small businesses, estimates have to be gathered from a number of sources.

Table 13.1 Estimates of the Size of the Small Business Sector, 1994

Golden Pages	96,000	(listings)
Dept. Social Welfare	105,061	(employers)
Rev. Commissioners	89,502	(employers)
	126,754	(VAT registrations)
Task Force estimate	160,000	(small firms)

The sources shown in Table 13.1 demonstrate the difficulty in agreeing on conclusive figures. The disparity between the figures quoted by the Revenue Commissioners and the Task Force on Small Business is explained by the fact that many businesses in the service sector are engaged in VAT exempt activities, are below the turnover threshold for VAT registration, or are actively avoiding taxation.

Table 13.2 Number and Types of Firms in the Small Business Sector

SECTOR	BUSINESSES WITH < 50 EMPLOYEES	% OF SMALL BUSINESSES	% OF TOTAL
Industry	3,759	5.9 %	78 %
Construction	7,518	11.9 %	98 %
Retail services	29,239	46.1 %	99 %
Wholesale services	2,885	4.5 %	96 %
Other services	19,958	31.4 %	99 %
Financial services	32	0.05 %	34 %
TOTAL	63,931		97 %

Source: Fitzpatrick and Associates, 'Background Report For the Task Force on Small Business', unpublished report, 1993.

Within the small business sector, services are the largest group of firms, consisting mainly of retailing and construction firms. Small businesses account for a markedly smaller share of employment than of enterprises. Enterprises with less than ten persons make up about 30 per cent of the private sector workforce, and those with less than fifty persons make up about half of it (Task Force on Small Business, 1994).

13.8.1 Start-ups, growth and closures

The problems encountered in trying to measure the size of the small business sector are again encountered in measuring the rate of start-ups. Table 13.3 draws on three data sources and shows a good start-up rate through the mid 1980s. The decline in more recent years is attributable to the recession and to the introduction of more stringent rules in giving grant assistance. Contrary to common belief, the level of start-ups in Ireland, if anything, has been slightly above the EU average in the last decade. By contrast, the closure rate is at the higher end of the European scale.

Table 13.3 New Company Start-ups, 1983–92

	New VAT registrations	New company registrations	New grant aided establishments Irish manufacturing
1983	12,652	6,336	443
1984	14,553	6,071	602
1985	13,794	6,486	627
1986	14,749	7,657	560
1987	12,698	8,063	541
1988	14,173	10,880	554
1989	15,857	14,631	441
1990	15,297	15,199	336
1991	13,380	14,840	299
1992	14,262	14,549	247
Total	141, 395	105,254	4,650

Source. Annual Reports of the Revenue Commissioners, Annual Companies Reports, Department of Enterprise and Employment Industrial Database.

Figure 13.1 Survival Rate of New Businesses Established in 1983

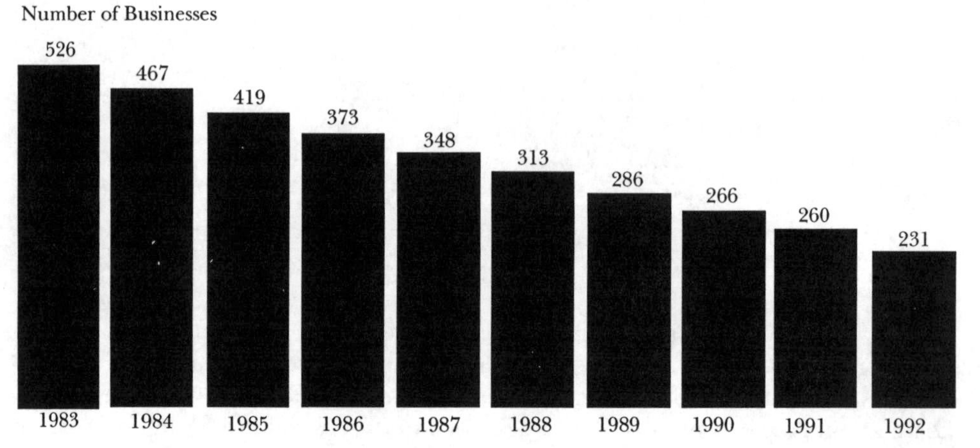

Number of Businesses

526 | 467 | 419 | 373 | 348 | 313 | 286 | 266 | 260 | 231

1983 | 1984 | 1985 | 1986 | 1987 | 1988 | 1989 | 1990 | 1991 | 1992

Source. Fitzpatrick and Associates, 'Background Report for the Task Force on Small Business', unpublished report, 1993.

Figure 13.1 shows the attrition rate of grant-aided firms in the manufacturing and international services sectors. By 1992, nine years after their first full year of operations, 56 per cent had gone out of business. Indeed, as these figures only include grant-aided enterprises, they almost certainly underestimate the overall closure rate.

Figure 13.2 1993 Business Failure Analysis

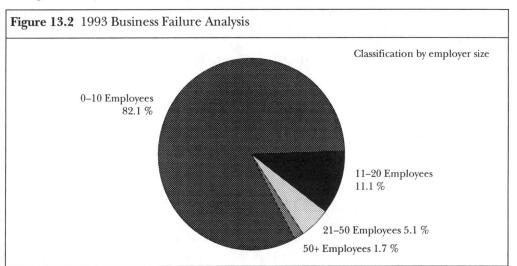

Source: Dun and Bradstreet.

Figure 13.2 shows that small firms experience the highest rate of business failure, with a remarkable 82 per cent of failures occurring in the category of firms employing up to ten people.

Interest also centres on the number of fast growth small businesses, which are regarded as significant contributors to job creation. Compared to the US and the UK, fast growth firms are less in evidence in Ireland and make a smaller contribution to employment generation. A survey of grant-aided firms carried out by the Task Force on Small Business (1994) showed about 1 per cent of all firms falling into the fast growth category. The international trend is that small business is a net creator of jobs; encouraging fast growth enterprises is vital in the context of Ireland's high unemployment rate.

13.9 SOURCES OF NEW PRODUCT/SERVICE IDEAS

It has already been stressed that a new enterprise does not necessarily have to be innovative. Table 13.4 shows the varying degrees of innovation in a typical market.

Table 13.4 Types of Innovation

Sector creating innovation	Branding innovation
Reformulation	Process innovation
Design innovation	Packaging innovation
Service innovation	
Performance extending innovation	
Technological reorganisation innovation	

Source: West, A., *Innovation Strategy*, Prentice-Hall, London 1992.

289

Research has shown that innovative new businesses drew their ideas from a wide range of sources:

1. **Work experience**: This is probably the most common source of ideas, and regarded as one of the most reliable. It is an important source of know-how, and also instils confidence in the innovator. Rothery (1977), in a study of thirty-eight entrepreneurs, found that each idea was linked to the person's employment or work activities.

2. **Domestic experience**: In the course of home and domestic duties, ideas for improvement can lead to business opportunities. Food products and household goods are typical examples.

3. **Hobbies and leisure interests**: Sporting or craft interests can act as a springboard to enterprise. Examples include furniture, jewellery, boatbuilding and sailmaking.

4. **Market knowledge**: Those who are experienced in, or keen observers of the market are in the best position to recognise an opportunity. One way to locate opportunities is by isolating trends, and then generating ideas that follow those trends.

Exhibit 13.2 Trintech Ltd

Trintech is the only Irish company manufacturing electronic credit card processing machines. The company's origins date back to a meeting between John Maguire, an engineering student, and a bank manager. Maguire, now managing director of Trintech, approached the bank manager, not for money, but for ideas relating to problems in the financial services sector. The bank manager pin-pointed credit card fraud detection. Trintech has developed a range of credit card and bank card payment terminals which provide electronic authorisation and processing of transactions. The terminals are bought by banks and placed in retail outlets to authorise payments and detect fraud.

Source: Joyce, C., 'Growth on the Cards' *Business and Finance,* 21 March 1991.

---

5. **Business contacts**: These often make or break a business. Many potentially successful ideas never make it because they have difficulty securing a backer or a sponsor. The increasing number of management buyouts can be partially attributed to their ability to attract financial backing and to their existing contacts in the business.

Exhibit 13.3 Waterford Stanley Ltd

Waterford Stanley Ltd, manufacturers of Stanley cookers, have enjoyed consistent profits since the company emerged from the receiverships of Pierce Engineering and Waterford Ironfounders in 1982. The co-founders Frank Cruess Callaghan and Owen Conway, had originally worked together in a Dublin management consultancy. Conway had worked in both Pierce's and Waterford Ironfounders, and along with Cruess Callaghan put together a rescue package financed by a merchant bank. The investment paid off handsomely. In 1993, the company reported profits of £3.03 million on a turnover of £22 million and employs 532 people. The Stanley cookers are the market leader in Ireland, the number two brand in the US and sell all over Europe.

Source: *Irish Times* 1994.

6. **Gap analysis**: This involves analysing a market and its constituent segments to find what gaps exist. There are always unfilled needs in a market, some of which are not articulated or even perceived by buyers. This technique is most widely used by marketing analysts in larger firms.

7. **Import substitution**: Up to 60 per cent of goods on the shelves in Irish supermarkets are imported. Both Forbairt and the Irish Trade Board have encouraged the development of more Irish-made products. In time, these firms themselves can become exporters. Beeline Healthcare, for example, was established in 1988 when the owner discovered that all branded vitamin supplements sold in Ireland were imported. The Beeline brand is now firmly established in the home market, as well as exporting to the UK and Europe.

8. **Foreign markets**: Studying another market, or observing buying behaviour while travelling abroad often sparks off a business idea. Many of the ideas for new food and drink products came from studying other markets.

9. **Competition**: Other firms in the industry can encourage competitive rivalry and further innovation. A 'me-too' product can of itself be a perfectly valid innovation, provided it meets market needs.

10. **Customers**: Buyers can often suggest ideas for product improvement or innovation. Observing customer behaviour can often be the inspiration for enterprise. Feargal Quinn got many of his ideas for enhancing Superquinn's level of service by standing around the shopfloor and talking to customers.

13.10 Screening New Venture Proposals

Investors and venture capital executives have to examine a range of potential enterprises and then decide which of them represents the best potential business. Ideas can be assessed from two angles: the acceptability of the concept itself in the market-place, and its technical feasibility.

Concept testing means relating the degree of innovation to the perceived risk involved, and then calculating whether or not the proposed new venture looks likely to succeed. For example, the search for a cure for cancer represents a high risk in terms of of the investment involved, but a huge market for the company which succeeds. On the other hand, many concepts turn out to have a low level of market acceptance even though the initial risk was not thought to be high.

Technical feasibility requires a study of the manufacturing know-how and service support required. Many Irish firms are taking advantage of technology transfer agreements to move into new markets. Faulkner Packaging, manufacturers of specialised packaging and bubblewrap materials, experienced its first significant success after striking up an informal technology transfer agreement with a British manufacturer (Keogh 1992).

Many designers and engineers are so enamoured with the technical features of their product that they fail to see it through the eyes of the customer. Some years ago, the British Design Council did a comparison of two air-conditioning systems, one from a British manufacturer and one made by a German company. The German version was custom built and scored very highly in design terms. The British product was poorly designed but used standardised parts, was cheap to buy and was the winner in the market-place (Foley 1989).

Some companies use a checklist or a rating scale to evaluate the business potential of an idea. For any idea there are ten key questions to be answered:

1. What is the potential return on investment?
2. What are the estimated monthly sales for at least the first three years?
3. How long is the estimated growth period of the product's life cycle? (This represents the highest profit period.)
4. What is the estimated start-up time before high volume sales?
5. How long will it take to pay back the capital investment?
6. What is the probability of achieving a unique market position for the product?
7. What effect will the business cycle have on the product or service?
8. What is the potential for selling the product at a premium price?
9. How easy is it to enter the market?
10. How long will it take to test-market the product or service?

The business knowledge contained in this text gives guidelines to the 'right' answers to the above questions. Unless at least six out of ten responses are promising, the project will most likely be a failure.

13.11 WAYS OF ENTERING BUSINESS

One of the most interesting aspects of enterprise is the variety of ways of getting started. Choice of entry method depends on the degree of control sought by the entrepreneur, the expected life of the business and the anticipated entry costs. The main methods of entry are set out under the following sub-headings:

1. **Sole trader:** This is an attractive route for the person who is concerned with retaining ownership and control of his/her own business. It means that the profits of the business accrue entirely to the owner. A *sole trader* is not required to register his/her accounts — apart from the usual reqirements for income tax, PRSI and VAT purposes. If the business name is different from the proprieter's name, it must be registered with the Registrar of Business Names. This form of business is most suited to an individual who wants to start small and stay small. It is most favoured by the proprieters of small retail outlets, pubs and small agency businesses.

Along with the attractions, there are several disadvantages that cannot be ignored. A sole trader is personally liable for the debts of his business, and so risks losing his home and other assets should he/she encounter difficulties. The second major problem is raising finance. When an investor is considering backing a sole trader, he/she is supporting the individual as much as the business. There may be may doubt as to whether the individual has all the necessary qualities for success. Many sole traders stay small, not by choice, but because of problems with working capital and cash flow. Problems with succession often mean that the business dies with the retirement or death of the owner.

2. **Partnership:** A partnership tries to deal with the limitations of the one person business by having two or more partners. In its simplest form, a partnership works in the same way as a sole trader, except that now there are two or more people to share the debts

and the profits. A partnership can have up to twenty members. Some of these may be 'sleeping partners' who have shares but take no part in the running of the firm.

Most partnerships start off by drawing up a formal agreement setting out individual responsibilities, profit shares, voting rights and the action to be taken when difficulties arise, e.g. the dissolution of a partnership, trading difficulties, withdrawal, retirement or death of existing partners, or the incorporation of new partners. In the standard partnership agreement, each partner is liable for the entire debts of the business. Voting rights and profits are usually allocated on the basis of equal shares, seniority, or capital invested.

A *limited partnership* is where one or more partners limits his/her liability to the amount he/she has invested in the partnership. However, limited partners cannot take part in the management of the business, and there must be one partner willing to accept limited liability.

Partnership offers the same advantages as sole trading, except it also tries to spread the risk and responsibility. It is cheap and easy to set up, but care has to be taken in selecting partners who are reliable from a business point of view and who have compatible personalities. Difficulties arise if there is a dispute among partners, or where one partner wants to withdraw his/her investment.

3. **Limited company**: A *limited company* is a separate legal entity, set up by reference to the rules of company law. The main advantage is that liability is limited to the company, so that the shareholders can only lose whatever amount of share capital they subscribe. A company can be set up from scratch, or an off the shelf company can be bought from a registration agent. A company must have a minimum of two directors, and a company secretary. Alternatively, this role can be performed by one of the directors or an outside agent such as a solicitor or an accountant. It must register a name which is acceptable to the Registrar of Companies. It files two documents which are essential for the formation of the company: the Memorandum of Association and the Articles of Association.

The Memorandum needs to be signed by the directors and states the company name, registered office, share capital and company objectives. The Articles of Association deal with the rules governing the internal workings of the firm and are signed by the directors. A Certificate of Incorporation must be received before the business can commence trading.

The limitation of liability means that a director's home and personal assets are safe. Sometimes the value of this clause is reduced in the case of a new company trying to borrow funds. The lender may ask for a personal guarantee as he/she may feel that the new business is a risky proposition. A limited company also operates around a more structured framework, as there are certain legal requirements with which it must comply. The main one is that it must file annual accounts with the Registrar of Companies. This means the trouble and expense of an annual audit. On the positive side, the preparation of annual accounts is a good method of control. There are also attractive tax advantages to a limited company. Income tax is paid only on salaries and benefits drawn, and retained profits are taxed at a low rate. There is a 10 per cent rate of Corporation Tax for companies engaged in manufacturing. A limited company can raise finance through the issue of shares or using the Business Expansion Scheme. Finally, it also has the advantage of spreading ownership, thereby diluting the risk.

The biggest drawback is cost — the cost of setting up and then complying with the requirements of the Companies Act. These factors deter many small firms from incorporation as limited companies. A tax disadvantage is that accumulated profits withdrawn from the company as dividends, salaries, benefit in kind or loans are subject to additional taxation. Service companies complain that the tax advantages favour manufacturing activities. For all these reasons, the limited company structure is most favoured by those entering business with a number of shareholders, or in a situation where there are diverse interests which need legal regulation.

4. **Buying an existing business**: An attractive option for the would-be entrepreneur is to buy a business that is currently trading. The size of such a committment can vary enormously. The buyer can purchase existing plant and equipment, agree to hire the existing workforce, or just buy the company's name and goodwill.

The attractions of the buy-out or buy-in are obvious. The business is already up and running, so many of the pitfalls of a start-up are avoided. It has most likely passed the break even stage, and is trading profitably. Its expertise, track record, earnings and reputation are known and act as a measure of its value. It may be possible to buy an existing business for less than it would cost to start from scratch. The purchaser hopes to turn the firm around from loss to profits, or improve on existing profits. The failure rate is higher, however, among those who aspire to turn around, than among those who buy businesses that are already in profit.

On the other hand, the first question to be asked by the buyer is 'Why is this firm for sale?' The most common reasons are:

(i) It is a recent, or consistent loss maker.

(ii) The market has changed. The firm's plant may be outdated, and the employees are in need of retraining.

(iii) The owner wants to divest to pursue other interests.

(iv) A company wants to sell an unprofitable or an unacceptable profitable subsidiary or division. Retirement or *divestment* are more attractive selling reasons than a history of consistent losses.

The buy-out (or buy-in) itself can take a few forms:

(i) The purchaser is an individual: He/she may fund the investment from savings, inheritance or a severance payment, or borrow part from a lending agency.

(ii) The buyer is an existing group of employees or managers who raise joint funds and get the support of an outside lender or investor. These management/employee buyouts are increasingly common, as it is easier to raise funds between a number of employees. If the business is already profitable, it is not too difficult to get lenders interested. An example of a successful buyout was the arrangement by the management of pharmaceutical wholesalers, Cahill May Roberts, to buy-out the owner, PJ Carroll plc.

(iii) The purchaser is a company: Many firms now feel it is less costly to buy-in than build a business from the ground up, and, as Table 13.5 indicates, the number of acquisitions has increased steeply. It makes sense to limit *acquisitions* to businesses in a similar line, or those that afford a degree of forward or background integration. Jefferson Smurfit and Kerry Group have made acquisitions in this way.

(iv) The buyer is a company specialising in buy-ins. Its business is to buy firms, improve their profits and then maintain or re-sell them. One figure well known in Ireland for this type of activity is John Teeling.

Table 13.5 Top Five Irish Acquiring Companies, 1994

Bidder	Target	Country	Value(£m)
Jefferson Smurfit	Cellulose du Pin	France	683,800
	Tower Park Leisure	UK	N/A
	Interlok Solid Board Division	UK	N/A
Kerry Group	DCA Food Industries	USA	250,000
	Mattesson Walls	UK	25,000
	Productos Vegetales de Mexico	Mexico	10,345
	Dermet de Mexico Ingredients	Mexico	3,449
Anglo Irish Bank	Mortgage Book- Canadian Imperial Bank of Commerce	UK	30,000
	Irish Business Bank-loan Book	Ireland	116,000
CRH	Marlux Group	Belgium	25,000
	A Rotondo & Sons	USA	14,600
	Templeglass Group	USA	13,500
	Sullivan Lafarge	USA	7,380
	Lebanon Rock	USA	7,380
	PJ Keating & Co	USA	7,380
	Bosse Concrete Products	USA	3,850
	Schuster's Blocks Inc.	USA	3,850
Green Property	Dublin City Properties	Ireland	42,000
	Setanta Centre group of companies	Ireland	20,000

Source: SKC Corporate Finance 1994.

The ideal business to buy is one which is well established in the market-place, with proven products and a strong earnings' record. The other cornerstone is cashflow: the buyer must be sure that the daily payment demands can be met, and that loans can be paid as they fall due. Only when this can be done with some margin of safety should the purchase contract be signed.

(v) Franchises: A *franchise* is an arrangement between a franchisor and franchisee, involving the sale or distribution of goods or services, using a particular marketing system and possibly with financial assistance provided. It is seen as an easy way to get into business because much of the groundwork has been done and a support system is usually available. Franchise agreements are of three different types. Manufacturers use franchises as a way of distributing their product, e.g. car dealers. A second situation is where the franchisor acts as a wholesaler to the franchisee. The third and most common situation is where the franchisor offers a system, which may include a name, a known image and a certain atmosphere, e.g. Bewleys. Table 13.6 shows the franchise names most recognised in Ireland.

Table 13.6 Top Ten Most Recognised Franchises

1. Burger King	2. Bewleys
3. McDonalds	4. Burgerland
5. Clarkes	6. The Body Shop
7. Benetton	8. Abrakebabra
9. Tie Rack	10. Four Star Pizza

Source: Management Training Services Ltd 1993.

The main advantage is that the franchisee can draw on an already established business. Most franchisors offer training and issue instruction manuals for the guidance of their franchisees. Many also help with site location and finance. Assistance is often provided with promotion and development. These supports help to shorten the learning curve and also help to reduce the payback period. Many franchises involve making a lump sum payment and a continuing royalty payment for the right to use the name. They may also use group buying systems and collect contributions towards group marketing efforts. The biggest advantage of a franchise is that some information about existing operations is available beforehand, eliminating some of the risk.

Table 13.7 Cost of Franchising

	Average	Highest	Lowest
Initial fee	£9,312	£15,000	£2,500
Franchise package	£18,750	£150,000	£2,500
Total cost	£58,340	£3.2 million	£5,000
Management service fee*	5.8 %	15 %	0 %
Advertising levy	3 %	6 %	1 %

* Some franchisors do not levy a management service fee

Source: MTS 1993.

A franchise usually sets down strict rules about every aspect of the business. The franchisee cannot individualise his/her own operation. If a franchise operation takes off, the first few licencees may suffer as they lose market share to those entering after them. The entry costs for a well-known franchise can be prohibitive (Table 13.7). As well as paying for the name, there are regular royalty payments which are usually a percentage of sales. A franchisee never totally owns his/her own business, and may be prohibited from selling it or passing it on to his/her family. There are some shady franchise operators who see franchising as a way of realising a quick profit, and offer little back-up. They can demand that franchisees buy all their supplies from them, at above market prices. It is best to sign with a well-established and managed franchise and to use professional advice before entering into any contract.

(vi) Licencing, joint ventures and co-operatives: These three are considered together as they represent a pot-pourri of opportunities that are often totally ignored. Manufacturing or service companies are often looking for licencees in new or peripheral markets. For instance, a US manufacturer of plumbing supplies may contract an Irish firm to produce these lines for the Irish or European markets. The licencee usually pays an initial fee, plus royalties. The plusses and drawbacks are similar to franchising. Many foreign firms, while not actively seeking licencees, would be willing to consider propositions from suitable individuals or firms. In general, Irish firms are underutilising the opportunities offered through licencing.

Joint ventures happen where two or more firms agree to join forces in some aspect of their business activities, e.g. marketing, distribution or technical development. The advantages are cost savings and the synergies gained by sharing experience and expertise. Irish firms find joint ventures particularly advantageous when tackling European markets. The joint venture between Aer Rianta and Aeroflot has led to the successful development of new duty free outlets in Eastern Europe, which have in turn opened up new channels of distribution for Irish giftware companies.

A co-operative is a venture where all the shareholders are entitled to a say in the decision-making as well as a share of the profits. The advantages are in the raising of capital and the feeling of democracy in the way the business is run. On the minus side, co-op shareholders may not be the best qualified to decide how the business should be run. Many co-ops suffer from a conservative attitude to product development and a difficulty in raising further funds from shareholders. Farmer co-operatives have been the most successful example of the model in Ireland.

13.12 FEASIBILITY STUDIES AND BUSINESS PLANNING

Having decided on the most suitable type of business organisation, the entrepreneur is now in a position to formulate a more concrete business proposal. If the proposal is a manufacturing or service idea requiring any significant investment, the initial step will be to carry out a feasibility study. If the results of the feasibility study appear promising and if the problems raised can be resolved, a business plan is then formulated. If the proposal involves a tried and tested area, or if it is already within the field of the entrepreneur's experience, he/she may feel confident enough to proceed directly to the business planning stage.

13.12.1 The feasibility study
A feasibility study is an examination of all the factors relevant to the establishment of the business. The purposes of such a study are to prepare a plan of the requirements necessary to develop the manufacturing plan or service operation, to arrive at an estimate of the finance required to set up the business, and to examine the underlying

key assumptions and timetable of events. It can be seen from the foregoing that a feasibility study demands extensive research and consideration. Professional consultants are often required to provide a research input, or assist with the preparation of the feasibility study document. Outside assistance is also helpful in viewing the business from a different perspective, and questioning the key assumptions and financial projections. Forbairt provides grant support (up to 50 per cent, with a ceiling of £15,000) towards the cost of preparing a feasibility study involving manufacturing or international services, provided the proposal is not in an area in which overcapacity already exists.

The typical headings for a feasibility study would be as follows:
1. Description of the business proposal
2. The market
3. The manufacturing plant or service operation
4. Finance
5. Staffing
6. Suppliers
7. Key assumptions and timetable of events.

Preparation of the feasibility study forces the entrepreneur into an examination of the crucial aspects of the business proposal. It also provides answers to the questions which will be posed by lenders and investors. If the outlook is positive, the information gathered for the feasibility study can be expanded upon in more detail in the business plan.

13.12.2 The business plan

The objective of the business plan is to set out in detail the proposal for the establishment and management of the business. The plan sets targets which can act as yardsticks for measuring progress once the business is up and running. The preparation of a business plan is also an exercise in communication: the clarity of expression is a reflection of the extent to which the proposal has been planned and considered.

Table 13.8 Differences between the Feasibility Study and the Business Plan

Feasibility Study	Business Plan
• A comprehensive analysis of information regarding the proposed venture	• A programme of action outlining how the business will be conducted
• Written for the benefit of the entrepreneur	• Often written for potential investors as well as the entrepreneur
• Regarded as a search for any factor which could prevent the project from succeeding	• A positive statement outlining the direction of the business
• Details of the feasibility of the project for a certain level of investment	• States the necessary financial requirements for the business
• Details alternative promotional/marketing strategies that the business can use	• Describes the marketing strategies that the business will use

Source: Bohan, P., *Notes on Enterprise Development,* The Marketing Institute, Dublin 1994.

A business plan may be prepared with a variety of audiences in mind:
1. The entrepreneur, or entrepreneurial team
2. The lending agency
3. The investor
4. The venture capitalist
5. The grant giving authority, at local, national or European level.

The actual writing of the business plan is the responsibility of the entrepreneur or members of the venture team, though it may be deemed necessary to call on expert advice as to the research and presentation of various aspects of the proposal. The plan should be professionally typed and presented, and be whatever length is deemed necessary to give a detailed description of the proposed business. A balance sheet, cash flow, and profit and loss statement covering five years of activity will be included in the financial plan. The financial forecasts will also give an analysis of the break even point, return on investment, and best and worst case scenarios.

The following headings show the contents of a typical business plan:
1. EXECUTIVE SUMMARY
2. PROMOTERS AND SUMMARY COMPANY DETAILS
3. OUTLINE OF PROPOSED VENTURE
   (i) Overview of proposed business
   (ii) History of the business
   (iii) Objectives and strategy
   (iv) Industry analysis
   (v) Proposed product/service
   (vi) Break even calculation
   (vii) Return on investment and financial ratios
4. MARKET RESEARCH AND ANALYSIS
   (i) Target market and customer profile
   (ii) Secondary research
   (iii) Primary research — method and findings
   (iv) Market positioning
   (v) Market size and share
   (vi) The competition
5. THE MARKETING PLAN
   (i) Sales plan
   (ii) Distribution strategy
   (iii) Pricing strategy
   (iv) Promotion plan
6. PRODUCTION/OPERATIONS PLAN
   (i) Premises
   (ii) Production/operations process
   (iii) Labour force
   (iv) Machinery and equipment
   (v) Materials
   (vi) Suppliers
   (vii) Manufacturing/process costs
7. THE VENTURE TEAM
   (i) Outline of proposed owners/shareholders

(ii) The management team

(iii) Responsibilities and organisation

(iv) List of outside agencies used to date — solicitors, accountants, state agencies etc.

8. FINANCIAL PLAN

(i) Sources of finance

(ii) Profit and loss projections

(iii) Cash flow projections

(iv) Sales forecasts by product/service

(v) Sensitivity analysis

9. STATEMENT OF STRENGTHS, WEAKNESSES, OPPORTUNITIES AND THREATS (SWOT) OF BUSINESS PROPOSAL

10. SCHEDULE OF EVENTS PROPOSED

11. APPENDICES.

Stokes Kennedy Crowley (1987) lists the nine most common reasons why a start-up venture might fail to attract finance and these are useful pointers to remember when preparing and presenting a proposal:

1. Weaknesses in management (lack of motivation, no financial expertise, no feel for the market, no track record)

2. Inadequate personal finance

3. Poorly presented proposals

4. Inadequate security offered

5. Too many risks inherent in the venture

6. Over-ambitiousness

7. Lack of detail as to how the finance will be repaid

8. Product or service weakness

9. Insufficient market research.

13.13 BUILDING UP THE BUSINESS

Even if a business secures the backing to get off the ground, the enterprising process does not end there. Once the firm gets started, the entrepreneur has to build it on foundations strong enough to secure its survival. Many small businesses think small and stay small. However, there is now more emphasis on pin-pointing fast growth small firms that can develop into medium and larger enterprises.

Kieran McGowan, chief executive of the IDA, suggests the following criteria as the key factors that contribute to the success of small businesses:

1. **Industry experience**: By starting a business in an area that is familiar, the risk is reduced and confidence increased.

2. **Being market driven**: The key requirement of a successful entrepreneur is that he/she be customer- and market-focused. A market focus, backed up by strong financial direction, is the model that has been found to work best.

3. **Team building**: The norm for high potential start-ups is a team of promoters rather than a strong individual. The ideal team would include strong competence in the areas of marketing, finance, human relations and production. Each member of the team would be a specialist in one of the areas and at the same time would be literate in all the others.

4. **Small firm experience**: International research shows that the best breeding ground for entrepreneurs is the small- and medium-size firm. A smaller firm gives exposure to a range of problems which have to be solved with the available expertise. This type of experience is invaluable in preparing for the real-life constraints which new firms always face.

5. **International experience**: This can be gained by working abroad, or by working for a multi-national in Ireland. International experience is important in terms of broadening the mind and becoming conscious of world class business standards.

6. **Building key relationships**: While this is not essential, many small businesses are built around a close relationship with a larger company. This could take the form of a contract to supply the larger company, a licencing/technology transfer agreement, or a marketing alliance.

7. **Single-mindedness**: Particularly at the early stages, the entrepreneur needs to be willing to fight all the way for his/her project. This means living with the project morning noon and night, negotiating, and presenting the business plan to a range of target groups. This single-mindedness should reflect itself in a longer term ability to push for new contracts and new markets. Burns and Dewhurst (1989) also emphasise the personal attributes of toughness and self discipline necessary for long-term success.

Among the other factors that can be added to the above, the first one worth considering must be quality (see Chapters 2 and 9). A reputation for quality goes hand in hand with a marketing orientation. Most customers now view quality standards as an absolute rather than a luxury. Quality standards must be established in the functions of manufacturing, delivery and aftersales service.

Many small firms are not seen as credible suppliers because they make late or short deliveries. If a firm wants to grow by reputation, it is absolutely essential that it makes delivery promises that it can keep. Foreign customers, in particular, will not entertain delays, and frequently purchasing agreements now include a performance clause which specifies a delivery date and possibly a cutoff time.

Good design is often considered an expensive luxury for the start-up firm, but it can be a competitive advantage and at the same time a barrier to entry. It gives the product a definite and distinctive appearance, bestowing a definitive image and impression. The design should have acceptable manufacturing costs while bearing in mind product reliability and safety features. Work on design can be carried out in-house or contracted out. In either situation, there are state subsidies available in specified circumstances.

The Irish market is now an international market in that the EU has opened up free competition. The experience gained in winning a competitive position in the home market can then be put to good use by examining opportunities in new markets. Most indigenous firms begin their international involvement by appointing a sales agent or distributor, or by placing their own salesperson in the market. As the commitment to the market grows, the firm may examine the options offered by joint ventures, licencing, manufacturing abroad, *mergers* or acquisitions.

Finally, no business will survive without having new products/services lined up to replace existing ones. Product life cycles are getting shorter, and markets are changing at an ever faster rate. Even if the market looks secure, there is always the prospect of new competition entering the field. Forbairt offers extensive help to firms developing new products or searching for joint venture or licence partners.

On the downside, many businesses fail in the first year of trading. In Ireland, there is an unusually low rate of second time start-ups, so the reasons for failure need to be considered and anticipated. The most common problems faced by new businesses are:

1. **Overtrading**: Businesses trying to expand too quickly often find themselves short of working capital. If buyers are slow to pay, the squeeze on cash flow can force the firm into liquidation.

2. **Inadequate capital structure**: Many businesses are burdened with high loan repayments, which are a particular problem at the early stage. The firm may use borrowings to pay wages and suppliers who often demand payment upfront at this stage, and then find itself burdened with more debt while waiting for cash inflows from its own sales. (See Chapter 8 for more information on financial management.)

3. **Inadequate managerial skills**: This problem is exacerbated by scarce resources limiting the ability to buy in expertise. Poor management often leads to over optimism in forecasting early sales, and a lack of contingency planning to cope with the shortfall. It also gives the firm poor credibility in troubled times, which may also go some way towards explaining the high failure rate.

4. **Poor research**: Many would-be entrepreneurs present incomplete market research as part of their business proposal. This may translate into a failure to secure the first few key customers. The firm may not have researched the buyer's ability to pay, or the standard terms required to do business with suppliers. Inability to identify market trends or changing preferences may threaten the long-term survival of the business.

The survey reported in Figure 13.3 concurs with these views.

Figure 13.3 Small Business: Main Reasons for Early Failure

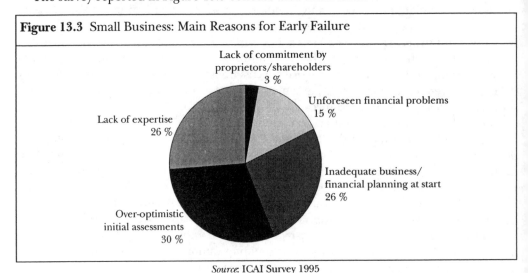

Source: ICAI Survey 1995

13.14 ENTERPRISE IN ACTION

In 1967, Patrick and Veronica Campbell established Campbell Catering Ltd. Their first piece of business was a cocktail party hosted by a college professor. They had both trained at the Dublin College of Catering, Cathal Brugha Street, married, and took over the running of a bed and breakfast business owned by Patrick Campbell's parents.

'When I told them we were getting out of B&B and setting up a catering company, my father thought we were losing the run of ourselves', commented Campbell. 'My mother prodded me in the chest, her eyes alive with excitement. "Go on, go on", she exhorted.'

Soon the firm was catering for larger events and tendered successfully for a contract to supply sandwiches to Dublin schools. Campbell has this view about the formation of entrepreneurs: 'I firmly believe that most businesspeople are conditioned by their experiences and exposure in childhood — as I was. The next most important factor comes from the development of their interests and attitudes during education.'

Campbell Catering decided to focus on catering for people in industry, education and healthcare. It also became involved in providing a complete hotel service — accommodation, cleaning and meals — for offshore oilrigs. This line of business offered many opportunities overseas, mainly in the Middle East.

After twenty years in business, Campbell Catering was one of the leading contract caterers in Ireland, and Patrick Campbell was considering retiring from his day to day involvement with the business. It was 1986, and he learned of the financial difficulties of Bewleys Cafes, a Dublin-based chain of traditional coffee houses. His initial impressions of the company were not favourable. 'I looked around at the customers. They were predominantly middle-aged nostalgics for whom Bewleys was a second home. Some shuffled in a Muscovite queue, hoping to attract attention from an indifferent staff. Others sat and reminisced about Bewleys in the good old days.'

Bewleys was being run as a workers co-operative. Both staff and premises were ageing, and pensions were being paid out of an unfunded scheme. The company had debts of £3.5 million, and owed the Revenue Commissioners £1 million. Campbell Catering bought the business and by 1992 Bewleys showed a profit of £1.3 million. The Bewleys Cafe concept has been franchised, and Bewleys products are sold in the US, Canada, Australia, Britain, Germany and Japan.

Along the route to success there have been problems. In 1989, Campbell Catering took a 50 per cent stake in a London-based vegetarian restaurant chain called Cranks. The hope was to emulate the success of the Bewleys turnaround. But within two years the investment was written off and the stake handed back to the other partner. Campbell blames this failure on poor management — the firm was short of staff to work on the ground with Cranks.

In the 1990s, Campbell Bewley has enjoyed further success through a joint venture with Aer Rianta, extending the distribution of Bewleys' products and expanding its handmade chocolate business. Patrick Campbell continues to preach the gospel of enterprise, for which he is a convincing ambassador.

13.15 SUMMARY OF KEY PROPOSITIONS

• The subject of entrepreneurship has been viewed in different terms by economists, psychologists and social commentators.

• 'Intrapreneurship' refers to intra-company enterprise and the effort to foster a working climate that encourages creativity.

• Defining entrepreneurship has proved problematic.

• There is an important distinction between entrepreneurship and innovation.

• The climate for enterprise has improved in Ireland, and the enterprise culture is beginning to bloom.

• The publication of the Culliton Report has resulted in a re-organisation of the government bodies responsible for industrial development in Ireland.

• There is a wide-range of agencies, both publicly and privately funded, involved in support schemes for new business. Support offered includes finance, training, business planning and mentoring schemes.

• There are approximately 160,000 small firms in Ireland. Most businesses are small (98 per cent), and most small firms are very small (90 per cent of all companies employ less than ten people).

• The level of start-ups in Ireland is similar to the EU average, but the number of business failures is above average.

• New product/service ideas must be put through a screening process in order to test their viability.

• There are a variety of ways of entering business — sole trader, partnership, limited company etc. Choice of entry method depends on the degree of control sought by the entrepreneur, the expected life of the business and the anticipated costs.

• The initial step in exploring the viability of a business proposal is the preparation of a feasibility study. If the results of this study are promising, a business plan is then formulated.

• Once the enterprise is established and stable, it must focus on building up its business. The management of a new firm must be aware of and anticipate the most common reasons for business failure.

DISCUSSION QUESTIONS

1. Review the definitions of entrepreneurship proposed by various authors. In your opinion, which of these definitions is most accurate?
2. Complete a personal profile of an individual entrepreneur, known either locally or nationally. How do his/her background and personal traits compare with those mentioned in this chapter?
3. What type of business structure (e.g. sole trader, partnership etc) is most commonly used by small firms? Why ?
4. Write a short case study of a recently established enterprise. The following headings should be addressed:

(i) Details of the proprietors of the business

(ii) Product/service offered

(iii) Level of innovation

(iv) Sources of finance

(v) Track record to date

(vi) Operational/managerial problems

(vii) Future prospects.

5. Select an enterprise known to you which has encountered failure/liquidation in the last five years.

(i) Why did the business fail?

(ii) Did the enterprise recommence business either in the same or a new format?

(iii) Have any of the employees, to your knowledge, become entrepreneurs themselves?

6. Can you think of any examples of successful businesspeople who encountered failure? What effect did it have?

7. Family-owned businesses often encounter problems with succession, leading to the sale or closure of the business. In your opinion, how can this problem be resolved?

8. Compare and contrast the level of grant support available for manufacturing and for service projects.

9. Which State bodies could offer assistance to an entrepreneur in the following situations:

(i) An individual buying a newsagent's shop.

(ii) An experienced shop manager currently in employment planning to start a business in the food industry.

(iii) The managing director of a timber firm examining the prospects for a new enterprise making pine furniture.

10. Visit your nearest campus innovation centre or Forbairt Enterprise Centre.

(i) Compile a list of the firms in operation.

(ii) How long has each enterprise been in business?

(iii) How is each business financed?

(iv) Write a short profile of the owner or manager of one enterprise.

11. Research the rates of interest and the terms being offered by lending institutions to start-up enterprises.

12. As a would-be graduate, do you consider your career prospects to lie in employment or in starting your own business? Why?

REFERENCES

An Bord Trachtala, *Annual Review and Outlook 1994/5*, Dublin 1995.

Bohan, P., *Notes on Enterprise Development*, The Marketing Institute, Dublin 1994.

Campbell, P., 'How to Start and Develop a Small Business', speech to Bank of Ireland Small Business Seminar, Dublin 1993.

Clare, Dr A., 'The Psychology of Risk Taking', speech to the annual conference of the Small Firms Association, Dublin 1994.

Drucker, P. F., *Innovation and Entrepreneurship*, Heinemann, London 1985.

Fitzpatrick and Associates, 'Background Report for the Task Force on Small Business', unpublished report, 1993.

Foley, E., *Irish Business Management*, Gill & Macmillan, Dublin 1989.

Henley Centre Ireland and Synectics Ltd, 'Innovation in Ireland', private report, 1994.

Hisrich, R. D. and Peters, M. P., *Entrepreneurship*, BPI Irwin, New York 1989.

Institute of Chartered Accountants, 'Small Business: Main Reasons for Early Failure', report presented to the Minister for Finance, 1995.

Joyce, C., 'Growth on the Cards', *Business and Finance*, 21 March 1991.

Kanter, R. M., *The Change Masters*, Simon and Schuster, New York 1983.

Kenny, I., *Out on Their Own: Conversations With Irish Entrepreneurs*, Gill & Macmillan, Dublin 1991.

Keogh, O., 'Peter Faulkner: Packaging the Family Business', *Irish Times*, 17 January 1992.

Management Training Services Ltd, 'The Irish Franchise Industry', report commissioned by the Irish Franchise Association, 1993.

McEnaney, T., 'Monaghan Tops for Enterprise', *Business and Finance*, 11 August 1994.

McGowan, K., 'The IDA and Small Business', speech to Bank of Ireland Small Business Seminar, Dublin 1993.

Meredith, G. G., Nelson R. E. and Neck, P. E., *The Practice of Entrepreneurship*, International Labour Office, Geneva 1982.

National Economic and Social Council, *A Review of Industrial Policy*, report no.64, Dublin 1982.

O'Connor, J. and Lyons, M., *Enterprise: The Irish Approach*, IDA Ireland, Dublin 1983.

O'Farrell, P., *Entrepreneurs and Industrial Change*, Irish Management Institute, Dublin 1986.

Report of the Industrial Policy Review Group, 'A Time for Change: Industrial Policy in the 1990s', Government Publications Office, Dublin 1992.

Rosenfeldt, R., and Servo, J. C., 'Facilitating Innovation in Large Organisations', in Henry, J. and Walker D., *Managing Innovation*, Sage, London 1991.

Rothery, B., *Men of Enterprise*, Institute for Industrial Research and Standards, Dublin 1977.

Stokes, Kennedy, Crowley, *Running Your Own Business*, second Edition, SKC, Dublin 1987.

Stokes, Kennedy, Crowley Corporate Finance (1994), 'Mergers and Acquisitions', private report 1994.

Task Force on Small Business, Government Publications, Dublin 1994.

West, A., *Innovation Strategy*, Prentice-Hall, London 1992.

'Waterford Stanley team wins award for restoring fortunes to cooker group', *Irish Times*, 17 November 1994.

14

The Management of Change

14.1 INTRODUCTION

This chapter examines the management of change within organisations. Due to the changing nature of the business environment (discussed in Chapter 3), the management of change has become a top priority for all managers irrespective of the organisation. Change is occurring at a far greater pace than before and the changes themselves are fundamental. While organisations face unique sets of factors forcing change, it is possible to identify four broad trends, along with potential sources of resistance to such change. A model of strategic change is then outlined and applied to an Irish example. Finally, factors which contribute to the successful management of change are considered.

14.2 THE NATURE AND IMPORTANCE OF CHANGE

The whole area of change and change management has become one of the most important issues in the field of management (Carnall 1990). Change can be viewed as perceived or felt differences in circumstances and behaviour, to such an extent that a situation becomes or is made different (Mills and Murgatroyd 1991).

Change has become an important issue for managers due to the nature of the business environment. Instead of a stable and certain environment, organisations are now faced with complexity, uncertainty and dynamism, all of which demand change. Such change, however, is very different in both nature and duration to other periods of change faced by organisations. Firstly, the current period of change contains fundamental rather than minor changes. These changes are so important that they require shifts in the way we think and view the world, sometimes referred to as paradigm shifts. Secondly, the period of change appears to be one long continuous process. Previous changes facing organisations had clearly identifiable beginnings and ends. For example, an organisation was able to recognise a given change and alter its behaviour in some way to accommodate the change and then carry on its operations. Today, however, as soon as an organisation responds to one set of changing circumstances it is faced with another. Organisations, therefore, have to constantly adapt to meet changes or to anticipate future developments in the business environment. Change, therefore, has assumed paramount importance for organisations due to its nature and duration.

The importance of change is not confined to particular regions, countries or industries, but is affecting organisations world-wide, including Ireland. Kanter (1991) has presented research conducted by the *Harvard Business Review* on the extent of change experienced by 12,000 managers in twenty-five countries. Respondents were asked whether their organisations had undergone a major restructuring programme recently. The results are contained in Figure 14.1 and demonstrate the extent of change undertaken by organisations especially in South Korea, the USA and Mexico.

Figure 14.1 % of Organisations Undertaking a Major Restructuring Programme

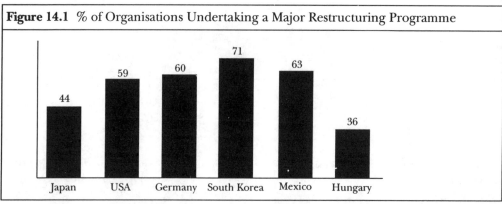

Source: Kanter, R., 'Transcending Business Boundaries: 12,000 World Managers View Change' *Harvard Business Review*, Vol.69, No 2, 154, 1991.

Not only is change occurring across all regions of the world, it is also affecting each of the major functions within the organisation. Departments and areas of the organisation that were traditionally responsible for co-ordinating change have been unable to provide the flexibility and adaptability to meet current requirements. Peters (1987) has outlined the extent of change occurring within individual departments and areas of the organisation. Figure 14.2 provides a summary of the prevalence of change within organisations and highlights the fact that the ability to manage change is no longer the exclusive concern of specialised areas, but that all parts of the organisation need to be adaptive.

Figure 14.2 Changes to Basic Organisational Functions

Function	Old Emphasis	New Emphasis
Manufacturing	Capital, automation, volume, low cost and efficiency	Short production runs, fast product changeover, people, quality and responsiveness
Finance	Centralised control with specialist staff reviewing proposals	Decentralised control, financial specialists who are members of business teams
Marketing	Mass markets, mass advertising and long market tests	Fragmented markets, small-scale market testing and speed
MIS	Centralised information control, information hoarded for consistency	Decentralised data processing, personalised computer proliferation, multiple data bases permitted
R&D	Centralised; emphasis on big projects; cleverness more important than reliability and service, innovation limited to new products and services	All functions hotbeds for innovation, not limited to new products and services, emphasis on portfolio of small projects and speed

Source: Adapted from Peters, T., 'A World Turned Upside Down' *Academy of Management Executive*, pages 231–241, 1987 and Peters, T., 'Prometheus Barely Unbound' *Academy of Management Executive*, pages 70–84, 1980.

In order to fully appreciate the extent of change facing organisations we need to examine in depth the main forces which are driving change.

14.3 FACTORS FORCING CHANGE

Organisations operating in both developed and developing countries are facing enormous pressure to change. Such pressures can come from two sources: internal and external to the organisation. While internal pressures for change (such as a new CEO or management team) are important, they are heavily influenced by developments in the external environment. For this reason our analysis will focus mainly on factors in the external business environment. Internal pressures will be considered later during the discussion on the change process.

Each organisation faces a unique set of factors which shape change depending on the nature of the industry and the characteristics of the organisation. However, it is possible to identify broad factors which are forcing organisations world-wide to change their strategies and operations as illustrated in Figure 14.3.

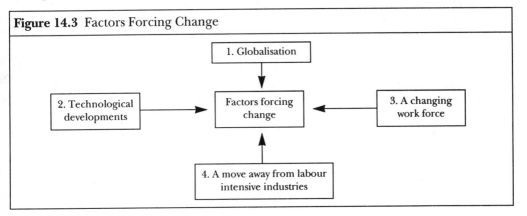

Figure 14.3 Factors Forcing Change

14.3.1 Globalisation

Organisations currently face competition on a global scale. Markets which were previously served by domestic operators have typically been opened up to foreign competition from aggressive new entrants. The trend towards globalisation has resulted from the emergence and development of a number of important industrial economies which have provided intense competition in established markets, especially high technology. Competition includes:

1. newly industrialised countries including the four dragons of South Korea, Taiwan, Hong Kong and Singapore
2. new and powerful trading blocks such as the EU and the 'Yen block' including Japan and its Pacific Rim trading partners (Peters 1990).
3. the move from planned economies to more open-market based economies in eastern Europe and the former Soviet Union.

All of these factors have heightened the trend towards global markets and consequently global competition and *global strategies*. Globalisation is now a powerful force facing organisations, and one that should not be ignored. An example of an industry that largely ignored the trend towards global competition during the early 1980s is the US automobile industry. Throughout the 1960s, and 1970s the US market had been dominated by US manufacturers; General Motors, Ford and Chrysler. However, the early 1980s saw the emergence of Japanese competitors into this domestic market. Within a few years companies such as Honda, Nissan and Toyota had overtaken the US manufacturers in their home market. The US manufacturers closed thirteen plants whereas the Japanese opened eleven plants (Hitt et al 1992). The Japanese success was primarily due to their high quality/modest price strategy and the fact that the US manufacturers failed to respond to the global competition that confronted them.

As a result of the trend toward globalisation, the numbers and strength of international and *multi-national corporations* (MNCs) have increased significantly. Such corporations are now the major players in the world economy. Trends towards privatisation and deregulation have also contributed to global expansion. Where markets have opened through deregulation large multi-nationals have frequently entered the scene. Privatisation of large state-owned organisations has resulted in leaner, more efficient and, therefore, more competitive organisations.

The emergence and expansion of corporations of this nature, such as Mc Donalds, Ford, Nissan, Intel and IBM, creates pressure for domestic organisations. In order to compete with emerging global players, smaller domestic organisations have had to introduce strategic change in relation to their structures, culture and operations. Telecom Eireann is faced with similar challenges. Competition within the telecommunications industry in Ireland will become global in 2003 when the market is opened up to competitors. To meet this prospect, Telecom is currently considering available strategic options, including the possibility of a joint venture arrangement with one of its future competitors Cable and Wireless, AT & T or British Telecom.

14.3.2 Technological developments

The pace of technological change in both manufacturing and information is occurring more quickly than ever before. The most dramatic and influential changes are in the area of information technology, where developments have far-reaching effects on the management and operation of work. Technological developments such as tele-conferencing, video-conferencing, faxes and electronic mail have greatly facilitated information exchange, regardless of the physical distance. A key result of such developments is that people no longer need to be in close physical proximity to work collectively. Increasingly, it has become possible for people to work from home and to communicate by phone, fax and computer. So, while the Industrial Revolution resulted in people moving to central bases such as factories, revolutions in information technology mean that the reverse can now happen with people working in isolation from their homes.

Systems such as Management Information Systems (MIS) and Financial Information Systems (FIS) have facilitated the dissemination of timely and accurate information throughout the organisation. These information systems have resulted in the elimination of layers of middle managers whose prime function was to relay information up and down the hierarchy. This has led to huge reductions in costs. These systems also make the control of operations much easier as the remaining managers can now spend more of the day facilitating the completion of work, rather than controlling the work of employees.

Technological developments have led to the introduction of CAD and CAM techniques in the design and manufacture of products. Recently, organisations have started to experiment with Computer Integrated Manufacturing (CIM). The CIM system involves the use of networks of computers to link the order, production, sale and distribution of a product. For example, a customer could place an order for a product by computer. This would then be relayed to a factory computer which sends instructions to factory machines outlining what needs to be produced, the mode of distribution and materials needed from outside suppliers. In this sense the organisation can operate a just-in-time (JIT) manufacturing system which reduces the costs of holding inventory.

Technological innovations and changing customer demands have resulted in a shorter product life cycle and reduced lead times for producing new products. Organisations can, therefore, no longer rely on technological leadership and innovation to provide a long-term source of competitive advantage. Product life cycles and lead times used to be as long as ten years, but currently they have been reduced to a few months. For example, when General Electric first produced X-ray machines it enjoyed a competitive advantage for many years based on that technological innovation. Today, General Electric has to innovate much more quickly to enjoy any form of competitive advantage from its technology (Potts and Behr 1987). The current pace of technological innovation demands that organisations be adaptive and flexible in order to compete effectively.

The outcome of all of the combined technological developments is that the modern organisation is in a state of transformation. The introduction of technological innovation can lead to significant cost savings and increased efficiency. As more organisations adopt such techniques, competitors are compelled to do the same in order to remain competitive. Therefore, technological developments, while producing enormous benefits in terms of savings, also force organisations to keep up to date with new technology.

14.3.3 The changing nature of the labour force

The nature of the world labour force is changing significantly both in terms of composition and values and expectations held. A number of important trends are emerging. The average age of the labour force is projected to increase significantly to the year 2000 as illustrated in Figure 14.4.

Figure 14.4 Age of the World Labour Force

Country	% Labour Force Under 34		% Population Over 65	
	1985	2000	1985	2000
Developed Regions				
USA	50.4	39.5	12.3	12.9
Japan	33.8	33.9	11.1	15.8
Germany	45.7	37.4	14.2	16.0
UK	43.6	38.8	15.5	15.4
Italy	48.0	44.6	14.0	16.7
Spain	49.9	49.0	9.1	11.5
Developing Regions				
China	63.7	53.3	5.5	7.3
India	55.6	52.0	3.4	4.1
Thailand	62.8	55.2	3.9	5.2
South Korea	54.7	44.2	4.5	5.9
CIS	50.2	42.9	9.3	11.9

Source: Johnson, W., 'The Global Work Force 2000: A New World Labour Market' *Harvard Business Review,* Vol.69, No.2, 115–127, 1991.

The trend towards an older labour force is most pronounced in the developed regions of the world. Older workers generally cost the organisation more as their wages are higher and healthcare and pension costs increase. As a result, organisations located within the developed world face the challenge of maintaining competitiveness in the face of increased costs. Unless such increased costs can be matched with higher productivity, organisations within these regions face the loss of competitive advantage. In contrast to the trends in most of the developed countries, Ireland still has a relatively young population as illustrated in Figure 14.5.

Figure 14.5 Irish Population by Age 1986–1993 (000s)

Age / Year	0–14	15–24	25–44	45–64	65+	Total
1986	1,024.7	617.5	922.6	591.4	384.4	3,540.6
1987	1,014.4	615.8	935.9	592.1	388.3	3,546.5
1988	944.0	608.8	939.2	595.6	393.2	3,530.7
1989	973.5	597.5	941.1	599.9	397.5	3,509.5
1990	954.6	594.1	949.1	608.1	400.0	3,505.8
1991	940.6	601.6	959.0	621.7	402.9	3,525.7
1992	930.9	608.2	967.2	637.1	405.8	3,563.3
1993	917.6	610.9	972.4	654.3	408.8	3,563.3

Source: Labour Force Survey, Central Statistics Office, Dublin 1993.

However, the Irish population is declining so it is likely that in years to come the Irish labour force will also age. In this sense, Irish companies can perhaps learn some lessons from other countries currently facing this situation.

The number of women in the labour force has also increased significantly, as shown in Figure 14.6. The developing regions show the most potential for future growth as relatively few women have entered the labour force to date.

Figure 14.6 Women in the World Labour Force 1987

Country	Female share of labour force % of total labour force	Female labour force participation % of all females aged 15–64
Developed Regions		
USA	44.1	66.0
Japan	39.9	57.8
Germany	39.3	51.3
UK	41.4	62.6
Italy	36.9	43.4
Developing Regions		
China	43.2	75.5
India	26.2	32.3
Thailand	45.9	74.8
South Korea	34.0	42.2
CIS	48.3	72.6

Source: Johnson, W., 'The Global Work Force 2000: A New World Labour Market' *Harvard Business Review*, Vol.69, No.2, 115–127, 1991.

Similar trends can also be found in Ireland where the number of women working outside of the home has increased.

Figure 14.7 Women in the Irish Labour Force 1988–1994 (000s)

	1988	1989	1990	1991	1992	1993	1994
Total number of women at work	353	358	381	386	399	410	428
Total female labour force	402	403	421	439	455	469	485
Total female population	1772	1765	1763	1772	1784	1792	1797
% of total labour force	30.6	31.2	32.1	32.7	33.4	34.1	–

Source: Labour Force Survey, Central Statistics Office, Dublin 1993.

As the number of women in the labour force increases, working conditions and patterns of consumer demand will change. It is likely that demand for fast foods, crèche facilities, day care and home cleaners will increase in line with female participation in the labour force. Organisations will continue to implement equal opportunities in the hiring and promotion of personnel. Women are likely to seek time away from work for family commitments. It is likely that the trend towards increased part-time and temporary work will continue to meet this demand. Figure 14.8 shows how both part-time and temporary work have increased in Ireland in recent years.

Figure 14.8 Part-time and Temporary Work Patterns in Ireland 1983–1989 (000s)

	1983	1985	1987	1989	% Change
Full-time temporary	27.6	38.5	41.8	40	+ 44.9
Part-time temporary	22.8	20.6	27.9	29.2	+ 28.1
Part-time permanent	29.8	29	33.8	37.7	+ 26.5

Source: Dineen, D., 'Atypical Work Patterns in Ireland: Short-term Adjustments of Fundamental Changes' *Administration*, Vol.40, No.3, 1992.

The labour force is predicted to increase significantly in the developing regions of the world. However, most of the well-paid jobs continue to be generated in the developed world. The result is a mismatch between workers and available jobs. Consequently, it is predicted that the labour force will be increasingly mobile. Employees are also expected to become less loyal to one particular organisation and to change occupations several times during their career (Handy 1989). It is predicted that the world's labour force will become more global in nature, with an increased standardisation of practices throughout the world. Already a degree of standardisation has developed in relation to holiday periods (five weeks) and the length of the working week (forty hours) in the EU, the USA and Japan. These trends are likely to develop further which means that organisations will have to keep up to date with the new trends.

The values and expectations of the labour force are also changing considerably. In general, employees are now better educated, less unionised and possess different values and attitudes. Younger workers are demanding more opportunities and more enjoyment from their work. They are less willing to accept traditional authority and demand more autonomy and a say over decisions which affect both themselves and the business. Improving the quality of working life has become an important goal for many employees. Organisations, therefore, have to respond to such changes and provide opportunities for employees in order to compete effectively in the labour market.

All of the foregoing changes in the world labour force herald changes for organisations which, in future, will be faced with an older labour force, higher rates of female participation and increased mobility of labour and standardisation of work practices.

14.3.4 A move away from labour intensive industry

In recent years there has been a marked shift in employment from traditional labour intensive industries (for example iron and steel and coal mining) to knowledge-based industries and services. According to Handy (1989), thirty years ago nearly half of all employees were involved in the manufacturing sector. In the USA alone the figure has dropped to 18 per cent in the early 1990s. Handy (1989) predicts that this figure could be as low as 10 per cent in another thirty years.

Traditional labour intensive industries employed large numbers of people at cheap rates who were heavily supervised by a hierarchical management structure. Employees were mainly hired on a full-time basis, to be used for the benefit of the organisation. The demise of the mass manufacturing organisation has seen the end of mass employment organisations.

While labour intensive industries have been declining, knowledge-based industries have increased in number (Drucker 1992). Examples of these industries include journalism, publishing, education and finance. In contrast to the traditional labour intensive industries, knowledge-based industries create added value from the information and creativity put in, rather than from muscle power. Organisations generally employ fewer, more creative people, aided by information technology. Even industries which were traditionally labour intensive, such as agriculture and construction, have recently invested in knowledge and machines to replace muscle power.

The move towards knowledge-based industries and organisations means that different people and indeed different forms of organisation are required. The organisations sub contract or out source work to specialist agencies, while retaining a core group of talented and energetic people. These organisations are also flatter and more adaptive.

There have also been moves towards the service sector on a world-wide basis. Figure 14.9 illustrates the trend towards employment in the service sector in Ireland from 1979 to 1989.

Social changes and increases in the female labour participation rate have led to a greater reliance on services provided by others. Society itself becomes more like the knowledge-based organisation in that it contracts out services that it is either not good at or does not have the time to complete. The result has been a significant increase in the services sector. While some services are knowledge-based, most are not, for example cleaning, transport and catering. It is in these areas that those who were previously employed in labour intensive industry will find employment. (Handy 1989)

Figure 14.9 Employment Changes by Sector in Ireland 1975–1989

	Agriculture		Industry		Services		Total
	000s	*%*	*000s*	*%*	*000s*	*%*	*000s*
1975	238	22.1	337	31.4	498	46.4	1073
1976	232	21.8	325	30.5	507	47.6	1064
1977	228	21.0	336	31.0	519	47.9	1083
1978	226	20.3	350	31.5	534	48.1	1110
1979	221	19.3	365	31.8	559	48.8	1145
1980	209	18.0	371	32.0	576	49.8	1156
1981	196	17.0	363	31.6	587	51.2	1146
1982	193	16.8	355	30.9	598	52.1	1146
1983	189	16.8	331	29.4	604	53.7	1124
1984	181	16.4	319	28.9	603	54.6	1103
1985	171	15.8	306	28.3	602	55.7	1079
1986	168	15.5	307	28.3	606	56.0	1081
1987	164	15.1	300	27.7	616	57.0	1080
1988	166	15.2	300	27.4	626	57.3	1091
1989	163	14.9	306	28.0	621	56.9	1090

Source: Dineen, D., 'Atypical Work Patterns in Ireland: Short-term Adjustments of Fundamental Changes' *Administration*, Vol.40, No.3, 1992.

Service based organisations have to be flexible to meet changing consumer demands. Such flexibility is ensured by the use of part-time and temporary workers in conjunction with a small core of full-time staff as discussed earlier. Therefore, the shift towards knowledge-based and service-based industries has had an enormous influence not only on the type of people employed but also on the type of organisation required. All of this has led to considerable change for traditional organisations.

Organisations can no longer ignore developments in the external environment as they now affect almost every aspect of the organisation from operations and production to employees and consumer demand patterns. Kanter (1989) has argued that the changes facing organisations today are similar to the croquet game in Alice in Wonderland. In that fictional game nothing was stable for very long because everything was alive and changing around the player, as Kanter states: 'The mallet Alice uses is a flamingo, which tends to lift its head and face in another direction just as Alice tries to hit the ball. The ball in turn is a hedgehog which instead of lying and waiting for Alice to hit it gets up and moves to another part of the court. The wickets are card soldiers ordered around by the Queen of Hearts who changes the structure of the game at whim' (Kanter 1989).

If we substitute the word technology for the mallet, employees and customers for the hedgehog and everyone from competitors to government regulators for the Queen of Hearts, the analogy fits the experience which many organisations are currently going through.

14.4 RESISTANCE TO CHANGE

Organisations facing change will inevitably encounter a degree of resistance even with sufficient planning. Organisations, by their very nature, are designed to ensure stability over time, so some resistance to change is natural. Such resistance can be overt and take the form of strikes, reductions in productivity and even sabotage. More covert examples of resistance to change include increased absenteeism, loss of employee motivation and a higher rate of accidents or errors in the workplace. The most damaging form of resistance occurs when employees refuse to participate in or commit to the process of change when given the opportunity to do so (Neumann 1989).

Resistance to change originates from two main sources: the individual and the organisation, as illustrated in Figure 14.10. In an environment characterised by constant change, it is vitally important that both managers and employees are aware of the reasons and sources of resistance to change if the process is to be successful (Spector 1989).

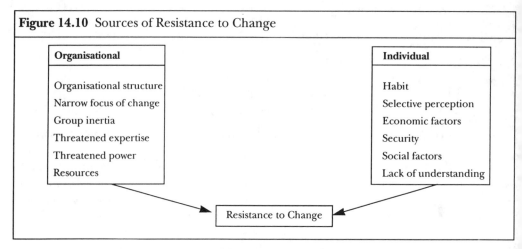

Figure 14.10 Sources of Resistance to Change

14.4.1 Organisational sources of resistance

Katz and Kahn (1978) have identified six main organisational sources of resistance to change.

1. **Organisational structure**: Organisational structure is designed to maintain stability over time. All organisations need a structure to ensure stability and continuity in order to function effectively. Consequently, employees are assigned established roles, and procedures are designed to achieve tasks. However, these structures (for example bureaucratic structures) become very rigid as they develop, which mitigates against change. Over time, tall hierarchies, narrowly defined jobs, and hierarchical authority block change. Due to the fact that they were designed to ensure stability, they emphasise a narrow and limited outlook and prevent the circulation of new ideas. Hannan and Freeman (1984) refer to this as structural inertia.

2. **Narrow focus of change**: Frequently, change programmes take a limited or narrow focus by attempting to introduce piecemeal changes in particular areas. In taking such an approach the important interdependencies between elements in the organisation, such as people, structures and systems, are largely ignored. For example, an organisation could change the structure of tasks by introducing teams, yet still reward employees for individual achievements and have a culture that emphasises competition between individuals. In this case, the organisation has changed the structure but not the culture

or the systems. Therefore, employees will resist change because the culture and systems do not back up the change. Organisations should carefully consider interdependencies between areas to avoid resistance to change.

3. **Group inertia**: Inertia is the innate desire to retain the status quo even when the present situation is inferior when compared to something new (Stanislao and Stanislao 1983). Group inertia occurs when the group, either formal or informal, refuses to change behaviour patterns. In this sense the groups norms act as a barrier to change especially if individual attempts at change are dependent on corresponding change by the group.

4. **Threatened expertise**: If the specialised expertise of an individual or group is threatened the natural reaction is to resist such change. For example, many organisations are introducing multi-skilling, whereby employees are trained to complete a wide range of tasks rather than one or two very specific skills. Craft unions resist such changes because they feel this dilutes the expertise of craft workers who have served an apprenticeship and have years of experience in a particular trade, such as mechanics or painting.

5. **Threatened power and influence**: Organisational change programmes frequently involve a redistribution of power and influence much like a political cabinet reshuffle, in that there are nearly always winners and losers. When an individual/ group or department controls a resource such as people, money or information, they have power. Once a position of power has been established such individuals or groups resist any change which is viewed as reducing their power and influence. For example, attempts to decentralise decision making from middle management levels to the shop floor have frequently met with resistance from middle managers. The reason for such resistance is the perception that such decentralisation will reduce the decision making power and influence of middle managers.

6. **Resources**: Organisational change programmes that attempt to alter the allocation of scarce resources will meet with resistance from individuals or groups that currently enjoy a favourable allocation and who are likely to lose out. Resources include people, money and information. For example if an organisation decides to reduce employment in Marketing from thirty to fifteen and concurrently decides to increase employment in Finance from twenty to thirty, it is quite likely that Marketing will resist this move as it marks a reduction in its prestige and resources.

The six organisational sources of resistance to change are primarily associated with people and social relationships. Many of the sources discussed are connected with the loss of either power, influence, resources or the status quo.

14.4.2 Individual sources of resistance

Researchers such as Nadler (1983) and Stanislao and Stanislao (1983) have identified a number of individual sources of resistance to change. In drawing together elements of this research it is possible to identify six main sources which are associated with the individual. Individual resistance to change arises from basic human characteristics such as attitudes and needs.

1. **Habit**: As individuals complete the various tasks assigned to them, habits develop. It becomes easier to do the job in the same manner each day whereby the steps are repeated over and over again. An established habit allows an individual to adjust to and

cope with the work environment and, therefore, provides a degree of comfort. Changing this habit may result in a resistance to change due to the fact that breaking a habit, by learning something new, is more difficult than leaving things as they are.

The extent to which a habit develops into a major source of resistance depends on whether individuals see any advantage from the change. If the rewards associated with the change are greater and more than offset the loss of breaking the habit, then resistance should not be a problem. If, on the other hand, no rewards or compensation are associated with the change, then individuals will more than likely be resistant.

2. **Selective perception**: Individuals tend to selectively perceive or view things that match their current understanding of the work environment or the world around them. When individuals have developed an understanding of reality through their values and attitudes, they are hesitant to alter this understanding. In resisting change, individuals frequently only listen to things that they agree with, 'deliberately' forget other viewpoints and misunderstand communications which, if viewed correctly, would not match their understanding of reality. For example, if an individual is told to make certain changes he/she may be selective about those areas to change and ignore those which are perceived to be at odds with the individual's beliefs and attitudes.

3. **Economic factors**: While individuals are not motivated solely by money, economic factors still remain important. Employees spend time learning how to perform the job successfully and getting good performance appraisals and possibly a bonus. Therefore, any change in established work practices or social relations threaten individual employee's economic security in two main ways: income may be reduced through change; the change may require learning other things to achieve the same level of performance as before, which means that income will be lower during the learning period.

4. **Security**: Individuals like to feel comfortable and secure in completing things the same way. In doing so they gain a degree of security in their jobs and in their lives. When the status quo is threatened by change, employees feel their security is at risk and, consequently, they resist such change. Confronting any form of unknown makes the individual anxious and insecure. Insecurity arises not only from the change itself but also from the prospective outcomes of such change. For example, employees may turn down an overseas promotion due to insecurity and fear of the unknown.

5. **Social factors**: Individuals may resist change due to social factors, particularly the fear of what others will think. The work group may exert peer pressure on the individual to resist change. The group norms serve as a guide to what is acceptable and unacceptable behaviour. If an individual's behaviour is contrary to the group he/she may be ostracised in some way which leads to resistance to change. If acceptance of the group is important to the individual then he/she will go along with the group view, even if that means resisting change which he/she would otherwise have supported. The opposite also holds true in that employees who may individually resist the change are carried along by the group which favours the change.

6. **Lack of understanding**: If the individual does not understand the rationale for the change, the change itself and any consequences, then he/she will resist the change. Employees will not take on board changes which they do not fully understand. In many cases individuals will resist the change rather than clarify the position. It is therefore up to the organisation to fully explain the change programme to its employees.

In combining both organisational and individual sources of resistance to change, there are potentially twelve different sources. An example in the Irish context can be seen in Team Aer Lingus and Irish Steel. In both cases the craft unions were initially unwilling to accept required changes in work practices, even when the survival of both organisations was in question. The main source of resistance centered around the loss of expertise by the craft workers which would result from the changes, coupled with a fear of the unknown and insecurity. Eventually, when it became obvious that both Irish Steel and Team Aer Lingus would close, agreement was reached, but not without intense resistance (Business and Finance 1994).

The organisation has to understand each source of resistance before it can attempt to manage or overcome it. Resistance to change should not necessarily be viewed as a bad thing; in fact it can have important contributions to make to the change programme. Where legitimate concerns about issues are raised, the organisation can benefit from a re-evaluation or checking of certain elements. It could be the case that important issues may have been overlooked. Resistance to change ensures that decisions are fully researched and considered before implementation. Re-evaluating a change programme in response to employee resistance can also have symbolic significance in that it shows management care about employees' views (Pfeffer 1981).

14.5 PLANNED ORGANISATIONAL CHANGE

It is important to distinguish between change that inevitably happens to all organisations and that which is essentially planned by organisational members. (Cummings and Huse 1989) According to Goodman and Kurke (1982), planned organisational change is a set of activities and processes designed to change individuals, groups, structures and processes. Organisations typically introduce changes in response to external pressures. However, they also make changes in anticipation of future problems. Effective organisations both anticipate future changes and react to current changes by planning and developing strategies.

Planned organisational change, either reactive or anticipatory, is the deliberate effort by organisational members to improve organisational performance. Planned organisational change programmes tend to have two main goals. Firstly, such programmes are designed to improve organisational flexibility and adaptability to respond to changes in the business environment. Secondly, they aim to change individual behaviour within the organisation which, according to Beer et al (1990), should be the primary focus of all planned organisational change programmes.

Planned organisational change requires a systematic process of moving from one condition or state to another. Two approaches to change which are based on this process are examined in the next section: Lewin's model of change and a model of strategic change.

14.6 LEWIN'S MODEL OF CHANGE

Lewin (1951) argued that efforts to bring about change should be viewed as a multi-stage process, rather than merely one step. His model of organisational change consists of three steps — unfreezing, change and refreezing, as shown in Figure 14.11.

Figure 14.11 Lewin's Model of Change

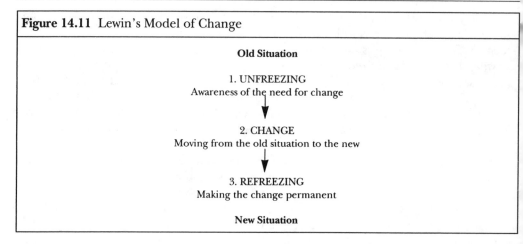

The first stage, *unfreezing*, is the process by which organisational members become aware of the need for change. Employees who are most affected by the intended change must be made aware of the need and rationale behind its introduction. This stage of the change process attempts to make employees dissatisfied with the current state of affairs, so that they will be motivated to change. For example, if employees know that a crisis is facing the organisation, they are more likely to feel the need for change and will be more open to it.

The second stage is *change*, which is the movement from the old situation to the new one. The change itself could involve the introduction of new technology or a change in the structure, systems or culture of the organisation. The final stage of the process is called refreezing which makes the new behaviour or change a permanent feature of the organisation. *Refreezing* can be achieved through training and development sessions and rewarding new behaviour. This stage is critically important in the process because, unless the new behaviour is made permanent, the organisation and its members will revert back to the old situation. Frequently during management training sessions new skills and techniques are learned. Yet, when the manager returns to the work environment the new skills are forgotten and the manager reverts back to his/her old behaviour. The reason for this reversion is that the new skills were not refrozen or made permanent in any way either through rewards or follow up training sessions.

Lewin's model is perhaps the most simple and straightforward available. For this reason it has been incorporated into many other models of planned organisational change. However, it has been criticised for viewing organisations as closed systems and for the notion of equilibrium which lies at the heart of the approach. Organisational life is rarely based on equilibrium, but on a constant battle for power. The model also ignores the role of factors forcing change, how change is actually introduced and what organisations can do to ensure successful change. The next model of organisational change to be examined seeks to overcome many of these inadequacies.

14.7 A MODEL OF STRATEGIC CHANGE

Strategic change is any change in the strategies pursued by the organisation. In this sense strategic change can occur in relation to employees, technology, structure and culture. The nature of the changes in the current business environment have forced many organisations to undertake significant strategy changes.

Strategic change can take a number of different forms. *Reorientation* or corporate level strategic change occurs when an organisation moves into new markets or industries and discards or reduces involvement in others. *Revitalisation* occurs when an organisation's performance is mediocre, but survival is still possible. For example, the organisation may have certain problems, such as a reduction in market share, which means that it has to revitalise its current market position. The most serious form of strategic change is a *turnaround* strategy which occurs when the survival of the organisation is at stake due to serious losses and poor performance. A turnaround strategy is, therefore, designed to turn around the organisation's fortunes.

Effective management of strategic change has become vitally important for managers in the current business environment. One of the biggest mistakes which organisations frequently make is to embark on a change programme without a carefully planned strategy for managing the overall process (Kotter and Schlesinger 1979). According to Nadler (1981), organisational change is successful when:
1. The organisation is moved from its current state to some planned future state that will exist after the change.
2. The functioning of the organisation in the future state meets expectations.
3. The transition is accomplished without excessive costs to the organisation and the individual.

These factors are important to consider when planning and implementing change. A model of strategic change is outlined in Figure 14.12 showing each of the main steps an organisation should go through when implementing change.

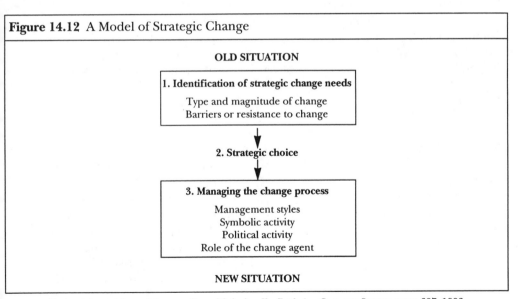

Figure 14.12 A Model of Strategic Change

OLD SITUATION

1. **Identification of strategic change needs**
   Type and magnitude of change
   Barriers or resistance to change

2. **Strategic choice**

3. **Managing the change process**
   Management styles
   Symbolic activity
   Political activity
   Role of the change agent

NEW SITUATION

Source: Adapted from Johnson, G. and Scholes, K., *Exploring Corporate Strategy*, page 387, 1993.

14.7.1 Identification of strategic change needs
The first step in the strategic change process is to clearly identify strategic change needs.

In other words, the organisation needs to identify and understand what factors are forcing change, why the organisation needs to change and what barriers to change the organisation is likely to encounter. An examination of the factors forcing change should indicate to the organisation the nature and extent of change required. Organisations are typically faced with two types of change — incremental and transformational. Incremental change is a step by step, non radical change, where the beliefs and values of the organisation are maintained. Transformational change is a radical form of change whereby the established beliefs and values of the organisation are challenged. Poor performance over a long period of time generally requires transformational change. Having established the nature of the change required, it then becomes necessary to identify the likely sources of resistance. The twelve main sources were discussed previously. It is vitally important that the organisation identifies potential sources of resistance to change so that attempts to manage and overcome them can be planned in advance.

14.7.2 Strategic choice
Strategic choice involves choosing the most effective strategy to meet the strategic change needs. In choosing the strategy, the issue is subjected to the normal decision making and problem solving processes. Alternatives are generated, evaluated and one particular strategy chosen. Organisations try to choose strategies that they think will meet the needs of environmental changes while minimising the sources of resistance to change. Top managers play a very important role in choosing the strategy to be pursued and, therefore, the process is influenced by their perceptions, attitudes and values.

14.7.3 Managing the change process
Having made a choice about which strategy to introduce, the organisation then moves on to implement the relevant changes. To successfully manage the change process, the organisation and those involved in implementing the change, should concentrate on management styles, symbolic and political activity and the role of the change agent.

• MANAGEMENT STYLES
Management styles are the techniques used by managers or change agents in introducing change. The change agent is the person responsible for managing the change effort. Styles used in given situations depend on the extent and nature of resistance to change. According to Kotter and Schlesinger (1979), there are six main styles of management associated with introducing change
1. **Education and communication** are appropriate where problems and resistance are caused by insufficient information or misinformation. Such a style requires an atmosphere of trust between both sides involved. Education and communication are generally more effective if they take place before the change is implemented. However, this style is costly and time consuming as it involves mass briefings. Organisations dealing with large numbers of employees use small group briefings to ensure effective communication.
2. **Participation** is appropriate where the commitment and participation of employees is vital to the success of the change programme It is an effective way of overcoming resistance based on lack of awareness or a narrow focus of change. Employees who are involved in the change process are also more likely to accept changes. Participation

322

usually involves project teams or task forces who generate ideas and give advice on implementing change. Once again, this style is time consuming and costly.

3. **Support and facilitation** are appropriate management styles when employees are experiencing difficulty in coming to terms with the new changes. In this sense, support and facilitation help to overcome resistance arising from fear of the unknown and the need for security. This style of management involves providing support mechanisms for employees to help them cope with change. Most frequently organisations provide additional training or extra emotional support while employees get used to the changes. A problem associated with this style is that while it may help people through the change process, it does not necessarily win their commitment and support. It is also time consuming and can fail.

4. **Negotiation and agreement** is a useful management style when groups or key individuals are negatively affected by the change, yet have sufficient power to resist and interrupt the introduction of change. A good example is a trade union whose primary concern is to protect the welfare of its members. By engaging in negotiation before implementation, the organisation may find the change process runs more smoothly. If any other problems arise during the course of implementation then both sides can refer to the written agreement to sort out problems. This method is most appropriate for overcoming resistance to change arising from threatened expertise, power, resources and group factors. Rewards such as increased wages or perks can also be examined to reinforce the direction of change (Nadler 1981).

5. **Manipulation** of the situation by the agent can make it easier to introduce change. For example, it has been established that crisis situations are more likely to motivate people to change. So, organisations can attempt to exaggerate the extent of the situation facing the organisation, to make it appear as if the organisation is in a crisis. This style is often used when resistance is caused by habit, resource allocation, economic and group factors.

6. **Coercion** involves the explicit use of power by issuing directives to employees about the changes being implemented. Managers or the change agent resort to coercion if all other methods have failed to reduce resistance to change. It is generally recognised as the least successful method. Even when coercion is applied, and employees accept change, it can have long-term negative effects on employee attitudes and behaviour.

Each of the management styles is appropriate for given situations and has both advantages and disadvantages associated with it. Education and communication are most effective for incremental change or where transformational change is being introduced over a long period of time. Manipulation and coercion are effective if there is a crisis or need for rapid transformational change. Participation and negotiation are intermediate styles whereby transformational change can be achieved with less risk but is also effective for incremental change (Nutt 1989).

• SYMBOLIC ACTIVITY

While styles of management used can help overcome resistance to change and can aid the implementation of change, symbolic activity plays an equally important role. In Chapter 2 organisational culture was referred to as the beliefs, values and attitudes of the organisation. In implementing change, managers must ensure that such change is apparent in the day to day experiences of employees and can be grasped by them. It is through symbolic means and organisational culture that the organisation can achieve this. For example, the organisation could introduce decentralised decision making, but senior managers could still make all decisions without delegating to middle managers. In this situation, middle managers do not see apparent changes in their experience of work. As a result, they will be reluctant to delegate any of their decision making power. All elements of the organisation's culture must reinforce the direction of the change if it is to be successful.

The most powerful symbol in any organisational change process is the behaviour of the change agent(s), whether it be the CEO, senior management or an external consultant. Either consciously or unconsciously the language and behaviour of the change agent must reinforce the changes. It is essential that his/her behaviour corresponds with the strategic change, to build commitment to the change process and ensure that the process is not undermined.

● POLITICAL ACTIVITY

When change takes place in the organisation, especially transformational change, there is nearly always an alteration of power structures. In order to achieve a reconfiguration of the power base, the change agent must understand the political processes and systems, and how strategic change can be implemented within the political context. Any manager who is faced with change needs to consider how it can be implemented from a political perspective. According to Johnson and Scholes (1993), there are four main political mechanisms which can be used to build a power base, encourage support, overcome resistance and achieve commitment.

1. The control and manipulation of resources: Identification by the change agent with important resource areas and the ability to withdraw or reallocate resources can be important in overcoming resistance to change and persuading others to accept.
2. Relationships with powerful groups: Association by the change agent with internal/external stakeholders and trade unions can become an important power base especially for an external change agent who does not have a personal power base.
3. Sub systems: Acceptance of and communication about the change process is important throughout the organisation. Therefore, how well the various sub systems are handled is important. An effective change agent will build up powerful alliances and networks of people within the sub systems. This can be very effective for overcoming resistance from groups. It is important, however, not to alienate existing elites within the organisation.
4. Symbolic mechanisms can be used to break with existing paradigms and to reward those who accept the changes. Creating stories and rituals around those who have facilitated the changes will help to spread the change.

These four mechanisms are important for introducing change through the political processes of the organisation. Problems arise when the change agent aligns himself\herself too closely to particular groups and alienates others. In addition, changing the power structure of the organisation can lead to instability.

● THE ROLE OF THE CHANGE AGENT

A change agent is responsible for managing the change effort. The change agent can either be an external consultant or an internal person or group. An internal change agent is likely to know the organisation, employees, tasks, politics and culture, which may help in interpreting data and understanding systems. However, an insider might be too close to be objective. An external person has the advantage of being objective and having a fresher outlook. However he/she will lack knowledge of the organisation and will have to build a power base from which to work. Many organisations still opt for an external change agent.

Unless the change agent is a top manager or CEO then his/her power base will not come from a hierarchical position and legitimate authority within the organisation. While support of the top management team helps the change agent he/she has to develop other sources of power to move the process of change forward. Beer (1980) identifies five sources of power which the change agent can develop:

1. High status afforded to the change agent by organisational members who believe that he/she shares similar attitudes and behaviour is an important source of power.
2. Another source of power is trust, which can be built up by consistent handling of people and information.
3. Expertise in the area of change management and previous experience can be an important source of power.
4. Established credibility from the management of other change programmes also establishes power.
5. Dissatisfied internal groups may see the change agent as an opportunity to introduce changes favourable to them and will consequently give the change agent a certain amount of power.

Source: Beer, M., *Organisational Change and Development: A Systems View,* Goodyear, California 1980.

The important characteristics for successful change agents are:
1. clarity of vision which can be communicated to others
2. ability to recognise the importance of the context in which the change is occurring and sensitivity to the type of change needed and the resistance to change
3. use of appropriate styles of management
4. use of symbolic actions where necessary
5. use of political processes to build a power base
6. good interpersonal skills and an ability to spread enthusiasm to others.

14.8 Successful Change Programmes

Following a clearly defined model of strategic change is not sufficient to ensure success. Organisations that follow models of this nature still end up with programmes which have been a failure. Yet, other organisations can introduce change with very positive results. So what is it about some organisational change programmes that make them successful? With this question in mind Pettigrew and Whipp (1991) conducted research in the UK in a number of industries from publishing to automobiles. They identified organisations which had introduced strategic change programmes and pin-pointed aspects of their success. Based on their research, they argue that successful strategic change depends on the presence of five interrelated elements as shown in Figure 14.13.

Figure 14.13 Managing for Competitive Success: Five Central Factors

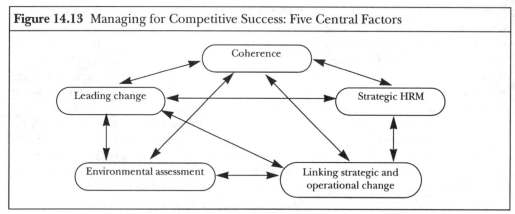

Source: Pettigrew, A. and Whipp, R., *Managing Change for Competitive Success*, Basil Blackwell, London 1991.

1. **Environmental assessment**: Organisations which introduce successful change programmes assess their external environment very carefully. In this sense, successful organisations went beyond acquiring and processing data and became open learning systems. External developments within the business environment were effectively communicated to employees and championed by a change agent.

2. **Leading change**: Pettigrew and Whipp (1991) found that success depended on the ability of the change agent to establish and develop a context for change both in cultural terms and the capabilities of the organisation. Styles of management were used which were tailored to the context, and the change agent altered the approach where necessary.

3. **Strategic human resource management**: Successful organisations integrated their HRM policies with their strategic changes. Training and development, employee relations and rewards were all designed to facilitate the introduction of the desired changes.

4. **Linking strategic and operational change**: Organisations that have successfully managed strategic change have effectively linked it with operational change. In other words, there has been a clear connection and consistency between strategic, tactical and operations plans.

5. **Coherence**: The most complex factor arises from the demands of the previous four — coherence. Pettigrew and Whipp (1991) have found that success depended on coherence across all aspects of the organisation as follows:

(i) consistency between intended strategy, strategic objectives, operational plans and the behaviour of the change agent

(ii) consistency between the direction of strategic change and the environmental changes

(iii) strategy must be feasible in terms of resources required, organisational structure and the changes required to the organisational culture

(iv) strategic direction must be clearly related to achieving competitive advantage.

Organisational change programmes that have been highly successful have displayed the above five characteristics. The next section applies the model of strategic change to an Irish organisation that introduced change and evaluates its success using the Pettigrew and Whipp (1991) framework.

14.9 MANAGING STRATEGIC CHANGE IN B&I

In 1965, the Government purchased the British and Irish Steampacket Co. Ltd (shortened to B&I and now called Irish Ferries). B&I, therefore, became a semi state body involved in the transport of both passengers and cargo from Ireland to the UK and Europe. By 1985, however, B&I was in severe financial difficulties. At the end of that year the company's consolidated balance sheet showed an accumulated loss of £90 million of which £57 million had been incurred in 1984 and 1985 alone.

In order to improve the competitive position of B&I, a private consultant was appointed as Chairman to revitalise the company and return it to profitability. Despite attempts to improve performance, B&I still incurred significant losses; turnover fell from £100 million in 1985 to 62 million in 1989 and the number of passengers fell by 20 per cent and cargo by 17 per cent over the same time period (Nolan 1994). Therefore, commercial viability had not been achieved for the long term and by the early 1990s, B&I was once more in severe trouble.

14.9.1 Identifying strategic change needs

Three main factors forced B&I to change by the beginning of 1990. One of the major factors was the company's poor financial performance. Between 1987 and 1991 B&I lost over £38 million as shown in Figure 14.14.

Figure 14.14 B&I Financial Losses 1987–1991	
	Millions
1987	19,953
1988	1,535
1989	1,462
1990	3,421
1991	1,708

Source: Nolan, J., 'The Management of Strategic Change in B&I Line', unpublished final year BBS project, University of Limerick 1994.

B&I was also burdened by high debts incurred through loans as shown in Figure 14.15.

Figure 14.15 B&I Loans 1987–1991	
	Millions
1987	34,121
1988	31,114
1989	28,809
1990	28,030
1991	30,080

Source: Nolan, J., 'The Management of Strategic Change in B&I Line', unpublished final year BBS project, University of Limerick 1994.

Turnover had also been declining since the early 1980s. While the turnover had increased since 1988, it was still much lower than it had been in 1987, as illustrated in Figure 14.16.

Figure 14.16 B&I Turnover 1987–1991	
	Millions
1987	81,779
1988	58,993
1989	62,339
1990	66,265
1991	72,528

Source: Nolan, J., 'The Management of Strategic Change in B&I Line', unpublished final year BBS project, University of Limerick 1994.

B&I was, therefore making significant financial losses, burdened by debt and below average turnover. If B&I continued to perform badly it could no longer exist as a viable entity without considerable state aid.

The second factor forcing change within B&I was its purchase by the Irish Continental Group (ICG) for £ 8.5 million in January 1992. ICG operated a ferry service from Rosslare to France and had been established in 1988, receiving BES funding. ICG recognised the crisis situation facing B&I and was determined to force through significant changes which would safeguard its investment. The image of B&I as an outdated and inefficient operator would have to be changed to make ICG's investment viable. The most important change produced by the ICG purchase was the move from a semi state body to a private commercial entity. In order to survive without state aid, B&I would have to improve its financial performance, compete against low cost operators and develop more harmonious employee relations.

The final factor forcing change was increased competition in the transport market between Ireland and the UK and Europe. Liberalisation of the air travel market between the UK and Ireland and the consequential fare wars between Ryanair and Aer Lingus from 1986 onwards led to a significant reduction in the number of people travelling by sea as it became cheaper to fly. As a result, demand for sea travel declined significantly.

Consequently, competition between established sea operators became more intense with each one fighting to maintain passenger numbers. Stena Sealink, B&I's most competitive rival operated with much lower costs which made it difficult for B&I to compete effectively.

The combined forces amounted to a crisis situation which demanded strategic change to turn around the fortunes of the company. However, like any long-established organisation B&I displayed an inherent resistance and suspicion to the proposed changes. The strongest resistance came from the trade unions as the changes threatened their power, expertise and membership base which would be reduced through voluntary redundancy.

14.9.2 Strategic choice
Having considered both the factors forcing change and the resistance to change, B&I

generated a number of strategic options. A choice was taken in favour of a strategy to reduce the price of the product and to increase quality in order to achieve competitive advantage. The strategic plan required a restructuring and rationalisation of each business area within B&I and contained the following important changes:

1. **Organisational structure**: B&I was restructured into three businesses.

(i) Ferry services which involves the transportation of passengers, vehicles and freight on two routes between Ireland and the UK.

(ii) European Container Service which operates container services between Ireland and the UK using a fleet of 1,200 containers.

(iii) Dublin Ferryport terminals which provides cargo handling for roll on roll off vessels by B&I and third party operators.

2. **Management Structure**: After the acquisition, ICG personnel were placed on the board of B&I. Old board members, who had been politically appointed non executive directors were removed. The new management structure, therefore, was a mixture of B&I and ICG.

3. **Reductions in staff**: In order to reduce the number of staff, cut costs and reduce the age profile of the company, which was heavily biased towards people in pensionable categories, 235 voluntary redundancies were planned. The expected cost of the redundancies was in the region of £8 million.

4. **Culture change**: The culture of B&I would have to change from a semi state to a private industrial enterprise. Therefore, the culture would have to be far more cost conscious and commercial in nature. The old image of B&I which had been built up in the public's mind would also have to be changed.

5. **Control Systems**: The final change was the introduction of more formal control systems to provide budgeting and estimates of future income and expenditure.

14.9.3 Managing strategic change

1. **Management style**: To overcome the main sources of resistance to change B&I embarked on a style emphasising education, communication, participation and negotiation. Before the take-over by ICG there were a series of written communications from ICG to all B&I employees explaining the changes. Once the official take-over had occurred, management continued using participation and negotiation to introduce change. Although the process was a long and drawn out, B&I persevered.

2. **Culture and symbolic activity**: It is important that change agents exemplify behaviour consistent with the planned change to generate commitment from employees. In seeking to make B&I more competitive, the company was willing to make a substantial financial investment in improving quality and image, showing the process of change was not all in one direction. The first symbolic move of this nature made by the company to demonstrate its faith in the programme and the employees was the introduction of the new Isle of Inishfree in 1992 and a £2 million refurbishment of the Isle of Inishmore in 1993.

3. **Political activity**: The main change agents who were the top managers in B&I used political processes to change the power base and to achieve commitment from employees. The change agents used symbolic political mechanisms to break away from established beliefs and values associated with the conduct of industrial relations. Essentially, management tried to reduce the power base of the unions by adopting a much tougher stance. The balance of power was shifted from the unions back towards

management. Previously, disputes went to the Labour Court which issued a recommendation that was used as a basis for further negotiations by the unions. The new management team made it clear that Labour Court recommendations were the final outcome and harshly implemented those decisions. At the same time, the company increased communications with employees and developed important alliances within the sub systems.

4. **The role of the change agent**: The most important change agent was the new Managing Director who spearheaded change within B&I, by attacking taken for granted ways of doing things. He dealt with resistance to change and earned the support and commitment of staff and possessed a vision to acquire bigger ships to achieve economies of scale in order to reduce costs, and implemented it with great success. Finally, he recognised the importance of communications in implementing change and built up an important power base.

14.9.4 A successful change programme?

Since the introduction of the change programme B&I has improved its financial performance significantly, increased turnover and has expanded into new commercial ventures. The successful management of strategic change was achieved by the application of the five key factors outlined by Pettigrew and Whipp (1991). The changing nature of the business environment was carefully considered including the trend towards larger ships to reduce costs and increase capacity (see Curran 1993). By identifying this trend B&I has been able to react successfully. The role of the change agent was effectively handled by the Managing Director who had the necessary vision and communications skills to implement the changes.

Strategic change and operational change was effectively linked through proper communications between different levels. A HRM director was introduced on to the board of B&I which was a significant move towards having HR polices integrated with strategic change. Finally, the B&I change programme was coherent, with consistency between the need for change, the strategy chosen, operational plans and the end result of achieving competitive advantage.

14.10 SUMMARY OF KEY PROPOSITIONS

• The management of change has become one of the most important issues for managers due to the nature of the business environment. The changes represent fundamental shifts and are occurring at a continuous pace.

• While each organisation faces a unique set of factors which shape the need for change, it is possible to identify four important developments affecting most organisations: globalisation, technological developments, a changing labour force and a move away from labour intensive industry.

• Organisations inevitably face resistance to change as the organisation itself is designed to maintain stability. Organisational sources of resistance to change include: organisational structure, narrow focus of change, group inertia, threatened expertise, power and resource allocation. Individual sources of resistance to change include: habit, selective perception, economic factors, security, social factors and lack of understanding.

• Change inevitably happens to all organisations. However, an organisation can plan to introduce change. Planned change is a set of activities designed to change individuals, groups, structures and systems. Planned change is normally introduced to increase organisational flexibility and adaptability and to change a particular element of individual behaviour.

• Lewin argued that the process of change occurred in three stages: unfreezing, change and refreezing. This approach, while having been widely adopted, has been criticised for its simplicity.

• Strategic change is a change in the strategy pursued by the organisation and occurs in three main stages: an identification of strategic change needs, strategic choice and, finally, the management of the change process.

• When managing the introduction of change, managers should pay special attention to styles of managing, symbolic activity, political activity and the role of the change agent.

• The change agent is charged with a very important role within the management of the change process. He/she should have a clear vision, recognise the context of change, use suitable styles of management, symbolic and political activity and have good interpersonal skills and an ability to spread enthusiasm to others.

• Pettigrew and Whipp found that organisations who successfully implemented strategic change had five things in common: a careful assessment of the environment, appropriate leadership, strategic HRM, a link between strategic and operational change and, most importantly of all, coherence between all of the elements.

DISCUSSION QUESTIONS

1. Why has the management of change become so important in recent years?
2. Explain the four main forces driving organisational change. Which one has most impact on Irish industry.
3. Explain the major sources of organisational resistance to change. Find an example of the one you think is most important.
4. Explain the major sources of individual resistance to change. Which one have you experienced?
5. What can an organisation do to manage resistance to change?
6. Explain Lewin's three step model of change. Why has it been criticised?
7. What is planned organisational change? What does it generally seek to achieve?
8. What is strategic change? Why has it become so important? Find some examples of organisations that have introduced strategic changes.
9. Explain the different management styles that can be used when introducing change. Under which circumstances are they appropriate?
10. What steps can be taken by the change agent to ensure that strategic change is implemented successfully?
11. Apply the model of strategic change to an organisation with which you are familiar.

12. Critically evaluate the five factor change framework developed by Pettigrew and Whipp. Can you think of anything else which should have been included?

REFERENCES

Beer, M., *Organisational Change and Development: A Systems View*, Goodyear, California 1980.

Beer, M., Eisenstat, R. and Spector, B., 'Why Change Programmes Do Not Produce Change' *Harvard Business Review*, Vol.68, No.6, 158–166, 1990.

Carnall, C., *Managing Change in Organisations*, Prentice Hall, New York 1990.

Cronin, C., 'ICG Battens Down' *Business and Finance*, 44–45, 14 January 1993.

Cummings, T. and Huse, E., *Organisational Development and Change*, St Paul, West 1989.

Curran, R., 'Stena Speed to Challenge B&I Route' *Sunday Business Post*, 11 July 1993.

Dineen, D., 'Atypical Work Patterns in Ireland: Short-term Adjustments of Fundamental Changes' *Administration*, Vol.40, No.3, 248–274, 1992.

Drucker, P., 'The New Society of Organisations' *Harvard Business Review*, Vol.70, No.5, 1952.

Flynn, G., 'Craftsmen: The Last of the Dinosaurs' *Business and Finance*, 18–23, 13 October 1994.

Goodman, P. and Kurke, L., 'Studies of Change in Organisations: A Status Report' in Goodman, P. et al (eds), *Change in Organisations*, Jossey Bass, San Francisco 1982.

Handy, C., *The Age of Unreason*, Business Books, London 1989.

Hannan, M. and Freeman, J., 'Structural Inertia and Organisational Change' *American Sociological Review*, Vol.49, 149–164, 1984.

Hitt, M., Hoskisson, R. and Harrison, J., 'Strategic Competitiveness in the 1990s: Challenges and Opportunities for US Executives' *Academy of Management Review*, Vol.15, No.2, 7–22, 1992.

Johnson, W., (1991) 'The Global Work Force 2000: A New World Labour Market' *Harvard Business Review*, Vol.69, No.2, 115–127, 1991.

Johnson. G. and Scholes, K., *Exploring Corporate Strategy: Text and Cases*, Prentice Hall, Cambridge 1993.

Kanter, R., 'Transcending Business Boundaries: 12,000 World Managers View Change' *Harvard Business Review*, Vol.69, No.3, 151–164, 1991.

Kanter, R., *When Giants Learn to Dance*, Simon & Schuster, New York 1989.

Katz, D. and Kahn, R., *The Social Psychology of Organisations*, Wiley, New York 1978.

Kotter, P. and Schlesinger, L., 'Choosing Strategies for Change' *Harvard Business Review*, Vol.57, No.2, 106–114, 1979.

Lewin, K., *Field Theory in Social Science*, Harper Row, New York 1951.

Mills, A. and Murgatroyd, S., *Organisational Rules*, Prentice Hall, London 1991.

Nadler, D., 'Concepts for the Management of Organisational Change' in Hackman, J., Lawler, E. and Porter, L. (eds), *Perspectives on Behaviour in Organisations*, McGraw-Hill, New York 1983.

Nadler, D., 'Managing Organisational Change: An Integrative Approach' *Journal of Applied Behavioural Science*, Vol.17, 191–211, 1981.

Neumann, J., 'Why People Do Not Participate in Organisational Change' in Woodman, R. and Pasmore, W. (eds), *Research in Organisational Change and Development*, JAI Press, Connecticutt 1989.

Nolan, J., 'The Management of Strategic Change in B&I Line', unpublished final year BBS project, University of Limerick 1994.

Nutt, P., 'Identifying and Appraising How Managers Install Strategy' *Strategic Management Journal*, Vol.8, No.1, 1–14, 1989.

Peters, T., 'Prometheus Barely Unbound' *Academy of Management Executive*, Vol.4, No.4, 70–84, 1990.

Pettigrew, A. and Whipp, R., *Managing Change for Competitive Success*, Basil Blackwell, London 1991.

Pfeffer, J., 'Management as Symbolic Action: The Creation of Organisational Paradigms' in Cummings, L. and Staw, B. (eds), *Research in Organisational Behaviour*, JAI Press, Connecticut 1981.

Potts, M. and Behr, P., *The Leading Edge*, McGraw-Hill, New York 1987.

Spector, B., 'From Bogged Down to Fired Up: Inspiring Organisational Change' *Sloan Management Review*, Vol.30. No.4, 29–34, 1989.

Stanislao, J. and Stanislao, B., 'Dealing with Resistance to Change' *Business Horizons*, Vol.26, No.4. 74–78, 1983.

Appendix 1:
Sources of Business
Information

(Each listing gives details of the organisation and type of information provided.)

GENERAL BUSINESS INFORMATION

Business Consultants
and Research Firms, for example;
A. C. Nielsen
36 Merrion Square
Dublin 2
Tel: 01 676 5122, Fax: 01 676 6621
— Marketing Research on Grocery Industry
— Statistics on Industrial Goods and Retail Trade
— Media Research

Business Information Centre
Dublin Corporation Central Library
Ilac Centre
Henry Street
Dublin 1
Tel: 01 873 3996, Fax: 01 872 1451
— Irish Companies and Business Associations
— Main Economic Sectors
— Government Information
— Ireland, Region by Region
— European Union
— Environment — ENFO, computerised environmental database
— Maps and Atlases

Central Statistics Office

Ardee Road	*and*	Skehard Road
Rathmines		Mahon
Dublin 6		Cork
Tel: 01 497 7144, Fax: 01 497 2360		Tel: 021 359 000, Fax: 021 359 090

— Labour Force Surveys
— Household Budget Surveys
— Demographic Statistics
— Foreign Trade; Facts and Figures
— Total Exports and Imports
— Transport
— Distribution
— Manufacturing
— Live Register
— Consumer price index
— Access to Reuters Terminal and world-wide database
— SAPS — Small Area Population Statistics showing breakdowns of population by
A) Age, Sex and Marital Status, B) Economic Status, Occupation and Transport

Chamber of Commerce
22 Merrion Square
Dublin 2
Tel: 01 661 2888, Fax: 01 661 2811
— Business contacts with other Chamber members
— Membership surveys
— On-line access to world-wide databases
— Access to members of Eurochambres, 800 other Chambers across Europe

Dublin Chamber of Commerce
7 Clare Street
Dublin 2
Tel: 01 661 4111, Fax: 01 676 6043

German-Irish Chamber of Industry
  and Commerce
46 Fitzwilliam Square
Dublin 2
Tel: 01 676 2934, Fax: 01 676 2595

— International Trade Information and Publications

On-Line Services

With over 150 topics covered, some of the more established host companies offering access to a wide range of databases are:

BRS-IT
Maxwell On-Line Incorporated
Achilles House
Western Avenue
London W3 0UA
England
Tel: 0044 181 992 3456, Fax: 0044 181 993 7335
— Financial Services Sector; the products, services and companies
— Marketing and Marketing Trends
— Telecommunications and Transportation
— Patents and Trademarks issued by the US Patent and Trademarks Office since 1971
— Trade and Business Sources on virtually all industries and products

— Up-to-date Research Reports
— Management-related topics

Dialog Information Systems
P.O. Box 188
Oxford OX1 5AZ
England
Tel: 0044 1865 730 275, Fax: 0044 1865 736 354
— Sales and Marketing Data
— Financial position of over 100,000 public and private companies
— Economics, policies, plans and research on energy in the US
— Accounting, Business Ethics and Industry Analysis Reviews
— Financial Management
— Insurance
— Telecommunications and Information Sciences and Systems
— All fields of Science and Medicine, with current and retrospective developments

FT Profile
P.O. Box 12
Sunbury-on-Thames
Middlesex TW16 7UD
England
Tel: 0044 1932 761 444
— Developments in the advertising industry
— Daily information on industries, companies and markets world-wide
— Enumerated business coverage from over 70 international newspapers and journals
— Major social, political and economic developments

Minitel
IPC House
Shelbourne Road
Ballsbridge
Dublin 4
Tel: 01 668 6600, Fax: 01 660 4044
— Agricultural market prices, production and farm business information,
— Car Sales
— Registered judgments
— Detailed Information on over 150,000 companies in over 30 European countries
— Central Statistics Office; the latest official details
— European manufacturers, prospective buyers for commercial and industrial equipment
— Company Commentaries and Financial moves
— Index of every limited company registered in Ireland
— European Transportation Networks
— Requirements when dealing in foreign markets and translation services
— EC regulations in Industry
— Co-operation between European Industries in advanced technologies
— Step-by-step guide on Finance, levels and costs of borrowing

— Media Facts, Broadcasting and details of readership/audience
— Travel and Tourism

PFDS On-line
Paulton House
8 Shepherdess Walk
London N1 7LB
England
Tel: 0044 171 490 0049
— Current and historical data on all UK and top European public companies
— British Standards and Codes of Practice
— Registered UK Trade and Service Marks
— 9000 Top Manufacturing Companies in Ireland
— New Sales Prospects
— Market Research on Manufacturing Industry
— Marketing and Management
— Sales Planning, Direct Marketing especially for small to medium sized business.

DIRECTORIES

Dun and Bradstreet
Holbrook House
Holles Street
Dublin 2
Tel: 01 676 4626, Fax: 01 678 9301
A large supplier of business information throughout the world
— World-wide Business Information Reports
— Country Risk Reports and Payment Analysis
— Financial Profiles
— Business Marketing — Identifying Sales Prospects, Direct Marketing, International Business Directories, Market Surveys and Marketing Research
— Receivables Management — Domestic and International overdue account collection services
— Database Services connecting into Thomsons Connection Database; European Marketing Database; UK Marketing Database
— Publishers of *Stubbs Gazette*

Kompass Ireland
Kompass House
Parnell Court
1 Granby Row
Dublin 1
Tel: 01 872 8800, Fax: 01 873 3711
— Information on approximately 16,000 companies
— Engineering, Electronics and Construction
— Financial Services
— Direct Mailing Lists
— Consumer and Household Information through An Post's Targetpoint

EMBASSIES, FOR EXAMPLE;

US Embassy
42 Elgin Road
Ballsbridge
Dublin 4
Tel: 01 668 7122, Fax: 01 668 2840
  — Potential business opportunities with US firms
  — Agent/Distribution Services
  — Trade Opportunities Programme
  — Matchmaker Events
  — Gold Key Services, introductions to overseas businesses

  (Other Embassies provide commercial services which are dependent on the scale of their representation in Ireland)

EUROPEAN INSTITUTIONS

European Commission
Jean Monnet Centre
39 Molesworth Street
Dublin 2
Tel: 01 671 2244, Fax: 01 671 2657
The Centre provides to the public;
  — a well-stocked library, including a complete set of the Official Journal of the EU
  — access to audiovisual material complementing the texts in stock
  — the INTERREG community initiative; providing support services to areas such as fisheries, tourism, agriculture, forestry and human resources, with strong emphasis on cross border co-operation
  — Business Development
  — Energy Development
  — Cinema and Television Advancements
  — EUROFORM; a training and employment programme
  — TELEMATIQUE; creating and developing communications among SMEs
  — CDI; promotion of binding agreements between SMEs and African, Caribbean and Pacific (ACP) firms
  — European Investment Bank (EIB); providing loans for capital investment projects
  — LEADER programme; aiding tourism, rural development and small and medium-sized businesses.

STATE AGENCIES, FOR EXAMPLE;

Forbairt — Development Services
Wilton Park House
Wilton Place
Dublin 2
Tel: 01 660 2244, Fax: 01 660 5019
  — Assistance available to indigenous Irish industries

— Financial advice available to small and medium-sized firms in Ireland
— Management Development
— Preparation of Feasibility Studies and Business Plans
— Networking with business partners/investors
— Financial Incentives
— Equity (Ordinary and Preference Shares)

Forbairt — Technology Services

Ballymun Road
Glasnevin
Dublin 9
Tel: 01 837 0101, Fax: 01 837 9620
— Advisory and grant assistance with product/process development
— Education programmes
— Access to an Irish Industrial Database
— Consultancy services designed to improve quality systems and to ensure safety and performance standards
— On-site library; a major source of industrial and technical information
— Providing research and development technology programmes of the EU

GOVERNMENT DEPARTMENTS AND OFFICES

Companies Registration Office

Dublin Castle
Dublin 2
Tel: 01 661 4222 (Ext. 3231), Fax: 01 679 5254
— New Companies; names and registration numbers
— Prosecutions
— Latest Annual Returns and Accounts
— Liquidations/Receiverships
— Re-registrations and Change of Name

Department of Enterprise and Employment

Kildare Street
Dublin 2
Tel: 01 661 4444, Fax: 01 676 2654
— Industrial Relations, Industry and Patents
— Employment Rights and Obligations
— Human Resource Development
— Enterprise Programmes
— Planning and Finance
— Commerce in Ireland

Department of Tourism and Trade

Kildare Street
Dublin 2
Tel: 01 662 1444, Fax: 01 676 6154
— All national policies connected with indigenous tourism and trade

Office of the Revenue Commissioners
Dublin Castle
Dublin 2
Tel: 01 679 2777, Fax 01 679 2035
— Tax Refunds through the New Enterprise Scheme
— Collection and administration of virtually all taxes
— Capital Gains and Corporation Taxes
— Import and Export Controls and Laws

INDUSTRY ASSOCIATIONS, FOR EXAMPLE;

Irish Business and Employers Confederation (IBEC)
Confederation House
Kildare Street
Dublin 2
Tel: 01 662 2755, Fax: 01 661 2157
— Information on exporting skills
— Domestic and International trade and industry
— Industrial policy
— Industrial Employee Relations
— EU policies
— New business and niche market opportunities
— Innovation and Technology
— Transportation

Irish Franchise Association
13 Frankfield Terrace
Summerhill South
Cork
Tel: 021 270 859, Fax: 021 270 850
— Code of Ethics established for franchising
— Educational Information
— Opportunities and Investment
— Current Market Trends
— Profiles on Established Franchises

Irish Small and Medium Enterprises Association (ISME)
32 Kildare Street
Dublin 2
Tel: 01 662 2755, Fax: 01 661 2157
— Credit Insurance
— Consulting Services through ISME Services Ltd
— Marketing and Financial Management
— Exchange Rate Services in conjunction with FexCo
— Joint ventures with European partners through its Reach Strategic Ventures Partners Programme (RSVP)
— Obtaining the ISO 9000
— County Enterprise Boards

— Health and Safety Regulations
— Debt Collection and Credit Control
— Facilitating Group Leasing

Small Firms Association
Confederation House
84–86 Baggot Street
Dublin 2
Tel: 01 660 1011, Fax: 01 660 1717
— Information on Business, Economic, Personnel, Regulatory, Technical and Trade matters
— Discount Services which can offer firms considerable financial savings
— Introduction and meetings with compatible business partners
— Contracts of Employment, Health and Safety at work
— Country-wide support services

Irish Trade Protection Association
Park House
North Circular Road
Dublin 7
Tel: 01 385 422, Fax: 01 386 897
— Judgments on Limited companies
— On-line data re Creditee and Crediscan
— Credit Control and Debt Recovery
— Publishers of its own periodical *The Gazette*

Local Authorities, for example;

Laois County Council
County Hall
Portlaoise
Co. Laois
Tel: 0502 22044, Fax: 0502 22313
— Local Authority Regulations
— County Enterprise Boards
— Planning Permissions
— Development Incentives and Controls
— County Infrastructure
— Agriculture
— Environmental Protection

Market Information Centre

An Bord Trachtála (Irish Trade Board)
Merrion Hall
Strand Road
Dublin 4
Tel: 01 269 5011, Fax: 01 269 5820

- Targeted Marketing Consultancy
- Growth and Trends in domestic and international markets
- Houses the European Business Information Centre and the Market Information Centre
- The Overseas Trade Service
- Sales Performance Incentives
- Trade Information and Promotion
- Market Representation abroad
- Marketing Investment
- European Regional Development

An Bord Trachtála — Regional Offices;
67–69 South Mall
Cork
Tel: 021 271 251/2, Fax: 021 271 347

Mervue Industrial Estate
Galway
Tel: 091 756 600/1/2, Fax: 091 756 606

'The Granary'
Michael Street
Limerick
Tel: 061 419 811/419 908, Fax: 061 413 683

Finisklin Industrial Estate
Sligo
Tel: 071 69477/8, Fax: 071 69479

Industrial Estate
Cork Road
Waterford
Tel: 051 78577, Fax: 051 79220

PROFESSIONAL ASSOCIATIONS, FOR EXAMPLE;

The Institute of Chartered Accountants of Ireland
87–89 Pembroke Road
Ballsbridge
Dublin 4
Tel: 01 668 0400, Fax: 01 668 0842
- Practice Advisory Service, especially for sole traders
- Cultivating a good communications network
- International advice available
- Auditing, Accountancy and Taxation
- Its association with FISC, a voluntary service, is offered providing free financial advice to less well-off members of the community

The Marketing Institute
South County Business Park
Leopardstown
Dublin 18
Tel: 01 295 2355, Fax: 01 295 2453
The Institute is the professional representative body for marketing people in Ireland, aiming to provide and develop high standards of marketing, to a wider business community
— Professional Development Programmes (PDPs)
— Publishes an annual journal, *The Irish Marketing Review*
— Publications on marketing topics
— Evening seminars on marketing related topics
— Access to similar institutions across Europe

TRADE ASSOCIATIONS, FOR EXAMPLE;

Construction Industry Federation
Federation House
Canal Road
Rathmines
Dublin 6
Tel: 01 497 7487, Fax: 01 496 6953
— Information on the construction industry
— Supplier associations
— Quality standards
— Guarantee schemes

RESEARCH INSTITUTIONS, FOR EXAMPLE;

Economic and Social Research Institute
4 Burlington Road
Dublin 4
Tel: 01 667 1525, Fax: 01 668 6231
— Economic commentary
— Economic forecasts
— Research reports

UNIVERSITIES AND COLLEGES

EXAMPLES OF SPECIFIC RESEARCH CENTRES INCLUDE;

National Microelectronics Research Centre
University College Cork
Lee Maltings
Prospect Row
Cork
Tel: 021 276 871, Fax: 021 270 271

— Design services, devices and processes
— Simulation, process and circuit simulation
— Evaluation on success or failure of processes
— Fabrication
— Education, through seminars and courses
— Consultancy, advice on process and product development

Regional Technical College Sligo
Business Innovation Centre
RTC Campus
Sligo
Tel: 071 44131, Fax: 071 44500
— Computer Aided Design
— Computer Aided Manufacturing training and consultancy
— Just-In-Time and Quality Production Systems
— Engineering
— Business Management
— Business Start-ups in high technology sectors
   (these facilities are available at most of the other Regional Technical Colleges
   throughout Ireland)

National Microelectronics Application Centre
University of Limerick Building
National Technological Park
Plassey
Limerick
Tel: 061 334 699, Fax: 061 330 316
— On-line search of world-wide databases to identify competitors
— Conceiving, designing and building prototypes for feasibility studies
— Developing prototypes for production
— Business Consulting Programme

The Innovation Centre
University of Dublin
The O'Reilly Institute
College Green
Dublin 2
Tel: 01 702 1155, Fax: 01 679 8039
— Many EU programmes run in association with an extensive list of industrial and
   academic partners at home and overseas
— Research and consultancy services available to small companies
— Availing of an Incubation Centre

An example of some Campus Companies at the University of Dublin Innovation Centre include;

Conservation Engineering Ltd
Majih Ltd (Statistics Consultancy)
IEunet Ltd (Networking Services to Unix Users)

344

Technology Systems Ireland (TSI) Ltd

Project Development Centre
Dublin Institute of Technology
17 Herbert Street
Dublin 2
Tel: 661 1910, Fax: 661 1973
  — Advise for start-up companies
  — Enterprise co-ordination
  — Project space for new enterprises
  — ESF grants, training and mentor advice

MEDIA REPORTS

There are a number of publications on the market which cater for all businesses. Some business magazines are more general than others, while some are very specific to just one industry or service area. Today most industries have at least one trade journal covering all activities within that industry, but other available titles disseminate vital market information and economic forecasts, relevant to any business.

The following are just some examples of Irish trade journals available:

Irish Hardware
Irish Computer
Irish Travel Trade
IRN — Industrial Relations News
MII News — The Marketing Institute of Ireland's magazine
Management — The Irish Management Institute's magazine
NEWS — IBEC's monthly magazine, they also public a 'Monthly Industrial Survey'
German — *Irish Business News* — published quarterly by the German-Irish Chamber of Commerce
Retail Business — *Market Surveys* — A monthly publication from the Economic Intelligence Unit, they also publish a number of quarterly and annual yearbooks on the Irish economy
D.O.E. News — the magazine published by the Department of Enterprise
Accountancy Ireland — A monthly magazine from the Institute of Chartered Accountants of Ireland
Business and Finance — a monthly magazine covering the developments and trends of the Irish economy, it also carries special feature articles focusing on topical industries

Within the past few years 'Business' has been dedicated more print media attention than ever before. Some of the better Business sections in the newspapers are:

The Sunday Tribune's Business section
The Sunday Business Post
The Irish Independent's Business section each Thursday, and
The Irish Times' Business section on a Friday.

Appendix 2:
Sources of Assistance for Entrepreneurs in Ireland

Allied Irish Bank Enterprise Development Bureau
Bankcentre
Ballsbridge
Dublin 4
Tel: 01 660 0311, Fax: 01 668 2508

Bank of Ireland Enterprise Support Unit
Head Office
Lower Baggot Street
Dublin 2
Tel: 01 661 5933, Fax: 676 3493

An Bord Bia
Clanwilliam Court
Lower Mount Street
Dublin 2
Tel: 01 668 5155

Bord Failte (Irish Tourist Board)
Baggot Street Bridge
Dublin 2
Tel: 01 676 5871, Fax: 01 676 4768

Bord Iascaigh Mhara
P.O. Box 12, Crofton Road
Dun Laoghaire
Co. Dublin
Tel: 01 284 1544, Fax: 01 284 1123

An Bord Trachtala (Irish Trade Board)
Merrion Hall
Strand Road
Sandymount
Dublin 4
Tel: 01 269 5011, Fax: 01 269 5820

An Bord Trachtála — Regional Offices
67–69 South Mall
Cork
Tel: 021 271 251/2, Fax: 021 271 347

Mervue Industrial Estate
Galway
Tel: 091 756 600/1/2, Fax: 091 756 606

'The Granary', Michael Street
Limerick
Tel: 061 419 811/908, Fax: 061 413 683

Finisklin Industrial Estate
Sligo
Tel: 071 69477/69478, Fax: 071 69479

Industrial Estate
Cork Road
Waterford
Tel: 051 78577, Fax: 051 79220

Business Innovation Centre
The Tower
Forbairt Enterprise Centre
Pearse Street
Dublin 2
Tel: 01 671 3111, Fax: 01 671 3330

Business Innovation Centre
South West Business and Technology
  Centre
North Mall
Cork
Tel: 021 397 711, Fax: 021395 393

Business Innovation Centre
Hardiman House
5 Eyre Square
Galway
Tel: 091 67974/5/6, Fax: 091 61963

Business Innovation Centre
Shannon Development
The Innovation Centre, Enterprise House
Plassey Technology Park
Limerick
Tel: 061 338 177, Fax: 061 338 065

Central Statistics Office
St Stephen's Green House
Earlsfort Terrace
Dublin 2
Tel: 01 676 7531, Fax: 01 668 2221

Central Statistics Office
Skehard Road
Mahon
Cork
Tel: 021 359 000, Fax: 021 359 090

Chambers of Commerce
22 Merrion Square
Dublin 2
Tel: 01 661 2888, Fax: 01 661 2811

Community Enterprise Programme
c/o FAS External Training Division
Cork
Tel: 021 544 377
also:
City of Cork Vocational Educational
  Committee
Emmet Place
Cork
Tel: 021 273 377/313 945,
Fax: 021 275 680

COUNTY ENTERPRISE BOARDS:

Carlow County Council
Athy Road
Carlow
Tel: 0503 31126, Fax: 0503 41503

Cavan County Council
Courthouse
Cavan
Tel: 049 31799, Fax: 049 31384

Clare County Council
Mill Road
Ennis
Co. Clare
Tel: 065 41922, Fax: 065 41887

Cork County Council
County Offices
Annabella
Mallow
Co. Cork
Tel: 022 21123, Fax: 022 219

Cork Corporation
City Hall
Cork
Tel: 021 966 222, Fax: 021 962 301

Cork County Council
County Hall
Cork
Tel: 021 345 128, Fax: 021 276 321

West Cork
County Offices West
8 Kent Road
Clonakilty
Co. Cork
Tel: 023 34700, Fax: 023 34702

Donegal County Council
County House
Lifford
Co. Donegal
Tel: 074 41066, Fax: 074 41205

Dublin Corporation
4–5 College Green
Dublin 2
Tel: 01 679 6111, Fax: 01 677 3612

Dublin County Council
46–49 Upper O' Connell Street
Dublin 1
Tel: 01 872 7777, Fax: 01 872 5782

Dublin South County Council
Tallaght Town Centre
Tallaght
Dublin 24
Tel: 01 462 0000, Fax: 01 462 0111

Dun Laoghaire/Rathdown County
    Council
Town Hall
Marine Road
Dun Laoghaire
Co. Dublin
Tel: 01 280 6961, Fax: 01 280 6969

Galway City and County Partnership
Woodquay Court
Woodquay
Galway
Tel: 091 65269, Fax: 091 65384

Kerry County Council
Aras an Chontae
Tralee
Co. Kerry
Tel: 066 21111, Fax: 066 22466

Kildare County Council
Naas
Co. Kildare
Tel: 045 897071, Fax: 045 876875

Kilkeny County Council
County Hall
John Street
Kilkenny
Tel: 056 52699, Fax: 056 63384

Laois County Council
County Hall
Portlaoise
Co. Laois
Tel: 0502 22044, Fax: 0502 22313

Leitrim County Council
Courthouse
Carrick-on-Shannon
Co. Leitim
Tel: 078 20005, Fax: 078 2149

Limerick Corporation
City Hall
Merchant Quay
Limerick
Tel: 061 451 799, Fax: 061 311 889

Limerick County Council
79–84 O'Connell Street
Limerick
Tel: 061 318 477, Fax: 061 318 478

Longford County Council
Great Water Street
Longford
Tel: 043 46231, Fax: 043 41233

Louth County Council
Jocelyn House
Jocelyn Street
Dundalk
Co. Louth
Tel: 042 27099, Fax: 042 27101

Mayo County Council
The Mall
Castlebar
Co. Mayo
Tel: 094 24444, Fax: 094 24416

Meath County Council
County Hall
Navan
Co. Meath
Tel: 046 21581, Fax: 046 21463

Monaghan County Council
Court House
Monaghan
Tel: 047 82211, Fax: 047 84786

Offaly County Council
Court House
Tullamore
Co. Offaly
Tel: 0506 21419, Fax: 0506 41160

Roscommon County Council
Court House
Roscommon
Tel: 0903 26100, Fax: 0903 25474

Sligo County Council
Court House
Riverside
Sligo
Tel: 071 43221, Fax: 071 44774

Tipperary North Riding County Council
Summerhill
Nenagh
Co. Tipperary
Tel: 067 33086, Fax: 067 33605

Tipperary South Riding County Council
County Hall
Clonmel
Co. Tipperary
Tel: 052 25399, Fax: 052 24355

Waterford Corporation
7 Lombard Street
Waterford
Tel: 051 73501, Fax: 051 79124

Waterford County Council
Aras Brugha
Dungarvan
Co. Waterford
Tel: 058 42822, Fax: 058 42911

Westmeath County Council
County Buildings
Mullingar
Co. Westmeath
Tel: 044 40861/5, Fax: 044 42330

Wexford County Council
County Hall
Spawell Road
Wexford
Tel: 053 42211, Fax: 053 43406

Wicklow County Council
County Buildings
Wicklow
Tel: 0404 67324, Fax: 0404 67792

Department of Enterprise and Employment
Kildare Street
Dublin 2
Tel: 01 661 4444, Fax: 01 676 2654

European Commission
Jean Monnet Centre
39 Molesworth Street
Dublin 2
Tel: 01 671 2244, Fax: 01 671 2657

European Business Information Centres
c/o An Bord Trachtala
Merrion Hall
Strand Road
Dublin 4
Tel: 01 269 5011, Fax: 01 269 5820
(*also at all An Bord Trachtála Regional offices*)

FAS — The Training and Employment Authority
P.O. Box 456
27–33 Upper Baggot Street
Dublin 4.
Tel: 01 668 5777, Fax: 01 668 2691

LOCAL FAS OFFICES

Government Buildings
Castle Park
Arklow
Co. Wicklow
Tel: 0402 39509, Fax: 0402 39413

The Townhouse Centre
St Mary's Square
Athlone
Co. Westmeath
Tel: 0902 75288, Fax: 0902 75291

FAS Centre
Riverside
Church Road
Ballina
Co. Mayo
Tel: 096 21921/21211, Fax: 096 70608

Main Street
Ballybofey
Co. Donegal
Tel: 074 31233, Fax: 074 31446

Fas Centre
Ballyfermot Hill
Ballyfermot
Dublin 10
Tel: 01 626 6211, Fax: 01 626 1433

Barrack Street
Bantry
Co. Cork
Tel: 027 50464, Fax: 027 50203

The Brace Centre
Main Street
Blanchardstown
Dublin 15
Tel: 01 820 1011, Fax: 01 821 1635

Royal House
Main Street
Bray
Co. Wicklow
Tel: 01 286 7912, Fax: 01 286 4170

Kennedy Street
Carlow
Tel: 0503 42605, Fax: 0503 41759

Goverment Buildings
Shannon Lodge
Carrick-on-Shannon
Co. Leitrim
Tel: 078 20503, Fax: 078 20505

Units 7 and 8
Humbert Hall
Castlebar
Co. Mayo
Tel: 094 22011, Fax: 094 22832

Magnet House
Farnham Street
Cavan
Tel: 049 31767/32532, Fax: 049 32527

Westward House
Main Street
Clondalkin
Dublin 22
Tel: 01 459 1766, Fax: 01 457 2878

6 Mary Street
Clonmel
Co. Tipperary
Tel: 052 24422, Fax: 052 24565

Northside Shopping Centre
Coolock
Dublin 17
Tel: 01 847 5911, Fax: 01 847 5770

Government Buildings
Sullivans Quay
Cork
Tel: 021 544377, Fax: 021 968389

14 North Quay
Drogheda
Co. Louth
Tel: 041 37646, Fax: 041 38120

D'Olier House
D'Olier Street
Dublin 2
Tel: 01 671 1544, Fax: 01 679 8240

27–33 Upper Baggot Street
Dublin 4
Tel: 01 668 5777, Fax: 01 660 9259

78–79 Park Street
Dundalk
Co. Louth
Tel: 042 32311, Fax: 042 36311

18–21 Cumberland Street
Dun Laoghaire
Co. Dublin
Tel: 01 280 8488, Fax: 01 280 8476

42 Parnell Square
Ennis
Co. Clare
Tel: 065 29213, Fax: 065 28502

Unit 14C
Finglas Shopping Centre
Finglas
Dublin 11
Tel: 01 834 6222, Fax: 01 834 6386

Island House
Cathedral Square
Galway
Tel: 091 67165, Fax: 091 62718

Irishtown
Kilkenny
Tel: 056 65514, Fax: 056 64451

Unit 1
Kenmare Place
Killarney
Co. Kerry
Tel: 064 32466, Fax: 064 32759

Ramelton Road
Ballyraine Industrial Estate
Letterkenny
Co. Donegal
Tel: 074 22200, Fax: 074 24840

18 Davis Street
Limerick
Tel: 061 228 333, Fax: 061 412 326

7 Market Square
Longford
Tel: 043 46820/46829, Fax: 043 45702

O'Brien Street
Mallow
Co. Cork
Tel: 022 21900, Fax: 022 22582

16 Church Square
Monaghan
Tel: 047 81511, Fax: 047 83441

Church Avenue
Mullingar
Co. Westmeath
Tel: 044 48805, Fax: 044 43978

Tara Mill
Trimgate Street
Navan
Co. Meath
Tel: 046 23630/23925, Fax: 046 21903

Connolly Street
Nenagh
Co. Tipperary
Tel: 067 31879, Fax: 067 31167

6 Georges Street
Newbridge
Co. Kildare
Tel: 045 31372/31090, Fax: 045 34446

Government Buildings
Gortboy
Newcastlewest
Co. Limerick
Tel: 069 62411, Fax: 069 61561

4 Meehan House
James Fintan Lawlor Avenue
Portlaoise
Co. Laois
Tel: 0502 21462/22198, Fax: 0502 20945

Castle Street
Roscommon
Tel: 0903 26802, Fax: 0903 25399

Industrial Estate
Shannon
Co. Clare
Tel: 071 471 133, Fax: 071 472 613

Government Buildings
Cranmore
Sligo
Tel: 071 43390, Fax: 071 44120

34 Main Street
Swords
Co. Dublin
Tel: 01 840 5252, Fax: 01 840 3751

Westpark
Old Bawn Road
Tallaght
Dublin 24
Tel: 01 452 5111, Fax: 01 452 5591

Government Buildings
Stradavoher
Thurles
Co. Tipperary
Tel: 0504 22188, Fax: 0504 23574

17 Lower Castle Street
Tralee
Co. Kerry
Tel: 066 22155, Fax: 066 22954

High Street
Tuam
Tel: 093 28066, Fax: 093 28068

Church Street
Tullamore
Co. Offaly
Tel: 0506 51176/21921, Fax: 0506 21964

28 Patrick Street
Waterford
Tel: 051 72961, Fax: 051 70896

Henrietta Street
Wexford
Tel: 053 23126, Fax: 053 23177

First Step
Jefferson House
Eglinton Road
Donnybrook
Dublin 4
Tel: 01 260 0988, Fax: 01 260 0989

Forbairt
Development Services
Wilton Park House
Wilton Place
Dublin 2
Tel: 01 660 2244, Fax: 01 660 5019

Forbairt
Technology Services
Glasnevin
Dublin 9
Tel: 01 837 0101, Fax: 01 837 8854

Forbairt Regional Offices:
Auburn
Dublin Road
Athlone
Co. Westmeath
Tel: 0902 72695, Fax: 0902 74516

Industry House
Rossa Avenue
Bishopstown
Cork
Tel: 021 343 555, Fax: 021 343 444

Portland House
Port Road
Letterkenny
Co. Donegal
Tel: 074 21155, Fax: 074 21424

Mervue Industrial Estate
Galway
Tel: 091 755 138, Fax: 091 756 539

IDA Industrial Estate
Cork Road
Waterford
Tel: 051 72911, Fax: 051 72719

57 High Street
Killarney
Co. Kerry
Tel: 064 34133, Fax: 064 34135

**Forbairt Enterprise Development
Programme**
Tel: 01 668 6633, Fax: 01 660 5019

Forbairt Mentor Programme
Tel: 01 660 2244, Fax: 01 660 5095

Forbairt Entreprise Link
1-850-353 333

ICC Bank
32–34 and 72–74 Harcourt Street
Dublin 2
Tel: 01 872 0055, Fax: 01 871 7797

ICC Bank
ICC House
46 Grand Parade
Cork
Tel: 021 277 666, Fax: 021 270 267

ICC Bank
Odeon House
Eyre Square
Galway
Tel: 091 566 445, Fax: 091 566 811

ICC Bank
ICC House
Charlotte Quay
Limerick
Tel: 061 317 577, Fax: 061 311 462

Industrial Development Authority
Wilton Park House
Wilton Place
Dublin 2
Tel: 01 668 8444, Fax: 01 660 5107

International Fund for Ireland
P.O. Box 2000
Dublin 2
Tel: 01 878 0655, Fax: 01 871 2116
also:
P.O. Box 2000
Belfast BT4 35A
Tel: 0232 768 832, Fax: 0232 762 313
(*operating in Northern Ireland and the
following counties; Cavan, Donegal, Leitrim,
Louth, Monaghan and Sligo*)

**Irish Business and Employers
Confederation (IBEC)**
Confederation House
Kildare Street
Dublin 2
Tel: 01 662 2755, Fax: 01 661 2157

Irish Franchise Association
13 Frankfield Terrace
Summerhill South
Cork
Tel: 021 270 859, Fax: 021 270 850

Irish Management Institute
Sandyford Road,
Dublin 16
Tel: 01 295 6911, Fax: 01 295 5147

Irish Small and Medium Enterprises Association (ISME)
32 Kildare Street
Dublin 2
Tel: 01 662 2755, Fax: 01 661 2157

Liffey Trust
117 Upper Sheriff Street
Dublin 1
Tel: 01 836 4645, Fax: 01 874 0298

The Marketing Institute
South County Business Park
Leopardstown
Dublin 18
Tel: 01 295 2355, Fax: 01 295 2453

The National Food Centre
Dunsinea
Castleknock
Dublin 15
Tel: 01 838 3222, Fax: 01 838 3684

National Irish Bank
7/8 Wilton Terrace
Dublin 2
Tel: 01 678 5066, Fax: 01 676 1672

National Microelectronics Research Centre
University College, Lee Maltings
Prospect Row
Cork
Tel: 021 276 871, Fax: 021 270 271

National Microelectronics Applications Centre
UL Building, National Technological Park
Plassey
Limerick
Tel: 061 334 699, Fax: 061 330 316

New Opportunities For Women (NOW)
Department of Enterprise and Employment
Davitt House
Adelaide Road
Dublin 2
Tel: 01 676 5861, Fax: 01 676 4852

or
Council for the Status of Women
32 Uppr Fitzwilliam Street
Dublin 2
Tel: 01 661 5268, Fax: 01 676 0860

The Bolton Trust
Powerhouse
Pigeon House Road
Ringsend
Dublin 4
Tel: 01 668 7155, Fax: 01 668 7945
(*run with the support of the Dublin Institute of Technology*)

Revenue Commissioners
Dublin Castle
Dublin 2
Tel: 01 679 2777, Fax; 01 679 2035

Saint Vincent de Paul
8 Cabra Road
Dublin 7
Tel: 01 838 4164, Fax: 01 454 0317

Shannon Development
Town Centre
Shannon
Co. Clare
Tel: 061 361 555, Fax: 061 361 903

Shannon Development
The Innovation Centre
National Technological Park
Castletroy
Limerick
Tel: 061 338 177, Fax: 061 338 065

Small Firms Association
Confederation House
84–86 Baggot Street
Dublin 2
Tel: 01 660 1011, Fax: 01 660 1717

Smurfit Job Creation Enterprise Fund
c/o Smurfit Finance
94 St Stephen's Green
Dublin 2
Tel: 01 678 1577, Fax: 01 475 3180

Udaras na Gaeltachta
Na Forbacha
Galway
Tel: 091 592011, Fax: 091 592037

Udaras na Gaeltachta Regional Offices:
Teach IPC
Shelbourne Road
Ballsbridge
Baile Atha Cliath 4
Tel: 01 660 7888, Fax; 01 668 6030

Na Doiri Beaga
Co. Dhun na nGall
Tel: 075 31200/31479, Fax: 075 31319

An Daingean
Co. Chiarrai
Tel: 066 51658/51417, Fax: 066 51788

Sraid na mBearaice
Beal an Mhuirthead
Co. Mhaigh Eo
Tel: 097 81418, Fax: 097 82179

Ulster Bank
Small Business Section
33 College Green
Dublin 2
Tel: 01 677 7623, Fax: 01 702 5875

NORTHERN IRELAND

Advisory Service to Industry Co-ordinating Unit (ASI)
Northern Ireland Technology Centre
The Queen's University Belfast
Ashby Building
Belfast BT9 5AH

Northern Ireland Business Club
Portview Trade Centre
310 Newtownards Road
Belfast BT4 IHT
Tel: 0232 453 260

Omagh Business Club
Omagh Enterprise Complex
Gortrush Industrial Estate
Omagh
Tel: 0662 49494

Business Innovation Centre
Innovation Centre Noribic
Springgrowth House
Ballinaska Road

Springgrowth Industrial Estate
Derry
Tel: 08 0504 264 242, Fax: 08 0504 269 025

Business Library
The Belfast Education and Library Board
Belfast Public Libraries
Central Library
Royal Avenue
Belfast BT1 1EA
Tel: 01232 243 233, Fax: 01232 332 819

Northern Ireland Chamber of Commerce
22 Great Victoria Street
Belfast BT2 7BJ
Tel: 01232 244 113

Northern Ireland Chamber of Trade
Bank of Ireland Buildings
92–100 Royal Avenue
Belfast BT1 1DL
Tel: 01232 321 980

Confederation of British Industry
Fanum House
108 Great Victoria Street
Belfast BT2 7PD
Tel: 01232 326 658, Fax: 01232 245 915

Co-operation North
7 Botanic Avenue
Belfast BT7 IJG
Tel: 01232 321 462

Department of Economic Development
Netherleigh
Massey Avenue
Belfast BT4 2JP
Tel: 01232 763 244

European Commission
Windsor House
9–15 Bedford Street
Belfast BT2 7EG
Tel: 01232 240 708, Fax: 01232 248 241

The European Technology Entrepreneurs Programme
ETEP Centre
Howard House
1 Bunswick Street
Belfast BT2 7GE
Tel: 01232 332 219

Federation of Small Businesses
3 Farrier Court
Glengormley
Newtownabbey
Co. Antrim BT36 7XB
Tel: 01232 844 079, Fax: 01232 342 441

Industrial Development Board
64 Chicester Street
Belfast BT1 4JX
Tel: 01232 233 233
(with offices in Germany, Belgium,
Chicago, Los Angeles, New York, Japan,
Korea and Taiwan)

Institute of Directors (Northern Ireland Division)
181A Stranmilis Road
Belfast BT9 5DU
Tel: 01232 381 591, Fax: 01232 681 795

Northern Ireland Innovation Programme
c/o L.E.D.U. House
Upper Galwally
Belfast BT8 4TB
Tel: 01232 491 031, Fax: 01232 691 432

Law Society (Northern Ireland)
Law Society House
98 Victoria Street
Belfast BT1 3JZ
Tel: 01232 231 614, Fax: 01232 232 606

L.E.D.U.
L.E.D.U. House
Upper Galwally
Belfast BT8 4TB
Tel: 01232 491 031, Fax: 01232 691 432

L.E.D.U. Area Offices:

13 Shipquay Street
Londonderry
BT48 6DJ
Tel: 01504 267 257, Fax: 01504 266 054

6–7 The Mall
Newry BT34 1BX
Tel: 01693 62955, Fax: 01693 65358

Livewire (Northern Ireland) Ltd
Action Resource Centre
103–107 York Street
Belfast
Tel: 01232 328 000

Newry and Mourne Enterprise Agency
5 Downshire Place
Newry BT34 1DZ
Tel: 01232 67011

Noribic
Asylum Road
Londonderry
Tel: 01504 264 242

Phoenix West Development Trust Ltd
Westwood Centre
Kennedy Way
Belfast BT11 9BQ
Tel: 01232 431 516, Fax: 01232 431 597

Small Business Venture Fund
22 Great Victoria Street
Belfast BT2 7BJ
Tel: 01232 244 113

Small Business Institute (Northern Ireland)
Enterprise House
University of Ulster at Jordanstown
Shore Road
Newtownabbey
BT37 OQB
Tel: 01232 365 060

Northern Ireland Training Authority
Direct Training Services
Swinson House
Glenmount
Newtownabbey
BT36 7LH
Tel: 01232 365 171

The Training and Employment Agency
Clarendon House
9–21 Adelaide Street
Belfast BT2 8DJ
Tel: 01232 244 300

Youth Enterprise Scheme
Belfast Enterprise Centre
103 York Street
Belfast
Tel: 01232 328 000

Glossary

Acquisitions The purchase of a controlling interest in one company by another. Acquisitions can be friendly or hostile.

Activity Ratios Ratios used to determine how efficiently an organisation uses its resources.

Amortisation The provision for paying off a debt, usually by means of a sinking fund. A sinking fund is created by setting aside a fixed sum of money each year to provide for the replacement of assets.

Asset Turnover Ratio The ratio between an organisation's sales and total assets. It indicates how efficiently an organisation is using its assets.

Authority Power that has been legitimised in a specific social context. In an organisation authority is the power to perform or command.

Autonomy The extent to which employees are free to take action based on their own initiative.

Bad Debts Bad debts arise when debtors can not pay the organisation what they owe. Such debts are essentially unrecoverable.

Bank Overdraft The permission granted by a bank for current account holders to overdraw on their accounts up to a specified limit.

Batch Production This relates to the manufacturing of a range of products on the basis of a pre-determined run or quantity (see **Production Management**).

Branding Giving a name, sign or symbol to items or services, so that they can be identified in a manner which would differentiate them from competitors' goods. Branding a good/service aids customers in differentiating between items/services offered by different companies.

Break Even Analysis A method of assessing the relationship between costs, revenues and the volume produced.

Break Even Point The point at which total revenue equals total expenditure and consequently no loss is made.

Budget A statement of plans and expected outcomes expressed in numerical terms for different organisational activities.

Bureaucracy An approach to management/structure which emphasises detailed rules and procedures, a clearly outlined organisational hierarchy and mainly impersonal relationships between organisational members.

Business Unit A distinct business area within an organisation usually producing a particular product/service.

Capacity Analysis Analysis to gain an understanding of the firm's core competence areas, in which it has a strong or unique ability.

Capitalist An individual investor in business who owns or shares in the ownership of the means of production.

356

Chain of Command A systematic ordering of positions and duties that defines a managerial authority.

Change Agent A person or group responsible for managing the change effort in the organisation. The change agent can be an internal or external person(s).

Classical Management An approach to management that emphasises universal approaches to internal efficiency in order to increase organisational success.

Closed System A system that does not depend on, is not influenced by nor interacts with its external environment.

Competitive Niche Specialisation by an organisation in a narrow segment of a given market.

Computer Aided Design (CAD) The use of computer technology to design products and services.

Computer Aided Manufacturing (CAM) The use of computer technology to manufacture products and services.

Computer Integrated Manufacturing The use of CAD and CAM to sequence and optimise a number of production processes.

Conceptual Skills The ability to see an organisation as a whole.

Concurrent Controls Controls that monitor the transformation of inputs into outputs to make sure that they meet standards.

Contingency A situation or the characteristics of a situation which affect the practice of management.

Contingency Management An approach to management that emphasises that managerial practice depends on a given set of contingencies or factors, i.e. the situation at hand. It therefore emphasises that there is no one best way to manage in all situations. It is sometimes called situational management.

Contingency Plans Sophisticated planning processes that identify alternative courses of action to be implemented if the key characteristics of a situation change.

Contingency Theory This is dedicated to examining the fit between a leader's behaviour and the specific environment in which he/she manages (see **Leadership**).

Continuous Flow Production This relates to the production of a high volume of output that flows in a continuous cycle (see **Production Management**).

Continuous Process Production A production system in which raw materials are transferred into finished products using a modern system in which the composition of raw materials is changed.

Control The management function which measures actual performance and compares it to established standards and then takes corrective action.

Coordination The process of integrating various individuals, work groups and business units to achieve organisational goals.

Cost Leadership A competitive strategy involving an aggressive pursuit of operating efficiency by an organisation so that it can be a low cost producer.

Critical Path The longest path or sequence of activities in a PERT chart.

Current Assets Assets acquired by the organisation for disposal in the course of trade and which are renewed again.

Current Ratio The ratio between an organisation's current assets and current liabilities used to assess liquidity.

Customer Departmentalisation A method of coordinating activities based on customer needs.

Database A collection of information stored in an orderly way in a computer.

Debt Equity Ratio The ratio between an organisation's total liabilities and total equities used to assess an organisation's debt financing.

Delegation The process by which new or additional responsibilities are assigned to a subordinate by a superior.

Delegation The process of assigning work activities and the related authority to specific individuals within the organisation.

Demarcation Lines The strict lines separating one area of work from another.

Depreciation This is the loss in value of capital goods over a period of time.

Differentiation A competitive strategy involving attempts by an organisation to develop goods or service that are viewed industry wide as unique in some important way.

Direct Marketing Interactive system of marketing that uses one or more media to effect a measurable response and/or transaction in order to communicate directly and personally with the would-be buyer.

Diversification A growth strategy whereby an organisation expands into new business areas outside of its original core capability.

Divestment To remove a vested right. Where a company gets rid of certain business operations that do not fit in with their mainstream strategy.

Dividend Payment from an organisation's post tax profits to its shareholders.

Dynamic Environment The degree to which environmental elements change.

Dynamism In relation to the economy — a phenomena of growth and change.

Economies of Scale Savings which arise due to the fact that the average unit cost of producing an item decreases as the volume of production increases.

Effective Manager An active leader who creates a work environment that both provides the opportunity and the incentive to achieve high performance.

Effectiveness The degree to which the outputs of the organisation correspond to the outputs that organisations and individuals in the external environment want.

Efficiency The achievement of objectives or targets at the least cost, resources or other undesirable outcomes.

Employee Relations This includes all employer-employee interactions, incorporating both union and non-union approaches to workforce management.

Employment Appeal Tribunal (EAT) A quasi-judicial tribunal that administers a number of legislative Acts in the area of employment and hears appeals from the rights commissioner service.

Enterprise Either a business organisation, as in a state enterprise; or an economic system in which people are free to do business more or less as they wish, as in 'free enterprise'; or in the context of this book, **the quality exemplified by the risk-taking businessperson.**

Entrepreneur A person viewed as undertaking a risk.

Entrepreneurship The entrepreneurial process involves all the functions, activities and actions associated with perceiving opportunities and creating organisations to pursue them.

Environment All factors affecting the organisation yet which lie outside of the organisation's boundary.

Environmental Complexity The number of environmental elements that affect organisational decision making.

Environmental Management Proactive strategies designed to change the environmental context within which the organisation operates.

Environmental Uncertainty A situation in which managers have little information about environmental events or their effect on the organisation.

Equality Officer This role was set up under the equality legislation to investigate claims of inequitable practices by organisations based on sex or marital status.

Existence-Relatedness-Growth (ERG) Advanced by Alderfer, it provides a means of understanding employee motivation. It argues that employee motivation can be understood with reference to these three key needs.

Expectancy The belief held by the individual that a specific level of effort will be followed by a specific level of performance (see **Expectancy Theory**).

Expectancy Theory Advanced by Vroom, this is a model of motivation. It argues that work motivation is a product of two distinct individual beliefs: the relationship between effort and performance; and the importance of particular work outcomes (see **Expectancy**, **Instrumentality** and **Valence**).

Expert Power Power that arises from the possession of knowledge or specialised skills.

Feasibility Study An examination of all the factors relevant to the establishment of the business.

Feedback Control Controls used to monitor outputs to make sure they meet standards.

Feedforward Control Controls used to monitor inputs to make sure they meet standards.

Finished Goods All items a manufacturer has made for sale to customers.

Fixed Costs Costs that do not vary with the level of output.

Franchise An arrangement whereby a company sells limited rights to use its brand name to a franchisee in return for a lump sum payment and a share of the franchisee's profits.

Franchise An arrangement between a franchisor and a franchisee, involving the sale of goods or services, using a particular marketing system and possibly with financial assistance provided.

Front Line Managers Managers responsible for directly managing operational employees and resources.

Functional Departmentalisation A method of coordinating activities based on each of the major functions undertaken by the organisation.

Gantt Chart A non financial method of control that illustrates across time the sequence of activities comprising a project.

Geographical Departmentalisation A method of coordinating activities based on the various regions served by the organisation.

Global Strategies A strategy of global competition based on the assumption that no differences exist among countries with respect to consumer tastes, competitive conditions, operations and political, legal, economic and social environments.

Goal Displacement A condition that occurs when people lose sight of the original goal and a new, possibly less important, goal arises.

Gross National Product The total value of output produced in a given country plus net property income from abroad.

Group Think The mode of thinking that people engage in when seeking agreement becomes so pervasive in a group that it overrides a realistic consideration of alternative solutions.

High Performance Work Teams A group approach to job design. Aimed at achieving the best person-environment fit, these are small work groups that work within the same facilitator and deploy acquired competencies across a broad range of areas (see **Job Design**).

Human Resource Management This refers to the management of employees through the development of a strategic corporate approach. The key principle is the incorporation of people issues into strategic decision making (see **Personnel Management**).

Human Resource Planning This refers to the specification and determination of future human resource needs in line with the organisation's strategic development plans.

Hygiene Factors Derived from Herzberg's 'Two Factor Theory' of work motivation, these are associated with the job context rather than its actual content.

Incentives A motivational force that stimulates people to greater activity or increased efficiency. Encourages an employee to work harder and be more productive.

Indigenous Company A company originated in the native/home country, that is, it is not a foreign-owned company.

Industrial Relations This refers to the rules, practices and conventions governing interrelations between management and the workforce; normally involves collective employee representation and bargaining.

Infrastructure The basic structure of a nation's economy, including transportation, communications and other public services on which economic activity relies.

Innovation A critical part of the business process. It is a new concept or approach in the product cycle. It is the addition of new elements to products or services, or to the methods of producing/providing them. Innovation is not the creation of an entirely new product, this is invention. Innovation allows one to gain a competitive edge over competitors.

Instrumentality The probability assumed by the individual that a particular level of achieved task performance will lead to specific work outcomes (see **Expectancy Theory**).

Interest The price paid to borrow money which is paid to the lender by the borrower.

Interest Rates Rates at which banks charge for the use of money.

Interpersonal Skills The ability to work effectively with other people.

Intrapreneurship This term refers to intra-company enterprise: the ability of a business organisation to create a climate that encourages innovation.

Inventory Turnover Ratio The ratio between an organisation's cost of goods sold and the inventory used to identify the number of times the inventory has been sold in a given period.

Inverse Correlation A relationship between two variables, such that movements/changes in large value of one variable tend to be associated with small item values of the other variable, and vice versa.

Irish Congress of Trade Unions (ICTU) The central co-ordinating body for the Irish trade union movement.

Job Characteristics Model Advanced by Hackman and Oldham, it seeks to identify job characteristics which satisfy higher order needs and which provide opportunities for achieving this satisfaction. It assumes that tasks are determined in terms of five core dimensions which are related to three critical psychological states and certain personal and work outcomes (see **Motivation Theory**).

Job Description An account of the responsibilities and tasks associated with a particular job.

Job Design Referred to as job design, job redesign or work structuring, it relates to the establishment of groups of tasks/activities to form a particular job.

Job Diagnostic Survey A measurement tool in the form of a questionnaire devised by Hackman and Oldham to test the job characteristics model.

Job Enlargement An individualistic approach to job design which focuses on the horizontal extension of the job as a means of broadening job scope and creating a more satisfying job (see **Job Design**).

Job Enrichment An individualistic approach to job design which focuses on the vertical extension of the job as a means of broadening job scope and establishing a more challenging, satisfying job (see **Job Design**).

Job Production This relates to the production of one-off or small quantities of a wide variety of specialised goods/items (see **Production Management**).

Job Shop An organisation with a large variety of products each produced in single quantities.

Job Specialisation Activities which are narrowed down to simple routine tasks.

Joint Venture A business venture entered into jointly by two or more partners. Their main aim is to share the risk of new ventures, or to benefit from synergy through the combining of each partner's resources.

Joint Venture A domestic or international subsidiary, jointly owned by two or more companies.

Just-In-Time (JIT) Manufacturing An approach to system waste determination, problem solving at source and continuous process improvement.

Key Result Areas Areas vital to the organisation's continued existence.

Labour Court It was established originally under the Industrial Relations Act of 1946 as the principal institution for facilitating the settlement of industrial disputes. This role was modified by the Industrial Relations Act of 1990.

Labour Relations Commission A tripartite body with statutory authority charged with the general responsibility of promoting good industrial relations.

Leadership The process of influencing an individual or group through deciphering his/her/its objectives and directing and motivating behaviour in pursuit of these objectives.

Legitimate Power Power based on an individual's position in the organisational hierarchy.

Lending Agencies A finance company, bank, loan organisation or the like that lends money and makes money by advancing money to others.

The Levelling Effect When an individual's thinking is brought into line with the average quality of a group's thinking.

Limited Company A separate legal entity, set up by reference to the rules of company law. The shareholders are limited by liability, so that they can only lose whatever amount of share capital they subscribe.

Limited Partnership Where one or more partners limits his/her liability to the amount he/she has invested in the partnership, but he/she cannot take part in the management of the business.

Line Authority The authority that follows an organisation's direct chain of command.

Line Unit A unit that contributes directly to accomplishing an organisation's goals.

Liquid Assets Assets which are available in cash or which can be easily converted into cash.

Liquidity A measure of an organisation's ability to cover short-term debts.

Management Activities that make up the management process. The major management functions are planning, organising and staffing, leading and controlling.

Management By Exception A control tool that permits only significant deviations between planned and actual performance to be brought to the manager's attention.

Management Development Leadership training for middle- or top-level personnel to upgrade their skills.

Management Process The process involving the four management functions of planning, organising and staffing, leading and controlling.

Managerial Grid Advanced by Blake and Mouton, it provides a framework for understanding and applying effective leadership. Five key managerial styles result from combining two fundamental ingredients of managerial behaviour — a concern for production and a concern for people (see **Leadership**).

Marketing Information Classified as any information that is relevant to making marketing decisions.

Marketing Information System A channel through which marketing information can be collected and disseminated in a timely fashion.

Marketing Mix A marketing concept, used to describe the alliterate constituents of marketing, that is, product, place, price and promotion in an integrated marketing program.

Market Research The process of methodically examining the market for an existing product or a new product. That part of marketing research that deals with the pattern of a market, measuring the extent and nature of a market and identifying a market.

Mass Production A production system in which large batches of standard products are manufactured in assembly line fashion by combining parts in a specified manner.

Matrix Structure A method of coordinating activities that crosses product departmentalisation with functional departmentalisation.

Merger The combining of two or more entities through the direct acquisition by one of the net assets of the other.

Middle Managers Managers in charge of plants and departments who have responsibility for the performance of their particular unit and how it relates to the rest of the organisation.

Motivation The forces that act on, or that are within an individual which cause him/her to behave in a particular, goal-directed fashion.

Motivators Derived from Herzberg's 'Two Factor Theory' of work motivation, they are related to job content or to what the individual does in his/her work.

Multi-national Corporation (MNC) An organisation that operates and competes in several different countries.

Open System A system that depends on, is influenced by and constantly interacts with its external environment.

Opportunity Costs The cost of not doing something. The opportunity cost is the reward that would have come from the best course of action that the business did not follow.

Organisational Chart A diagram of all the positions in the organisational hierarchy.

Organisational Culture The common set of beliefs and expectations shared by members of the organisation.

Own-branded Products Items bearing the names or brands of the store selling the item as opposed to bearing the producer's name if different.

Partnership A contractual relationship between two or more people in a joint enterprise who agree to share, not necessarily equally, in the profits and losses of the organisation.

Perceived Value The value people feel they should obtain by purchasing a particular product.

Performance Appraisal The process of evaluating an employee's job and organisational-related performance and his/her future potential.

Personnel Management This refers to either the specialist professional function performed by personnel managers or to all those people in an organisation with responsibilities for people management issues.

Person Specification This sets out the knowledge, skills, abilities and other characteristics required by an individual to perform a given job.

PERT Analysis A network analysis system whereby events in a project are identified along with the time taken to complete them. A network is developed showing relationships between the sequence of each event. A critical path can then be established.

Plant Layout This refers to the physical arrangement of all production facilities.

Portfolio A collection of securities owned by an individual or an organisation.

Price Competition Competition based on offering the lowest price.

Principal The original cash sum borrowed which has to be repaid, excluding the interest.

Privatisation The transfer of ownership of an organisation from the public to the private sector. Public sector organisations are sometimes called nationalised organisations or industries.

Product A bundle of features both tangible and intangible which are presented to the prospective customer.

Product Departmentalisation A method of coordinating activities based on the products produced by the organisation.

Production Management This refers to the management of the transformation of the material resource inputs into outputs of goods and services (see **Job**, **Batch** and **Continuous Flow Production**).

Production Planning and Control System A means of ensuring that the correct quantity of a product is produced at the right time, at the right quality and at the most acceptable cost.

Product Life Cycle The stages of market acceptance of any goods. The stages are: introduction, growth, maturity and decline.

Product Mix A composite of items offered for sale by a company.

Productivity The relationship between the total amount of goods or services being produced (output) and the organisational resources needed (inputs) to produce the goods or services.

Quality circle A group of employees who meet regularly to identify and solve quality problems or to make suggestions as to how quality can be improved.

Quick Asset Ratio Ratio between an organisation's total liabilities and total assets less inventory. It is used to measure an organisation's ability to meet financial obligations.

Rate of Return (on investment) The amount earned in direct proportion to the capital invested.

Ratio Analysis A control tool based on the process of generating information that summarises the financial position of an organisation by calculating ratios based on various financial measures appearing on balance sheets and income statements.

Recruitment The process of identifying and attracting potential job candidates.

Refreezing The process of making new behaviour permanent after a change programme has been introduced.

Reorientation A process that occurs when an organisation moves its resources into more attractive markets and industries.

Revitalisation A process an organisation goes through when its performance is unsatisfactory, designed to give the organisation new life.

Reward System This refers to the organisation's approach to compensating employees for job performance.

Rights Commissioners People charged with the responsibility for investigating individual disputes relating to pay and conditions. The recommendations made by them are generally not binding.

Sales Promotions Short term incentives to encourage product trial, shift brand loyalty, or increase product usage.

Scalar Principle A structure in which each person is part of one chain of command that extends from the top to the bottom of the organisation.

Science Organised knowledge of relevance to an area of practice.

Scientific Management An approach to management that emphasises the one best way to perform a task by applying scientific methods of inquiry.

Scientific Method A problem solving approach that involves 1) observing a system; 2) constructing a framework that is consistent with the observation and from which the consequences of altering the system can be predicted; 3) predicting how various changes would influence the system, i.e. cause and effect relationships; 4) testing to see if these changes influence the system as intended.

Secondary Data Information not received by a user from its original source, but coming instead from references gathered earlier.

Segmentation The categorising of consumers into a number of different segments, each of which has a distinctive feature. Its purpose is to identify more precisely the target market for a particular product or service.

Selection This refers to the process of evaluating and choosing the most suitable candidate from a pool of candidates established through recruitment.

Self Managed Teams A group of employees who have the day-to-day responsibility for managing themselves and the work they do.

Small Open Economy An economy which is small relative to its trading partners and is open in that it imports and exports a significant amount of goods and services.

Sole Trader At the end of the day, whatever profit is made accrues to the sole trader, the sole owner of the business.

Specialisation The number of distinct occupational titles or activities accomplished within the organisation. High specialisation means that there are many different functions or activities within the organisation.

Staff Authority The authority to provide advice and expertise to help line units in achieving their goals.

Staff Unit A unit that contributes indirectly to accomplishing an organisation's objectives.

Statistical Quality Control A process used to determine how many products from a larger number should be inspected to calculate a probability that the total number of products meet the organisation's quality standards.

Strategy A general and broad plan developed to achieve long-term organisational objectives.

Strong Man Theory Associated with leadership style, this is based on the principle of autonomy.

Structural Imperatives Factors that determine how the organisation should be structured for effectiveness.

Subjective This relates to or arises from a person's emotions or prejudices.

Substitute Products Items that can easily replace one another in either production or in consumption.

Sub-system A system created as part of the process of the overall management system.

SuperLeadership An approach to leadership that emphasises the central role of the followers. The central role of the leader is to help the followers to become self-leaders.

SWOT Analysis An analysis of the internal strengths and weaknesses of the organisation, and also studying the external factors of opportunities and threats, all of which effect the organisation.

Synergy The creation of a whole that is greater than the sum of its parts.

System A set of interdependent parts or elements which function as a whole in achieving certain goals or objectives.

Team Building A conscious effort to develop effective work groups throughout an organisation.

Theory The systematic grouping of interdependent principles that provide a framework for drawing together significant knowledge.

Theory X This focuses on managerial assumptions about employees. It argues that managers perceive employees to have an inherent dislike of work and will avoid it where possible (see **Theory Y**).

Theory Y This focuses on managerial assumptions about employees. It argues that managers perceive employees to enjoy work and derive satisfaction from the performance of their duties (see **Theory X**).

Time and Motion Study The study of the time and number of motions necessary to perform a task.

Top Managers Managers who determine the form of an organisation and define its overall character, mission and direction.

Total Costs The total of fixed and variable costs.

Total Quality Management (TQM) A systematic approach to improving the production of goods and services.

Trade Union An organisation dedicated to uniting workers with common interests, and defining, articulating and collectively advancing those interests.

Trait Theory This argues that leaders are born and not made, and are endowed with key characteristics which other individuals do not possess (see **Leadership**).

Turnaround A situation in which a business has sustained serious losses and needs radical changes if it is to survive.

Two Factor Theory Advanced by Herzberg, it provides a means of analysing employee motivation. It suggests that factors leading to job satisfaction are distinct from those leading to job dissatisfaction (see **Motivators** and **Hygiene Factors**).

Unfreezing The process by which people become aware of the need for change.

Unit Production A production system in which either one or a small number of finished products are manufactured according to customer specifications.

Unity of Command The idea that no subordinate should report to more than one supervisor. It is designed to ensure that conflicts in instructions are reduced and that personal responsibility is increased.

Universal Principles of Management Management principles that are universal or applicable to all types of organisations and all organisational levels.

Valence The value the individual attaches to specific work outcomes (see **Expectancy Theory**).

Variable Budget Budgets that distinguish between fixed and variable costs and which show how budget expenses vary as the volume of output increases.

VAT Value Added Tax is an indirect tax levied by the government on particular goods and services. VAT is added on at the point of purchase by the selling organisation. It is therefore a commercial tax.

Venture Capital Capital provided by financial institutions specialising in loans to unquoted companies.

Working Capital The amount of capital needed to carry on a business from day to day.

Zero Based Budget A budgeting process whereby each budget starts from zero and carries nothing forward from the last one. It is designed to eliminate inefficiencies which are carried forward from one budget to the next.

Index